COMPENSATION

COMPENSATION

Fifth Edition

Robert E. Sibson

American Management Association

*This publication is designed to provide accurate and authoritative
information in regard to the subject matter covered. It is sold with
the understanding that the publisher is not engaged in rendering
legal, accounting, or other professional service. If legal advice or
other expert assistance is required, the services of a competent professional person should be sought.*

Library of Congress Cataloging-in-Publication Data

Sibson, Robert Earl, 1925–
    Compensation / Robert E. Sibson, — 5th ed.
        p. cm.
    Includes index.
    ISBN 0-8144-5977-3
    1. Compensation management. 2. Job evaluation. I. Title.
HF5549.5.C67S588   1990
658.3'22—dc20   *90-55210*
                                                              CIP

Printing number

10 9 8 7 6 5 4 3

Contents

Contents

Contents

Preface

For those who work in compensation, it is important to recognize basic changes in the field of their work. This must be done by understanding the changes in the personnel field generally. There have been four distinct phases in the evolution of personnel work, and three of these have occurred during my working life.

Personnel activities emerged shortly after World War I. Those who were in personnel work at that time mostly had two responsibilities: selecting employees and keeping out labor unions.

By today's standards, those who worked in personnel in the first phase practiced what were crude employment techniques—mostly "gate hiring." Job selection depended upon one person's firsthand knowledge of the applicant. In keeping out unions, the personnel representative carried out the activities in whatever way he thought was best.

Those who first filled what can now be recognized as personnel jobs were typically ex-plant foremen or former industrial engineers. They had no knowledge or experience in "personnel"; there wasn't any experience. That was the first phase in the evolution of the personnel function.

The second phase started in the 1930s with the passage of legislation such as the National Labor Relations Act, the Social Security Act, and the Fair Labor Standards Act. The National Labor Relations Act fostered unionization and created the need for bargaining knowledge and skills. Unions presented issues in employee relations, and work on such issues required basic personnel data and analysis.

The Fair Labor Standards Act created the need for the first basic elements of wage and salary administration. Social Security laws and union pressures for retirement plans required the development of experience and expertise in employee benefits.

In the second phase of the evolution of the personnel function, it essentially experienced two dramatic changes. For one thing, the function took on a number of new activities, which were essentially administrative or service-oriented. These included the maintenance of basic compensation information, rules and guides for various types of pay programs, and practices that were intended to guide pay decisions.

In the second phase, the personnel function also evolved new technologies that were unique to this field of work that were of considerable importance to management. For example, job evaluation plans were developed and broadly instituted. Merit increase systems were also applied in many companies during this period. It was new technologies such as these that brought about a new type of personnel activity and a new type of personnel person who viewed personnel work as a career. During this phase of work in personnel, there was a greater need for both technical competence and a facility for establishing good working relationships with others in management.

The third phase in the evolution of the personnel function started in the 1950s and was mostly characterized by the evolution of a full-service staff organization in personnel. In the third phase, personnel departments grew to be large organizations, requiring many skills, including skills in managing a large personnel department.

During this third phase, personnel people started assuming important elements of authority. For instance, labor relations people negotiated contracts—including wages and benefits of employees represented by unions. Considerable responsibility and authority were vested in personnel people in the field of compensation also. As this third phase evolved, for example, many compensation people had authority to make decisions about job grades in many companies.

In the third phase, the personnel department assumed new roles. For example, it investigated problems such as turnover. From such experience, personnel people developed unique knowledge and experiences that were usable throughout the company.

Most of all in the third phase, personnel people developed new programs and practices. These were developed in every facet of personnel and at a most impressive pace. Many compensation programs were developed.

Increasingly in the third phase of the evolution of the personnel department, those who worked in the personnel field did so because they chose this line of work as a career. Many of those who started to work in the field had taken college courses in personnel work. In varying degrees, the function had become an accepted and respected part of the organization.

Phase 4 started to emerge in the early 1970s. The characteristics that distinguish personnel in the fourth phase are the role of the personnel group, the resulting expectations of work by personnel people, and the standards of performance that management set for them. In the fourth phase, the personnel department has become an integral part of the management of the business.

In the fourth phase, it is not sufficient for those in personnel just to be a full-service organization that is available to management. Personnel must take a far more affirmative role in management issues. Those in personnel must not only respond to problems but they must identify issues and develop solutions before they become major problems. Personnel is no longer an organization apart from operations, but personnel, and all its specialist parts, must be an integral part of the business system.

The technical excellence of personnel people must be maintained, but excellence in the knowledge of personnel alone is insufficient in the mature personnel organization. The special knowledge of personnel people must be to effectively relate their experience and know-how in personnel work to the operations of the enterprise. Actions must be geared to the operation's needs and the strategic plans of the company. Personnel actions must visibly make positive contributions to the achievement of the goals of the enterprise.

The mature personnel organization is more than a collection of functional departments, such as compensation and benefits. These departments still exist, but their work is so interrelated with others in the personnel function and with other facets of management that they are working as an ongoing project group in personnel matters rather than as separate entities. Each function of personnel must recognize that each area has an impact on every other area of personnel and that everything done in one area, such as compensation, is affected by every other area.

Each of these recognizable phases in the evolution of the personnel function has lasted about twenty-five or thirty years. If this is a pattern, then we should start to see the early signs of a new or fifth phase in the evolution of the personnel function. Never think that any function in business is set and unchanging.

In the past few years, I have given speeches on the fifth phase of the personnel function to various management groups, and some think I am predicting the demise of the function; one organization, in fact, subtitled my speech, ''The Last Ten Years.'' I am not really predicting that, although it is a possibility. What seems clear, however, is that the personnel function is going through a rapid and dramatic change.

A number of basic factors are bringing about the rapid change in human resources management. One example is the increased knowledge of personnel work by line managers. The average line manager today knows as much about compensation as the average compensation director did not many years ago.

Another example of basic factors changing human resources management is the exploding computer and communication technologies. With these technologies, we are moving in the direction of zero staff at the corporate level. We will never get to a zero corporate staff level, but the emergence of such things as expert systems and the skills and knowledge of managers in networking are changing compensation roles. More and more, compensation experts will be putting knowledge into the expert systems, and, more and more, they will become central switching systems in the networking.

There are some reasons to be concerned about the personnel function in business. If indeed the function and all of its major parts, such as compensation, are to continue to be a respected and integral part of the management of the business, the personnel departments must take more affirmative action in identifying and dealing with fundamental issues.

Human resources management people in few companies have dealt with key business issues involving personnel in an affirmative and effective manner. For instance, most companies have still not developed a personnel data base that contributes in a substantive way to personnel decision-making. Downsizing did not occur at the initiative of personnel, and in most cases, the personnel department was only incidentally involved in this critical work. In many companies, personnel is the last major activity to start work in the area of expert systems. Compensation, particularly, should be the leading edge in developing expert systems.

If those who work in personnel don't meet the challenge of being part of management, then the function will likely backslide, and the fifth phase in the evolution of the personnel function might be similar to the third. In some companies, that is already happening.

This is the fifth edition of this book, which was first published in 1960 and originally titled *Wages and Salaries—A Handbook for Line Managers*. The purpose has always been to present a comprehensive work on compensation. In 1960, it was possible to do that in little more than two hundred pages in a small book with big print. The work was written originally for line managers, partly because there were few people in the field of compensation. Today, the work is prepared for a far broader audience, including managers of personnel, those who work in the field of personnel management, and compensation professionals.

To get a sense of where we are in the field of compensation, it helps to look back to the practices of the field in 1960. Having looked back thirty years, we can then look forward thirty years to the year 2020.

I remember well the state of the field of human resources management (then called personnel management) in 1960, because that was the time when I was talking to many companies about possible consulting assignments. Back then, there were usually two units in the field—one labeled labor relations and the other labeled personnel relations; a business version of the marine corps and the peace corps. Labor relations usually was the larger, more important, and better-paid unit.

Personnel relations consisted mostly of employment, training, and compensation—in that order. The head of college recruiting, for example, would usually be one of the top three members of the personnel department. Training mostly involved basic instruction in plant operations. Few companies had a compensation department at all.

Few organizations had a corporate interest in compensation. Most often, if there was a formal compensation program at all, it was at location levels, applied mostly to nonexempt persons and involving point (NMTA) or factor comparison (Hay) job evaluation plans.

It was shortly after 1960 that management pay plans started to emerge, with the development and implementation by a few companies of annual incentive payment plans for managers in operating divisions. It was mostly the development of these management pay programs that led to the formation of compensation functions at the corporate level.

Compensation work in 1960 was crude by today's standards. The few who did the work did compensation alone. When compensation work *was* done, the tools included a slide rule for calculations and a piece of string, which was often used in determining regression lines.

There is much that is new in this fifth edition, and it is far different from what was published in earlier editions. We shouldn't consider this as criticism of what was formerly done. Different ideas, approaches, and practices have become necessary because of changes in business and the work force. Most important has been the increase in technology and a greater diversity of jobs.

Looking ahead thirty years and making predictions is always risky. However, we must plan for the future.

Clearly, the human resources management job will be very different by the year 2020. The work force, the style of managing, the values of employees, the tools used, and the human resources management know-how of managers will be very different from what they are today. But most of all, the human resources management job will be different because of computer and communications technology.

Before very long, computer use in human resources management will reach a level of sophistication that is equivalent to CAM in manufacturing and CAD in research. Then we will have computer-aided personnel (CAP) and computer-aided compensation (CAC).

There will be a great deal of modeling in all areas of human resources management, particularly compensation. Operating managers throughout the company will have direct access to vast amounts of reference information in compensation from computers through the communications system.

All of this will expand the capabilities of professionals in human resources management and extend their reach. One result will be that personnel ratios* in companies may be under 0.5—down from 1.2 in 1989.

More than half of those who work in human resources management will earn in excess of $50,000 (1989 dollars). Therefore, personnel organizations will be composed of a few high-level knowledge experts, whose know-how will be leveraged greatly through computers and communications equipment.

Compensation professionals will largely be internal consultants, and

---

*Personnel ratio is the number of personnel employees per one hundred employees in the company.

they will spend a large portion of their time putting knowledge into the management information system. Those who do work in compensation will also be involved in major developmental projects and spend a great deal of their time monitoring the work and decisions of managers throughout the company.

Consistent with these predictions, the compensation job will probably be much broader in scope than it is now. The function will likely at least include benefits, human resources information systems management, and needed research in human resources management.

The first edition of this book was mostly based on the practices and experiences of thirty companies. The second (1967) and third (1974) editions were based largely on consulting experiences. As the founder and head of Sibson & Company, Inc., during this period, I had hundreds of compensation project experiences, either directly or by monitoring the work of associates.

By the time the fourth edition was published (1981), I had sold Sibson & Company and was living year-round in Vero Beach, Florida. But I kept fifty clients and held four conferences each year, two of which were in compensation. Attendance at the conferences was by invitation only and included the top people from the largest companies, so these conferences provided especially valuable additional inputs for the fourth edition.

The conferences are still being held, and I still do a substantial amount of consulting work, mostly by telephone. Both have been valuable inputs to this edition. For this edition, I also invited a random sample of subscribers to *The Sibson Report* to write to me and describe principal compensation questions they faced, and these were then discussed with each person by phone. There were thirty-two such cases, which were most helpful in preparing this edition. A questionnaire on compensation management priorities was also sent to eight hundred compensation professionals. There were 212 responses, which were also extremely helpful.

If there is a sixth edition of this book, it will not likely be done by us. For this reason, and for all those prior editions, Sally and I have worked very hard to make this book special.

Robert E. Sibson

Chapter One

Compensation and Management

The single most important thing to be said about compensation is that it is an integral part of human resources management—which, in turn, is a vital component of management. This is why "Compensation and Management" is the first chapter. Specifically, it is vital to emphasize that compensation work in all its forms should contribute to the success of the operation and serve properly all the direct participants of the enterprise. Work in compensation must also recognize that all the functional areas of human resources management are interrelated and that, in combination, they ultimately have to do with employee-employer relations. Compensation is a part of management, and therefore the style of management must be reflected visibly in the methods of compensation. That style of management is increasingly a delegative style, and compensation programs must reflect that style. Compensation programs and practices must also reflect the policies of the company, and these must be the conscious policies of its executive managers. Last and certainly not least, in all that is done in compensation, there must be an accountability to the employees as well as to the enterprise.

Compensation Work and Enterprise Success

Compensation is a part of management. Quality work in compensation should contribute significantly to the success of the business. Compensation impacts on business success in a variety of ways. Here are a half-dozen key suggestions for performing compensation work in a manner that contributes to enterprise success:

1. Make certain that pay is competitive.
2. In compensation work, recognize that people are income-producing assets.
3. Don't let proper accounting practices cause improper compensation practices.
4. Make sure that compensation supports productivity management.
5. Manage payroll costs, not just pay-rate levels.
6. Recognize that not every dollar of payroll is the same type of expense.

Pay Must Be Competitive

It is sometimes considered insensitive to talk about wages as prices, but pay is the price paid for work. That applies to the minimum wage required by law, and it applies to the pay of an executive who is paid $10 million a year.

The use of compensation in terms of attracting and retaining talent has always been recognized as a critical management activity. As a means of allocating resources, pay is only starting to be recognized as a key management tool—largely because labor scarcity has caused more attention to be directed to the competitiveness of pay. As a form of motivation, pay contributes to the competitive success of the enterprise.

Competitiveness of pay is one basic aspect of compensation that impacts on enterprise success. The constant need for competitiveness is often lost on the agenda of daily work. This issue requires constant attention, and is the focus of considerable detail in later chapters.

Those Paid Are Income-Producing Assets

Human talent should be considered an asset, and in an increasingly technological world, human talent represents the only truly unique asset of an enterprise. Those who work for it produce for the company—they produce its products or services. Thus, pay for workers represents pay for work, and employees are income-producing assets of the company.

There is no accepted relationship between talent and business success. Yet it seems logical that significantly better than average talent, well-directed and well-managed, will yield at least somewhat greater enterprise success. Management practices of all types, including those in compensation, should always consider how pay can contribute to the optimum use of talent.

Sometimes managers have difficulty accepting any relationship between talent and success; therefore, they have difficulty accepting any actions, including compensation practices, designed to improve the use of talent, partly because those managers were brought up to think differently. Those who learned about business before the 1980s were taught to think about physical resources—plants, equipment, material, warehouses. The sole model of business taught in the formative years of many of today's managers was geared to the capacity of physical facilities. With these facilities in place, then it was assumed that the number of people with the knowledge required to run the facilities could be recruited and put on the job. In the model of business that was taught for many years, human talent was always expected to be bent and shaped to meet the requirements of a company's inorganic resources. The limit of production was thought to be the limitation of the plant, not the people who worked for it, in what I call the Model A of business, which was the only business model for many years.

When these notions were the dogma, businesses and business thinking were dominated by smokestack industries like automobiles and steel, where these ideas were partially true. It also was very much the way General Electric used to be.

In this traditional model of the business, pay was for time alone, and efforts were made to keep an inventory of people and their time and talent for when it was needed, to be released as needed. Today there is reason to think that these views are less true in all types of businesses and untrue in many businesses. In compensation work, it is necessary to know the true nature of the model of the business and to do compensation work that is supportive of that model.

In fact, there are now a number of distinct business models. For example, technology businesses and those that serve the personal care and leisure time fields are numerous, and these business areas are growing rapidly. In these businesses, the primary limitation on output is the capacity of people; for example, you can always rent more space and lease computers.

To be translated into greater success, talent must be managed well. There must be excellence in the management of personnel, and compensation must be a tool for that excellence.

The development of compensation programs and the advice and counsel given to managers of personnel by compensation professionals must reflect the needs and realities of all contemporary enterprise models. Those who work in compensation management must recognize first and foremost that compensation has to do with the acquisition and use of a company's most critically important producing asset—human talent.

In light of these circumstances, compensation professionals must concentrate not only on technical excellence and administrative tidiness but on compensation practices, information, and advice that support the effective management of people. The view urged on those who do compensation work is to consider that talent represents a unique asset.

Management is the acquisition, allocation, optimum utilization, and retention of resources. It is the management of all resources that obviously provides the competitive edge for the enterprise. But people are the truly unique asset, and, therefore, the management of people is the critical management skill. In my opinion, everything that is done in the field of compensation should reflect these basic principles.

Accounting Practices and Compensation Work

Also recognize that there is something in the tradition and practices of accounting that impedes the effective management of people, and this thinking has dominated the compensation practices of companies in many cases. We say that employees are our most important assets, but the fact of the matter is that employees aren't treated as assets in our accounting statements. On the balance sheet, they are treated as liabilities; on the income statement, employees are treated as expenses.

To some extent, many managers say that employees are liabilities and not assets. For example, managers constantly emphasize wage cost containment, but rarely do you hear managers talk about increasing the income-producing potential of employees.

Many who say they manage mostly manage costs, including employee costs. Some manage nothing but costs and have nothing to do with revenue production. With this view, it is inevitable that there is overemphasis on simply cutting the payroll and no emphasis on increasing the output per payroll dollar.

In some corporations, the entire process of management focuses on expenses. It all starts with a budget. There is no doubt that budgeting is a useful business practice. But budgeting is now often overdone and has become a preoccupation with negative thinking. The most destructive part of the budgeting process, as practiced in many companies, is that it treats employees as expenses and liabilities only and budget review systems become an obstacle course to the development of the company's only unique asset, the people who produce wealth.

Compensation Must Support Productivity Improvement

In the next twenty years, it is possible that productivity will increase at 4 percent a year, compounded—an unprecedented rate of productivity improvement. This great increase in productivity will occur largely by the traditional method that has been used in this country: capital substitution. The capital substituted will mostly be computers and communications equipment.

A big difference in this case of substituting capital for labor is that employees, not the capital, will control output. This means that human assets will be even more critically important to enterprises. Capital substitution when output is labor controlled means that the management of personnel will have to be elevated to a new high of excellence.

Compensation work must support management in achieving higher productivity partly by providing relevant information and partly by giving better guidance on compensation matters in a responsive manner. New programs will be required to meet changing needs, although most of these programs will likely be variations of former programs and simplifications of existing practices.

Manage Payroll Costs

Most clearly, compensation affects business success because pay is a major expense item. Payroll costs should be managed like any other cost—even though payroll costs aren't always like other costs.

In every enterprise, a model of pay costs should be constructed on computers. This is not difficult to do and would be usable many times. This model should show the impact of each additional dollar of payroll cost on the business's financial results. The computer model should show costs of various organizations and the payroll costs of alternate work methods. Such information is required by the compensation professional for work that must be done today and provides information inputs to the management process.

Computer models are primarily useful in compensation work as a method of managing compensation costs. However, the models can also be useful in designing new compensation programs and in organizational structuring work. Compensation models can also contribute to redesigning products or services to be less capital-intensive. There are cases where payroll models were key in entering new business areas. It is work such as this that gets compensation people really involved in the management of the business.

Take an Investment View of Payroll Costs

By proper accounting rules, every dollar of payroll is an expense, and each dollar of payroll is an equivalent expense to every other dollar of expense. That's sound accounting, but it isn't good compensation management. In compensation, there are:

1. Direct costs
2. Opportunity costs
3. Investment return
4. Cost-reduction spending

Direct costs represent a straight expense: pay for time worked, regardless of the value of what was done. Such payroll costs are just like the expense of materials purchased, whether or not the materials are used well.

Opportunity cost compensation payments are made only if something favorable happens to the business. Profit-sharing payments would be an example of opportunity cost compensation payments. Payments are a pre-determined cost, but they are made only in periods of good business results and are paid only in most cases if a reasonable threshold of profits has been achieved. Similarly, payments above a threshold and *up to* a standard business goal under a management incentive compensation plan are oppor-tunity costs.

Payments *above* a reasonable business goal under a management in-centive compensation plan represent investment spending. In this case, profits are higher than expected or planned. At least to some extent, it is reason-able to think that it was the opportunity for higher pay that contributed to more effective management. It was more effective management that re-sulted in greater profits, and only a part of these profits is paid to the managers. This is investment spending for higher than expected business achievement.

Salary increases that are based on performance increases are also in-vestment spending in compensation. One reason why pay for performance continues to be a subject of great interest to business executives is because salary increases based on improved performance don't cost the company anything.

Cost-reduction spending occurs when any performance award pay-ment is less than the performance improvement. When there is promotion from within and the new person comes up to performance levels of the person replaced but is paid a lower salary, then there is cost-reduction spending in compensation. The types of cost avoidance cases in compen-sation are few, but the instances may be many.

Managing compensation costs is a serious matter in human resources management. Controlling compensation costs doesn't mean minimum wage payment levels but rather an optimum spread between the output of people and the pay costs of those people. *Compensation management means op-timizing the margin between output and payroll costs.*

Compensation and Human Resources Management

There is never any disagreement with the notion that compensation work is an integral part of personnel management—and that personnel management is an integral part of the management of personnel. The prob-lem is always in the application.

In my consulting career, I have often been called upon to deal with a compensation problem and then found out that the problem was really something else. Part of the talent of the true professional is in identifying the true problem, and you learn with experience that what is presented as a problem is very often the surface symptom.

It isn't enough to generalize about the interrelationship of each functional specialist area of personnel. It must be part of the mind-set of those who do the work. Compensation professionals must think management of personnel to achieve the goals of the business. Compensation is an integral part of human asset management, and human asset management is an integral part of business management (see Figure 1–1).

Cases are often needed to demonstrate the fact that each facet of human resources management affects every other function and, in turn, is affected by every other function. Cases occur regularly, so a few should serve the purpose of illustration.

I have been asked many times to deal with the issue of pay compression. The problem has *never* been compensation. Mostly, what was reported as a pay compression problem was really an organizational problem.

A very hierarchial organization inevitably causes pay compression problems. Most companies today have at least two organizational levels more than is appropriate, and that alone would cause serious pay compression, at least between some levels of jobs.

Recognize that compensation practices may also contribute to organizational problems. For example, job evaluation plans often weigh heavily the number of employees supervised. This creates a pay incentive to create hierarchial organizations.

Figure 1-1. Compensation, Human Asset Management, and Business.

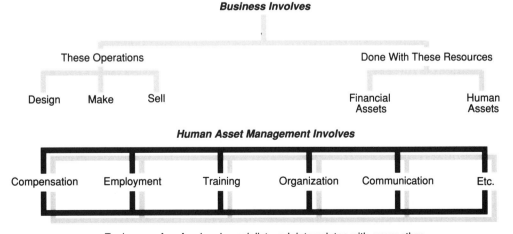

Each area of professional specialist work interrelates with every other.

Turnover is often reported as a pay problem. No doubt, pay often does cause people to seek work elsewhere, but many times pay is the reported reason for turnover and not the causal reason.

Problems of excessive pay costs may very well involve areas other than compensation. When companies report that compensation costs are too high, the real issue is often that revenues are too low. More sales, higher prices, and greater productivity are often better answers to high compensation costs than pay cost containment.

Ineffective manpower management is another major cause of excessive compensation costs. There are more noncompensation actions to deal with the problem of excess compensation costs than there are compensation actions. In fact, lower job pay is seldom a cure for excessive compensation costs.* That should be enough cases to illustrate the interrelationship of compensation and other professional specialist areas in personnel.

At some of the compensation conferences I have held for the past fifteen years, I have challenged the group to identify anything they do in compensation that is important and consumes any serious amount of time that does not impact the work of other areas of human resources management. You can identify a few activities, but not many. Try it yourself.

Overspecialization in compensation work can cause serious problems. For example, one result of specialization can be that a compensation question is given to a compensation person who then fashions a compensation answer. But the result is often the right answer to the wrong question, because the core problem was in some area of personnel other than compensation.

Specialization has resulted in compensation professionals learning more and more about less and less. This has the tendency of making specialists even narrower and insulating those who do only compensation work from the real world of work and the real questions about work. With time, such greater specialization will mean that even pure compensation questions will tend to get answers that are too technical for the users and that information provided by compensation specialists will be incomprehensible to others.

In compensation work, there can be high levels of specialist knowledge *and* more effective use of that knowledge. This must be done, and it can be done in a number of ways.

First, in allocating time, the compensation person must allocate *more* time and attention to the application of know-how and relatively less time to the development of more programs. Remember that most of the programs that will ever be developed in the field of compensation have already been developed.

---

*Pay for performance increases are *never* a cause for excessive compensation costs. Yet in every recession, there are cases where companies cut their ''merit increase budgets.''

There needs to be effective networking of knowledge. The compensation professional can't know everything and, therefore, needs to know what must be networked either with other human resources management professionals or with outside experts. The compensation person must be able to network the expert knowledge in computers and from expert human beings.

Not many years ago, specialist knowledge was the most highly prized quality of candidates for specialist positions, and it was a scarce resource. Today, broad human resources management knowledge and a proven ability to identify questions and translate know-how to others who are not specialists in the field are as highly prized as specialist knowledge.

Most of all, human resources management people must have the ability to relate what they know to what the managers of personnel do in their jobs. There is a broad trend in business for far more delegation of decision-making to operating managers. This means that each manager of personnel makes more decisions and that increasingly the compensation specialist's job is to help managers make better decisions and be more effective managers of personnel.

Delegative Management in Compensation Work

Compensation work must always reflect the style of management in effect in the enterprise. There has been a broad trend in all types of businesses toward a far more delegative style of managing. Compensation practices must change to be consistent with the trend toward a more delegative style.

Delegative management means real delegation of authority—authority to determine tasks done, schedules, and correct work processes with respect to each individual worker.

Some matters, such as the work to be done by the operations, needed corporate policies, procedures affecting the interworking of jobs, quality standards, and safety requirements, must be handled centrally, and everyone must adhere to these corporate needs. In addition, a manager must usually be advised about changes in work methods, with the authority to concur or not concur. But within these parameters, each worker must increasingly manage his own work, and each immediate supervising manager is more and more accountable for effective work.

One thing you find out when you deal with issues of delegative management is that you need to use cases, because people often mean something different when they use the expression "delegative management." Here are two cases that reflect my view of what delegative management should mean.

Case #1: Salary Grade Decisions. Assume that about 10 percent of all jobs are slotted into the company's salary structure by market pricing done by the corporate human resources management department. Then under my vision of delegative management, the correct salary grade of all other jobs would be decided by the immediate supervising managers throughout the company. There would be no prescribed system for doing this work and no individual review procedure for any specific decision.

Case #2: Performance Management. Decisions relating to the performance of each worker and the determination of action steps (if any) to improve performance would also be decided by each direct manager of personnel with only a general review—usually after the fact. There would be no specific review and approval process.

Until recently, most firms had essentially a programmatic method of management. Under a programmatic style of management, companies develop programs, practices, and processes. Such programs are then implemented. Managers and supervisors throughout the company make key management decisions in accordance with the programs. In fact, all managers are trained to apply the programs "correctly," which generally means "the same way" under a programmatic system.

Under a programmatic style of management, it is the goal to embody the decisions and thinking of top management in the programs. In effect, under a programmatic method of management, it was the programs to a large degree that made decisions.

The programmatic method evolved when there were many employees doing relatively few jobs. Programmatic management worked when businesses were simpler and less technological than they are today. The difficulties in an increasing technological environment that were experienced by companies led to the evolution of a more delegative managerial style throughout business.

The delegative method of managing has four essential interrelated elements:

1. Policy management
2. Guideline management
3. Delegative practices
4. Quality management

Policy management sets the objectives and describes the thinking of top management. It is the foundation of delegative management. Policies under a delegative management style tend to be much more descriptive than the general platitudes or vague statements that were typical of policy statements under the programmatic style of management. For policy management, it is often necessary to have recorded cases; precedents that describe critical cases and therefore illustrate what the policy means. These cases become part of the policy. This is the common-law approach applied to corporate policy making.

Guideline management establishes few rules and requirements in human resources management. The requirements are set only when they are prescribed by law or when essential corporate matters are involved.

Delegative practices are the third part of the delegative management style. Delegative practices refer to whatever is done to empower managers throughout the organization with the authority and the accountability for making more managerial decisions. Delegative practices also facilitate the delegation of more decisions to first levels of work—to the workers themselves.

Quality management is a system of reviewing, monitoring, analyzing, and auditing, which, in combination, assure that the decisions and actions of managers and workers throughout the company are consistent with policy, conform to requirements, reflect guidelines, comply with safety requirements, and contribute to the accomplishment of the objectives of the company. Quality management is so named because its purpose is to ensure a high quality of decision making, a high quality of work, and a resulting high quality of products and services.

Quality management is an essential part of the delegative style. To delegate without quality assurance would be to abdicate accountability.

Delegative management is free choice at the work station—potentially as powerful as free choice in the marketplace. The cumulative impact of independent decisions and actions to improve work methods, done every day and at every work station throughout an organization, is very great.

Those who do work in compensation are caught up in the groundswell of movement from programmatic to more delegative methods of management. Compensation work is part of management and, therefore, must change to reflect and support this evolving method of management.

Delegative Practices and Scientific Management

With delegation has necessarily come different attitudes by workers and toward workers. With the evolution of delegative management has necessarily come a different view of how to manage and how to manage people. Compensation professionals must also adapt to these changed ways of work.

In the recent past, business thinking was largely in terms of programs such as MTM systems, work layout, job evaluation, time studies, and other tools of "scientific management." Management was a system whereby perfect work methods were designed by geniuses to be carried out by clones in a prescribed manner. This is a brief and perhaps harsh description of programmatic management, but it is an accurate description.

The tools of scientific management are still usable; particularly because they can be linked to computers. But "perfect systems" aren't; and they may involve risks that are unacceptable. Systems that assume workers are physically identical clones also cause discontent in the work place, probably result in lower than optimum productivity, and almost certainly result in less excellence in work quality.

There is no place in delegative management for group think, anarchy, chaos, randomness, or consensus decision making. Group work is an organizational aberration. "Group management" and "consensus decisions" are oxymorons anyway. Individuals think; there is really no such thing as group think. Individuals decide; groups compromise. Individuals act; groups meet again. So delegation is to managers of personnel and then to individual employees. If an individual goes to others in a group and asks a question or seeks inputs, the response is usually helpful and supportive. If that individual has his work subject to review or mandatory comment by another person or group, that is interfering and meddling.

Delegation of decision making is greater in an increasingly technological and more rapidly changing work environment. The problems and issues today are in the "doing." Part of the problem of doing is a state of mind and overcoming the traditions of the past.

Under the past styles of programmatic management and the Model A of business, which were based partly on scientific management, the view of the business is from the top. Management decided most things, directly or through programs, and management was all-knowing in the Model A of business.

It was reacting in part to this totalitarianism in the work place that Theory X and Theory Y evolved. That wasn't enough, however, so organizational development evolved, followed by a whole series of other practices, until we reached today's participative management era.

Each step in that chain may have represented efforts for a more flexible and considerate way to exercise programmatic management—a way to adapt the view from the top to a new environment. But it now seems clear that there is a need for an entirely different view.

The center of the work universe needs to be the individual worker—whoever that individual is in the organization. It would be degrading and patronizing to talk about "a view from the bottom" as much as it would be to talk about "a view from the top"—or "participation."

Delegation, as it should be used in business, is not well-defined in the dictionary; and that may cause confusion. In plain English, delegation in management is best defined in the dictionary by the word *empower-*

ment—and some companies have so designated their delegative management system.

Empowerment means to "give power or authority"—and that is what is done under a delegative style. The chief executive officer is empowered; and every employee who works in the organization is equivalently empowered.

It isn't necessary to playact any of this. It isn't necessary, for instance, to call workers "team members" or to call the managers of personnel "coaches." "Employee" isn't a dirty word. An employee is a person working for another person or business for pay. We all do that: the chief executive officer and the lowest-paid worker alike.

Playacting and using funny words are artificial and will seem devious to some. If you empower people, they will work with equivalent effectiveness at every level of the organization and in every field—and they won't mind at all if you call them employees. But they must still be managed—the subject is delegative *management*.

Management isn't a dirty word either. Look it up in the dictionary. We all need management. Today, the management of employees must be increasingly delegative.

Compensation Policies

Policy making is an essential part of management and a key element of delegative management. This applies to all areas and activities in an enterprise. There needs to be effective compensation policies also.

Too often in business, policy is set from the bottom up. Practices are evolved at the operating level in reaction to daily issues, become part of the company's way of doing business, and over a period of time they become the policy.

Policies should, of course, reflect the thinking, the values, and the basic strategy of the company. Policies must be set consciously and thoughtfully by top management. That seems so obvious and so reasonable, but it doesn't happen like that very often.

Policy issues must be identified. There are relatively few compensation policy issues that apply broadly. Here are the issues I consider to be basic policy matters in the field of compensation that apply to most enterprises.

- What should be the pay of jobs compared to comparable positions in relevant markets?
- What is the policy with respect to pay for performance?
- Is there a commitment to pay in relation to inflation, and what is that commitment?

- There is the matter of providing health and retirement benefits and the reasons for providing such benefits. This also involves the issue of employee contributions to benefit coverage.
- Equivalency of compensation treatment is a policy issue—whether all persons and all jobs are treated in the same way.
- Communication questions relative to the right to know and the need to know are policy matters.
- What is the basic philosophy of pay—for example, do you buy people's time, use their knowledge, or pay for results?
- Should all employees or some employees share in the company's success?
- What are the "at-risk" and contingent compensation policies?
- Should compensation consider employee needs or corporate ability to pay?

In my opinion, these are the key policy matters in the field of compensation, except for a few that occasionally apply in special situations or in specific operations. There are, of course, other important matters and key issues or problems. But the ten items noted are the policy issues relevant in most firms that need to be addressed and answered by top executive management and then followed and referenced by all who work in the enterprise.

There aren't many policy issues in compensation, but they are complex issues of enormous importance to the company and to those who work in it. The issues require a high intelligence by top executive management, guided by sound information and counsel by compensation professionals. The process of evolving policy is important, if for no other reason than the importance of the issue and the level of the policy decision-makers.

When it comes to the matter of the correct process for developing policies, you may hear different ideas. My view is based on hundreds of experiences. It's not the only effective way, but it's my way, and it has the virtue of being simple and direct. Here, in brief form, is that process for developing policy.

First, identify the specific compensation policy issues. Also provide an opportunity for all senior managers to say what they think the policy issues are. One simple way to do this is to have a checklist of all possible compensation policy items.

Next, write brief statements about each policy matter for presentation to top management. At this point, what you present to top management is not what you recommend, but rather statements designed to get their views. Executive managers react better to statements or specific questions than they do to open-ended questions or philosophical discussions. Present the statement; have follow-up questions; then listen and take notes.

Third, evaluate the information you get. Also evaluate relevant data that are available and the experience of professionals in the field. From all these sources, write a set of policy statements that you recommend. Make sure that each policy statement is no more than one typewritten page.

Submit the results of your work as recommendations to top management. In some cases, the reaction of top management will send the policy issue back to the starting point. Sooner or later, however, you get to the point where there is only detailing and wordsmithing to be done.

Some firms think it is appropriate to engage in strategy sessions with respect to each policy. That involves top management broadly in the implementation phase. Strategizing is partially a matter of top executive preference or style, but properly done it also ensures that implementation faithfully and correctly mirrors the thinking of top executives. Compensation strategy work with top executives requires the use of samples and models and a judicious use of what-if questions.

The compensation policies and strategies that have evolved should meet certain specific requirements. For one thing, they should be specific enough to serve as a screen. When somebody makes a proposal about some action, it can be screened against the policy statements. Policies must also be the basis by which managers throughout the organization make specific decisions and judgments about compensation matters. The various policy statements about compensation can also serve as one basis for reviewing the performance of managers and how well they are managing people. Finally, policies must be specific enough and comprehensive enough so they become an important communications tool.

Accountability to Employees

Part of management is accountability. This should include accountability to employees.

For me, consulting work always involved two customers: the customer who paid and the customer served. It's much like a medical practice, where an insurance company pays the bills but the patients are served. For me, the company paid. (More specifically, the person who signed my bills authorizing payments was the customer who paid.) But the employees who worked there were the customers served. It is an attitude I urge on those who practice in human resources management. It is an attitude I particularly urge those who work in compensation to consider.

Compensation professionals are part of management. As such, they have an accountability for the enterprise and for the employees. Working in a manner that properly meets accountability to the business and to those who do the work in the business is part of the compensation job.

Accountability has a special meaning in business. Strictly speaking, accountability means the obligation to justify, report. or explain; but in an enterprise, accountability also means the authority to act and the responsibility to exercise that authority. Note that accountability, strictly speaking, is only to people. You never need to make explanations to things.

In human resources management areas of work, accountability means the possibility of a reaction from employees. You aren't really responsible to some person or persons unless they can do something when pleased or displeased. Actually, the passage of the National Labor Relations Act and the historic growth of unions in the 1930s were based on this truth and tended to give some classes of workers the ability to react. Then in collective bargaining, employers were accountable to those classes of employees.

Discussions on change always focus on technology changes, and those are breathtaking. But it seems that there is an equivalent change in relationships, and there isn't much focus on changing employee relationships.

For example, there are so many more people who affect your work life today in so many more ways. And while accountability to individual owner-stakeholders has decreased greatly, accountability to employees has increased. That changes accountabilities in the management of human resources greatly.

Accountability involves the use of authority. There are changed dimensions in the use of authority that are also occurring and that affect compensation work.

In some ways, Theory Y made authority seem evil. Actually, what Theory Y essentially said was that the totalitarian attitude of managers of that time was insufficient. Those who preached Theory Y said that the use of authority should be accompanied by help, suggestions, persuasion, and participation.

Keep in mind, of course, that Theory Y was evolved in the 1950s, when business was very different from the way it is now and management practices in large businesses were almost as authoritarian as the army. Management should clearly include persuasion and so forth—even more in the knowledge era of the 1990s than in the industrialized age of the 1940s and the 1950s. But there still must be authority, and it must be exercised.

In work today, it isn't just a question of X or Y. There are times when authoritarian methods can't be used at all, and permissive management is just too costly. Some combination of XY is often the only way, or no authority at all may, in fact, be inevitable.

As important as the use of authority is, the question is also when to exercise authority and on what subjects. The consideration of the use of authority is now two-dimensional. When and where to use authority are now a second grid to consider—a major consideration—and often changes the answer to how to use authority.

As a practical matter, you simply cannot exercise authority in many jobs today on some subjects—at least at some times. It isn't a question of what's nice but what's effective; authority can't be exercised sometimes. For example, you can't make people know something or use what they know. You can't order mental processes.

One of the great ironies of history may prove to be that political tyranny and totalitarianism can no longer exist in a world where economics are dominated by technology. The dictators, bureaucrats, and autocrats can't make people know something or compel the effective use of that knowledge; they can't dictate work quality or work process in knowledge jobs. Technology is the parent of *perestroika* everywhere.

Legal liability to employees relates mostly to conditions of work, particularly health and safety. Theoretically, there is no managerial liability for the material success of employees or their personal fulfillment. The law only requires bargaining with the representatives of employees over wages, benefits, and conditions of work. Otherwise, matters like employee welfare are only subject to free choice. Nevertheless, I would urge you to consider these ideas. First, there must be fairness at work and a commitment to employees' personal goals if there is to be employee accountability to work and a sufficient employee commitment to excellence of work. Second, while physical assets belong to the owners, knowledge belongs to the employees. I think these issues can be resolved by compensation answers rather than by psychological or legal answers. For example, one answer is an employee stock ownership plan.

More work needs to be done on accountability to employees on the part of management. Compensation professionals must particularly consider these accountabilities in the work they do, because pay is a very personal matter.

Chapter Two

The Basics of a Compensation Program

A compensation program is a management method. The programs and practices of compensation should be an integral part of the company's human resources management programs. Human resources management, in turn, is a subsystem, a part of the management of the enterprise. The compensation program is, therefore, an important and integral component of the overall system of managing an enterprise. The basic ideas and principles that reflect this thinking are presented in this chapter.

Basic #1: Serve All Stakeholders

A sound compensation system is composed of programs and practices that help make pay decisions and resolve pay problems in an effective and efficient manner, consistent with the interests of all participants in the enterprise. The participants are the company and its owners, the managers and the employees. All are direct participants in the enterprise.

Owners are basically interested in profits, which are affected greatly by the payroll costs of the business and the productivity of those who work there. Therefore, the owners are interested in a sound compensation program that helps to control the costs of the company and that also contributes to greater employee productivity in return for each dollar of payroll cost. The owner wants compensation programs and practices that broaden the margin between sales and payroll.

Individual managers of personnel need a sound compensation program in the sense that it helps them do the management job more effectively. Managers are the ones who must make decisions and explain programs as well as take specific actions. A sound program is one that helps managers do *their* jobs.

Managers are in a special position in that they are members of all three groups—owners, managers, and employees. They have their management job to do, and a compensation program should facilitate that part of their responsibility. Because they are managers, they are the representatives of the owners. Managers are also paid a salary and receive benefits and are, therefore, employees who are directly affected by the compensation programs.

Pay establishes a standard or style of living for each employee. It also represents the employer's evaluation of an employee's worth to the business—the value of each person's experience, knowledge, and ability. Thus the compensation program is of vital interest to all employees, for it determines their families' standard of living and affects their self-esteem.

The company's compensation program is, therefore, important to owners, managers, and employees alike. When the objectives of these three are in conflict, a sound compensation program should balance the interests of each of these groups.

All those who work in compensation have two customers. That's true in some ways for operating managers of personnel, human resources management generalists, and compensation specialists.

The easier part of this split accountability is to serve the owner-stakeholders and their manager representatives. Answer their questions and resolve the company's problems. Do this in a way that supports the achievement of enterprise goals and reflects all facets of human resources management.

Serving the employee-stakeholders is the more difficult task. Do your best, but recognize that when owner-stakeholders' and employee-stakeholders' interests are in conflict, the owner-representatives' views are predictable and very difficult to change. But do your best, and remember free choice. If accountability to employee-stakeholders is not met, then there will be reactions. But it is often the compensation professional who must monitor these matters and report consequences to owner representatives.

Basic #2: Keep It Simple

The best compensation plan is certainly not the most elaborate, nor is it the most complicated. It is the plan that works best in a particular enterprise. The objective of compensation persons should not be to administer a program that gains admiration in the compensation profession. The compensation program should be useful to the enterprise, helpful to managers, facilitate the achievement of reasonable employee goals, and balance the interests of all the participants in the enterprise. But it should be as simple as possible.

With a trend toward a more delegative style of management, there is a trend toward simpler compensation programs. When everything was directed from the top, there may have been need for considerable complications to make possible programmatic management from a central location under every circumstance. With delegative management, it is possible to get results with far more simple programs. The policies and guidelines of delegative management must be applied by many different managers throughout the organization under many circumstances, and logic argues for simple programs. Generally, the trend from a programmatic to a delegative style of management permits greater simplification and results in lower costs in compensation administration.

Over the years a great deal of technology has been developed in the field of compensation. The very presence of so much technical matter encourages elaborate, complicated, and institutionalized programs. One of the many skills of the compensation manager today is to avoid art for art's sake and recognize that, in spite of a great deal of information and technology, a key skill of the compensation professional is the ability to develop the most practical, useful, and efficient application of the knowledge of the field.

A criterion for excellence of work by compensation professionals today is their ability to simplify. For the many years when there was programmatic management, the professionals were complicators; now they must be simplifiers.

Basic #3: Start by Identifying Compensation Needs

A practical business approach to compensation administration starts by identifying needs. These may be problems in the area of compensation, or they may be special opportunities. Identifying needs is the most critical aspect of compensation work. Clearly, excellent answers to the wrong questions are wasteful. Often, a clear understanding of the need is itself a major step in determining correct actions.

Compensation experts must always know what the problems are. Never let yourself be surprised. Have reasonable proof or evidence that the need is real, not an opinion, anyone's red herring, or a compensation fad. Be sure to have a sketch of an answer and a proposal for how to proceed with respect to any problem identified.

There are some compensation needs and opportunities that are caused by broad economic, political, and social trends. To some degree, these impact all companies and are, therefore, needs to be identified for every enterprise. These *current* trends and developments are information inputs and represent "must-have" information.

Other needs and opportunities vary from company to company, based on company operations and management-initiated actions. In a given company, needs will also vary among divisions and different business units. In each business, division, or unit, needs and opportunities will vary at different times.

There are a number of ways in which compensation needs can be determined, but the critical thing is to have a reliable process, which is part of the management process that can be always used to identify needs and opportunities. The process I recommend for identifying needs in compensation (and in other areas of human resources management) involves some regular and ongoing monitoring, occasional audits, and purchasing reliable information on current trends in human resources management.

Here are some specific methods companies should use in order to determine specific compensation problems and needs. First, always reference your own company's business plan. These plans will tell you how management intends to change the business. Second, make sure you observe the compensation experiences and problems that people encounter in their work. You can do this in the normal course of your work, but try to do it in a somewhat organized manner; at least have some specific questions that you ask frequently.

Use statistical analyses and personnel data whenever possible. Usually, the use of such data will not tell you what the problems are, but they will most likely be diagnostic and suggest problem areas that need to be investigated and analyzed.

You might consider employee opinion polls. I rarely have favored the use of broad-scan opinion polls among employees for a variety of reasons, but it is an option. And a focus poll might be appropriate on special occasions when there are critical matters.

Always listen to the managers. Nurture their questions. Try to gain their confidence so they will tell you their problems.

In addition to all these matters, consider having a formal personnel audit from time to time. The audit should be in all areas of human resources management, not just compensation. It should not be an audit in the accounting sense of looking for errors or mistakes. The audit should try to identify opportunities and problems. Audits will certainly identify compensation problems. If done in an affirmative way, I have always found that personnel audits yield immediate results, and the value far exceeds their costs.

Make sure that an objective intended to resolve one problem does not create a larger problem. Needs must be analyzed qualitatively before they can be translated into realistic, specific, and obtainable objectives.

Translating needs into objectives also requires assessing the importance of a problem or opportunity, how and when it may affect the business, the probability of success in resolving the problem or exploiting the opportunity, and the costs involved. This is art, not science. The process sometimes relies heavily on precedents, intuition, and judgment.

There are three criteria I always apply for evaluating the appropriateness of any program or practice. The criteria are usable to evaluate new proposals and as a tool in a personnel audit.

First and foremost, there must be a clear and compelling need. You must be able to prove the need beyond a reasonable doubt and translate this into a tangible impact on business results and employee aspirations or both.

Second, the proposal to deal with the need must assuredly deal with the problem. "Maybe" or "probably" won't be sufficient—the proposed action must provably solve the problem and not create new problems.

Third, the value of the new program or practice must be clearly greater than the cost, including the time costs of company people and the costs of disruption. As a rule of thumb, I recommend that values exceed costs at least four times; partially because value estimates are always squishy, but cost estimates are usually firm.

Most companies have neither the time nor the financial resources to deal with every identifiable pay problem and opportunity. Compensation needs must also be melded into overall personnel priorities, which, in turn, must take their place in general business priorities. By the time this process of integrating is completed, a high-priority item in compensation may not make the high-priority business list at all. The compensation professional who is a part of management may be frustrated, but he will understand the business needs and the necessity of prioritizing business issues.

Basic #4: Group Employees Properly

The proper development of compensation programs also involves issues of the proper grouping of employees for purposes of human resources management generally and compensation administration specifically. Different types of jobs may require different types of pay programs and practices. Therefore, how employees are grouped and how programs are tailored to the different needs of groups are a basic issue in compensation.

Historically, companies tended to establish groups of employees on the basis of legal and accounting requirements. Employees were exempt or nonexempt in compliance with the Fair Labor Standards Act, and people were divided between direct and indirect work for accounting convenience. The fact is that employees can be grouped by logical business standards and the organization can still comply with the provisions of the

Fair Labor Standards Act. The accounting profession can accommodate any grouping now that it has computers.

For management purposes, jobs must be grouped so that work elements and characteristics are similar in each group; so that the types of training and recruiting methods required to fill the jobs are appropriate; and so that the backgrounds of those who fill the jobs are similar. When this is done, many personnel practices, such as recruiting, communications, training, and compensation, can be developed to meet the needs of the jobs and the people who fill the jobs in each group.

There are at least five groups of employees who should be considered. These are:

1. Operations employees
2. Sales employees
3. Administrative, technical, and supervisory employees
4. Professional employees
5. Management employees

There are frequently subgroups within each of these. For example, large companies sometimes distinguish between the management group and an executive person. Figure 2–1 shows the historic distribution of these groups in a Model A smokestack company and in a professional business.

At the top of the company hierarchy are management employees. These are people who make decisions and judgments that affect business results. Those at the top represent a small group of high-level managers whose actions and judgments affect the long-term success of the business.

Professional employees are those who apply formal knowledge to the solution of company problems. Included in this group are physicians, law-

Figure 2-1. Grouping of Employees.

Groups of Employees	Percent of Total Employment	
	Model A: Industrial Firm	Model P: Professional Business
Executive	0.2%	0.2%
Management	1.2	1.7
Administrative, Technical, and Supervisory	6.9	10.2
Sales	3.4	3.2
Professional	1.1	42.2
Operations	87.2	42.5

yers, engineers, and others who apply recognized academic disciplines. Also included are business disciplines such as personnel and finance.

Sales employees include all those in the field organization. This would include those who have direct contact with customers and those who distribute the company's products or services. This group generally does not include home office sales personnel in such areas as advertising, merchandizing, and market research.

Other middle-group positions include supervisory, administrative, and technical personnel. Supervisors are those whose primary purpose is to direct the work of others. Technical employees are subprofessional people. Administrative employees are those who genuinely cannot be classified in other categories.

Operations workers include both factory and office personnel. Their jobs involve the performance of basically unskilled or semiskilled work that can be defined or proceduralized. Sometimes it is useful to subdivide the operations jobs. For instance, they may be divided into those who are represented by unions and those who are nonunion.

It used to be that the distribution of employees by census count in these various groups could be depicted by a triangle, with management jobs at the apex and many operations jobs at the base. In fact, the numeric distribution of the work force by groupings was illustrated this way in the first four editions of *Compensation*. Then for a time we tried to depict the distribution of employees as a bowling ball or a red beet; but no picture will work anymore. The census distribution and grouping of employees varies greatly for different models of businesses, and no one diagram illustrates all models.

The differences between employee groups are decreasing. Even when different job group labels are used, the compensation practices are the same or equivalent or the differences are less and less. There are a number of reasons why there has been a great deal of movement away from grouping employees and why there are fewer differences between the groups that still exist.

The reasons that caused groupings are no longer relevant or are less compelling. For example, computer technology makes it possible to meet legal requirements and accounting analysis needs without any employee groupings.

Technology has also diminished the need for groupings. More jobs are high-tech; and jobs that were low-tech have more technology. This not only means that there are more ''professionals'' but that, as one example, distinctions between lower level professional work and high-level operations work are more difficult to make.

Management once meant accountability for men and money. Now we manage people, money, and *knowledge*. Many who manage knowledge have no employees reporting to them and only an incidental accountability for assets. They are managers anyway.

The decline of unions is another reason for greater equivalency of treatment in wages, benefits, and conditions of work in different groups of jobs. Unions negotiated special status. Company labor relations negotiators wanted to contain union conditions, and one way to do this was by maintaining hourly status for union members in negotiations and extending salaried status to others.

The trend for greater fairness at work is another reason for eliminating groupings. Special status and privileges for some groups were thought to be rewards and forms of compensation in the era when tenure in one firm was lengthy and company loyalty was an important element of human resources management. Today, there are shallow roots at work, and fairness requires equivalent treatment of all employees.

Consider eliminating differences in pay and treatment between employees as much as possible. Consider as few groups of employees as possible. Never have differences of pay and conditions of work unless such provisions are typical in a labor market and/or required for the effective conduct of work.

Basic #5: Have a Proper Process for Developing Compensation Programs

Always start with needs; never start with programs. Identify the questions—the problems or the opportunities. Then develop the programs or practices that solve the problems or exploit the opportunities. Starting with a program is an answer to a question that wasn't asked.

The correct approach to developing proper compensation programs is illustrated in Figure 2–2. It is the correct approach to problem solving—a traditional approach in business. You should always follow this process. Some key points about the process for developing programs are presented in this section.

Custom-Designed Programs

Essentially, every company is unique, different not only in terms of its size, products, locations, and organization but also in more subtle ways. For example, companies have different management styles: things get done differently, and decisions are made in various ways.

It necessarily follows that if each company's needs and questions are different, then the answers must also be unique. This suggests that compensation programs and practices must be tailored to each company situation.

Similarly, in large diversified companies, the divisions and other organizational units may be different. While part of the overall company, they too may have unique needs and questions. Therefore, it is also nec-

Figure 2-2. Recommended Process for Developing Compensation Programs.

1. Identify needs, problems or opportunities, focusing on such methods as:
   - Data analysis
   - Reported issues
   - Discussions with managers
   - Discussions with employees
   - Personnel audits

2. Develop objectives
   - Set specific goals
   - Consider impact on other human resources management programs
   - Schedule
   - Consider resources available

3. Conceptualize the answer early in the work and at first as a broad sketch, considering:
   - Company characteristics
   - Competitive practices
   - Company culture
   - Employee reactions

4. Testing and specific program design, which may involve:
   - Legal, tax, and accounting considerations
   - "What-if" gaming and modeling
   - Comparative analysis with alternative answers
   - Evaluation against company plans and forecasts

5. Implementation

6. Evaluating the effectiveness of the program

7. Review

essary to tailor compensation programs and practices to some extent to each operating unit.

For effective corporate management control and internal equity, it is necessary to tailor programs and practices in different units to fit within an overall company framework of policy and guidelines. But in terms of specific practices and programs, some tailoring to the needs of different units is almost always essential.

The need for a tailored program means that canned programs are inappropriate in almost any situation. The predesigned program may meet the needs of the supplier, but it cannot meet the needs of the users. To argue otherwise is to say that every company is essentially the same, whereas, in fact, they are all different.

Those who offer canned plans are people walking around with an answer in a briefcase looking for a question that matches. They are at an advantage as salespersons, because they have hardware to sell; something visible that can be shown on flip charts. They can also say that others have used their canned programs, but that likely means that others erred.

Goals and Objectives

The basic goals of a compensation program are to meet the needs of the organization, support the achievement of objectives, resolve problems, exploit opportunities, and meet the reasonable aspirations of employees and owners. It is sometimes useful to translate such general objectives into more specific goals.

In my consulting work, I am always very specific about objectives for a program and have always urged human resources management professionals in all fields to do the same. Ours is a soft science that requires deep knowledge. This means that we can rarely prove anything or identify with certainty a predictable cause and effect relationship. So much of our work is based upon the knowledge and precedents of experience. However, you can be specific about objectives and build models that provide some factual inputs to costs and values.

Never set as an objective squishy, generalized, or do-gooder goals, such as "improve morale," "provide greater internal consistency," or "create a better quality of work life." Such goals don't mean anything to anyone—or they can mean whatever is desired. Such word blobs will likely cause wonderment and distrust on the part of managers and employees.

Set specific goals, such as "reduce the cost of classifying jobs by 80 percent" or "delegate pay decisions to managers." Then set up data systems that help judge cost and value.

Conceptualize the Answer

It is desirable to conceptualize the ideas for an answer as early in the process of program development as possible. Long, stretched-out study programs cost too much and often fall of their own weight. Worst of all, programs that take a long time waste a lot of time if the ultimate conclusion proves to be incorrect or requires rework.

Traditional notions of program development differ from the recommended early postulation of an answer in important respects. According to the problem-solving lessons of the past, you gathered all the information, did all the staff work, carefully considered all alternatives, had many meetings, and finally came to a conclusion. It was thought that this was a fail-safe way of solving problems, making decisions, and developing programs. But it never seemed to work like that. If nothing else, we *never* have *all* the information.

These traditional methods of problem solving evolved in an era where change was slow and work was more predictable. In compensation work today, there are enough alternatives available and enough experience and know-how to make judgments about the correct program or practice very early in the project—provided needs have been correctly identified, objectives have been set, and senior and experienced people are directing the project work.

The main advantage of early conceptualization of an answer is that it leaves more time to test the tentative answer. It leaves time to detail and make sure that everybody understands exactly what is being done and why. There is also more likely to be time for proper design for change and for involving those who must approve and support the new program in one way or another.

Testing and Detailing

Testing may involve a few minutes of reflection, some networking, or a major part of the total time required to develop a compensation program. If a project is important enough to be undertaken in the first place, then it's important enough to be tested.

Part of testing is to ensure that all technical aspects of the work are absolutely correct. This is the time to review the work with tax and accounting experts.

Sometimes detailed testing is required. This may involve setting up computer models and elaborate testing tabulations. This is very often the case with sales incentive compensation plans.

Modeling is increasingly a useful way to test. Modeling carries the "what-if" exercise into the world of technology.

If there are going to be meetings with others in the field or people in other functional areas of personnel, then it is in the testing and detailing phase that they should be conducted. Here's where you need input from other people.

Implementation

Implementation means more than simply getting things done. Implementation means putting programs into operation and establishing the various procedures and reviews that are a necessary part of any program. Implementation, in effect, puts flesh on the bones of a designed program. The specifics of administrative practices and cases that are experienced become part of the substance of the program.

It is difficult to be specific with respect to implementation because implementation practices must be tailored so much to each operation, each company situation, and the people involved.

In a sense, the implementation phase of any activity never ends. Compensation problems are not solved by adopting a program or practice but only by ongoing application. Furthermore, the application of a program or practice inevitably involves decisions on matters not answered in detail, or perhaps not anticipated, when the program or practice was initiated. Such decisions add to, frequently modify, and, over a period of time, change the program. Finally, the nature of operational and administrative work involved in implementation will change, and the staffing required to do the work must similarly change to meet current requirements.

There is often a series of implementation phases covering the life of an activity. Normally, a new compensation program requires a great deal of attention and special practices when it is first implemented. But the practice needs and staff support should usually diminish with time.

Review and Revise

Programs that involve a major use of time should have built-in systems for subsequent review. This should be just one part of the design specifications. Ultimately, however, every program should be subject to the personnel audit program.

Adaptations that occur with time may accumulate to a point where a major revision is necessary. A major revision may also be necessary because of a change in operations, regulations, or management. The company's needs may change, or there may be changes in priorities. There may be a change of management or a change of ownership. Finally, the technology of compensation changes, and this may result in the development of new programs and practices that serve the organization better and justify revisions or replacement of programs.

There are few decisions more difficult to make than when to change a program or make major revisions. This is particularly true if the program has been successful and is well understood by managers and accepted by employees.

It is also difficult to revise a program at the right time. Suggestions for revisions or new programs are, in fact, sometimes perceived as criticisms. There is also a natural tendency to put off such revisions until there is a clear need. By then, however, there may also be a major problem.

Some companies have established "sunset rules" for many programs, including major compensation programs. When a program is implemented, there is a date when it automatically expires or comes up for review and possible revision. In fact, most programs and practices will inevitably become obsolete. In compensation, the life expectancy is rarely more than ten years. As long as businesses change and the environment in which business is conducted changes, revisions or periodic adaptations of complete new programs are inevitable.

Basic #6: Program Design Must Reflect Company Culture

Business circumstances and operating characteristics must also influence the proper design and management of compensation programs. Those who work in the company know these characteristics and circumstances. But even the company staff needs to reflect on this important matter from time to time, particularly if a major new project is being considered.

Companies are as unique as people and as changeable with time. Before undertaking a project, consider writing a profile description of the firm that will be relevant to the work. This need not take more than a few pages and should deal with such issues as the inclination of the organization to innovate, its management style, and the inclination toward bureaucratic practices. This written document is valuable in assuring that any project is truly tailored to the company involved.

Two examples should be sufficient to illustrate this important input to the proper development of compensation administration. One would be company growth characteristics and proper compensation practices. A second would be the administrative time and effort involved in compensation activities at different phases of their evolution and implementation.

Students of business have established that there are essentially four phases in the evolution of an organization from its foundation to maturity. The first phase involves the early formation of the company and its beginning operations. The second involves the growth phase, when a company's sales and earnings are growing in excess of 15 percent a year above inflation. The third phase represents high levels of profitability and a slowing growth, but a growth rate that matches or slightly exceeds inflation. Finally, there is the phase of maturity. Each of these phases of company growth requires substantially different compensation programs and different emphasis in the mix of pay for some groups.

A new compensation program usually requires a considerable amount of staff time. It is a new system, unfamiliar to managers. It requires constant communication. Managers may need assistance in working with the program. After the program has been in effect for a number of years, supervisors become familiar with it. This should permit broader delegation of decision making, administration, and communication to the managers of personnel, and less staff time.

A sound compensation program must always reflect the culture of the organization. Culture is a fancy word that in business means "the way we do things around here." In an era of rapid change, company culture is an important issue. This always means work that reflects company culture. It may also involve changing company culture.

The issues of company culture are human resources management issues. Company culture relates only to people: how we manage people, our human resources management policies, basic executive management attitudes toward the management of people, how people work together (including the structure of the organization), how people are paid, and how decisions are made. In this sense, every company has a culture, and it is of obvious importance.

If you work on company culture, the first essential step is to define, explicitly and in detail, the company culture that exists in your firm at the present time. How can you change your company culture unless you begin with a knowledge of what it is?

The second step requires a careful identification of changes that are occurring in your business, and/or an understanding of why your business is not doing well, and/or an understanding of current trends and developments that are significantly impacting your business.

Such changes in the business must then be examined against the company culture that exists. This examination must determine the following:

- What changes in culture must be made?
- What actions need to be taken to bring about these changes?
- What is the probability of success of these actions in changing culture appropriately?
- What is the cost of these actions?

Work on company culture requires the highest level of professional knowledge, a deep understanding of the business, and high sensitivity. Be mindful of the fact that there are few areas of work where company culture is more important in determining the success of a program than in compensation; and that is particularly true of management pay issues.

Basic #7: Install a Formal Program

A somewhat formal system in compensation is needed in all but the smallest businesses. A formal program, in the sense of establishing standards that are predetermined and in writing and serve to guide individual pay decisions, seems reasonable and necessary. Such elements of a formal structure in compensation should contribute to better decisions, more consistency, and greater fairness.

A formal program should never mean that the program itself makes decisions and that the program becomes mechanical. The program or its procedures cannot be the decision-making process.

A formal program does not necessarily mean an elaborate program, although a minimum amount of structure is required. In fact, the more elaborate a program is, the more difficult it is to implement and communicate. Ideally, a program should be the simplest plan that meets the company's needs and objectives.

The complex compensation programs that evolved in the third phase of the evolution of the personnel function are now obsolete. The use of formal programs in the sense of rigid, overly ceremonious, and directional rules and regulations is not appropriate now, and any that exist need to be modified or replaced.

Business went through a substantial downsizing in the middle of the 1980s, and I maintain that the downsizing process is only half over as of 1989, when this was written. The focus of downsizing was a reduction in staff—mostly support staff. Compensation departments were drastically reduced in many cases. While the focus was on the need to reduce personnel, the real issue was the need and opportunity to downsize *work;* and that often meant eliminating or streamlining overly complex and rigidly formal compensation programs.

The methods of downsizing were harsh but quick, effective though not necessarily correct. The target should have been bloated and obsolete programs, not the people who did the work on these obsolete programs.

Now that the first wave of head-count downsizing is over, companies are looking at programs, and in most enterprises, there is still a substantial opportunity for more effective compensation programs. Consider a process for reviewing your programs, keeping cost and value in mind. Because of downsizing and the pressure for cost reduction, the need for formal compensation programs will have close scrutiny.

Some companies review programs by some form of activity value analysis, a system of zero-basing activities. Activity value analysis can involve elaborate and costly activities in its own right. My preference is simply to work with the compensation staff and go back to the basics. Working with a professional and starting with a figuratively blank sheet of paper gets better results, in my experience, at a far less cost and can be completed in an elapsed period of time of one month.

Basic #8: Be Skilled in the Art of Managing Change

In an era of rapid change, all who do compensation work must be able to adapt to change. The popular phrase is to manage change, but what most of us do is manage well in an environment of change. Those who do compensation work must learn to manage in an environment of change. Often this means a quick change of programs.

Management skills in managing change must mostly mean skills in the management of people, because employees are the company's only resource that reacts to change or resists it. Here are a few ideas and suggestions for managing change.

There are some things we know about change and the art of managing people in a climate of change. We know, for example, that change occurs most quickly and most effectively in response to a crisis. Much of the work that has been done in the field of personnel also suggests that you can manage change best by getting the involvement of all the people who would be affected by that change. The logic is that involvement gets a greater acceptance of the change because of the participation in the process. Such participation seems reasonable on the surface, but there are also very high costs when many people become involved. Furthermore, the change process may often move too slowly. Involvement and participation frequently mean compromises, and they may not deal effectively with change.

There is a different attitude toward change at the bottom of an organization than there is at the top. Those who work at the bottom levels generally resist change only if such changes reduce their pay, benefits, or conditions of work. Thus compensation practices are extremely important in managing change in operations-level jobs. Here are a few brief principles of managing change.

As you get higher in the organization, the resistance to change is protective *plus* a commitment to the status quo. Higher-level people tend to like to leave practices the way they are, particularly if those higher-level people were the decision makers who implemented existing practices.

Age is a factor to consider when dealing with the issues of managing people in a climate of change. Younger people are more used to change. Change existed fifty years ago, but most change occurred at a more leisurely pace.

Executives often think that making a change is managing a change. It is obviously the top policy makers who make the decisions that result in the big changes. But they make the decisions and don't communicate the decisions or implement required modifications of practices.

You can change people or change inorganic things like programs. Given the choice, recognize that it is always easier to change things.

Some teach very organized methods of dealing with change. That has not worked well for those I know who tried it, particularly because there isn't anything orderly about change.

If you are going to deal with change and manage people effectively in a climate of change, the first step must always be to identify the change. If you are going to manage change, it is essential to know what the changes are. That sounds simple, but it is becoming increasingly difficult to track current trends and developments.

34

Many changes that must be managed are unique to a business and initiated by the management of the business. Existing systems of management identify these changes. Increasingly, however, broad social, economic, and political trends impact on all organizations.

When selecting the correct course of action, it is always important to "engineer for change." This means that the practice selected for implementation should be determined by the excellence of the practice and by the degree to which managers of the firm will understand it, accept it, and use it effectively.

In compensation, programs have changed dramatically over the past thirty years; in fact, they have changed greatly since the fourth edition of this book. In compensation work, however, this change has been uneven. Many firms have adapted well and quickly. Others, unfortunately, still operate with the programs of the 1960s.

A fair evaluation of those who do compensation work would have to be very complimentary in most respects. But if that same evaluation were to list failures, then very likely the number one fault of those who work in compensation in general is resistance to change and a desire to direct and control highly programmatic and formal work in compensation from a central point.

Chapter Three

The Elements of Compensation

Employees receive their pay in various forms. Each form or element of compensation serves a different objective for the company, having evolved over time to deal with specific company needs. Each element of compensation also tends to meet different employee aspirations or objectives.

Identification of the elements of compensation is a cataloging of forms or methods of pay. It represents hardware information but is important because different forms of compensation are available; each serves somewhat different needs; and it is the total that represents costs to employers and income to employees.

The elements of compensation may be categorized in a variety of ways. One useful breakdown is as follows:

- Salary
- Premium payments
- Bonus payments
- Long-term income payments
- Pay for time not worked
- Benefits
- Extra pay plans
- Nonfinancial rewards

Some of these elements are more applicable to some groups of employees than to others. For instance, overtime is applied only to operations

Figure 3-1. The Elements of Compensation.

Salary
  + Overtime
  + Bonus
  _____
  = TOTAL CURRENT COMPENSATION

Total Current Compensation
  + Long-Term Income
  _____
  = TOTAL COMPENSATION

Total Compensation
  + Pay for Time Not Worked
  + Benefits
  + Extra Pay Plans
  _____
  = TOTAL INCOME

Total Income
  + Perquisites
  + Environment
  _____
  = TOTAL REMUNERATION

The elements of compensation add up to total remuneration.

persons. Long-term income plans are typically restricted to higher-paid persons.

Salaries, bonuses, and premium payments of one sort or another all represent cash income earned in the course of the year. They are, therefore, the current compensation for an employee (see Figure 3–1). Current compensation, plus long-term income, is the dollars actually received by an employee and might be properly labeled total pay.* Benefits, pay for time not worked, and estate-building plans represent values for employees, even though they may never receive cash payments from some of them. However, these elements of compensation represent a part of the total income of the employee and have values that can be calculated. Finally, there are items of income, such as perquisites and the nonfinancial aspects of income, that cannot be put into monetary terms. They are of value, however, and, added to total income, represent the total remuneration of employees.

---

*The word "pay" is a generic term referring to any or all elements of compensation. However, it is also often used to mean salary, bonus, and premium payments.

FINANCIAL REWARDS

Each of the elements of financial income serves a different need and objective for the company. Identification of these elements of compensation is not, therefore, a theoretical breakdown. Rather, it is a classification of the elements of compensation that evolved over time to meet specific needs and sometimes legal requirements or other conditions of the time.

Objectives of Financial Elements of Income

Some of the basic needs served by different elements of compensation are illustrated in Figure 3–2. This exhibit identifies some of the principal values of the elements of compensation that are generally applicable. Each of the elements may serve additional special objectives for some companies and in some circumstances. Note that these different elements of financial income also satisfy various objectives for employees, as indicated in the exhibit.

Figure 3-2. Company and Employee Needs and Objectives Served by Different Forms of Compensation.

Form of Compensation	Employee	Company
Salaries or wages	Sets standard of living Reflects employer's evaluation	Key to pay competitiveness Basis for administering other forms of compensation
Premium payments	Extra income; frequently permits special purchases	Legal requirement Induces employees to work longer hours
Bonuses	Extra current income Reward for achievement of short-term goals Opportunity for above-average income Impact of lump-sum income on lifestyle	Variable cost Motivation for attainment of short-term goals Attract key personnel Favorable short-term cash flow

(continued)

Figure 3-2. Continued.

Form of Compensation	Employee	Company
Long-term income	Reward for achievement Opportunity for high income Possibly lower net tax Key estate-building mechanism	Favorable financial aspects Holding power Motivation for attainment of long-term goals Attracts key personnel
Pay for time not worked	Rest from work Recreational opportunities	For some employees, low-cost item of high value Competitive need
Benefits	Tax-sheltered income Protection against economic risks	Meet company's social responsibilities to employees
Extra pay plans	Leveraged savings High-level fund management	Flexible supplement to insurance programs Build favorable employee attitudes

Each of the specific elements of compensation serves company objectives and employee goals.

The basic features of each of the elements of compensation and their essential role in overall remuneration are summarized in the following paragraphs.

Salaries or Wages

Salaries or wages are periodic payments to employees. For the company, they represent a fixed cost of doing business. They are also one basis for administering some other forms of compensation. Salary represents the principal basis for attracting and retaining the people needed to operate the business.

For employees, salaries or wages are the basic income that sets their standard of living. Rarely are premium payments sufficient to materially affect their standard of living, and premium payments cannot be guaranteed. Bonus pay is also at risk and, when paid, can vary a great deal from year to year. The salary or wage also reflects the employer's evaluation of the worth of an employee's job.

Premium Payments

For most operations-level employees, overtime pay is legally required. As a matter of policy or collective bargaining, many companies have enriched the rate of payments for work beyond standard work weeks.

Shift premiums came about because of the need to pay more to recruit employees to work outside of the standard daytime working hours. Widespread use of such premiums also resulted from collective bargaining. There are other types of premium payments in some industries, such as pay for unusually hazardous work.

Bonuses

Bonuses involve periodic lump-sum payments. They may be annual payments, such as those under an annual incentive award plan for managers, or bonus or commission payments to salespersons, which would more likely be made monthly. Bonuses may also be special awards for such achievements as cost savings.

For the employer, all such payments represent a variable cost. Perhaps most important, many firms believe that some types of bonuses contribute substantially to improving operations by providing financial motivation.

A bonus award for the employee represents extra income and an opportunity to attain above-average earnings. Moreover, the fact that the bonus is paid in a lump sum may enable the employee to buy goods or services that can have a meaningful impact on the employee's way of life. If the same amount of money were paid to the employee in equal amounts over twenty-four or fifty-two periods in a year, the employee might not save the funds for such special purchases. Frequently, a bonus also represents a reward for special achievement; it signifies recognition as well as income.

Long-Term Income Payments

Long-term income plans are bonuses paid for achieving goals or standards over a period of time, which is longer than one year. They include stock option programs and various performance reward programs geared to earnings improvement. Generally, these plans are applied only to higher-paid employees.

For the employer, long-term income plans represent a variable cost.

Long-term income plans may motivate employees to achieve the long-term goals of the enterprise. Long-term income plans also represent a principal method of building "golden handcuffs" into the compensation program; frequently, they provide that employees who leave the company voluntarily forfeit values accrued under the plan.

For the employee, the long-term income plan is an opportunity to accumulate very large sums of money. For some, it has meant the opportunity to become rich.

Pay for Time Not Worked

Pay for time not worked includes vacation time, holidays, sick-leave days, and special time off for such things as jury duty and military service. There is also pay for time not worked during working hours, such as scheduled rest periods or coffee breaks. Sick-leave days represent a form of self-insured sickness pay, providing employees with continued income in the event of a short-term illness. Vacation and holiday payments allow for a paid rest from work. For the employee, they obviously provide more time for their families and for recreation.

Benefits

Employee benefits provide protection against economic risks, including death, disability, and illness. Many of these are insured benefits, with the employer paying some or all the cost of the insurance premium.

These benefits offer needed protection at a lower cost to the employee than would be available on an individual basis. In some cases, employer-sponsored benefits also provide coverage the employee could not obtain as an individual.

Benefits meet certain company needs. Pensions, for instance, were designed to solve the company's problem of how to treat long-service, valued employees who have become too old to work. Because some benefits are so widely practiced today, the presence of a benefit package is now necessary in order to attract and retain employees.

Extra Pay Plans

Extra pay programs include stock purchase plans, thrift plans, some forms of profit-sharing trusts, special stock purchase plans, and estate counseling services. All such plans help employees accumulate savings or manage their savings better, sometimes on a tax-deferred basis, at a lower cost to the employee or with professional investment advice.

Magnitude of Financial Payments

Each form or element of compensation can represent a significant part of the overall remuneration of an employee. Only the financial elements of compensation can be expressed in dollar terms. Estimated values typical at different salary levels are illustrated in Figure 3–3.

Salary still represents the key element of compensation at almost all job levels and is certainly the major part of income in lower-paying jobs. Even in very highly paid jobs, where salary represents less than half of total remuneration, salary is still key, because it is the largest single element of compensation year after year and is frequently one basis for determining other forms of compensation. For these reasons and because salary represents a fixed cost for the employer and the basis for living standards for employees, the design of the salary system is critical to the success of a compensation program.

Even for lower-paid employees, compensation elements other than salary represent about one-third of the overall cash values. In higher-level jobs, bonuses and long-term income can equal salary and, in very good years, can far exceed salary. In fact, key executives in large companies receive only one-third of their total remuneration from salary.

Pay for time not worked is difficult to report with precision. Higher-level employees often are entitled to as much time off with pay as they wish, but many do not use it.

Benefits are clearly no longer "fringes" at any salary level. They tend to be slightly lower as a percentage of salary at higher levels of pay mostly because of prescribed maximum benefits in some plans and flat payments regardless of earnings in others.

Figure 3-3. Magnitude of Income From Different Elements of Compensation (as percentage of base salary).

Element of Compensation	$10,000	$25,000	$60,000	$100,000
Salary	100%	100%	100%	100%
Premium pay and bonus	5	2	20	30
Long-term income	0	0	15	26
Pay for time not worked	10	9	7	5
Benefits	30	29	28	27
Extra pay plans	2	2	3	3
	147%	142%	173%	192%

This exhibit shows the portion of total pay in basic elements of compensation at different salary levels.

NONFINANCIAL ELEMENTS OF PAY

It is correct to say that money isn't everything. It is equally correct to say that for almost all employees, during at least part of their work careers, money is far ahead in importance of whatever it is that is in second place. Nonetheless, nonfinancial elements of remuneration (sometimes referred to as "conditions") are important and should be an integral part of the management of compensation.

Basic Types of Nonfinancial Remuneration

There are a number of identifiable different forms of nonfinancial remuneration. Management needs to identify specifically these items in its own organization. It may help to do this identification in terms of:

- The company and the environment the company creates
- The work
- Physical conditions
- Work environment
- Perquisites of the job
- Fairness

Company Environment

What the company does can be of perceived value to the employee and, therefore, is an element of nonfinancial remuneration. This value can relate, for instance, to the social merits of the enterprise, as in the case of a hospital. The value can relate to the visibility of company activities; this is true, for instance, in many public transportation companies. The value can be related to the fact that the company and its employees are "where the action is," as in many news media organizations.

What the company does can be of value in the sense that the company is a pioneer in its field or working in the frontiers of knowledge. Classic examples are the work done in the Manhattan Project and work at NASA. Working for a prestigious organization can be of value. This may simply be that the company is extremely well-known or that it has been outstandingly successful. These characteristics can be perceived to be a work benefit or of value to employees and, therefore, are inherently a part of remuneration.

There is also some value in working for a quality company. This is a company that is known for its integrity and its fair dealings. It may be a company that is a good neighbor in the community and, therefore, is well thought of by friends and neighbors. It can be a company the employee is proud to be associated with, and this pride of association can be a value that, in fact, is a part of remuneration.

The Work

Clearly, the job the person does can be of great value aside from the rate of pay received for doing the work. Anyone values more highly a job he enjoys doing, which he does well, which is visible, and which is highly regarded by fellow employees. Thus the work itself not only determines direct pay but has a psychological value as well.

The associates one works with can also be a plus or a minus in terms of psychological income. For some, this may mean others to learn from or a strong leader. Congeniality and mutual helpfulness can contribute to or detract from productivity and, to some degree, are always elements of nonfinancial remuneration.

Whether the employee has the proper tools to do the work can affect how he does his work and whether he enjoys it. Sometimes it is just a matter of the independence a person is given to do the job.

Physical Conditions

The element of nonfinancial remuneration that has been most studied and examined involves the physical conditions of work. These include such items as cleanliness, light, decor, and, more important, comfort and safety. It is in these areas, not surprisingly, that there are some tangible experiences and data to indicate values and costs.

Work Environment

There are also aspects of the work environment that can have value to employees. The location of a company can be important. Access to shopping centers, transportation facilities, and similar things can be important. Particularly with the high cost of transportation, a company near population centers with ready access to public transportation can be highly regarded by employees, and that can be an element of nonfinancial remuneration.

The management style in the company can be another important element of the work environment and overall remuneration. How employees' questions and grievances are handled, the type of job security that exists, and company policies regarding employee relations can also be important elements of nonfinancial income.

The degree to which the company helps employees to not only perform more effectively but to grow in their work and in their careers may also involve nonfinancial income. A positive work environment mostly means excellence of supervision, but it can also mean having the right tools or equipment to do the job, as well as a management style that permits employees to do their best.

Perquisites

There are also various forms of perquisites that add income values to the job. Purchasing company products at discount, parking facilities, and company-subsidized cafeterias are all examples of perquisites that have value to employees.

Titles can be important to some employees. Using titles as an element of reward can have its own set of problems. Frequently, each new title creates the desire for such recognition in other jobs. Over time, some companies have added titles to the point that it diminishes the value of titles for all.

If titles are to be used as a nonfinancial reward, rather formal ground rules for titling should be established. Usually, this involves multiple criteria, such as organizational level and salary grade. Some companies have concluded that the armed forces have a better system with respect to titles. This system awards titles to the individual rather than to the job.

Service awards, prizes, and special recognition in company publications are other examples of perquisites. None of these has great value, of course, but they do add to total remuneration. Sometimes their value in the minds of employees is all out of proportion to the cost to the employer.

Fairness

Working for and with those perceived to be fair is of value to many people. Therefore, it should be added as an element of nonfinancial compensation. More than most elements of nonfinancial remuneration, the value of fairness can't be numericized, but the value is real for some people, and fairness at work is an important business matter.

We know that fairness is of some importance to employers and to employees. Clearly, however, such an item has unproven values and undeterminable costs.

For many years, in many large companies, a form of corporate niceness has been practiced, and some have come to regard this as a valued nonfinancial element of compensation. Corporate niceness, however, has largely been applied to the management ranks. In companies where it is used at the top, it becomes part of the corporate culture and it is valued. Sometimes it has been reported as a value and discussed as a positive element of company remuneration. Little of that kinder corporate environment, however, has trickled down below the management ranks. Furthermore, downsizing, leveraged buy-outs (LBOs), and takeovers have largely ended corporate niceness as a form of nonfinancial remuneration.

Value of Nonfinancial Elements of Pay

There is little understanding about the elements of nonfinancial remuneration. It is possible to list many elements of indirect pay, but what is lacking is an exhaustive listing based on sound study methods. Furthermore, there are inadequate methods for costing different elements, determining their value to employees, or understanding how such elements of nonfinancial remuneration affect enterprise results.

. Nonfinancial elements of pay represent real values to employees and, therefore, are a form of remuneration. They similarly involve a real cost to the employer. These costs sometimes also involve capital expenditures. The largest item of the cost of nonfinancial elements of remuneration is, however, a time cost.

There is need for an analytic method for determining and evaluating items of nonfinancial remuneration. With computer technology, models can be developed that help to manage conditions or at least provide guidelines for a better valuing of such items, support the development of more effective management of conditions, and help management make better decisions with respect to conditions.

Business has relied largely on opinion surveys and the work of behavioral scientists with respect to the management of conditions. Opinion polls tell management what it should already know: that conditions of work are important to employees, affect their attitudes, have some impact on the effectiveness of work, and also that employees tend to want what they do not have.

Work by behavioral scientists has been instructive but not directly useful. Some action programs stemming from work done by behavioral scientists have done more harm than good. The problem has been that too much of the work by these professionals has been clinical and theoretical. Resulting programs fail to recognize the dynamics of the real world of work. The value of these academic efforts lies in the *information* gained from them, not in the conclusions that were made.

Employees have certain *expectations* with respect to conditions of work. These represent *requirements* for an employer. Unless these requirements are met, there is negative remuneration, and failure to meet such requirements is viewed as a job negative. Requirements vary among different companies and different job groups, but there is a rather specific list, and they are relatively easy to identify. For example, work cannot be hazardous because of equipment failures or lack of concern by the employer. Also, employees expect to have reasonable tools to do their work, whether these tools are grinders, typewriters, conference rooms, or computers.

Unless requirements are met, unproductive practices will evolve, resulting in lower productivity. Employee attitudes will be unsatisfactory, often reflected by resistance to necessary business changes and disinterest in productivity or work quality. Given the opportunity, effective employees will look for other jobs unless such requirements are met, and no level of pay is likely to dissuade them from seeking employment elsewhere.

Requirements truly represent a necessary cost of doing business. In the minds of workers, failure to meet requirements is a failure of the enterprise.

Some conditions or elements of nonfinancial remuneration may be *supportive* or *motivational*. The degree of improvement in work effectiveness from these nonfinancial elements of remuneration and their impact on business results vary for different elements of nonfinancial reward and for different individuals. Much work needs to be done in this area. The primary opportunities for these elements of nonfinancial remuneration are in work-oriented areas: better equipment, improved layout, and stronger leadership.

Continued improvement in nonfinancial items of remuneration will inevitably reach a point of *sufficiency*. Beyond this, there is *redundancy*, and further improvement of conditions does not result in additional nonfinancial reward in the perceptions of employees, nor is it likely to contribute to improved operations. Additional improvement in conditions beyond the point of redundancy may, in fact, result in a *negative return* if it is not valued by employees and fails to contribute to higher productivity.

Changing one element of nonfinancial reward will probably change employees' perceptions of and desires for other elements. Thus the management of conditions is a systems activity, with few guidelines or analytic models. The tools of management are now mostly understanding, a framework for thinking, and guidelines for decisions.

The Management of Conditions

The elements of nonfinancial remuneration are little understood, and sometimes they are not well managed. These elements are important to employees, involve real values of substantial magnitude, and cost the employer significantly. They must be managed.

To manage these conditions, personnel staffs and particularly compensation professionals must first identify all the elements of nonfinancial remuneration. The author's list includes dozens of items, so this phase itself is a task. Most of the items apply to almost all firms. It is, therefore, a job that can be done best and with the greatest assurance on a group basis. However done, you must start by identifying the elements of conditions.

Using available information and known techniques, the next job is to determine methods of costing and valuing items. There are better methods and more experience in costing than in valuing items of conditions. In most cases, judgments about costs and values are all that is possible, and the company would be well advised to build a considerable safety margin in its assessments of requirements for nonfinancial elements of remuneration. The cost of failing to meet requirements is very high.

Companies should consider a case-by-case review of proposals to improve conditions beyond requirements. This screening should include a very specific identification of needs, estimates of costs (including the time of company employees), and some description of objectives and values.

How a firm identifies and categorizes conditions can also be a helpful step toward the effective management of these nonfinancial forms of remuneration. Although there are no clear-cut categories of conditions, the approach I recommend identifies:

- Work support items
- Extra income items
- Intangible items
- Status items

Work support items are all those that help employees do a better job. Companies should seek out these items. All those that involve a moderate time or cost or for which the benefits of resulting effectiveness clearly exceed cost should be considered favorably.

All "extra income" items should be either taxable income or reimbursements for business expenses. Some business expense reimbursements, such as meal allowances, have a tangible value to employees, reducing their families' expenses. Companies need to monitor these items carefully to assure their legitimacy.

Intangible items include things such as company image or work location. Once established, these items cannot be easily influenced; nor does their value in the minds of employees change. All intangible items, by nature, are difficult to manage.

It is the status items that have proven to be troublesome and frequently counterproductive. Usually, an enhanced status for one person means a diminished status for others. Furthermore, focus on status items may encourage employees to seek the symbols of success rather than the substance of achievement.

When considering conditions, it is also important to realize that the values sometimes lie mainly in perceptions. One individual may love travel; another may dislike it intensely. For one person, a job may be "hazardous;" for another, it may be "man's work." Such factors further complicate the management of conditions.

There is one other critically important subject relating to the management of conditions that has value to employees and is of great importance to the organization that is far beyond the subject of compensation alone. This is the matter of leadership.

During the past ten years, some helpful work has been done on the subject of leadership. Perhaps of greatest value is the prudent-man *proof* that leadership in the operations substantially improves results and that working for a person with leadership attributes is highly prized by almost all employees.

There is also information about leadership attributes among operating managers. In fact, there are two types of attributes: four of which always apply and at least one additional attribute that is highly individualistic. The four operating manager leadership attributes that are always required are:

1. Credibility
2. High competence in managing nonsupervisory work
3. A positive "can-do" attitude
4. A people-sensitive person, in the sense that the manager listens and cares

The additional attribute is highly individualistic and often very personal. The extra individual leadership attribute may be a personality trait like charisma. The extra attribute may be a former accomplishment unrelated to work. The additional attribute is one or more characteristics that make that person stand out, is perceived as being something special, and becomes a subject of person-to-person identification.

I often talk about leadership at my conferences for compensation professionals as well as those for personnel generalists. Some human resources management areas are important to every functional area. Leadership is not, for example, an area of exclusive importance to training. Actually, you can't teach most leadership attributes, so leadership is more a subject of employment and promotion or selection rather than training.

Leadership considerations will become more important in the next decade. This is largely due to the fact that communication technology has extended the reach of leaders in much the same way that recordings extended the reach of musicians.

THE ELEMENTS OF COMPENSATION AND COMPENSATION MANAGEMENT

All the elements of compensation have management importance because they serve special goals of the employer and special needs of the employees. The elements of compensation also represent the working tools of persons who do work in compensation.

It is useful to make the distinction between compensation management and the management of compensation. The management of compensation is what operating managers throughout the company do in the normal course of their work. Operations managers manage the pay of those who work in their units. This means making decisions about pay and communicating those decisions. Compensation management is basically what the specialist professionals who work in compensation do in their work to support the effective management of compensation.

Elements of compensation have the most practical values in compensation management. The compensation professional should identify the basic elements of compensation that exist for each of the groups in the enterprise where he works. What is urged, however, is that there is also an identification of each item within each element of compensation. For example, it is not just that you identify benefits as an element of compensation, but that you then proceed to identify each separate benefit item.

Simply identifying all the elements of compensation can be a difficult activity. This is partly because there are so many of them, but also some are only partially official and others are hard to categorize. I would then urge the compensation professional to examine each item in each element of compensation and identify its value and its cost, and that is also difficult. These things must be done, because it isn't possible to manage the elements of compensation without such information.

Sometimes it appears that the elements of compensation are simply a convenient way to present information in the field of compensation. They are that, and the organization of this book is based on the elements of compensation. More than that, however, each element of compensation does have a particular reason. If you find that for a group of employees—any group of employees—there is any element of compensation that does not serve a special objective of the company or a special need of employees, then it should not be part of your compensation package.

One final value of analyzing the elements of compensation and identifying items within each element of compensation would be to work toward the simplification of compensation programs. When you identify the elements of compensation and see all the specific items or programs under each element, there may be opportunities to eliminate or combine some, thus simplifying compensation.

Chapter Four

Pricing and Surveying

Compensation information is the base of sound compensation management, and that is particularly true when a more delegative style of management is in practice. Compensation information is the basis for determining competitive pay directly and is key to dealing with issues of fair pay. In response to the need for more and better compensation information, a great deal of effort has been expended over the years to develop and use survey information more effectively in compensation management. As a result, a great deal of pricing and surveying information is available; and a number of useful pricing and surveying techniques exist.

Market Data: Cornerstone of Salary Administration

Thirty years ago, job evaluation was necessarily the essential cornerstone of a sound salary administration program. In effect, job evaluation was essential because it had to substitute for such unknown factors as market salary levels and the salary relationships between jobs in the marketplace. There was limited and sketchy information about market pay information. Today, we do not need administrative or proxy measures for determining market salary levels and salary relationships. There is a great deal of market data that are directly usable. Therefore, the first essential step in salary administration is to get sound market pay data.

Availability of Market Data

Extensive salary data are available in published reports, and hundreds of salary data sources are sold. In addition, there are many industry surveys, area surveys, and surveys by special groups of companies that work to exchange salary and other compensation information. Various functional surveys for professional engineers, attorneys, physicians, personnel specialists, and consultants are also conducted. Finally, almost all companies conduct some surveys of their own. These are generally conducted to get salary data that are essential to some firms but are not broadly available. Increasingly, companies are seeking out others with similar needs so they can share the cost of special surveys that must be conducted.

A recent study about surveying shows that larger companies, on the average, *at the corporate level,* buy four published surveys. On the average, the corporate staffs of these companies also participate in five surveys conducted by other companies, and the companies themselves conduct three surveys each year, on the average. That's a total of 11 survey sources of salary data conducted each year at the corporate level. In addition, many surveys are always conducted at the division and location levels. This study indicates the magnitude of salary survey data that is available.

When using published surveys, it is essential that the company's staff knows basic information about each source. Compensation professionals need to know how the survey was conducted and by whom. They must know whether audits were performed on the information submitted. The company's staff needs to know the degree to which jobs in the sample change from one survey period to another. Above all else, it is necessary to know the sample of companies participating in the survey.

Selecting Jobs for Market Pricing

One key to the usefulness of job pricing information is the selection of jobs that are to be priced by the survey. Company jobs selected for market benchmarking must match those surveyed by firms that participate in the survey. Job content as well as the title of jobs selected for surveying must be reasonably typical of jobs in the marketplace. Another practical consideration is that there should be large numbers of employees in jobs to be surveyed.

The jobs selected for surveying should represent a good cross section of all jobs in the unit. This should mean basically four things:

1. The sample of jobs priced should be a cross section by level of job. The company must avoid surveying all high-paid or low-paid positions.

2. Jobs should also be a cross section in the sense that they include all important job families.
3. Jobs selected for pricing should include at least the basic areas of manufacturing, marketing, engineering, finance, and personnel.
4. The jobs should also represent a cross section in the sense that they represent a reasonable sample of jobs from each of the operating units of the company and from each location.

In order to use market data as a cornerstone for salary administration, a minimum of 5 percent of all jobs in a unit must be priced. Ten percent gives an ideal cross section of jobs for pricing, and there really isn't any purpose served by pricing more than one in ten jobs. In practice, companies find that a higher percentage of jobs can be priced among operations-level workers, among high-level management positions, in professional work, and in first-level supervisory positions.

It must be remembered that the pricing process is fact-based. If there is substantial doubt about the comparability of any job that is priced, or any other technical issue, then that job should not be used at all. Job pricings that can be accepted as reliable and valid are the facts as determined in the marketplace and not in the minds of anyone or by some administrative process. They cannot be changed for any reason. To do so would be to change fact into a point of view.

There is a need to apply demographic sampling techniques to compensation pricing and surveying. If it is possible to predict election results on the basis of one percent samples, it should be possible to price all jobs with a sample of no more than 2 percent of a proper cross section of all jobs in a firm.

Nature of Labor Markets

The objective of job pricing is to determine the salaries paid for benchmark jobs in appropriate labor markets. Only in this way will a company be pricing jobs in a manner that is fair and equitable to employees. Only in this way can a company know that salaries are competitive and fair.

Appropriate markets are increasingly difficult to define. The "market" for a company is comprised of those companies from which the organization recruits or would logically recruit people, or to which it is most likely to lose its people. Appropriate markets are companies that have the same or similar jobs in the appropriate geographic area.

Markets vary geographically for different levels and types of jobs. For operations-level jobs, there is typically a local market. This basically means the immediate community. In job pricing work, define the immediate community carefully for each location. Market areas will vary a great deal from one community to another, mostly depending on transportation, facilities, and the costs of commuting to and from work.

For high-level management and professional jobs, there is a national labor market that must be priced. For middle-level employees, there is a regional market. Just what is "regional" is a function of the type of job, the number of jobs being filled, the number of people available, and the costs of relocation.

In the past, companies often used data of salaries paid by product competitors as a gauge of their labor market. Today, however, it is rare that labor market competitors are limited to product competitors. Surveying product competitors for salaries is not even necessarily useful anymore in determining "competitive labor costs" because businesses are not as well defined today as they were in the past.

Ideally, a company will identify a sample of companies that are *most like* itself and have a high percentage of jobs similar to the jobs in its own company. This is particularly useful in pricing general management positions. Selecting such a sample requires a careful examination of the operating and economic characteristics of the firm and then an identification of other firms in the labor market areas with similar economic and operating characteristics.

In one study, for instance, the following criteria were used to select peer-group companies for surveying management positions:

- Companies should be roughly the same size.
- The basic technology of the company must be chemistry.
- They should not be high-technology companies; for example, the research and development (R&D) budget should not exceed 2 percent of sales.
- They must serve multiple markets or have more than two separate distribution systems.
- The major share of sales should be to consumers through either company-operated or company-controlled retail outlets.
- There should be little product differentiation.
- The business should be characterized by a high degree of stability and not be subject to any basic changes in structure, markets, or business areas.

Finally, businesses should recognize that a substantial part of their labor market is their own company. A high percentage of the jobs in most companies are filled from within. There must be logical career paths, and salaries must be priced so these moves represent career opportunities and encourage career growth.

It is the job of compensation professionals to do survey work. However, all those who depend on the survey data must be assured that the survey has validity and that comparable jobs are being appropriately priced in relevant labor markets.

Changing Nature of Labor Markets

Increasingly labor markets are being affected by changes in business, by economic trends, and by social factors. For instance, people are less inclined to relocate for any reason. Companies are finding that an increasing number of people, particularly middle-level people, will not move even for substantial improvements in positions. They are less willing to relocate for the good of the company. This narrows labor mobility.

Increasingly, families have more than one working spouse. Therefore, relocation affects not only the company's own employee or candidate but the employment of all the working members of his family. This, too, tends to restrict mobility.

Markets are also being restricted by difficulties in relocation because of a scarcity of housing, higher housing costs, and high mortgage costs. Aside from these practical economic factors, increasing numbers of people are weighing lifestyle preferences as well as economic opportunities.

With greater technology and more technology, there are more specialist professional fields. Each of them can become a distinct labor market. On balance, greater technology tends to narrow labor markets.

On the other hand, companies are becoming more diverse in their operations. This provides broader experience for many in the organization. Also, job and industry changes are becoming more common in work careers. Multiple careers will be increasingly common in the next few decades, and this trend also will tend to broaden labor markets. All these factors broaden labor markets.

Companies must also recognize that they operate in multiple labor markets. There are different markets for different areas of a business, markets for each major functional area of work, and different markets for each functional position. Even a moderate-size organization will compete significantly in at least a dozen different labor markets.

Standard industry classification systems are no longer valid as a basis for comparison. Companies have diversified to the point where they do not really fit into any of the standard industry classifications. Many business areas of the new segments of our economy are related to health care, knowledge, and enjoyment, and don't fit well into any of the standard business classification systems.

Proper Sample of the Markets

It is not likely that any survey, whether one published by an organization selling the survey or a company-initiated survey, would get the pay for all jobs in the total labor market, and that would also be unnecessary. What is necessary is a reasonable sampling of the labor market.

The market sample must be reasonable in order to have credibility. Unless there is a sound sample, there will be a question as to whether there is selective reporting. Unfortunately, a number of well-known published surveys are based on inadequate samples. Some market data that is sold as a product have distorted samples because of the companies that just happen to respond to their survey; other survey samples are badly distorted because only subscribers or clients are used for the survey.

Mailed survey responses must be carefully monitored to make certain that a reasonable sample is reported. Additional mailings are sometimes required to make sure this happens. Mailed surveys also have a distinctly downward bias. Lower-paying companies are more inclined to participate in mailed surveys than higher-paying companies.

The rules of statistics apply to work with market data. The accepted practice of sampling in statistics therefore applies. In market data, a small number of cases are sufficient if sampling is correct, jobs are comparable, and surveys are done in relevant labor markets.

Market Data Sources

Many have gone into the business of pricing jobs. Unfortunately, the marketing skills of some of those suppliers are sometimes better than their professional skills in compensation surveying. Check particularly the job selection and company participation of survey products.

When surveys are conducted and sold, always make sure you understand the seller's motive. Apparently, they are in the business of surveying to make money. Some are in the survey business to get clients. When this is the case, there is always the possibility that data will be skewed to serve the interests of business development.

For most companies, there are sufficient sources of market data so that purchase or participation will meet all needs. Market data should be group work or supplied by one source for the benefit of all. It is the cost-effective way of getting needed market data. Avoid work done by your own company's staff in getting market data. This work represents a costly commitment that is rarely needed.

Survey Methods

There are a number of methods for pricing jobs. The selection of proper techniques and the methodology of surveying are the job of the compensation professional. Pricing is a basic job of compensation work and should always be done very well. In fact, the quality of many surveys conducted by those who claim to be compensation professionals is very poor. Sometimes the most elaborate surveys are technically the worst.

Methods Used

The most valid system of surveying jobs is through job-matching surveys. When this method is used, each job to be surveyed is first identified and described. The surveying organization then distributes these descriptions to organizations that are to participate. Participants are asked to supply data on salaries paid to individuals for each of the jobs in the survey.

This may be done by mail alone. The validity and reliability of the information obtained are enhanced considerably, however, if there is at least telephone monitoring. The ideal method is by personal visits and discussions about jobs. In fact, some survey groups meet regularly so that all participants understand clearly the jobs to be priced and the methods used.

A second method, and one that has considerable validity, is the information-based survey. In this case, jobs are selected that have already been priced by some ongoing survey, usually using the job-matching method. Jobs that have been priced by other surveys go into an information bank. They become the basis upon which other jobs are then priced.

One well-established information-based survey collects about a half-dozen priced jobs from each of more than three dozen ongoing surveys. These provide a core group of more than two hundred priced jobs. Most of the surveys used are conducted by companies in which there has been considerable discussion, resulting in a high degree of validity of job matching. There is information about each of the surveyed jobs and the surveys in the information bank. The jobs that are priced represent a cross section by industry, function, and level. They serve as a framework within which any position can be reasonably priced. This pricing can be done at a very low cost.

Consider your own benchmarking system. Perhaps your company participates in enough surveys so that a sample of jobs can be taken from each and an information-based survey established. More likely, a group of ''peer-group companies'' should join together for various information exchange activities, and the establishment of an information-based survey could be one such goal.

There are a few surveys that are conducted on the basis of job evaluation matching. Surveyed jobs are, in effect, ''priced'' by evaluating other companies' jobs in terms of the surveying firm's job evaluation system. This approach assumes some correlation between the points of the job evaluation system and actual market pay relationships. That assumption isn't justified, but job evaluation pricing, nonetheless, is another system of job pricing and surveying that is used.

Data bank surveys are widely used. Usually, they employ the techniques of regression analysis. Various characteristics of the job, and sometimes of the people who hold the jobs, are fed into a computer that then calculates the correlation between each of the elements and salary levels paid to those in the sample. This becomes the basis for regression analysis. Then the elements of any other jobs and the persons filling the jobs can be entered, and the ''market price'' is mathematically calculated.

There are other ways of pricing jobs besides surveying. For instance, some companies have developed reliable systems for monitoring their employment experience. For this method to work, those who do recruiting work must keep some basic records, have access to knowledge about company jobs, and have some training in job matching.

Recommendations

Pricing job salaries in the marketplace is the foundation of a sound compensation system. Surveying to accomplish that goal is surely one of the most basic activities in the field of human resources management. In my opinion, pricing and surveying are often done poorly, and the pricing and surveying work costs too much. On occasion, inappropriate management decisions of great importance have been made partly on the basis of poor survey data. These cases have proven to be very costly business mistakes.

It is really simple to price jobs. The pricing of jobs can be done at a very low cost.

Assuming that special surveys are not required, market benchmark jobs can be priced initially at one-tenth of one percent or less of payroll and maintained for one-tenth that cost each year. The pricing work can be done by intermediate-paid persons. Here are my recommendations for job pricing.

To do job pricing, you need to identify jobs (at least the jobs that are to be priced), and they must be described in writing, usually in one paragraph. You must also have a companywide salary structure that is used as a basic company information system.

Start the actual pricing with your employment experience. Next determine jobs (if any) that *must* be surveyed; for example, college hiring rates. Also identify the logical career path in your company. Very often, these actions alone will be all the job pricing that is needed; no surveys will be required at all.

Job pricing by employment experience is by far the most relevant pricing. There is no need to define the labor markets of the company in some logical or administrative manner; when recruiting, you are in the real labor market. The recruiter can be trained to do the pricing with little incremental time. Pricing by employment experience can be structured to help the recruiting process, and this should be done.

Don't use other pricing and surveying methods unless it is necessary; don't get survey information because it's available at what seems to be a low cost. If you use surveys, use reliable methods only. It is better to price a few jobs very well than many jobs in any manner besides very well.

Remember that how jobs are priced is a professional specialist's issue and an activity that experts must always do correctly. In job pricing and surveying, many experts have often been terribly wrong. The classic case is using regression analysis to price jobs.

Regression analysis is a mathematic method. As used in job pricing, regression analysis first relates actual salary paid mathematically to a number of variables. Unfortunately, none of the variables used in regression analysis relates necessarily to free choice in the marketplace and the real world of competition for talent. Don't be seduced by arguments about statistical proofs in regression analysis; regression analysis is a mathematical self-proof.

Use computer and communication technology to monitor pricing. Simple software can be designed to test the appropriateness of job pricing activities and survey methods: for example, by the company's recruiting pay, quits, current pay, and salary progress.

Use of Survey Data

Regardless of the method used, surveys yield data on salaries paid to people. Therefore, they indicate how the surveyed companies value the job *and* the people who perform the work. Resulting pricing also reflects company policy. This may be a conscious policy of positioning a company in the marketplace, or it may be a simple, informal policy of attempting to get and hold people at the lowest pay possible.

When you use surveys, it is necessary to assume that performance of all in the market is, by definition, average. Similarly, job pay of all is assumed to be at statistical average. In a small sample, however, these assumptions may not be true, and the professional must make statistical adjustments.

There is always a question about the accuracy of salary pricing. Done properly, particularly by the job-matching-method or by employment experience, salary survey information should be accurate plus or minus 5 percent. Even this, of course, is a judgment, If we knew what ''accurate'' was, then we wouldn't have to conduct any survey. Nevertheless, by various testing methods, it is probably correct to conclude that, when done properly, the surveying of salaries is accurate within plus or minus 5 percentage points. Anything as much as plus or minus 10 percent of accuracy is usable.

Survey results are generally recorded as an average figure. In fact, this average is a result of widely differing numbers. Even if one eliminates the highest-paid 10 percent and the lowest-paid 10 percent of the people in a typical survey, there may still be a spread from as little as 75 percent to as much as 150 percent from the lowest-salaried to the highest-salaried person for a job reported in a survey. Furthermore, this range, and the dispersion within the range, can vary substantially from job to job.

The schematic in Figure 4–1 is quite representative of the dispersion of individual data that results from traditional methods of surveying in middle- and higher-level positions. Even though job C pays more on the average, one-third of those in job A earn more than persons in job C. Note also the greater dispersion of reported salaries. In the illustration, job C is likely very competitive, and job B likely includes the reporting of more than one job. Jobs priced by employment experience take on the characteristics of the curve illustrated in job C.

There has been enough experience in surveying that standard distri-

Figure 4-1. Range and Dispersion of Salaries as Reported in a Typical Salary Survey.

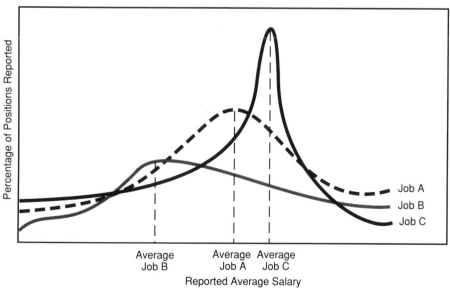

This illustrates the great dispersion of actual salaries reported in a survey (eliminating the top and bottom 10 percent of reportings.) The average is a single number, resultant of broadly different actual salaries paid.

bution curves have been developed that reflect the distribution under different circumstances, such as geographic dispersion, which usually occurs, providing jobs are well matched. Such curves can be used as an audit in surveying to pinpoint cases were valid data may not have been attained.

A single salary number for each job is usually used in reporting survey results, and those are the salaries that are most representative of competitive and fair salaries. A single salary number will be the statistical average or median, which becomes the standard salary for the job in your company compared to comparable jobs in similar companies. This benchmark salary is also a guide for salary structure midpoints.

The single salary numbers must be used to link your structure and salary standards (midpoints) of all jobs in your company to jobs in the labor market. The compensation professional needs a deep understanding of the linking process and the nature of the markets that have been mirrored.

The labor market is a four-dimensional continuum, reflecting different levels of the same job, similar work at different levels in the same job family, different but related jobs, and jobs in different but contiguous geographic areas. In each of these dimensions, there is a great deal of overlap in the pay for jobs.

It is these characteristics of labor markets that make benchmarking pricing practical and the use of a single salary number a necessary practice. Theoretically, every job is competitive with other jobs through multiple linking. You can make comparisons through competitive links with almost any job. Furthermore, in labor markets increasingly dominated by technology work and multicareer workers, the number of links between jobs are far greater; as is the transference of personal talent from one job to another.

Job markets are also reflective of decisions by many employees and by many employers. But these decision-makers are not always the same persons. For example, we know from common experience that some people are looking for jobs most of the time and others never look for jobs until they are outplaced. There are clearly different decision-makers in the market at different times. It is not necessary to survey on an annual cycle. A survey, done well, need not be done again for at least three years and perhaps as many as five years. In between salary survey years, job salary levels can be adjusted based on surveys of salary increases.

In surveying, recognize that you are always determining what salary levels *were*. There is generally a two-year difference between the time salary surveys were set and the time the salary levels you will set as a result of your survey. Factor that time warp into your salary-setting process.

It is relatively inexpensive to *determine* ''competitive salaries.'' To *prove* that the market price determined is correct can involve an enormous amount of money—in some cases, twenty times as much as it costs to determine the correct amount. This argues for selecting qualified compensation persons and then delegating to them the necessary authority and responsibility for determining market values.

Market pricing is a job to be done centrally by the compensation professional. There isn't anything contradictory with delegative management in such a centralized activity. In fact, the delegative process involves many more decision-making areas delegated further throughout the organization *and* a few activities more tightly centralized. That's why some people call delegative management ''loose-tight'' management.

Market pricing is a job the professional must do extremely well every time. The goal is only to determine average salaries for market benchmark jobs; it will often be necessary to prove the correctness of the data.

The use of market data is the key to effective salary administration—it is necessarily the cornerstone of a formal program that is to be competitive and fair. Data about pay of comparable jobs in relevant markets are what make any formal program competitive and fair. The compensation professional must have a sound knowledge of the methods and uses of pricing jobs and surveying. He must be truly expert—the final reference. The professional must have an in-depth understanding of the characteristics of labor markets and the survey methods and uses that have been outlined.

Compensation Increase Surveys

Determining salary increases in the market is an important separate activity in pricing and surveying. Such data is necessary to assure that salary levels continue to be competitive. Information about salary increases is also directly usable as an input in determining salary increase budgets and in financial management work.

There isn't nearly as much work required in determining salary increases as there is in the pricing of job levels. A few days of work and modest fees for survey organizations will get all the data required each year relating to compensation increases.

The amount of attention given to pay increase amounts each year is very impressive. Each year, in fact, there is publicity about pay increases. It seems that this is always considered by editors as being newsworthy, with the volume of reporting about pay increases about the same when increases are small as when they are large.

The information reported about pay increases is often incorrect and misleading. The stories about pay increases are frequently what the pay increases will be—reported months before the increases take effect. Not surprisingly, newspaper stories always emphasize the dramatic. If a legitimate survey has reported three or four different survey figures, the highest will usually be highlighted.

It is crucial to recognize that there are different salary increase figures. Each is a different number, and each serves a different purpose. Here are definitions of salary increase data that should be used as guides each year.

Increase in Average Salary by Position

This figures shows the increase for everyone who is now on the payroll. It is the figure that is most useful to companies in developing salary increase budgets.

Increase in Average Personal Salary

This shows the effects of promotions and organizational changes. It is most useful in tracking the salary progress of individuals.

Average Increase of Those Receiving Increases

This is obviously the average increase of those now on the payroll receiving increases; excluding those who received no increase, even if it was only because their salary increase period had been stretched out beyond the twelve-month reporting period. This figure is a useful supplement in salary increase planning.

Average Increase in Payroll

This is how much the payroll at year-end will exceed the current payroll. It is most useful in financial planning.

To illustrate how different these salary increase numbers can be, look at Figure 4–2. This data happens to be for management salaries, but the same point is relevant for salary increases for any group. If you use the wrong budget numbers, that error can be a costly mistake. The press will likely always report the higher numbers and compound that by using ''pay increase data''—which includes bonus payments. Note that none of these numbers corresponds with changes in the consumer price index except by coincidence.

In most organizations, surveys of salary increases are translated into salary increase budget numbers. Salary increase numbers in budgets can lead to two types of management problems or issues. For one thing, the amount budgeted tends to become the amount spent, whether sufficient, appropriate, or superfluous. Even prudent managers must hesitate about

Figure 4-2. Management Salary Increases.

	Increase				
	1985	1986	1987	1988	1989
Increase in average salary by position	7%	7%	6%	5%	5%
Increase in average manager's salary	9	8	7	6	7
Average increase: those receiving increases	10	9	8	7	8
Average increase in manager's payroll	7	4	2	3	3
Percentage of managers receiving increases	90	90	80	90	95
Average interval between increases granted (number of months)	13	13	14	13	13

Each of these salary increase numbers differs in most years, and each serves a different purpose in compensation management. The data happens to be from issues of *The Annual Management Compensation Study,* and such data is available for the twenty-five years the report has been published. In years when available, data shows the same differences in salary increase categories in any type of job.

varying from budget in any direction, because at least that raises the risk of them having to explain and be criticized.

Also remember that in many years some companies you survey actually grant increase amounts that are quite different than planned at the time the survey was conducted. Sometimes these are small differences due to administrative reasons. Often, however, the difference in increases budgeted and increases spent is substantial, due to a corporate decision to cut increases or to pay more.

I recommend that companies do the following with respect to surveying salary increases:

- Price job levels only once every three to five years, and establish salary levels in the between years from salary increase survey information.
- Assuming that the fiscal year is on a calendar-year basis, don't start the process of determining salary increase budgets until October of each year. Two to three months are plenty of time to get salary increase information and to set budgets.
- First get data about trends and pay increase practices (historic not

prospective), changes in Consumer Price Index (CPI) measures, and employment experience. Get opinions from those who work in human resources management, particularly those in recruiting, about what salary increases should be. Get the opinions of key management persons—particularly those dealing with jobs in the category of scarce positions. Also calculate the levels of salaries within range, and compare that with prior years.

- From such information, prepare planning information. Consider separately "budgeting" of performance increases: submit only budgets for salary increases other than those based on performance.
- Finally (in early November), find out what other companies are doing. Use this information to confirm or question your own conclusions: don't let the decisions of others determine your firm's budgets.

Surveying Extra Compensation and Benefits

Surveying extra compensation and benefits has essentially the same characteristics and problems as the pricing of salaries. In addition, each item in extra compensation and benefits has some very special problems of pricing. Because of these special problems, the pricing of extra compensation items is often not accurate or reliable.

For instance, surveying incentive pay awards at any level of the organization requires understanding far more than the amount of bonus awards paid. To survey bonuses, it is also necessary to understand the plans of every company included in the survey. In some types of plans, it is important to know the "standard awards" prescribed by the plan (amounts that are intended to be paid when performance standards are achieved). Finally, critical to the evaluation of the amounts paid under any bonus plan is some understanding of the level of business performance or activity experienced in every company in the survey group. Unless there is a small group and a great deal of information is exchanged, the resulting survey data lack usefulness altogether.

Comparisons of long-term income plans have all the problems of bonus plans plus some questions of tax and accounting treatments. With long-term income plans, there is also the problem of elapsed time. For example, do you count income from options in the year the income is expended, the year income is reported to the government, or over the period of time in which the option values accrued?

One problem in surveying benefits is that there are so many widely different practices in the various items that might be included. Furthermore, in some benefits, there are elements that considerably affect the value and cost of benefits, yet such information is generally not available to any company in the survey group. For instance, the cost and value of pensions are a function of the age and length of service of employees.

In benefit comparisons, there are mathematic and actuarial assumptions that should be understood. Assumptions are broad and many are questionable. Yet reported benefit survey results are presented with the appearance of precision.

Determining the appropriateness of benefits requires a review of each benefit item. Because of the nature of the work force, local or industry practice, company policy, or employee preferences, companies will emphasize some items of benefits and provide lesser amounts of others. No company is tops in every benefit item. In fact, few companies will be "average" in every benefit item.

The purpose of surveying is necessarily different with respect to benefits than it is with respect to salaries. A dollar of compensation value or cost cannot be an objective of benefit surveying for practical reasons. If there is surveying of benefits at all, it is to get information about practices.

Companies should get information on extra pay plans, but primarily for reasons of information. It doesn't cost much to find out what others do, and it's part of the need to be well informed. However, if information is for the purpose of being informed about the practices of others, then the companies surveyed should often be a different sample of companies than would be appropriate for setting compensation levels or payroll costs. Companies surveyed for practice information should be those companies that, in your judgment, are likely to have sound, appropriate, and innovative compensation and benefit practices. This doesn't have to be many companies, and information can be accumulated over a period of time, at a very low cost, mostly in the course of doing other necessary work.

To get a measure of the total pay in the marketplace involves all the problems of pricing salaries, extra compensation, and benefits. To undertake total pay comparisons requires developing a model that, of necessity, will be based on a considerable number of assumptions. Thus the validity and usefulness of total-pay comparisons are quite limited. Yet it seems to be important to some people to know the total pay amounts in other companies. Any computation and comparison of total pay is completely without validity; total pay comparison figures are just numbers on a piece of paper. Be assured that if each of the elements of compensation is competitive and fair, then mathematically the sum of the total must be equally fair and competitive.

Practices Surveying

Practices surveying aims at gaining information, understanding, and insights, rather than tabulating numbers. Increasingly, the effective management of compensation requires an understanding of practices, insights into how different programs and practices have worked in various circumstances, a knowledge of what is going on in other companies, and what important trends are developing.

The practices information surveying approach is necessary, for example, to get information on nonfinancial elements of reward used in other firms. Items of conditions cannot be quantified. Useful information cannot be obtained from "yes" or "no" answers, checklists, or multiple-choice answers. What is needed is to identify items and then engage in a dialogue. It's also helpful to make personal observations of some items.

Practices surveys are also required to obtain useful information about the programs of other companies and how they work. It is useful to know what other companies do, why they do it, and how practices have worked under different circumstances.

It is also useful to monitor trends and developments. Such information should include what is being eliminated as well as what is new. From time to time, careful and selective monitoring of new practices will identify programs or practices that may be useful.

Practices surveys must be conducted in a selective manner but with deep understanding. A company does not need to know everything about everybody. Nor could it afford such an information-gathering effort. It must focus on those subjects of greatest importance to its particular business and its specific circumstances. There must also be selective contacting of those whose experience is most relevant.

Getting practices information is increasingly a need in all companies, but getting this information is a special time-consuming effort. As already noted, the sample will be different from that required for surveys to determine competitiveness and fairness. Questionnaires and other written material can provide only a small part of the total information output of qualitative information that is useful, so that much of the required practices information must be obtained by phone or visit. This means that quality information gathering is time-consuming and costly, which emphasizes the need to do this work selectively and on a joint-venture basis whenever possible.

There are opportunities to get practices survey information in an efficient manner. An industry or professional association may be one way to obtain such information from a number of organizations. Workshop conferences provide the same opportunity if the groups are small and the sessions are structured for interchange. Representatives of different companies may form a group, with each person assigned a special item and occasional meetings scheduled to exchange information about what each member learned. Finally, such information may be obtained from an individual who, in the normal course of his work, gets a great deal of information. Staff persons in large corporations are an example, but consultants should also have such knowledge.

Those who conduct practices surveys must be rather high-level and experienced. They must know the questions to ask. They must know what to explore in more depth. They must understand what they hear, and they must evaluate the information provided.

Management of Pricing and Survey Information

Market pricing and surveying are a vital part of compensation management today. The technology and art of surveying are a necessary part of the knowledge and skill of the compensation professional.

One of the basic uses of such surveying is for pricing benchmark jobs, which is now the cornerstone of the compensation program of most companies today. Pricing and surveying are the cornerstone of modern compensation because this information is accessible. We want pay to be sufficient to ensure competitiveness for the company and fairness for employees.

This is technical work that companies are inclined to delegate to compensation professionals. It is work that must be done very well. Unfortunately, it is work that has been done poorly in many cases.

Surveying methods are also critical as one measure of competitiveness. Salary levels alone, of course, do not reflect competitiveness. Using appropriate recruiting practices, for instance, can affect the ability to attract people as much as salary levels. Similarly, the types of compensation programs and nonfinancial elements of reward can influence the ability of a company to attract and retain employees.

Information inputs are the third basic area in the use of surveys. More and more, there is a need for practices information surveys and surveying items other than salaries.

Surveying is not complex work. Simple methods can often be used. In this work, there is a need for care, good judgment, and correct reporting.

Most for-sale surveys flunk all three of these criteria of excellence in surveying. In fact, there have been a lot of fancy systems that lack relevance and technical correctness altogether. Surveying has developed a number of maladies, and it is up to the users and the buyers to straighten out the defects in compensation surveying.

Of a dozen of so *essentials* of human resources management, three would relate to compensation, and two of these involve pricing and surveying.* This is a basic job of compensation. It is technical work that is necessarily delegated to compensation professionals. It is work that must be done well.

---

*Three of a dozen or so essentials of human resources management that involve compensation are: pricing to assure competitiveness and fairness; pay for performance; and managing the spread between output as measured by sales and payroll costs.

Chapter Five

Recruiting, Retention, and Allocation

A very special purpose of pricing jobs is to ensure that the firm is competitive when recruiting new employees. Similarly, the pay of current employees must be sufficient so that it does not cause turnover. Pay must be competitive in a real-world sense of attract and retain. Then pay can play an affirmative role in getting needed talent.

RECRUITING PAY

There is no problem in personnel that has existed any longer or that is more important than effective recruiting. Never underestimate the importance of effective recruiting. In recruiting, obviously, a company brings in the talent with which it must compete. The people you recruit are your organization's human assets, and human talent very much affects business results. Adequate recruiting pay is clearly an important component of effective recruiting.

Effective Recruiting, Recruiting Pay, and the Management of Personnel

In personnel management and in the management of personnel, we spend a great deal of time on increasing the effectiveness of the work force. However, there is evidence to suggest that increasing the work of a group is more difficult than recruiting more talented people in the first place. That suggests that better recruiting can be a major productivity improvement effort, and recruiting effectiveness is an ongoing method of improving productivity. As far as we can tell, it costs no more to recruit productive workers than it does to recruit less productive workers.

Companies spend a lot of time and money on training employees, and there must be training. But if a firm hired all self-motivated quick learners with a strong work ethic in the first place, then, logically, training would be much easier, and training costs would be much less.

Companies also spend a lot on supervisory training—and there must be supervisory training. Here also, if a highly talented group were recruited in the first instance, less supervisory training would be needed. It is equally correct that if misfits were recruited, no amount of supervisory training could make up for such deficiency of the work force.

Observations of many cases make me think that productivity improved more by recruiting capabilities in the first instance than by making a person or group more productive by training and better supervision. Generally, it is easier and less costly to bring in more capable people than it is to upgrade the people you have.

Of course, we should increase productivity by more effective management *and* by more effective recruiting. You are more likely to have more of an impact more quickly and at a lower cost, however, by improved recruiting than by productivity management. For all these reasons, always at least start by "putting your personnel dollars up-front"—by doing better recruiting.

Pay is a critical element in effective recruiting. Recruiting pay and the impact of recruiting pay on effective recruiting are an issue at some times and in some ways in every business.

It isn't often that the issue comes up directly about whether recruiting pay is appropriate. That happens sometimes—usually in terms of "we need to pay more to get people." Most of the time, when the issue first reported is "we need to pay more," the real problem turns out to be something else—usually ineffective recruiting. The issue of recruiting pay often starts as something else, such as excess turnover, low productivity, or inadequate upward mobility.

Recruiting pay should be set at the 75th percentile of pay for jobs targeted for recruiting, provided you do vertical recruiting. That would make your recruiting pay rate about 10 percent higher than the statistical average of pay for jobs targeted for recruiting, and more than three-fourths of all who work in jobs targeted for recruiting would currently earn at least 20 percent less than your recruiting pay.

If you do horizontal recruiting, then the 75th percentile pay of targeted jobs would only permit a raise of any type for less than one-fourth

Figure 5-1. Recruiting Pay and Market Potential.

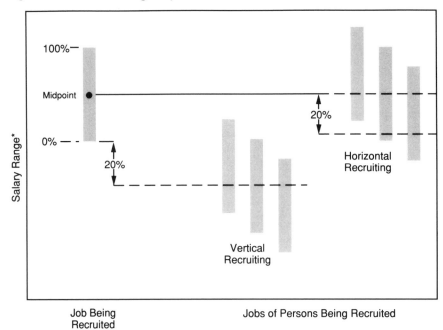

*Salary range of jobs targeted in the market equal average — eliminating the high 20 percent and the low 20 percent of actual pay in the marketplace.

The exhibit illustrates that in vertical recruiting of two to four pay grade promotions firms can offer a 20 percent increase in salary, hire at the minimum of the salary grade, and attract more than half those in the labor market. It is difficult to recruit horizontally from the view of pay alone, even if you hire at the midpoint, which, of course, causes problems in internal equity and future pay increases based on improved performance.

of all in the labor market even if you brought in those persons high in your salary range for the job being filled by recruiting. This salary relationship regarding recruiting pay is illustrated in Figure 5–1. While only an illustration, the exhibit provides an accurate picture of recruiting pay and labor market relationships in nineteen of twenty cases.

There is a tendency to offer more pay when recruiting difficulties are experienced. Pressure for increases in offering pay can be intense and often appear to be compelling. Jobs need to be filled, and it seems so reasonable to raise the pay for just those persons to fill one particular job that is open. Filling the job is essential, and doing it by more pay for that job doesn't cost much overall—or so it seems. Recognize, however, that even in a few cases, higher recruiting pay will have a ripple-effect impact on the pay of others throughout the organization.

If pay is the problem in recruiting, then usually there must be substantially more pay—at least 20 percent more in the offering salary. Small increments, like 5 percent, rarely make much of a difference in recruiting.

More likely, recruiting problems are due to some issue other than pay, provided there is vertical recruiting. Unrealistic or unnecessary background requirements are often the obstacle to effective recruiting. If jobs are positioned average to the market and vertical recruiting is used, then inadequate recruiting pay cannot be a problem in more than one of twenty cases.

Problems are rarely raised about recruiting pay that is too high. In fact, there aren't enough reported cases of overpayment in recruiting to have a sense about how widespread overpayment in recruitment really is. Experience as well as logic tells us that there are probably many cases of overpayment in recruiting. Overpayment in recruiting could be a serious matter, partly because of the upward pressure this causes on the pay of existing positions. Overpayment in recruiting can also cause pay compression and may seriously narrow future opportunities to reward those recruited who are better performers. Overpayment in recruiting must be monitored.

There are times when experts urge companies to pay more when recruiting. Sometimes the experts urge this for a given job or a given class of jobs. Sometimes the recommendation is for a policy of generally high recruiting pay.

A firm must always listen to its experts. Recognize, however, that in this case at least some of the experts are advantaged in their work or in their compensation or in both by higher recruiting pay. For example, an employment agency has a somewhat easier time recruiting and gets larger fees for the same job when paid by a percentage of starting salary if the recruiting pay is higher. Others may be advantaged by higher recruiting pay, including your firm's recruiting professionals.

These experts may be quite sincere in their urging, yet they may be wrong in their advice. The employment agency, for example, may be responding reasonably to its experience but is seeing pay requests of but a small part of the recruiting market. All recruiters' views are also biased because their views of the market are dominated by job changers and those who seek advancement by job change and employer change. The recruiting company's view of the labor market is often the result of its recruiting effectiveness.

A company can raise the level of human talent or lower the level of pay in a short period of time. In the past ten years, a number of my client companies have done both.

From 1975 to 1985, when many companies embarked on productivity improvement programs based on the application of human resources management methods, one action I often recommended was called "organizational enrichment." In this work, the performance appraisal of those who vacated a position was used as a selection criterion for replacements. This was done in promotion from within and it was done in recruiting. Those who filled the jobs had to be judged to be more effective than those who were replaced.

Through organizational enrichment alone, productivity was increased noticeably, if not measurably. Then companies got a substantial return within a few years for a zero investment of money, because there was no change in recruiting pay.

Be advised that it can work the other way. Talent can decline with no decrease in recruiting pay offered. That has happened in many large companies in recent years, because the historic recruiting advantage of large companies in the marketplace has eroded, and the blue chip companies must now do their labor recruiting on an even playing field.

If you like numbers, a rule of thumb is that each instance of 5 percent more in recruiting pay above market average for jobs targeted for recruiting will increase the pay in your firm overall by one-fifth of one percent in one year. Thus twenty-five cases of even modest premiums in recruiting pay can raise the average salary by 5 percent in an operation, regardless of the number of employees who work in that operation.

No one has ever published research on the impact on productivity when people with greater effectiveness than those who currently work in the company were recruited at less pay, but the opportunities can be very great. This affirmative action by recruiting and recruiting pay can impact an organization far more favorably than most companies achieve through downsizing.

For many companies, there are great opportunities for business improvement by greater recruiting effectiveness at less or no greater recruiting pay. The near-term favorable impact on business results can be significant. Business improvement through more effective recruiting has a double value. In addition to immediate results from more effective recruiting, there are ongoing strategic improvements in the effectiveness of work. These substantial values—double values—can be achieved with short lead times and low investment costs. There isn't anything to invent, and there are no new programs to develop and implement: we know how to do effective recruiting and how to set recruiting pay correctly.

There is one final and very important point relating to recruiting and the management of personnel: the relationship between recruiting pay and payroll costs. Generally, each additional $1 more in recruiting pay is equal to $4 in recruiting costs. Thus if you are recruiting for a position with a starting salary of $30,000 and decide to pay $33,000 in order to increase recruiting effectiveness, this is equivalent to $12,000 more spent in recruiting costs. Obviously, that would pay for a great deal more recruiting excellence. Work out your own models for recruiting costs and recruiting pay. You will find that the 1:4 ratio is a good average overall.

Recruiting Pay and Elements of Compensation

There is a tendency to generalize about recruiting pay. In fact, salary, bonus payments, capital-building programs, and benefits all have a different impact on recruiting effectiveness.

Job salary levels obviously have an important impact on the ability to recruit people into a company. You can be up to plus or minus 5 percent of market average and still be fully competitive. But if you get beyond plus or minus 10 percent, you have a different market position.

The *presence* of basic benefits has importance in recruiting, although benefits are far less important than salary. How good the employee benefits are is not usually a factor in recruiting. Some benefits have no impact at all on the ability to attract new employees. Prepaid legal benefits are an example. Some benefits have no relevance in recruiting in some cases; for example, retirement plans have little relevance to a young person.

Some companies have had success in utilizing the concept of the "unique benefit." This would be a truly unusual situation offered by a company that is not offered by competitors. Sometimes the unique benefit can have an importance in recruiting that is all out of proportion to the dollar values of the benefit. The trouble is that unique benefits become widespread practices, partly because of surveying. Then you only have more costs.

When bonus plans of any type (near-term or long-term) are prevalent in a type of job or a class of work, then the *presence* of a bonus plan can be essential to effective recruiting. The payments made in prior years of distribution have less importance and the types of bonus plans have little recruiting importance. Exaggerated claims about bonus plans are deplorable but have been used with some success in recruiting, particularly in high-turnover positions.

Extra pay plans of all types (stock-purchase plans, profit-sharing plans, thrift plans) generally have little marginal impact on recruiting—except when a type of plan is traditional or widely practiced for a group of people or a class of jobs. The specific types of extra pay plans or amounts of past payments have little impact on recruiting.

It is only with respect to salary that there are mathematically proven experiences that are good enough to be usable as predictive tools in recruiting. As far as recruiting is concerned, with respect to bonus, extra pay plans, and benefits, you should have the plans that are expected by people, but the design of the plan and the payment system should be geared to your own company's operations and not to competitive considerations.

Recommendations on Recruiting Pay

Matters of recruiting must be regarded as being at least as important as purchasing. Just from the view of acquisition of income-producing assets, employment recruiting should be done well. And the price of recruiting should be a matter of great importance. Here are my recommendations with respect to recruiting pay.

Recruiting Pay at Statistical Average Compared to the Market

Make sure your salaries for jobs are *competitive*—set at statistical average. Then when any job opens up, you will be able to offer salaries that are sufficient to attract suitable people who are fully capable of doing the work that is to be done. Usually with jobs at market statistical average, you can offer 20 percent raises to more than three-fourths of all persons in the marketplace who are reasonable candidates, provided there is vertical recruiting.

Statistical average to the market is fully sufficient to get the number and quality of persons required to do the work. This is not a matter of opinion—it is a matter of fact. It is a matter of fact that has been proven statistically many times, and you can prove it with your own employment experience.

Paying salaries that are 10 percent above the market (at the 75th percentile) improves labor market competitiveness somewhat but not very much. Recruiting pay at the 75th percentile is a waste of company resources, because in most cases considerable amounts of the company's cash are expended unnecessarily.

However, you must pay statistical average compared to *relevant* jobs. This is where many company practices with respect to recruiting pay become unraveled.

Relevant jobs means a fair sample of jobs you recruit from (or reasonably might recruit from) and jobs you lose people to (or reasonably might lose people to). That is a practical definition of comparability.

The comparability of jobs means transference between jobs: any job in the relevant market where a person doing the job being considered could move into the job and perform it. That's broader than ''same job'' (or worse yet, ''same job title''). Fortunately, this proper basis for determining comparable jobs (and therefore appropriate recruiting pay) improves your company's ability to get useful information about appropriate recruiting pay.

Vertical Recruiting

Another critical issue of recruiting pay is vertical recruiting. Vertical recruiting means that you search for a person who is capable of doing the job but who is now doing a lower-level job; the next lower-level job in the career path.

Vertical recruiting is what you always do in promotion from within.

Vertical recruiting is a basic policy issue; one I always include in personnel policy and strategy discussions with top management. Obviously, unless there is vertical recruiting, there is a strong bias against promotion from within. Vertical recruiting has other substantial values. Certainly, one of these relates to recruiting pay.

Always do vertical recruiting. If there are exceptions at all, they should be less than one in a hundred. Make sure that such exceptions are subject to the approval of the chief executive officer of the enterprise or some other top executive who is very close to the chief executive officer. This matter deserves the attention of top management.

There is always pressure for exceptions to vertical recruiting and support for horizontal recruiting. Some arguments for horizontal recruiting seem logical. For example, some will say that they need fully experienced persons. But the logic and business reasons for vertical recruiting are even greater.

A Range of Recruiting Pay

You often need a range of recruiting pay and must consider developing guides for pay offers. In most jobs above entry level, you should provide a range of offering salaries to give the recruiters needed flexibility. Concentrate on a single figure, but have a policy known to everyone involved about a range of recruiting pay and the circumstances that might justify more than the set amount of recruiting pay established.

There are many employers who just set a rate of recruiting pay and then consider only those in the marketplace who will work for that amount. The government is one employer that often does this, and all the government's jobs are full.

My own opinion is that an employer is well advised to have somewhat more flexibility than that. The top candidate may simply not accept the recruiting pay. Just a few extra dollars will often do it. Give your recruiters some flexibility. Inflexibility in recruiting pay has the tendency to push recruiting pay higher—higher than necessary because of pressures to get desired people who want more money.

Never pay less than the recruiting pay figure. If you find candidates who will accept less, pay within the recruiting range anyway. Savings by paying less than the recruiting range are usually small, but the result in good will by paying the higher recruiting rate can be great. Paying less than your own set recruiting rate is also risky if the person recruited turns out to be a high performer and later finds out that he has been paid lower than company policy prescribes. You can lose good people that way.

Some argue that if the candidate is willing to work for significantly lower than recruiting pay, then you should pay him that. But when this happens, institute some very careful checking. Something may be very wrong. A willingness to accept much less than current salary can mean that a background is being misrepresented or the candidate is a social misfit.

Recruiting Pay Offer Guidelines

If it is necessary to offer more than the set recruiting pay, try to confine the premium to 10 percent—and rarely greater than 20 percent above recruiting pay. If a candidate is unemployed at the time of his recruitment, then recruiting pay equal to former pay is fully satisfactory. With respect to those currently working, you should expect to pay at least a 10 percent salary increase over their current pay and likely as much as 20 percent. Occasionally, the spread will be 30 percent, but that should be the exception, not the rule. Don't believe search firms that tell you that you must always offer 30 percent more.

For many years, one of the standard salary administration guides was that starting salaries in a job (in promotion and recruiting alike) should be in the bottom third of the salary range. That guideline still holds true and is a very useful administrative tool. In promotion and vertical recruiting, a candidate below the 75th percentile of band position who gets a 15 percent raise and moves into a position that is a full three grades higher would be within the bottom third of the range. Even if a person promoted to a job three grades higher were at the top of the range and received a 10 percent raise, he would still be in the bottom third of the range of that new job. Unless the structure is flawed, this almost always works out, so I recommend using the bottom third of the grade range as a guide for recruiting pay.

Never pay recruiting bonuses. Don't pay lump-sum cash bonuses, and don't do it in indirect ways by unusual entertainment, as one example. Make the focus be the job, the conditions, and the salary.

Don't pay recruiting bonuses for referrals by your employees. These produce problems and not more or better candidates. Doesn't it seem reasonable to assume that if your employees think well of the company they work for, they will want capable (though not necessarily competitive) people as co-workers in their joint venture?

Quick Response to Recruiting Pay Problems

There will always be specific questions and issues about recruiting pay. This is an area where your firm needs a quick-response procedure. In at least nine of ten cases, the review will reaffirm the recruiting pay if you have followed the recommendations outlined. But if you don't have an effective and quick-response system, then more than half the cases will result in higher recruiting pay, and in a very short time, you will have an expensive, chaotic situation.

There must be a quick-response system because there is a job opening that must be filled. There is no time now for a study, so the system for responding to problems in recruiting must be effective and quick. This must include responses to questions about recruiting pay.

I have seen many such review systems that work, but all that work the fastest and best are hinged on a person (or persons) in personnel who does compensation work and who is accountable for recruiting pay issues. Of course, your company must have systems for getting information that reliably identify correct market pay, but it is the use of such available information by a professional that is critical when the pay for recruiting is questioned and challenged.

More volumes of data and costly endorsements by brand-name consultants are not the answer. Substantiation of data and information by a knowledgeable person who has a high skill in this work is the key. That person finds answers and helps get jobs filled. This in-house expert gains the confidence of the "users" of the recruiting services: the managers in your organization.

Here, in summary, are my recommendations with respect to recruiting pay:

- Set recruiting pay at 75th percentile statistical averages for jobs that would be logical sources for qualified candidates.
- Use the idea of job transference not just job titles to determine jobs you may recruit from.
- Always do vertical recruiting.
- Set a range of pay for recruiting: generally, a range that covers the bottom third of the salary grade.
- Rarely hire a person for less than your recruiting salary amount.
- Never use recruiting bonuses.
- Have a system for quick-response solutions to questions about recruiting pay.

• Set guidelines, delegate decisions to the recruiters, and monitor closely what they do.

The Importance of Recruiting Pay

It is my opinion that the recruiting activity is second to none in its importance, that the excellence of recruiting has been eroding, a bit at a time over a long period of time, and that it is now not good enough in many organizations. Insufficient attention to setting recruiting pay and verifying recruiting pay, when appropriate, are obviously critically important parts of effective recruiting, and that also is not being done well enough in many companies.

Failure to recruit the caliber of persons required to run your operations and achieve enterprise goals is simply unacceptable. Therefore, errors in recruiting practices or recruiting pay are not acceptable. In addition, recruiting pay that is higher than necessary is wasteful and can involve major costs. In business generally, better recruiting and more appropriate recruiting pay saves more money than downsizing.

Sometimes the problem goes back to job evaluation. If recruiting pay is incorrect, it is sometimes because job slotting generally was done by a job evaluation process that was unrelated to the real world of attract and retain. In addition, many traditional methods of surveying don't sample real labor markets. Frequently, both job evaluation and survey methods are wrong. When this happens, recruiting pay can be very wrong.

There are forces at work in companies that cause a drifting toward excessive recruiting pay. Without restraints, recruiting pay will drift to at least 10 percent above what is appropriate. That involves very high costs, serving no useful purpose.

There are companies that go into the recruiting market with the thought that they have money and they can buy any talent they want. That approach won't work in the long run. You may buy the talent, but you cause enormous disruptive conditions with respect to the talent you have. Furthermore, the talent you get from buying it came to you only for money. Remember that every other company in the marketplace has money also.

Recruiting effectiveness generally and recruiting pay issues specifically will become more important if it is correct, as most business plans indicate, that we are in a period of chronic labor scarcity. Higher recruiting pay generally is not an acceptable answer to labor scarcity for most companies because of high costs. However, all companies will experience greater pressure in more cases to increase recruiting pay on a selective and strategic basis, and there are ways to do that.

Mostly because of increasing technology, there is greater turmoil in labor markets, more job changes, and, increasingly, more career changes. Every business plan I have seen suggests that activities in labor markets will continue to increase for the next twenty years. More transactions will result in more attention to recruiting pay and require greater excellence in managing recruiting pay issues.

There have not been good models developed about the relationship between recruiting pay and recruiting effectiveness. It would be useful to build such models. The difficult part would be in the building of the model itself. After that was done, many companies could utilize basically the same software at a low cost.

Experience with such models, and observations and judgments based on experience, suggest:

- Plus or minus 10 percent in recruiting pay is necessary to make a noticeable difference in the ability to recruit required persons.
- Even 10 percent more in recruiting pay is not really as important as even modest differences in recruiting effectiveness.
- A 10 percent reduction in turnover doesn't affect recruiting pay at all in the lowest-paid jobs, but it is equivalent in impact to an increase in recruiting pay of 10 percent in middle-level jobs.
- There is not a fixed relationship between recruiting pay and the effectiveness of recruiting.
- The range of recruiting salaries that can be used is quite narrow— probably no greater than 30 percent in two-thirds of all cases.

Recruiting and recruiting pay have always been central and basic matters of human resources management. With increasing labor scarcity and extreme pressures in many companies for greater business competitiveness, recruiting pay is one of the truly essential matters in human resources management.

RETENTION PAY

You often read about pay to attract and retain as though recruiting pay and retention pay were the same. They are not the same. Both with respect to form and amount of compensation, the two are very different. The issues are also different, with the issue of retention pay being mostly to avoid voluntary turnover. Retention pay thus relates to compensation levels and practices that avoid turnover.

The Issue Is Turnover

Pay should be such that the compensation programs and practices of a company do not cause problems and induce turnover. The avoidance of turnover is the minimum goal of compensation.

Look at the issue from the other view. Wouldn't you agree that a compensation program that indeed induces quits among valued employees was unacceptable? There isn't any necessity for compensation programs or practices to induce quits, and you shouldn't have these practices.

The relationship between compensation and turnover has never been formally studied, which, in itself, is remarkable in view of the many millions of dollars spent each year on compensation studies of various types. Therefore, it is necessary to rely on individual cases and on the precedents of experience in evaluating the impact of retention pay on turnover.

Most employers keep some records on turnover; specifically, records on the reasons for leaving. Usually, the information is largely incorrect, because "more pay" and "better opportunity" are convenient reasons for an employee who has quit to give that will not likely offend a former employer. Data on reasons for leaving can be kept in a reliable manner and in a way that is quickly accessible at a low cost or at no cost.

Survey information among groups of companies on the subject of the causes of turnover and the role of retention pay on turnover is lacking. This is the type of personnel data survey information that is so badly needed. Based on my own experience, I would rank the causes of voluntary quits generally throughout enterprises of all types (in all but the highest-paid and lowest-paid positions) as follows:

1. The work being done was boring or very disagreeable for the individual.
2. There was a lack of pay progress.
3. The person thought there were limited opportunities for growth and/or, in fact, career growth was minimum.
4. There was dissatisfaction about pay level or pay relationships.
5. There were relations issues that mostly involved relationships with supervisors.
6. All other causes combined, including benefits, retirement pay, and perquisites.

Pay progress and pay relationships are the principal retention issues in compensation for jobs other than very high-paid and very low-paid positions. Furthermore, it is often the perception of pay progress or pay relationship that causes turnover.

In managing turnover, always make a distinction between reasons for leaving and reasons why a person started looking for another job. The reasons listed for quitting are usually not the reasons why people start looking for another job. In matters of voluntary turnover, why people start to look for another job is the relevant factor. Be assured that when a capable person starts to look for another job, he will find another job, and most of the time he will get higher pay.

Recommendations on Retention Pay

Pay is an important factor in retention, although not important as often or to the same degree as it is a factor in recruiting. Pay considerations are contributors to voluntary quits often enough to make it an important subject, particularly because in compensation management it is essential to have pay programs and practices that are not dissatisfiers and cause turnover.

It isn't difficult to manage compensation so it does not become a cause for turnover. Here are seven suggestions:

1. Understand the cost of turnover. Have numbers and cases for executive management. For example, in a company with a thousand employees, avoidable turnover related to pay dissatisfaction may cost the company $1 million each year. That's the kind of figure that will get the attention of management.

2. Make certain, by assured monitoring methods, that salaries for jobs are competitive (market average) and that salary increases match labor market inflation. Be sure to communicate this to employees.

3. Make sure that pay increases for individuals are what the company says they are. If some amount in addition to that necessary to match inflation is said to be for performance improvement, make certain that this is true. Lack of credibility is a cause of voluntary quits among valued employees.

4. Emphasize fairness in the administration of pay. Start by being fair, which I will always argue means being competitive in setting job salaries to market averages and gearing pay increases to job market inflation and to individual performance improvement. Being "fair" is the biggest objective, and you need to communicate what you do and at least state why the company thinks its practices are fair.

Fair doesn't mean fancy, and it doesn't mean complicated. Complex point-factor comparison job evaluation systems or elaborate rating systems for pay increases are indecipherable to employees. What employees don't understand they are likely to distrust, and many companies' pay programs are as unexplainable to employees as the federal income tax is to me.

Too many compensation systems are so complicated that even the managers of personnel don't understand them. A manager can't explain something he doesn't understand; and very likely the manager won't think that complicated systems he doesn't understand are fair.

5. Keep track of why people leave. Reasons for leaving are basic information in human resources management. Standard exit interviews and exit interview records are experience-proven in their value. Consider supplementing this with simple questionnaires to others—particularly the immediate supervisory managers of those who quit.

Also consider a telephone follow-up on a sample basis. Wait at least three months after a person has left the company and no more than six months. Then have someone in the personnel department call the person who quit at his home and ask him why he left. Be sure to explain that you are doing this so you can improve personal relationships in the organization. Almost all people will cooperate under these conditions. Now you will get a sample of information that is highly valid and that will improve the quality of the turnover information greatly.

6. Keep track of the pay progress of high performers. Every employee is valued, and all employees should be treated equivalently. But high performers are equivalently greater contributors and should be treated especially fairly.

7. The loss of any high performer should be regarded as a major company loss. It should be regarded as a loss of such magnitude that it should be reported to very high levels of management. Any significant increase in the rate of voluntary quits, particularly among high-performance people, should be a matter of company crisis, requiring specific executive action.

It's been said by some experts, in different ways, that a small percentage of the work force does a major share of the work. That isn't accurate, but it is true that a small percentage of employees account for a high percentage of the *improvement* in operations and set a standard of work excellence for others. That makes the high performers a very special human asset; with a value that is usually far in excess of the premium amounts paid to high performers. Make sure you are never surprised by a high performer quitting for pay reasons.

High-performing employees and those who are difficult to replace occupy such critical positions in the corporation that it is logical that such persons should be managed closely, in the sense that they are observed carefully and continuously. In the case of a company with one thousand employees, there wouldn't likely be more than fifty high-performing people who are difficult to replace. Watch them very carefully, and pay particular attention to the salary progress of these people.

Golden Handcuffs

There is another extremely important issue with respect to retention management that involves compensation. This is *contingent compensation,* which is often referred to as "golden handcuffs." These compensation practices involve amounts of money that the employee gets only if he stays with the company for a prescribed period of time.

The theory of contingent compensation is very simple. By having money dependent upon staying with the organization, there would be another reason to stay. Contingent compensation was a positive and tangible compensation retention management tool for many years.

There was a time not many years ago when contingent compensation was a standard part of compensation and was considered to be an important method of controlling turnover. Unvested pension benefits and options that did not even start to vest for five years were two principal practices of contingent compensation for many years. Over the years, for different reasons, contingent compensation has diminished, and in most companies today, it is not a significant part of the compensation package.

Contingent compensation never really prevented turnover. What it did was discourage turnover and reduce frivolous or impulse turnover. Golden handcuffs also increased substantially the amounts of recruiting pay that would have to be offered by those attempting to recruit employees for a company that has contingent compensation.

I urge every company to build golden handcuffs into their compensation programs. My urging is not based on current tax laws, which will likely change anyway. Nor do I think that much about accounting rules, which merely keep track of how much a company is making or losing and don't affect turnover at all. The reason I think contingent compensation is important is because retention of human talent is important, and golden handcuffs contribute in a significant way to effective retention management.

Laws have changed so that vesting in pensions has been substantially reduced and will likely be eliminated with full portability. Most long-term income plans aren't long term and start vesting almost immediately, with full vesting within five years. For various reasons like these, compensation plans that were used in the past are less effective as retention management tools today or are not used at all.

In an era of increasing technology, more rapid change, and multiple work careers for an increasing portion of the work force, the value of retention is changing also. Thinking based on the assumption that it was desirable for every employee to work for one company all of their work careers isn't valid any longer. Compensation plans geared to those historic goals and values of the past are therefore obsolete. Retention management needs to be more selective.

Today, companies need to consider the new breed of contingent compensation plans. These may have been around for some time, but the first I was aware of any was in 1984. The new contingent compensation plans have the following characteristics:

- Employees must be full-time employees with at least three to five years of experience before they are even considered for eligibility.

- "Tests" are applied to candidates, particularly a rather elaborate multiple evaluation system not dissimilar to multiple interview techniques used in the employment process in many firms.
- The focus is on the high performers and those whose work is such that they are difficult to replace. The focus of the new contingent compensation plans may be on only 5 percent of all employees.
- The funds involved for each participant are substantial.
- After inclusion in the program, the person must remain on the payroll for a specified number of years, and in most cases, this is at least five years.

In 1986 I predicted that by the year 1990, 10 percent of all companies will have contingent compensation plans with the characteristics outlined, and that prediction is on target. I also predicted that by the turn of the century 95 percent of all companies will have these plans. Retention management is an important issue. Retention pay is an important consideration in retention management. Contingent compensation is an essential part of retention pay.

ALLOCATION OF TALENT

In the economy generally and in labor markets specifically, pay allocates talent. In this view, pay serves the classic role of prices of all types.

The pay of plumbers is more than the pay of secretaries, not because the work requires more skill, is physically more demanding, or is typically performed by males. The pay for plumbers is more than for secretaries because it is more valued in the marketplace. If at any time secretarial work became more valued, then the pay of secretaries would increase substantially relative to that of plumbers, and more people would go into secretarial work and relatively fewer into plumbing work. That is a very simplistic model, but that's the way labor markets work.

Supply and demand determine the price of labor—the pay for jobs. And the price of labor helps to allocate scarce resources by encouraging people to move into jobs where there is a greater need for people and discourages people from moving into jobs where there is an oversupply. Some think pay should reflect fairness. For them, we must ask, "Who's criteria of fairness should apply?" For almost thirty years, the criteria (factors) of job evaluation plans influenced judgments about the fairness of pay and, in many large corporations, resulted in an artificial and wasteful allocation of talent.

In free-choice labor markets, the criteria of fairness of workers and those who need work determine fairness. Union leaders and corporate labor relations executives argue that brute economic strength should determine values, although they probably aren't really serious. Now some intellectuals argue that knowledge is the standard, and more pay should correlate with more knowledge. But intellectuals who are bright will know that knowledge *used* is what is of value, and the free choice of those in labor markets now value knowledge used.

If some criteria other than value determine pay, then those will be the criteria that allocate resources. What else besides the need of employers for talent and the interests of workers in job choices should apply?

Supply and demand pricing of labor is very different than it is for corn or any other commodity. For the price of labor to cause reallocation of talent, there must be a significant difference in pay; likely at least 30 percent. Even then, the market correction will take time, at least the length of time it takes for people to go through formal education, formal training, and required experience. Furthermore, for the price of labor to affect the allocation of talent, the need for the work must be great; *and* there must be a substantial difference between supply and demand; *and* there can be no material adjustment to a talent shortage such as the redesign of a product to require fewer people. Small or moderate differences in supply and demand won't cause reallocation, because market imbalances will be resolved by job transference in the labor market.

The characteristics of the prices of labor in allocating talent in no way prevent the power and inevitability of wages to adjust the supply and demand for jobs. Substantially higher prices-wages attract more people into the field of work over a period of time. Substantially higher price-wage costs get employers to find ways to use less of the high-cost talent. These things really happen with great force and predictability. This impact of wages as an allocator of manpower and talent is very powerful.

Don't underestimate the power of pay to allocate talent. The difference in pay rates may not seem great, but remember that there are probably one million job-pay decisions made every working day.

As a management method of dealing with scarcity, pay has relevance in a number of practical ways. For example, employers will have to pay relatively more in recruiting for scarce talent in the first place. Salaries and career paths will have to be managed consciously to retain current employees in areas of work experiencing scarcity and to encourage talented current employees to transfer into work where talent is scarce, even when periods of education and training are required.

My advice is to deal with labor scarcity in a number of ways. Labor scarcity is a major and complex problem, requiring multiple approaches. First, concentrate on increasing the excellence of recruiting. There is also a productivity answer to labor scarcity, and companies should concentrate productivity management efforts in areas where there are numbers of labor-scarce positions. Reducing turnover is another major opportunity for dealing with labor scarcity; pay particular attention to retention pay management in labor-scarce jobs. Inevitably, however, there are compensation issues relating to labor scarcity.

Don't even consider increasing salaries of jobs across the board to deal with labor scarcity. Few companies can afford such costs. What must be considered is selective adjustment of job salaries based on labor scarcity.

For some, the idea of selective pricing is radical or at least untidy. And some argue that, at least in large companies, the company can deal with scarcity in the future as it always has in the past. But those who think this way have been living in a corporate cocoon too long and fail to recognize that the past in this respect is no longer relevant. A selective pay pricing strategy is an essential method of allocating scarce resources. Selective wage pricing is required to get people for labor-scarce positions. Selective wage pricing must be factored into the pay of the many employees in order to allocate the human resources that a company has.

Selective pay pricing strategies simply urge companies to do, at their own initiative and in a timely manner, what labor markets do. The pay of scarce jobs tends to go high in labor markets over a period of time, as required. My suggestion is to identify highly valued, long-learning-time, scarce positions and raise their job pay by as much as one full level (three salary grades) at the company's initiative. Anticipate the market, and adjust pay selectivity based on importance and scarcity quickly.

Selective pay pricing turns a problem into an advantage. Your company becomes a preferred employer in labor-scarce positions. If necessary for cost reasons, adjust other jobs downward relative to the market (by less than market average upward adjustments). If you adjust 4 percent of your jobs upward 30 percent, you can "lower" all the others a few percentage points to equalize costs.

Among market-priced jobs, reallocation of talent has been going on for some time. Starting in the early 1980s, the pay of operating jobs in manufacturing and marketing has increased at a far greater pace than other jobs. * This should reflect itself in salary relationship changes among market-priced jobs in your company.

---

*Data in large companies will not support this observation, and survey data dominated by very large companies will be inconclusive. But this is largely because many large companies survey each other and the fact that some large companies consciously attempt to insulate themselves from labor markets, even though they have been increasingly unsuccessful in doing so.

Unionized operating jobs have not increased much during this period because of get-back bargaining and the loss of so many of these union jobs with regulated pay to foreign operations.

Also note that R&D jobs have not increased at the same rate as operating jobs in manufacturing and marketing, which may, in part, reflect a near-term view by executive management.

Only some jobs in the company are market priced, and others are regulated by administered systems. These systems of internally regulated pay don't often weigh very much in the market valuing systems, including the importance of the work to the company or the scarcity of talent. In fact, regulated internal pay was biased against operating jobs for more than four decades prior to the 1980s. This needs to be corrected, and selected internal pricing is an affirmative action for doing this.

In recent years, I have increasingly asked whether companies were allocating their human resources properly. It is a subject of great sensitivity, partially because the case is rarely presented to manufacturing and marketing managers in the operations. It takes real executive leadership to deal with this issue.

In its most simplistic description, the executive operating job is to assure the proper allocation of company resources and the effective utilization of talent. Companies spend a great deal of time and attention with respect to the allocation and use of financial resources. Now, particularly in a period of labor scarcity and increasing technology, there is reason to pay similar attention to the allocation of human talent.

There is reason to have concern about the way companies have been allocating talent in the past twenty or thirty years. Relatively too much of the best talent has gone into legal, financial, public relations, advertising, and personnel. Relatively too few highly talented people have gone into marketing and manufacturing.

Relatively too much of our top talent has gone into law firms, consulting firms, and investment banking. Relatively too little of our talent has gone into the operating companies.

There is a need for a conscious reallocation of human talent in companies into production, sales, and R&D. To do this requires substantial changes in how we manage people. Such a reallocation would run some risks and may involve some special investment costs. Reallocating talent would require changes in specific practices. It would mean changes in compensation plans and practices.

It wouldn't be easy to reallocate human resources talent into operations areas, but it seems to me that it's at least worth considering. Certainly, one of the things that must be done is to establish a different pay strategy and policy for these operations positions.

Pay a 30 percent premium for labor-scarce, critical operations positions in research and development, marketing, and manufacturing. Make sure that career paths encourage the best people to move up the organizational ladder through operations, marketing, and R&D, and then into executive management.

A conscious allocation of scarce human talent in an era of labor scarcity seems obviously to be a major job for human resources management people. Allocation pay must be a part of compensation management.

Chapter Six

Salary Structure

A salary structure is a basic tool for managing the salary component of compensation. Structures serve administratively to translate pricing and surveying data into competitive salary rates to be paid to employees. A salary structure is also a key tool for setting recruiting pay, retention pay, and for manpower management. The classification of jobs requires a salary structure. Increasingly, a structure is an integral part of a firm's human resources information system. Finally, a salary structure is used in actions of all types, including pay for performance increases.

Technical Features of a Salary Structure

A salary structure is a formal numeric organization of a number of steps. Each step or scale (which are called grades) reflects a distinguishable difference in pay for jobs, and the range of numbers for each grade is a reasonable spread of pay for individuals who work in jobs of similar scale, from the beginner to the top performer.

The structure reflects how the firm consciously positions salaries for its employees against the market. Thus pay for jobs reflects the competitiveness of salaries against the market.

A typical salary structure is reproduced in Figure 6–1. This particular structure has 10 percent between grades and plus or minus 15 percent from midpoint to maximum and from midpoint to minimum.

Some argue that a structure should be tailored to each company.

However, this is an elaborate and costly process, and differences that result from tailoring are so small that they make little practical difference. Therefore, standard structures, such as that reproduced in Figure 6–1, are increasingly used.

There are various technical questions of some importance with respect to a salary structure. One of these involves the correct between-grade progression: the percentage difference from the midpoint of one grade to the midpoint of the next grade. The practical minimum for between-grade progression is 7 percent, because of the limited precision of market data and the administrative methods of slotting jobs into the structure, such as job evaluation.

Figure 6-1. Salary Structure.

Grade	Minimum	Midpoint	Maximum
50	$810,229	$931,763	$1,071,528
49	736,572	847,057	974,116
48	669,611	770,052	885,560
47	608,737	700,047	805,055
46	553,397	636,407	731,868
45	503,088	578,552	665,334
44	457,353	525,956	604,849
43	415,776	478,142	549,863
42	377,978	434,674	499,876
41	343,616	395,159	454,432
40	312,378	359,235	413,120
39	283,980	326,577	375,564
38	258,164	296,888	341,422
37	234,694	269,899	310,383
36	213,359	245,362	282,167
35	193,962	223,057	256,515
34	176,329	202,779	233,196
33	160,299	184,344	211,996
32	145,727	167,586	192,724
31	132,479	152,351	175,203
30	120,435	138,501	159,276
29	109,487	125,910	144,796
28	99,533	114,463	131,633
27	90,485	104,058	119,666
26	82,259	94,598	108,787
25	74,781	85,998	98,898
24	67,983	78,180	89,907
23	61,802	71,073	81,734
22	56,184	64,612	74,303
21	51,076	58,738	67,548
20	46,433	53,398	61,408

(continued)

Figure 6-1. Continued.

Grade	Minimum	Midpoint	Maximum
19	42,212	48,544	55,825
18	38,374	44,131	50,750
17	34,886	40,119	46,137
16	31,714	36,472	41,942
15	28,831	33,156	38,129
14	26,210	30,142	34,663
13	23,827	27,402	31,512
12	21,661	24,911	28,647
11	19,692	22,646	26,043
10	17,902	20,587	23,675
9	16,274	18,716	21,523
8	14,795	17,014	19,566
7	13,450	15,467	17,788
6	12,227	14,061	16,171
5	11,116	12,783	14,701
4	10,105	11,621	13,364
3	9,187	10,565	12,149
2	8,351	9,602	11,045
1	7,592	8,731	10,041

This is an example of a sound salary structure. The numbers in grade 1 consider the minimum wage. Between-grade progression is 10 percent. Within-grade progression is plus or minus 15 percent from midpoint.

On the other hand, there should not be such large between-grade progressions that jobs of substantially different values are slotted into the same salary grade. Jobs that by basic logic, by administrative judgment, or because of career paths are clearly of more value than others should obviously be in a higher grade. To meet this requirement, between-grade progression should be a maximum of 15 percent in most jobs.

Logically, there is a need for broader between-grade progression in highly technical jobs and for higher-level management and administrative jobs. This is due mostly to problems of measurements of the differences between jobs. A 15 percent between-grade progression is often used in high-tech companies. Because more jobs have more technology, generally throughout the economy, there has been a trend toward a somewhat greater between-grade progression in salary structures in the past ten years, and this trend will likely continue in the future.

Some favor an increasing percentage between pay grades in positions of increasingly higher-level grades. The logic is that it is more difficult to make distinctions in higher-level positions. There have also been some analyses as to whether the progression should be arithmetic or geometric, but such exercises are usually more theoretical than useful.

Whether a company uses a flat or progressive between-grade progression and whether progression is arithmetic or something else is not of great importance. Sound salary administration is possible in any of these cases. The value of the uniform structure is simplicity and equivalency at all levels.

The within-grade spread should be sufficient to manage salaries or wages properly for given jobs. It should, for instance, provide enough range or spread to recognize different levels of job performance. The within-grade spread should also provide guidelines for recruiting and be broad enough to provide necessary flexibility in administering salaries or wages in special situations.

The structure shown in Figure 6–1 is somewhat narrower than is typical in business, at least in higher-level jobs. Quite frequently, in fact, structures have as little as a 25 percent spread in the lower grades and as much as a 50 percent spread in higher-level positions.

There is some logic in a broader range in higher-level jobs. There are greater differences in performance from minimum to maximum levels in higher-paid positions. Also, incumbents typically are in higher-level jobs for longer periods of time. On the other hand, broad ranges can be counterproductive. For one thing, it is generally more difficult to determine the appropriate position within a range than it is to determine which grade any particular job should be slotted into. A broader range results in greater latitude in an area where there is less precision and necessarily less confidence in results.

Broad within-grade spreads may contribute to basic errors in critical human resources decisions. For instance, a very broad range may make it possible to continue to give increases to a high-potential individual who is approaching the top of the range, whereas what is really needed is to redesign the job to provide more challenge and to make sure that the individual has a promotional opportunity within a reasonable period of time.

The technical features of a salary structure are the responsibility of compensation specialists. The work must be done correctly, because the technical features of the structure impact the excellence of salary administration. Issues like within-grade spread directly affect pay decisions and indirectly affect other human resources decisions, such as promotional decisions.

Slotting Benchmark Jobs Into the Structure

Jobs that are priced by surveying can be slotted into the salary structure. Procedurally, this is done by putting each market-priced job into the structure where the average of the market data most closely matches the salary structure midpoint.

This is the market approach to salary classification. For benchmark jobs, salary structure midpoints reflect the market. The market also necessarily determines *relative* job worth. Thus the answer to the question, ''Why is my job in a level lower than that job?'' is that the market has set that pay relationship.

This puts salary administration on a more objective basis than that which is inherent in judgments under any job evaluation plan. In market classification, the employer's representatives gather facts as best they can and match those facts against jobs in the company. The process is not perfect by any means, but it is impersonal and free from bias. In job evaluation, there are judgments about the criteria that value jobs. These are selected by the employer's representatives, and there may be some doubt about the objectivity of evaluation, regardless of how well the evaluators do their work.

A market-pricing approach is simple. It is an approach that is understandable by all supervisors who must explain salary classification decisions. Generally, a market-priced basis of classifying jobs is far more acceptable to all the employees who are affected.

Employees may not like the decisions of the marketplace, but they tend to accept them. They want to be paid fairly. To them, being paid fairly is, in large part, being paid as well as others who do similar work in other companies. The facts of market pay are typically more meaningful to employees than what someone's judgment says their jobs are worth, regardless of how elaborate and sophisticated the system for making the judgment may be.

Before market salary data were available, companies had to use administrative systems such as job evaluation to classify jobs. Now, with market data available, the salary levels of some jobs—the market-priced jobs—and the salary relationships between market-priced jobs are established by the marketplace. With market data, the price of benchmark jobs is known, and administrative proxy measures are not needed to determine the fair and competitive pay for these jobs.

Market pricing *is,* in effect, job evaluation. The market evaluates jobs. The market, in millions of free-choice decisions, determines the real factors that determine job value and the real weighing of these factors. The market sets fair pay and fair pay relationships.

Some experts are uncomfortable with market pricing as the basis for the classification of jobs. Sometimes their discomfort is caused by the fact that they were trained to use job evaluation as the basis for job classification. Experts also see the technical imperfections of surveying. There are, of course, job matching and other types of problems, which are covered in detail in the chapter on surveying. Experts sometimes have concern about whether there is a sufficient sample, whether the sample is large enough and whether there is a proper cross-section of jobs. Not all who do market pricing are equally qualified to do the work. There even may be questions of objectivity in slotting market data, particularly the slotting of professional specialist jobs by compensation professional specialists. These are the issues that need to be managed in a system of slotting jobs into a structure.

Market pricing must be done well; the issues must be recognized and dealt with. Classifying jobs by market pricing is not perfect, but it is as technically sound as any other system such as job evaluation, is far less costly to administer, and is more acceptable to most managers, personnel, and employees.

The market-pricing system particularly requires that the data be valid and the jobs matched appropriately. In fact, if there is any substantial doubt about the comparability of any job with market data, then that job should not be used as a benchmark position. There is such a large amount of data available today for most levels of jobs in most industries that only those jobs for which job matches are clearly correct should be used.

If you want proof that slotting market-priced jobs into a salary structure and not job evaluation should be the basis for job classification, it isn't difficult to get. Pick any job evaluation system and any reasonable sample of jobs. You will find that the resulting job evaluation total points set different levels and different relationships than the market does. Consultants who sell job evaluation systems may say that the market is therefore wrong. But note that they very often then proceed to establish adjustment factors for their points to adjust them to the market.

Not all jobs can be slotted into a salary structure by pricing them in the labor market. Market pricing can be the base, but jobs that cannot be priced directly in the marketplace by surveying techniques must be set by some other way, and traditional methods of job evaluation represent one of the alternatives.

Positioning the Structure to the Market

A company has flexibility in positioning the salary structure to the market. The structure should be consciously set to the market by policy determination. No company necessarily has to follow the leader and establish its salary structure relative to the market the same as other companies. What each company does in positioning pay for jobs to the market is an important policy issue that each company should consider.

Five significantly different levels of competitiveness are possible, as shown in Figure 6–2. The statistical average is, of course, exactly that. But it must also be recognized that there are imperfections in any survey-

Figure 6-2. Levels of Competitiveness.

Level	Description
Superior	High enough above statistical average to influence ability to attract and retain people. Generally 25 percent above statistical average.
Above Average	High enough above statistical average to negate possibility of statistical error. At least 10 percent above reported average.
Average	At statistical average of reported data.
Competitive	Far enough below statistical average to negate possibilities of statistical error. At least 10 percent below reported average.
Conservative	Far enough below statistical average to affect costs significantly. Generally 25 percent below reported average.

ing technique. The data must be accurate plus or minus 5 percent. Positioning the structure at "statistical average" places the company at the reported market data average and assures that statistical error does not place the company structure significantly above or below the market average.

Above average means a level sufficiently higher than statistical average so that it is clearly not due to statistical error. In effect, this means that in order to pay above average, the company must set its salary structure at least 10 percent higher than reported market data. Similarly, a competitive posture to the labor market would have a salary structure set at least 10 percent below reported statistical averages.

Either superior or conservative positioning of salary structures must be substantially above or below reported statistical average for salaries of comparable jobs in similar firms. Generally, at least 25 percent above or below reported averages is necessary to significantly affect a company's competitiveness and cost. A difference of this magnitude is also necessary for people to see clearly that their pay is above average or below average.

A company can set its structure at positions other than these five levels. While that may have some administrative purpose, such intermediate positions would not affect the company's competitiveness in a meaningful way. Nor could intermediate positions be explained convincingly.

Each of five levels of competitiveness of job salaries puts the company in a significantly different position with respect to attracting and retaining qualified workers. Above-average levels, for example, make it somewhat easier to attract persons, or measurably easier to attract more talented persons. Superior levels of competitiveness would provide recruiting pay levels that would mean that the company could almost always offer substantially more salary than its competitors. The five levels of salary competitiveness similarly involve five very different levels of payroll costs.

There are a number of factors that companies must consider in consciously establishing and implementing a policy of positioning themselves relative to the marketplace. Whether a company is active in recruiting is one such consideration. Generally speaking, the more active a company is in the market, the higher its salary structure relative to labor markets must be. A company may also have a conscious strategy of paying a higher or lower than typical percentage of total pay in the form of salary; for example, somewhat less salary but superior benefits.

A growth company will tend to pay job salaries below market average by at least 10 percent. Similarly, a mature (nongrowth) company will tend to pay somewhat above market average. A highly capital-intensive company may pay more, on average, because employee costs seem less important than the utilization of capital.

Personnel practices affect the appropriate level of salary competitiveness. Excellence in recruiting will make an average or competitive salary level more practical. The degree to which the company does vertical recruiting also has a major impact on whether it must position the salary structure at average or above average relative to the market.

Assuming that your structure is average to the market, then your structure midpoints are average salary compared to the market, assuming those in your company and those in the labor market are average performers. Workers in the market are average in performance by definition, but those workers in a company or in a location of a company may net out in their performance at something different than average. You should know what performance is in your company.

A practical factor in positioning the structure relative to labor markets is the current level of pay for jobs within the existing structure. If, for any reason, employee pay is high in the range, this creates pressures to raise the structure. If employee pay averages below midpoint, that creates pressure to leave the structure as it is, regardless of the amount of wage inflation in the market.

There should never be significant differences between structure midpoints and actual average pay—considering performance. If actual pay is unexplainably high or low in your ranges, you have a serious problem. Most often, the problem is either that the professional specialists have not done a good job of pricing or your pay for performance program is working poorly.

These are examples of the factors that must be considered in setting a salary structure. The nature of the salary structure and how it is positioned against labor markets are key matters. These issues affect human resources management and compensation costs.

Adjusting the Salary Structure

The salary structure must be adjusted from time to time. Structure adjustments are necessary to assure that job salaries will remain competitive; that the company's policy of gearing jobs to labor market pay is maintained.

While companies need to consider a number of factors in adjusting the structure, a principal criterion should be to maintain market competitiveness. Thus salary structures should be adjusted to match increases in market salary levels.

Never adjust structures to increases in the cost of living as measured by any consumer price index. Structures should be linked to labor market pay changes, and these are not the same from year to year as changes in the Consumer Price Index. Furthermore, the CPI's measure of change is the price of goods and services typically purchased only by employees in a few grades.

Structure adjustments reflect changes in market pay for all employees in the marketplace. Structure changes match market pay trends and are always less than salary increase budgets, mostly because of turnover, promotions, and retirement.

Actual increases in salary structures that are reflective of general industry practices over the years are shown in Figure 6–3. Note that salary structure adjustments are about 25 percent less than the amount of salary increases budgeted. Data on increases in structures provide a key piece of information that materially affects the competitiveness of the company, and they are also the correct figures to use in financial budgeting to reflect increases in payroll costs.

The result of market salary adjustments during a period of inflation is a continuing increase in structures. For employers, this represents an element of increasing cost. For employees, it represents salary progress, although not necessarily progress that is equal to changes in their cost of living. It does mean, however, that during an inflationary period, employees tend to get increases even if they do not receive promotions or are not recognized for improved performance on their jobs.

Have a process for reviewing increases in salaries in relevant labor markets. Be certain that the reviews are at regular intervals. The salary structure should be matched to average market increases.

In making annual adjustments, never mind that salaries for some types

Figure 6-3. Increases in Salary Structures Over a Twenty-Year Period.

Year	Increase in Structure**	Salary Increase Budgets*		
		Management	Middle Group	Operations
1969	3%	7%	7%	8%
1970	5	9	7	8
1971	4	7	6	7
1972	4	7	7	8
1973	5	7	7	8
1974	6	8	8	9
1975	8	10	9	10
1976	7	9	8	9
1977	7	9	8	9
1978	8	8	7	9
1979	9	8	8	9
1980	9	10	10	11
1981	8	11	8	7
1982	7	10	7	7
1983	7	9	8	6
1984	7	8	7	6
1985	6	9	6	6
1986	5	8	4	5
1987	4	7	3	4
1988	3	7	3	2
Average	6.0%	8.4%	6.8%	7.4%

*Includes salary increases for those on payroll through the year who did not change jobs and includes those receiving zero increases.

**Average increases in structure for sample groups studied.

Source: Data from published reports over the twenty-year period.

and levels of jobs increase more than others. These differences occur over time and will be reflected automatically in market-priced jobs.

The Use of Salary Structures

A salary structure essentially records decisions about classifications of jobs, whether by market pricing or any other method. Salary grades serve to differentiate between jobs as to their value. The structure is useful in positioning company pay, in accordance with company policy, in some predetermined relationship to pay in relevant labor markets.

A salary structure serves as a vital part of a company's human resources information system; in the field of compensation it is a uniform accounting system. A "level 6 job" has a meaning, regardless of the labor market, the labor market area, or the dollar values attached to the structure. It is a tool for managing compensation and salaries, not just with respect to the market but internally as well.

The salary structure has many uses as a management tool. For example, structures can help in determining promotional opportunities and correct career pathing. The structure can provide information about high-potential persons and provide an information alert to make sure there are appropriate opportunities for high-performers. Structure information provides information on manpower planning, complement control, and payroll cost management.

Salary structures have special uses in employment and internal promotion decisions. Generally speaking, the bottom of each salary range should be sufficient to recruit people into the company, provided the recruiting strategy and recruiting methods are effective. Structures assure that job moves within the company are as intended—that if it is intended to promote a person, the job move indeed represents a move to a higher-level job.

Salary structures also serve as a useful administrative tool. For example, eligibility for various pay programs, benefits, and perquisites may be based, at least in part, on salary grade.

Salary structures are guidelines, not boxes. They are not so precise as to be used rigidly or without exception. Any plan that allows no exception (an individual above or below the salary structure) is probably being administered too rigidly. However, in general, no more than one of twenty jobs should be outside the established salary structure.

A salary structure is such a simple and mechanical tool of management, yet it is key to sound compensation. If you strip back your salary practices to the minimum basics, two things will have to be kept: You would need a salary structure, and you would need to do market pricing.

A salary structure is an affirmative tool of salary administration and a key piece of information in the management of personnel. Today, a salary structure is a tool of management more than a control mechanism.

Special Problems and Issues

There are special problems in the management of salary structures. One faced by large companies with multiple locations is whether they should have one structure for all locations and businesses or a number of structures. Similarly, should there be different structures for different types of work (professional, management, operations, and so on)?

The answer to those questions is that it is never necessary to have different structures for different areas, for different businesses, or for different disciplines of work. One structure, such as that shown in Figure 6–1, is sufficient. There may be different numbers attached to the salary grades for some levels, some categories of jobs, or some areas, but one structure can accommodate all. This has the advantage of the appearance of equivalency of treatment for all employees. A single salary structure is essential to the use of the salary structure as a uniform information system for the company.

A related question involves the use of ranges. Not all jobs need to use the same parts of the range in each grade. Some jobs may be single-rate jobs and not use a salary range at all. Other jobs may use a broader range from minimum to maximum than your structure calls for; others may use only a part of your spread from minimum to maximum. In all such cases, a single salary structure can still be used—with variations.

There are special cases where multiple structures may have some value. When this happens, consider only supplemental structures for special uses. For example, some believe that professional career development and pay reward in high-technology industries are handled more positively and effectively if a separate professional structure is in effect. However, this is not a technical requirement; it is used simply because it better reflects the style of the organization and the thinking of the managers who make decisions in these professional disciplines. Similarly, in the health care industry, some hospitals have established separate structures for registered nurses, technicians, managers, and operations people. Again, such actions are not necessary, but some find them to be a helpful supplement.

There have been problems when, for whatever reason, there is concentration on structure as though the structure was pay and the structure represented pay costs. Employees judge fairness by what they are paid and not by the fairness of the structure. Never communicate pay matters to employees in terms of salary structure. Don't even mention salary structures to employees unless it is absolutely necessary. Salary structures are only management tools, with no necessary meaning to employees.

Some confuse structure increases with salary increase budgets or individual pay progress. The latter figures are always larger, and if structures are increased the same amount as salary increases, then structures will be far above market in a very few years.

You must be prepared for many types of questions involving structure and actual pay. Take the case of a fully satisfactory person at the midpoint of the range. If that individual gets the average ''merit increase,'' then he will likely be higher in the range because the average merit increase would be higher than the structure's increase. Supervisory managers are often concerned about this situation. The answer to this small dilemma is, ''Yes, he will be higher in the range, but that doesn't make any difference.'' Structures are guides for all salaries and not a specific determinant of the salary of any individual jobs. Structures represent general guidelines for viewing the appropriateness of salaries within range based upon performance, length of service, or whatever standards are used to set individual pay for different people in the same or similar-level jobs. Small differences in band position lack significance.

Finally, there are the special problems relating to the use of salary structures as controls. The bottom of the range in each grade is a guide to the lowest salaries for jobs in that grade that are fair. The bottom part of each range also serves as a guide for recruiting pay. The maximum of the range should similarly be a guide to fair pay for top performers in the grade. The midpoint reflects average salaries paid for jobs like the same jobs in your company in the marketplace; it is fair pay for work done to your company's standards.

How much a company uses the guidelines as controls is a matter of management style. Even in firms that use structures as absolute controls, there must be exceptions. Just as clear is the need to require explanations for deviations from the guidelines; and most should be explainable. Don't make managers explain every exception; ask for explanations from the managers of personnel who make frequent exceptions.

Salary Grades, Levels, and Classes

Salary *grades* differentiate between degrees of value of a job. For all the reasons noted, salary grades, as used in the traditional salary structure, are a key tool in the management of compensation. The material presented thus far relates only to the use of traditional salary grades.

Salary *levels* are a second management pay tool. Salary levels reflect different jobs in terms of organizational level, a distinctly different level of professional attainment, or reasonable supervisor-supervised pay differences. Salary levels should significantly differentiate between higher levels of management responsibility and authority, and such differences should, in turn, roughly follow the organizational structure of the company.

Actually, salary levels encompass about four salary grades, as shown in Figure 6–4. Data in this exhibit reflect many organizational studies made over the years, studies of career paths, and are consistent with long-standing guidelines for promotions.

Figure 6–4 shows the salary levels used in a number of companies. The data comes straight out of the salary structure (Figure 6–1), but only a single salary number is used, and overlapping is not appropriate with respect to salary levels.

Salary levels are directly usable in salary administration. In fact, for many years some companies have used only salary levels and had no sal-

Figure 6-4. Salary Levels.

Salary Level	Benchmark Salary	Salary Grade*
12	$694,324	45–48
11	474,232	41–44
10	323,817	37–40
9	221,233	33–36
8	151,105	29–32
7	103,207	25–28
6	70,491	21–24
5	48,147	17–20
4	32,884	13–16
3	22,460	9–12
2	15,341	5–8
1	10,478	1–4

*See Figure 6-1.

Note: Each salary level is approximately 46 percent higher than the next lower. The specific numbers are used for mathematics and are not intended to suggest precision to the nearest dollar.

ary grades. Other companies have found that using salary levels instead of the more conventional salary grades for some jobs in salary administration is helpful. This is particularly true for higher-level and professional positions.

Companies have also found that using salary levels is frequently more practical than using traditional grades in the administration of some extra pay plans, for benefit administration, for succession planning, and for organizational analysis. Some companies have successfully used the salary level concept in administering bonus payments and granting long-term income awards for all eligible positions.

Salary levels can also be useful in career pathing. A career change or a career path is more readily and more easily tracked by levels than by grades. Therefore, in jobs where career pathing within a family of jobs is relevant, translate their grades into levels—or use both numbers.

Salary levels can be used to audit compression. For example, a supervisor and someone supervised by that person should never be in the same salary level.

Organization structures can be monitored by the use of salary levels, and salary levels can be a useful tool in the developmental phase of organizational work. First-level managers of personnel should be in a base salary level, which would normally be the first exempt salary level. Second-level managers should be in the second organizational level and the second salary level. The results won't be exactly like that; the organization is not that precise. But this one organizational level/one salary level concept is useful in organizational structuring work.

Some students of business have said for many years that there should only be six organizational levels in a company. In large enterprises with multiple businesses, there may be two extra levels, for a total of eight salary levels—at the very most. No one has ever publicly argued against the eight-level organization maximum. Yet if you use that guideline, no executive in the United States should have a salary of more than $700,000 in even the largest firm (see Figure 6–4).

In concept, salary levels are quite similar to the use of slope data. However, slope data are usually used only with the salary of the chief executive officer of a firm or an organization as base 100. In addition, slope guidelines reflect only existing practices, whereas salary levels are an affirmative guideline.

Salary levels do not involve extra work. They are just another useful salary administration guideline that can be keyed mathematically to the salary structure. If anything, time is saved by using salary levels for some work because there are fewer levels than grades.

Salary *class* is the newest idea with respect to salary structures usable in compensation administration. Salary classes distinguish between significantly different standards or styles of living. Salary classes are illustrated in Figure 6–5. Each salary class is about ten salary grades and two or three salary levels. There are only eight salary classes.

Workers obviously never want their standard of living to decline. Sometime in their careers, almost all workers also seek to achieve more. They want to improve their standard of living. They want their families to move from one style of living to the next higher style of living.

Figure 6-5. Salary Classes.

Salary Class	Approximate Annual Salary Amount
8	$6,000,000
7	2,250,000
6	850,000
5	325,000
4	125,000
3	53,000
2	23,000
1	10,500

Note: Each salary class reflects a significantly different style of life, and there are only eight salary classes with respect to earned income.

During at least a part of their work careers, most people are motivated primarily by a desire for more money. This is not to suggest that money is everything, but that for most people, at least during part of their careers, money is number one.

Salary classes measure income needed to live at substantially different lifestyles. Therefore, one use of salary classes is to provide information for salary increase planning.

A person's pay progress can be tracked to see if he is on a trend that may lead to a higher salary class or whether he has peaked in the salary class in which he is now positioned. If this tracking is at variance with judgments of the person's potential, or the manpower plans of the company, then future increases must be adjusted. If the pay progress and movement toward another salary class are inconsistent with the person's expectations, then some discussions and counseling may be appropriate.

Class 8 represents an income that supports the lifestyle of the rich and famous. At this income level, pretax income is about $20,000 each day; the person in class 8 earns almost twice as much more in one day than the person in class 1 earns in a year. The people in class 1 are at the poverty threshold. There are only eight measurably and significantly different styles of life that are achievable by earned income.

The eight different styles of life have been recorded in family budget items. In this way then, the different standards of living are translatable into tangible family income: for example, no car; one five-year-old car; a recent model car. In terms of tangible differences of family asset accumulation and expenditures, it really isn't practical to have more than eight styles of living.

Chapter Seven

Job Evaluation

Thirty years ago, job evaluation was the centerpiece of work in compensation. Necessarily, a book on compensation was largely about job evaluation. Probably more than a third of all those who worked in compensation did job evaluation work at that time. Today, most enterprises don't use job evaluation at all. Market pricing, market classification, and delegative management practices are now the basis of compensation work. Job evaluation is still used, usually as one alternative in slotting jobs into a structure where the jobs cannot be priced directly in a salary structure.

The Traditional Job Evaluation Approach

The basic method of traditional, administrative systems of job evaluation has remained unchanged for almost fifty years. This approach, illustrated in Figure 7–1, calls for the measurement of job duties against a predetermined yardstick in order to assess, by administrative judgment, relative job worth. The duties and responsibilities of work assigned to the job are measured, not the individual's performance of that work. Thus the process is impersonal and has nothing to do with how well the work is performed or with the ability, potential, attitude, or background of employees. Existing job duties are determined through job analysis, and the appropriateness of the job analysis is ultimately based upon the knowledge of the job.

Job evaluation measures job worth in an administrative rather than

Figure 7-1. The Job Evaluation Approach.

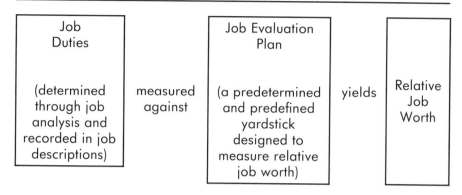

| Job Duties (determined through job analysis and recorded in job descriptions) | measured against | Job Evaluation Plan (a predetermined and predefined yardstick designed to measure relative job worth) | yields | Relative Job Worth |

economic or social sense. Economic worth can be determined only by the marketplace; social worth can be assessed only by the forces operating in such activities as individual or collective bargaining. The administrative concept of job worth involves the importance or difficulty of the work performed. This assumes that market worth correlates with difficulty or importance, which is not always correct.

Job evaluation sought to administratively set job salaries that were competitive. The system was also thought to be fair, largely because the system was impersonal and the same system was applied to all persons.

All of this was clearly true during the period when job evaluation was widely adopted and used. That period started in the 1930s and continued through the 1960s. In essence, job evaluation was better by far than the pay system that preceded it in most companies, which was largely informal and arbitrary.

Job evaluation also brought thinking and discipline into setting pay as well as competitiveness and fairness. The system was based on fact—the duties performed on the job. The system detailed the criteria (factors) that were to be used in valuing every job and quantified these different factors, sometimes mathematically with points. Job evaluation represented a great leap forward in personnel management in the 1930s and 1940s.

The system of job evaluation represented the classic case of programmatic management. A single system designed by experts and personally approved by top executives was applied throughout the organization. Managers were trained to use the system the correct way, which meant largely the same way. In large part, then, the system made the decisions.

Today, there is a need for a far more delegative management system, and this trend will clearly continue into the future. Programmatic tools aren't operative in a delegative environment: Programmatic and delegative are contradictory in meaning.

With an increasingly technological economy, it is also more difficult to describe jobs, and this means that job evaluation systems increasingly weren't factual. Job evaluation was never successfully applied to top management jobs and professional jobs anyway, mostly because job duties could not be recorded in a way that was sufficiently clear for persons in some central locations to make job evaluation judgments. More and more jobs cannot be described because of increasing technology, and this is a major reason for the declining use of job evaluation.

Job evaluation was always known to be flawed, because the factors for valuing jobs were not consistent with market values, which, in turn, are based on supply and demand. Not surprisingly, then, as more market data have become available, more companies moved directly to methods that determined competitive pay directly.

There was always one other major issue with traditional job evaluation, and that was cost. In today's competitive era, with cost containment and downsizing, the high cost of job evaluation is something companies are increasingly less willing to incur, particularly when the same objectives can be accomplished at a far lower cost.

The net result of these considerations is that job evaluation is used less often in business. It is still a technique that can be used, but it never should be a key part of compensation systems and programs.

Traditional Job Evaluation Methods

Evaluation plans that are used to translate job duties into relative job worth may take different forms. Essentially, however, the principal measuring techniques for determining relative job worth differ from one another in three ways:

1. What is measured—the whole job or identifiable elements of the job.
2. Whether or not point values are assigned to establish quantitative measures of job value.
3. How jobs are measured—against other jobs or against a predetermined yardstick.

The application of these techniques can result in four basically different types of job evaluation plans, as shown in Figure 7–2. These are, and have been for many years, the ranking system, the classification system, the point evaluation plan, and the factor comparison plan. Combinations of these systems can also be used.

The Ranking System

The most widely used method of job evaluation is the ranking system. Under this plan, one job is ranked against other jobs, without assigning

Figure 7-2. Traditional Methods of Job Evaluation.

1. What Is Measured?	2. How Is Job Weighted?	3. How Is Job Measured?	
		Job against Scale	Job against Job
Overall job	No point values		Ranking
	Point values assigned	Classification	
Elements or factors of the job	No point values		
	Point values assigned	Point evaluation	Factor comparison

point values. Evaluators simply compare two jobs and judge which one is more difficult. Once this determination has been made, a third job is compared until all jobs have been ranked, from the most difficult to the least difficult.

The greatest advantage of the ranking system is its simplicity. The evaluation process is quick and inexpensive. In addition, the ranking system uses a job-against-job comparison, which is the most accurate method of evaluation, because it is far easier to judge which of two jobs is more difficult than it is to judge the absolute difficulty of either.

On the other hand, the system does little to guide the judgment of evaluators. There is a tendency to judge each job on the basis of its dominant characteristics, which can result in inconsistencies. In addition, it is extremely difficult to explain or justify the results of rankings to employees or managers, because there is no record of the judgments of the evaluators. Finally, the ranking system can indicate only that one job is more difficult than another, not how much more difficult it is.

Several techniques have been devised to refine the ranking system. One of these is the paired-comparison ranking system, in which evaluators are given a list that pairs every job with every other job. Evaluators are asked to decide, in each case, which job in the pair ranks higher. The evaluator's rankings are then analyzed statistically to produce a master list of overall rankings.

Another refinement of straight ranking is the factor-guided ranking technique. Under this system, evaluators rank jobs not just in terms of overall difficulty but in terms of their difficulty with respect to certain factors, such as knowledge and physical effort required. When the evaluation is complete, a separate ranking is established for each factor. These separate rankings serve to audit or confirm overall rankings.

The Classification System

In the classification system (sometimes called the rating system), each job is measured against a predetermined yardstick whose various categories define overall job value or difficulty. The evaluator compares each job against the yardstick and slots each job into the grade that best describes its characteristics and difficulty.

While this system is simple and inexpensive to install and administer, it has several limitations. For one thing, classification has most of the shortcomings of the ranking system. For example, it is difficult to explain resulting decisions. Furthermore, it is very difficult to define levels of overall job worth in any meaningful way. As the number and diversity of jobs increase, the definition of an appropriate yardstick becomes increasingly difficult.

Nonetheless, the classification system does have some applicability, particularly in operations with a large number of employees who work in relatively few jobs. In addition, in recent years some companies have applied the classification approach to professional positions and think the work was helpful in establishing professional levels. In these cases, classification levels were written for different levels of professional jobs, defining, in essence, the level of professional attainment and the type of work typically performed at each level. Similarly, classification methods are increasingly found in use, sometimes in the business disciplines of accounting, personnel, law, industrial engineering, and investment.

The Point System

Under the point evaluation system, various factors that measure a job are selected and defined. A separate yardstick for different degrees of each factor is prepared. A job is then rated against every yardstick. In essence, this is the same process as the classification system except that the job is evaluated on a separate scale for each factor. In addition, each degree of each factor has point weightings. In this way, evaluations under each of the factors can be combined to get a measure of the overall job value.

Point evaluation systems provide a written record of judgments made. In addition, the degrees in each factor provide a guideline for judgments. Because points are assigned for each factor, each job can be given a total numeric point value, which provides a measure of how much more difficult one job is than another.

The main problems of the point evaluation system are the difficulty of selecting relevant factors, defining degrees for each factor, and assigning appropriate point values. In addition, there is the problem of determining the correct number of degrees. Ideally, just enough degrees are established to identify minimum measurable differences in each factor. Finally, the various degree definitions must be written to serve as guides that are both useful and meaningful in terms of the jobs being measured in each specific company.

Factor Comparison

The final basic approach used in traditional job evaluation is the factor comparison system. In this system, factors must also be identified, as under the point system. Within each factor, however, a ranking system rather than a classification system is used. That is, for each factor, the evaluator ranks all jobs from the highest to the lowest. Various degrees result, but they are not defined or described. Points are assigned to each of these degrees.

Factor comparison has two basic advantages. First, it uses the job-by-job comparison technique. Second, it does not involve the semantic problems encountered in defining factor degrees. However, because of the lack of definitions, it is always difficult to explain the results of factor comparison evaluations to employees or supervisors.

Combination Systems

In practice, most companies use combination plans. The most typical approach is to use a combination factor comparison and point system. In this way, the advantages of each system are obtained, and the difficulties of each are neutralized.

A combination system I used for many years involves the following steps:

1. Factors are selected and defined. These are usually the five basic factors of responsibility, authority, knowledge, skill, and working conditions. In some cases, such as high-technology firms, different factors will be used. In special situations, factors are selected on a customized basis.

2. Benchmark jobs are selected. About half of these are jobs that can be priced in the marketplace.

3. The benchmark jobs that can be priced in the market are so priced.

4. All benchmark jobs are ranked under each factor. This includes both those that were priced in the marketplace and those that were not. The ranking of market-priced jobs, however, must reflect market pay relationships. The ranking of other jobs is done primarily by comparison with jobs that have been priced.

5. Points are assigned to each degree of each factor on the basis of a standard system. The relative maximum weight of each factor is a function of the number of degrees established in the ranking process.

6. Job points are totaled for each benchmark job, and an overall ranking is established. For market-priced jobs, this overall ranking is again compared with the rank order established in the marketplace, which may not be changed.

7. Each degree is defined. This is done in terms of the company's jobs that have been ranked in each degree.

8. Jobs are slotted into a structure. This must be consistent with the job pricing of those benchmark jobs that were priced, or else a reconciliation process must follow.

9. All other jobs are evaluated, by comparison against degree definitions and on a job-against-job ranking system, particularly using benchmark jobs priced under each factor.

Multiple Evaluation and Cross Evaluation

In some companies, multiple evaluation plans are used. One such plan calls for evaluating each position three times by three different factor comparison techniques. If the results in each case are identical, the evaluations are reviewed and approved. If not, a reconciliation process is applied. This involves triple work, and the increase in precision must be weighed against such costs.

Cross evaluation is another technique used in combination systems. It is used primarily for auditing the results of job evaluation. In some companies, cross-evaluation systems are a formal part of the salary classification program. Usually, however, they are informal, unofficial techniques developed by staff personnel or line managers.

One type of cross-evaluation system involves reviewing the results of all evaluations for each family of jobs, such as accounting. Another cross-evaluation system involves comparing evaluation results with normal career movement patterns. Other cross evaluations include:

- Ranking all jobs by point values assigned, and reviewing results by overall judgments
- Grouping all jobs whose total point values are similar, and checking each group to make sure that jobs are worth about the same, as indicated by survey data and/or company experience

Technical Questions About Job Evaluation Methods

When traditional job evaluation methods are used, those who apply and explain the program must understand some of the key technical aspects of such plans. These particularly involve the validity of the factors used, point assignments, and the grouping and grading techniques that are used. These are problems particularly associated with the point evaluation system and the factor comparison system.

Those who use the system and have to explain it must understand what factors are used and how these measure job worth. In theory, the factors in a job evaluation plan must meet the following requirements:

- Each factor must have some relationship to job difficulty or job value.
- In combination, the factors should correlate reasonably well with job difficulty—and, at least roughly, with market values.
- The factors selected must be both observable and measurable.
- The factors that are used must be explainable.
- Important elements of every job must be measured by one or more factors.
- Every factor should serve to help distinguish between jobs.
- Two factors should not measure essentially the same characteristics.

Having developed a number of job evaluation plans over the years and having audited others, I can say with confidence that it is extremely difficult to establish factors that would meet all these criteria. Most job evaluation plans used over the years would not pass the test of these criteria.

If factors used do not meet these criteria, then the plan is not fair to all employees and almost surely will not evaluate positions in a manner consistent with market pay relationships. In such cases, then, job salary level grades are not competitive, and they are not fair.

Don't feel good about your plan if it has no factors. Then the criteria actually used in evaluating jobs will surely fail to meet the seven criteria for appropriate factors in job evaluation.

In effect, factors are proxy measures of job difficulty and job worth, which in turn are proxy measures of market worth. Those who use the system must understand this and keep it in mind as they apply the factors. They must be prepared to explain the relevance of these factors and how they aid in making judgments of job value.

The assignment of point values within each factor is important because it establishes the relative significance of the factors used in the plan. This is a matter that must be considered in the design of the program. Those who manage the program and explain it must understand that the weightings affect the value of each factor and, therefore, indirectly the valuation of jobs. Points are simply a means of coming to a total value, which establishes the relative values of jobs. Therefore, point weightings affect the valuing of all jobs.

How these points are then grouped into salary grades must also be understood by those who manage and explain the program. Since different grades have salary values attached to them, the method of grouping indirectly affects the actual dollar values of jobs.

Theoretically, it would be possible to give dollar values to all jobs in direct proportion to the total points assigned. This is administratively impractical, since it could result in almost as many different pay grades as there are jobs in the company. In addition, since even small changes in duties would probably require adjustments in total points, pay grades would be changing constantly. The results of job evaluation can never be accurate enough to justify such distinctions anyway; therefore, for technical as well as administrative reasons, jobs need to be grouped into salary grades.

Therefore, jobs are grouped to arrive at logical and practical distinctions between jobs. The mathematical method of grouping points to make this happen is a technical matter. What is important is that a range of points establishes salary grades, and any point within that range falls into the same salary grade.

Technically, this means that a one-point difference can make a distinction between salary grades, while, on the other hand, two jobs with a significantly greater number of points may be in the same salary grade. This obviously raises questions and difficulties. But borderline cases will always exist. It must simply be recognized as one of the inevitable administrative aspects of any traditional job evaluation system. This does not dilute the usefulness of the technique. The system can still be a useful guide for management decisions and judgments. But it is hardly precise and cannot be used as though it were.

There are problems in explaining the degrees assigned. In ranking and factor comparison, there are no written explanations. In point systems and classification plans, the degrees are defined, but these are seldom specific enough to explain why a particular job was slotted in a given degree. In traditional job evaluation, therefore, the only justification of degrees and therefore grades is that someone or some consultant thought that judgment was correct. Few employees or managers of employees find that to be an acceptable answer.

Finally, remember that every company is unique. Therefore, a technical problem of any canned job evaluation plan sold broadly to many companies is that it really fits none of them.

The sales skills of some who market job evaluation plans are wondrous, and the vendors of job evaluation plans have slick, well-honed answers to each question. But that's another problem: Sales excellence costs, and that cost is ultimately paid for by those who use their plan.

Market Classification Systems

The market classification system is an alternative to any of the traditional job evaluation methods. Market position classification systems were first described publicly in 1974 in the third edition of *Compensation*. Today, more than half of all operations use some form of market classification (and more than half of the others don't use any system of job classification at all).

Market classification systems were made possible by the increasing availability of market pay data. With the answers to fair pay available directly, there was no longer any reason to go through the elaborate evaluation systems that were costly and administrative in nature. You didn't have to go through the administrative methods of job evaluation to get proxy or estimated values for jobs—they could be obtained directly.

Operations managers increasingly had greater knowledge about the field of compensation. They knew more about job evaluation. This meant more questions and challenges.

While the accessibility of data and the know-how of operating managers made market classification systems more practical, there were trends that made traditional job evaluation less usable. Increasing technology of work meant jobs were more difficult to understand. The trend toward more delegation of management made a highly programmatic system like job evaluation an anachronism.

It was the combination of increasing difficulty and high cost on the one hand and greater delegative management styles plus greater management know-how about compensation that has made market classification the centerpiece of salary administration. Market classification is simple and direct.

The first step in the market classification system is to set a structure. Note that this is the last step in the traditional method of job evaluation.* When a company adopts the market classification system, it can use the structure or structures then in effect.† Increasingly, it is important to have a single structure throughout the organization, but this is for reasons of information management, not compensation management. If a company has no structure when it first adopts a market classification system, it must adopt one. The salary structure shown in Chapter 6 can be used by any company. Always be certain that the current minimum wage is within the lowest salary grade.

The second step in the market classification system is to price jobs. This should be done by the methods described in Chapter 4. In my opinion, every company must use its own employment experience in pricing. In addition, use surveys that previously have been used successfully.

The determination of market-priced jobs must be done centrally, by an experienced compensation professional. That professional determination

---

*I last described the full process of job evaluation in the third edition of *Compensation* (New York: AMACOM, 1974), pp. 36–65.

†Note that those who convert from old traditional job evaluation plans to the market classification system can start with all the classifications then in effect.

should not be subject to anyone's opinion. Pricing is not an exact science, but it is objective in approach and mathematic in nature. Conclusions cannot be changed by anyone's opinion—not even the chief executive officer. Even your chief executive officer does not command the labor market.

The third step in the market classification system involves slotting market-priced jobs into the structure, and that process has also been described. This is arithmetic—matching market averages against structure midpoints. You can be confident that at least 5 percent of all your jobs will be slotted by market pricing. However, make certain that these include samples from all levels of pay, all functions of work, and each of your company's operations.

The fourth step requires slotting nonmarket-priced jobs into the structure. My preference is to start by delegating this to operating managers throughout the organization. Give each manager complete authority to slot jobs not priced directly in the marketplace by any method he chooses. Let each manager choose a different method if he wants. It isn't important that he chooses the same method or what you consider a sound method. All that's important is that he does a good job.

If managers aren't doing a good job, then you can consider some method or some more requirements for them to use in making these judgments. But why borrow a problem until you know it exists?

The human resources management department should be available to render advice in slotting nonmarket-priced jobs. Operating managers might even ask those in the company's compensation department to do the job of slotting for them. Be careful, however, of permitting operating managers, at any level of the organization, to use their own outside consultants. Require that operating managers use the corporate compensation professionals as their consultants. The corporate compensation professionals then, in turn, can hire consultants if that seems appropriate.

The fifth and last step in the market classification method involves some system of monitoring and auditing. This is easy to do with a personal computer and a general personnel data base. If you don't have a personal computer, you can buy one, and if you don't have a general personnel data base, the compensation department can develop the software to do this at a very low cost. There's no additional work in inputting information; you must record all pay data anyway.

The monitoring should make all kinds of auditing processes feasible. The auditing can be done every day—every hour if you wish. It can include elaborate auditing processes, such as cross-evaluation comparisons.

The biggest advantage of the market classification system is that it directly relates the salary grades of each job to competitive markets. It is a fair system. The system is simple and easily understood.

The cost of market classification systems is no more than one-tenth of the cost of a traditional job evaluation system. This represents a substantial cost savings to implement a far better system.

Invariably, employees accept the results of a market classification system because what is determined in the marketplace may not be liked but it is accepted. At least your market results are always perceived by employees and managers as being impartial.

With all these strong advantages, it's hard to understand why any employer would use anything other than a market classification system. The system is far better than no system. Market classification systems are far better than traditional job evaluation and can be installed and administered at a far lower cost.

The Administration of Job Evaluation Programs

The ongoing administration of any job evaluation plan is as essential to a sound compensation program as the correct design of the system. There are many facets of proper administration. Four common areas of concern are: providing job information needs; keeping the program up to date; proper consideration of compliance matters; and communicating results to employees.

Job Information Needs

In compensation work there is need for information about jobs and people who fill the jobs. Information about jobs is critical to job classification. It is necessary, of course, to have information about benchmark jobs and to be able to compare these against the jobs in surveys that are used to price the benchmark jobs. There is an equal need for information about the content of nonbenchmark jobs so they can be appropriately slotted, regardless of the classification system.

Without knowledge of the jobs measured, there can be no useful job classification system. The knowledge of jobs should be substantial on the part of the direct managers of those jobs. Then job classifications can be made by managers without any need for additional work in job analysis or job descriptions for the purposes of job classification. At the other extreme, a central committee or compensation professional who makes job classification decisions for many jobs would need rather complete written information about the job prepared for that purpose, including a written job description.

Even for simple nontechnical jobs, the proper preparation of job descriptions is time-consuming and costly. For high-level jobs, it is not possible to analyze a job or write a job description that can be understood by a central person with little or no knowledge of the job.

The preparation of descriptions is very costly. It costs from $100 to $1,000 to write each job description. The cost of keeping the descriptions up to date is $50 to $500 annually for each person covered by the program. That is a very high cost, whose purpose is only to make decisions centrally rather than having managers throughout the organization make essentially management decisions.

The need for job information is not confined to compensation. Therefore, in thinking about the kind of information needed in job evaluation, the company must consider total information needs. Compensation administration and job evaluation are likely to be but two of these needs.

Think of total job information needs in terms of the overall job of the management of personnel. In its most elementary form, management's job of getting things done through people can be said to involve six activities:

1. Thinking through what work must be done and organizing that work efficiently.
2. Staffing the job to accomplish objectives.
3. Assigning work to individuals, communicating duties, and setting work standards.
4. Observing and judging how well employees are performing the duties that have been assigned.
5. Improving performance by appraising how duties are performed and identifying ways in which work can be improved.
6. Rewarding employees for their performance or taking appropriate corrective action.

Job information can play a vital role in all these key management activities. Basically, the manager must make certain that all work assigned is essential and that essential tasks are grouped and organized in the most efficient and economic manner. Using job information, the manager can develop specifications that, in employment, promotion, or transfer decisions, will help assure that properly qualified employees are selected. Job information can also assist the manager in showing employees what is expected of them and making sure they understand how to do the work assigned. Moreover, knowledge of job duties helps the manager determine reasonable standards of performance. This can be a sound and objective basis against which actual performance can be evaluated.

Job information can be used in improving manpower utilization. Through an understanding of the duties that have been assigned, the manager can identify time-consuming tasks that are below the overall level of work assigned and reassign these tasks to use employees' efforts in the most economical way.

In addition, the manager can study job duties in terms of work loads to determine approximately the proper manpower levels. Managers must obviously be concerned about wage costs, not only in terms of salary levels but in terms of the number of employees at each level.

Job information can be used as a basic management tool for improving operations. It can pinpoint duplication of work, indicate a better work flow, and suggest a better use of job skills. Knowledge of jobs enables managers to assess each job duty in terms of its importance to the success of the operation.

Job knowledge that serves such purposes as these will be more than appropriate for job classification and market pricing. Therefore, the important thing to do is to assure that job information serves the needs of *managing*.

The manager who doesn't have job knowledge as described can't manage. The manager who does have such knowledge surely has sufficient information about jobs to make job classification decisions. The only need for job information is that required to make classification decisions at a central location by people who don't know much about the job. For their purpose, material provided must be substantial. The analysis in writing such information requires a great deal in time costs. The assimilation of this information by the central decision-makers requires more time costs. These are all factors that must be considered when deciding on a method of job classification.

Keeping the Program Up to Date

In any organization there is constant change in work to be performed and in the organizational structure. Theoretically, as the duties performed in jobs change, evaluations should be reviewed. As a practical matter, only significant changes in job responsibility should result in a review of job evaluation decisions. Frequently, even in this case, the changes turn out to be insufficient to cause a different job classification.

However, managers throughout the organization as well as in the staff organization must make sure that the program is ongoing. Job evaluation is not solved by the implementation of a program. The implementation is the initiation of the program. The excellence of ongoing administration and the sustained effort necessary to keep the program up to date are critical. At any given point in time, the validity of the program is, in fact, a function of the degree to which it has been kept up to date.

With the many priorities in business today and the many pressures faced by people throughout the organization, there is a tendency to postpone reviewing jobs for purposes of job evaluation. But that activity cannot be deferred forever. In a rapidly growing company, postponing evaluating jobs can obsolete the program within a year.

In a typical organization, serious erosion of the program can occur within months; and in any company, or any department of a company, neglecting to adjust job evaluations to reflect changes in job duties for more than two years is likely to render the program useless. Furthermore, even a few cases of evaluations that are based on obsolete duties can diminish the confidence that both supervisors and employees have in the appropriateness of the program.

If job descriptions are centrally written, there should be a system of notification every time a job is significantly changed. Then a job analyst must analyze the job and write another description. The same is true when a new job is created.

In addition, every job must be reviewed formally at some interval to make sure that such change notifications or new job notifications are made appropriately and because changes very often occur a bit at a time. In a company experiencing rapid change in its business or in its operations, this can mean that a job description must be reviewed at least once each year.

If classification decisions are delegated to the managers of personnel, no system for maintaining job descriptions is required. The monitoring then only needs to make sure that classification decisions are being kept up to date.

Compliance

In designing their job evaluation programs and in administering these programs, companies must make sure that they are in compliance with government requirements for equal opportunity and equal pay. In essence, the law is very simple: in pay matters, the company may not discriminate against any employee on the basis of sex, age, or minority status. This is a legal requirement. It is also good business.

It is unfortunately a fact that job evaluation plans, by their very design, grossly discriminated in the past. They were not designed to discriminate; that was simply the result. This was primarily because factors in job evaluation plans used indirect measures of job worth, such as years of experience and the degree of education. Such measures of job value inherently discriminated against people who had not had an opportunity to gain experience or get an education.

Equal care must be used in market pricing. Jobs in which females or minorities have typically worked and where discriminatory pay practices have existed must be avoided in benchmarking, or special adjustments must be made in recognition of discrimination.

In the ongoing administration of such programs, it's most important that both managers and staff are sure that evaluation judgments continue to focus on the job and not on the individual who fills the job. Obviously, special care must be exercised when jobs are filled, for whatever reason, by females and minorities. This is where discrimination is most likely to occur. This is certainly where Equal Employment Opportunity (EEO) investigators would look first.

Companies should follow a business approach to EEO, recognizing that compliance is both a legal requirement *and* sound business. It serves the objectives of the business and *all* employees to fill jobs with the best qualified persons and to provide equal opportunity to all, without bias.

If, in fact, the company is managing pay without bias, then it is in compliance. Unfortunately, some firms have had EEO representatives who seemed, by their thinking and behavior, to enforce their vision of social justice rather than assuring compliance with the law. Companies must resist such improper intrusions with all their resources, however disagreeable that effort may be.

Communication

In the last analysis, the pay program of the company is what employees understand it to be. What they understand about the program is primarily what they experience. What they know about the program is primarily what they are told about it. Their experiences and what they are told about job evaluation are primarily in relation to their own pay and how their supervisor explains how results are obtained.

In ongoing administration, what is communicated is mostly in response to questions asked. It is never possible to anticipate the questions that employees might ask in any situation. It is clearly impossible to do so for all employees in all companies. However, supervisors should have basic information about the program, whatever the program is, so they can describe it accurately. They must refer questions to staff specialists when they do not know the answers.

In addition, supervisors should be prepared and, if necessary, trained to answer the most basic types of questions—those that employees are most likely to ask. The following points should be kept in mind:

- When communicating job evaluation results, it must always be made clear that it is the job that is being measured and not the individual.
- The basic objective of the program—to pay fairly and competitively and to relate the pay of each employee to the marketplace—must be constantly restated.
- Employees tend to think that every change in their job duties should result in an upgrading (never a downgrading). It is, therefore, important to review job classifications and job evaluation results with employees when job duties change, even when it is not likely that a change in salary grade will result.
- Employees make comparisons with other jobs on the basis of a par-

tial knowledge of those jobs or their observations. Their concerns must be handled in terms of the company's job evaluation system.

- Employees often have questions because of what they read in the press or what they see on television. Aside from the correctness of such reports, the response must be in terms of the company's own program.
- Unless their supervisor evaluates their jobs, employees may wonder if the evaluator really knows what work they do. It is important to be sure that the evaluator does know the job and then to assure the person that this is the case.

Other matters that might be communicated, and which certainly must be understood by supervisors, include the reasons why the company established job classification programs in the first place. Supervisors must understand the way job evaluation or market classification works and why the particular system used by the company was selected. Employees must understand, by practice and communication, that the company's classification methods are applied consistently to all jobs.

Even from this briefing on the methods of job classification, it is plain that process is very time-consuming and, therefore, very costly. Traditional job evaluation requires a great deal of management attention. Market-priced classification takes far less management time, but the management job still must be done well.

The Management of Job Evaluation

I was privileged to be invited to give the keynote speech at the 25th Anniversary Meeting of the American Compensation Association. In that speech, my emphasis was that *managers* should manage compensation in the 1980s; that the era of compensation management by professionals in a central office was over; and that the period of the management of compensation was beginning. Not everyone at that meeting liked the message, and some still don't. But ten years later, that message seems even more to be correct.

Typically, operating managers today know as much about compensation as did those compensation professionals who attended ACA's 25th Anniversary Meeting. You must also believe that managers want to pay competitively and be fair to employees as much as central staff persons do. And clearly, operating managers throughout the firm should manage compensation. The reason they should make job evaluation decisions—except those priced in the marketplace—is because no person has more interest in or should have more concern about competitiveness and fairness than the operating managers.

Operating managers throughout any company should make nonbench-mark job evaluation decisions because it is their job, because they are qualified to do that job, and because they can be counted on to do that job. Certainly, determining the pay of employees is an inherent part of the job of managing people. All facets of compensation are an integral part of the management job, including the proper pay classification of all jobs managed. No one can seriously argue about managers' qualifications to do this job, particularly when they have compensation experts in the central office who can provide assistance and advice.

However, there is still substantial resistance to the idea of delegating decision-making authority to managers in areas of compensation such as job evaluation. Concerns are related to control and to personal errors.

Those who worry about loss of control point out that managers are less qualified to make job evaluation decisions than the central staff experts, and many argue that differences in the degree of capability among managers to make such decisions argue against delegation. There is also the thought that even if qualified managers make these decisions, they have many reasons not to do it correctly. These concerns are only occasionally correct, but please note that when they are correct, such errors are easily identified and can be corrected.

Perhaps a more important objection to the management of pay by managers is a concern about personal loss by compensation specialists and by some compensation consultants. For some compensation consultants, for example, the concern is very real and very great. For those in the business of selling elaborate job evaluation systems that are designed to be managed centrally, there is concern about the loss of their business. But they must remember that this is free enterprise, and horse-buggy manufacturers had to modify their products also. Compensation professionals should not be concerned about the trend toward managers managing compensation. The result of that trend will be fewer compensation jobs, but those that remain will be evaluated in higher salary grades.

Chapter Eight

Individual Salary Actions

Establishing the correct salary grade for each job is only part of the salary-setting process. What is also required is some system for setting salaries within the range for each person who holds each job in each salary grade. In many respects, determining individual salaries is more complex than setting the correct salary grade for each job. It involves more basic issues, and a number of very different approaches can be followed. Every manager is involved in deciding the correct salary for every person in each job within grade.

One of the fundamental issues involved in salary increase decisions is whether employees as a group should be granted a general increase from time to time. Another issue is whether there should be a single rate for everyone performing the work properly or a range of salaries. If there is to be a range, then the question is what factors management should consider in determining individual salaries within each range. Another issue that must be considered is what salary actions should be taken in the case of transfers, promotions, demotions, and other job actions. Each of these matters is important to all companies, and each is covered in this chapter.

General Salary Increases

General increases or, as they are sometimes called, across-the-board increases, involve salary or wage adjustments for all employees or for a group or class of employees, such as office workers. When such increases are granted, all employees receive the same increase on either a percentage or a dollars-and-cents basis.

Need for General Increases

General increases are designed to deal with economic factors that affect all employees. The issue of general increases deals directly with the need to have employees keep pace with the pay of peers in the marketplace. To the degree that such increases genuinely deal with economic factors that affect all employees, there is reason for serious consideration of this issue. Without such increases, employees' pay will become less for the same job and the same level of performance. Their pay may become uncompetitive in the marketplace, and their real earnings may decline.

For most employees, keeping abreast of the market is a basic element of equity or justice, and at least maintaining the real earnings level is a core objective. They expect to be paid at least as much as they have in the past if they are doing the same job and performing it as well as they did before.

For the company, general increases represent a direct way of staying competitive in the marketplace. It is not the only way to remain competitive; but it is the most direct and assured method. In fact, unless the company does stay reasonably competitive in the marketplace by some method, its ability to attract and retain the number and quality of people necessary to operate the business may be affected.

When a company grants a general increase it is paying more for essentially the same level of performance. These higher costs must be matched by improvement in productivity, passed on to customers in the form of higher prices, or absorbed by lower profits. Such increases in payroll costs are no different from increases paid for the rising costs of energy, materials, or supplies. Increases in pay during inflationary periods simply represent part of the increased cost of doing business.

A critical part of the management job is to manage the spread between increasing prices and increasing costs. This is sometimes called margin management. If a company grants general increases linked to market inflation, then maintaining this spread between revenues and costs must be managed by methods other than the containment of wage increases. That may be thought to make the management job more difficult. Cutting or containing payroll is an option to maintaining the revenue-cost spread that managers have often used. A commitment to general increases eliminates this option.

Management wants every possible amount of flexibility in dealing with the cost-price spread. This is why managers often have concerns about general increases that are automatically tied to any economic factor. Management may think that a commitment to general increases is a blank check, representing a substantial risk for the business. Management would usually prefer to have at least some flexibility in the timing of general increases and in the choice of factors to be considered in determining the amount of the increase.

Over time, company pay levels must match changes in market pay, or the competitiveness of the firm and the fairness of salary levels will erode. So there is need to grant increases with increasing pay in the marketplace. The issue is whether general increases are the proper way of doing this.

The issue of a general increase sometimes involves weighing human values along with business needs. For workers, the need for increases in inflationary periods is critical to the welfare of their families. For the company, it may be a difficult business problem. But, in most instances, it is not likely to be as critical to the business as it would be to employees, particularly lower-paid employees. These are complex matters, and they require the best advice and information inputs from compensation specialists. I can't offer a specific solution that can be applied in all cases, but I think the following ideas are important to consider:

- I would always advise management never to write blank checks: don't make commitments to the future, regardless of circumstances. Always maintain the option to review and judge again in the future.
- I do recommend a general policy commitment to match wage inflation. This should apply to income classes 1 and 2.
- Have a valid system for monitoring pay increases in your labor market (see the section on compensation increase surveys in Chapter 4). Review this material periodically: once every six months in periods of rapid inflation and once every two years in periods of moderate inflation.
- Make sure employees know the truth about how you keep job salaries in line with the market.

Management must also seek new ways to deal effectively with the spread between costs and prices, other than by withholding or stretching out general pay increases that are required to match inflation. Margin management is a serious issue that requires far more attention in the future.

Methods of Granting General Increases

The exact method a company follows in dealing with inflationary pay increases and the basis of granting general increases are important matters. The primary issue involves the question of whether general increases should be tied to increases in wages of people doing similar work in the marketplace or whether they should be tied to increases in the cost of living.

Companies recognize the need to be competitive in the marketplace. A central objective of compensation administration is to provide programs and practices to assure competitiveness. Therefore, tying wages in some way to market inflation is a logical and reasonable approach.

The simplest and most direct method of providing general increases is to grant an appropriate increase to all persons. If this method is used, a company should have an annual review date. Then grant increases at that time and always communicate actions or lack of action to employees.

Some companies would prefer to keep pace with the market by recognizing inflation from time to time by the budgets formulated for granting individual increases throughout the year. If this alternative to general increases is followed, amounts included in salary increase budgets include provisions for general increases and amounts that provide for performance pay increases. This provides a method for remaining reasonably competitive, but still provides flexibility in the timing of increases and an opportunity to vary amounts accorded to individuals.

Companies are more inclined to grant across-the-board increases for lower-paid than for higher-paid employees. They recognize the greater impact of inflation on lower-paid people. Furthermore, the pay of higher-level employees tends to be only partly in the form of salaries; incentive bonus awards and long-term income awards also affect the pay level and pay progress of higher-paid employees.

Cost-of-Living Adjustments (COLA) and Indexing

Management rarely agrees willingly to cost-of-living increases. Tying wages to the cost of living is not a market necessity. It represents a substantial blank check that can have profound economic consequences for the business. As a result, employee and manager views may differ on the appropriateness of cost-of-living increases or the indexing of pay to the cost of living.

From a broad economic view, tying pay to the cost of living in a formal manner through a cost-of-living provision or any method of indexing is an economic contradiction. Furthermore, such practices, if widely used, become a self-fulfilling economics problem.

If, in fact, broad economic forces are causing a decline in real earnings, there is nothing that a cost-of-living or indexing system, broadly practiced, can do about it. Declining earnings occur because of such things as declining employee productivity, unfavorable balances of trade, and inflationary government policies. Cost-of-living indexes do nothing to deal with these substantive issues. Real earnings will decline anyway. If everyone had a cost-of-living increase, it would merely mean that it would feed the inflationary spiral and cause everyone to fall further behind in real earnings.

An individual company, however, cannot take the broad economic view. It is the job of elected and administrative officials in Washington to manage the economy. Management's job is to run its own company. Similarly, groups of workers or union representatives who speak for them cannot take the broad economic view. They represent only their constituents; and that's where their responsibilities are.

For the individual or one group of workers, COLAs are protection against increased prices. The economic burden of declining real earnings may then be put on other workers, but those covered by COLAs are protected. So an individual, group, or a union may benefit from COLAs, but the company incurs risks and other employees take up the costs and burdens of lower real earnings.

Always recognize the technical issues in COLAs. For example, there is no measure of the "cost of living." The Bureau of Labor Statistics publishes an index of changes in the prices of goods and services in a market basket. The market basket is based upon goods and services typically purchased by a family of four of a semiskilled factory worker, where the head of the household is the only family worker.

The Consumer Price Index (CPI) is a useful measure for economic purposes and as an input to compensation planning and administration. The data do not measure the cost of living but rather changes in the prices paid for goods and services at a style or class of living. Specifically, the CPI is applicable to class 2 in Figure 6–5. It is usable but not specifically applicable to the working poor (class 1 in Figure 6–5). The CPI is of doubtful value in measuring the changes in prices of those things bought by persons in class 3 and has absolutely no relevance at all to those whose salaries are in excess of $75,000 (1990 dollars).

There are cost-of-living measures in different areas. For the same base family unit, these show the relative price of goods and services typically purchased in different communities. Again, these data are only directly applicable to those whose earnings are in class 2. Higher-level workers have very different expenditure patterns, and the cost of the goods and services typically purchased varies substantially from data published in the CPI. There are no measures of consumer price changes or intercity price differences for employees above income class 2 (see Figure 6–5).

Always remember that the CPI and an index of wage levels are very different. They do not move together. In fact, over time, wages have increased more than relevant CPI measures—real earnings have improved. But in periods of from one to five years, the CPI can outstrip wages measurably. And for certain groups of workers and in certain industries, the measures of consumers' prices can increase much faster than wage inflation.

Some Thoughts About General Increases

Every employer should consider some type of commitment to increase job salaries with market inflation. Recognize that with time the company must make adjustments to keep up with market pay inflation or company policy will change.

There are a number of procedures for accomplishing this. The important thing is that the employer makes the commitment and communicates that policy to employees, including how that policy will be carried out.

Management often has concerns about such a commitment. A major question is the cost exposure of such a commitment. By all means, analyze the costs. Make sure such factual questions are dealt with numerically, to the extent possible. The results of cost analysis are often surprising. In a fast-food chain, as one example, the "cost" of a wage commitment in each of the years 1986, 1987, and 1988 was such that the price of their big hamburger would have had to be increased by a few cents more each year, assuming they increased the salaries of jobs because of the wage commitment and would not have increased salaries across the board without the commitment.

Another concern is that the general increase to match inflation is too inflexible. These concerns must be balanced against employee needs for assurances against the erosion of competitive pay. Consider all factors, and most likely your company will have some form of commitment to general increases for some groups of employees.

In lower-paid jobs, general increases should be equal to wage inflation. Compelling reasons can be presented against the use of COLAs, *except* in jobs whose current annualized pay is below the poverty threshold now. At these levels, any erosion of living standards has a serious impact on family welfare.

In higher-paid jobs, a different method of assuring pay progress that at least measures wage inflation is appropriate. In higher-level jobs, the Consumer Price Index doesn't measure the cost of living at all, and wage inflation is difficult to assess. Furthermore, many jobs in these levels are paid bonuses; and most persons receive promotions from time to time. At these levels, an individual pay review system is more appropriate, with consideration of the amount of general increase granted to others as one major input to individual salary review systems.

Basic Approaches to Individual Salary Actions Within Salary Grade

There are four basic approaches to granting individual salary increases. These are the single-rate approach, the automatic approach, informal systems, and the "merit" pay approach.

The Single-Rate Approach

Salary or wage differences for individuals are not necessarily desirable for each job. For instance, when all employees work essentially to the same standards, single rates make sense. For instance, this would apply to a day-work system where standards for equivalent output are set for every job.

When there is a short learning time on the job, single rates are frequently paid to everyone, since all are working at the same pace or attaining essentially the same standards. Single rates also apply in automated work or where the assembly line controls the pace of work. Here too, all employees are essentially producing the same, and it is logical to pay each at the same rate. Finally, in some office jobs, work standards are about the same for all employees because of the set routines of the jobs or schedules of work. In all these situations, there is little opportunity for efforts or ability to affect output, so single rates are logical.

Step rates are sometimes used in conjunction with single-rate systems. For instance, an employee may be given a starting rate while learning the job. That employee's pay would then progress at stated intervals to the standard rate as performance increased to job standard. Typically in these situations the learning period is relatively short.

There has been widespread use of single rates in factory positions, because many of these jobs have relatively short learning periods and are fairly well prescribed in terms of the standards followed and the work volume to be produced. To vary pay under these circumstances would be to pay a premium for no purpose or to penalize some employees for no reason. Employees would tend to view such variations as favoritism. To many employees, the standard of equity is "equal pay for equal work."

Increasingly, companies are also applying this logic to many operations jobs in the office that have the same characteristics as factory jobs: a relatively short learning time, set quality standards, and approximately the same volume of work for all employees.

Don't assume that single rates only apply to lower-paid positions. Airplane pilots, for instance, all get paid the same as long as they fly the same equipment and are qualified. The thinking is that we only want fully qualified pilots in the cockpit, a view we can all subscribe to every time we step on an airplane. Somewhat the same thing applies to a number of other higher-paid fields. For example, there are those who think that only fully-qualified teachers should be standing at the front of each classroom, and that argues for single rates for teachers.

Many managers are biased against the use of single rates. Some want to reward employees for qualities other than performance—usually such things as attendance and cooperativeness. While such qualities are admirable and desirable, employees are essentially paid to do their work. Flexibility can be of value in any activity—business included. Always have some concern, however, about the exercise of flexibility. If flexibility is exercised to take into account the facts and circumstances of each occasion, then latitude may often be more constructive than harmful. However, have monitoring that can quickly sense latitude that is used for bias, favoritism, or to exercise personal power.

Others think long service should be rewarded by higher pay. Aside from practical problems, service can be rewarded by other methods, such as greater job security. Furthermore, money used to grant raises for length of service may have to be taken from higher performers, which can be a disincentive for excellence. More individual pay based on time alone is a form of tenure, one of the worst compensation ideas in history.

Automatic Approach

Under the automatic approach to pay increases, the salary or wage of an employee increases automatically with time. Usually both the amount of increases and the period between increases are predetermined. Neither operating supervisors nor personnel staff, therefore, can exercise judgment in granting increases.

In jobs where employees need only gain experience or familiarity with routines in order to attain standard performance, the automatic approach has proven to be useful and practical. It is used under essentially the same conditions as step rates under the single-rate system, except that the learning periods are usually longer. For such an approach to be effective, there must be well-defined standards of work performance at each of the automatic increases. Progress must also be fairly uniform for all employees who do a particular job.

Frequently, the automatic approach is in effect because a union will not allow management to retain the sole right to decide on pay increases. Sometimes this is because companies have not done a good job of observing and appraising the performance of employees in the past.

One feature of the automatic approach is that it removes individual merit or performance from compensation decisions. If, in fact, employee effort or talent affects the output or quality of work, this could be an inequity. Inability to reward better performance also removes the financial incentive for improving performance. Under an automatic approach, the only incentive an employee has is to stay with the company long enough to reach each pay increase level.

The automatic approach is extremely inflexible. Once it is adopted, it may be difficult to change, even if the economic circumstances affecting company operations change materially.

In fact, in some companies and in some sections of companies, the automatic approach is in effect by reason of practice and precedent rather than policy. Increases are called merit salary increases, but they tend to be automatic.

Increment increases have sometimes been a system of cost savings, hiring below job rate and stretching out automatic increases even though employees are working to standard. This is one way to lower payroll costs. This form of payroll cost containment rarely works. Any savings that result from the application of this method are usually more than offset by higher recruiting costs and greater turnover.

Informal Approach

Under the informal approach to wage or salary administration, supervisors make individual pay decisions for people on a job without formal guides or controls. Supervisors have knowledge of the job and the individual. They may have facts such as the pay history of the individual. They may even have some very broad limits or controls, such as budget limitations. With these limits, the manager has complete discretion for making pay decisions under an informal approach. These decisions are rarely monitored in an effective manner by any source under an informal approach to individual salary actions.

To be effective, an informal system requires that the supervisor knows the job and the employee well and is in a position to observe the work of the employee regularly. The informal approach also requires that decisions are consistent among all employees. Finally, the informal system requires that managers have basic facts available concerning rates of pay and prior increases.

Under these ideal circumstances, managers must have skill, experience, and judgment to make good pay decisions without guides and controls. Under the pressure of daily operations, managers may not devote sufficient time and effort to obtaining and analyzing all the information needed to make intelligent pay decisions under an informal approach.

There are other drawbacks to an informal approach. For one thing, each manager in a company may have somewhat different standards for granting pay increases. Different supervisors may even have different things in mind when they make pay increase decisions. Such differences in thinking may lead to inequities. The application of different standards by different managers may also lead to confusion on the part of employees regarding what is expected of them.

In addition, lack of standards, guidelines, and controls may result in pay decisions that are influenced by personal favoritism. Because there are no standards or guidelines for increases, it is also difficult to explain pay raises to employees, even if they are completely equitable.

Simply requiring the approval of higher-level management on pay decisions does not necessarily overcome such problems or improve the quality of pay increases. Immediate supervisors are inclined to rationalize their pay recommendations in whatever terms are necessary to gain approval. Furthermore, unless higher-level managers are informed about the day-today performance of employees, approval reviews will not necessarily bring about more equitable or logical pay decisions.

It's important to distinguish between discretionary actions based on favoritism or random consideration on the one hand and management on the other. What may appear on the surface to be informal and random judgments may, in fact, be measured judgments of management.

Some want too much order in business. Too often this has meant rule by programs and sameness in decision making rather than management.

Those who manage well must make judgments and decisions to match circumstances. Decisions made must be based on information, consistent with policy, within established guidelines, and in keeping with past practices and decisions.

Completely informal individual salary increase actions represent total delegation of individual salary decisions. The trend is toward more delegation and, therefore, toward more informal practices. But delegation does not mean abdication and informal does not mean arbitrary. A delegative, more informal approach toward individual salary decision making requires experienced managers of personnel, is aided by information and guidelines, and must involve monitoring results.

Merit Pay Approach

If individual performance of employees differs for any reason, the employees should be compensated in part for performance. Otherwise employees will not be rewarded for greater contributions, which means there would not be financial motivation for higher performance in salary increase administration. This would seem like bad business and would be unfair to higher-performing employees.

Any merit system is by definition a management practice designed to relate differences in pay for the same job to differences in work performance. If there are indeed opportunities for employees to affect output through greater effort or greater talent, then the absence of a merit pay system would mean a lack of financial motivation to improve performance.

Merit pay systems assume that performance can be observed with reasonable accuracy even if it cannot be measured objectively. Therefore, the first essential step in any merit pay program is supervisory evaluation of employee performance.

Performance pay increases or the merit portion of an increase means more money for the employee but does not represent additional expense for the company. If, indeed, the extra increases under merit awards are for better performance, then they are payments for greater output. Regardless of the accounting practice, this is a form of investment spending.

The issue of rewarding employees for performance is central to the effective administration of pay in many positions in the company. It is so central that the features and practices of performance pay are covered separately in the next chapter.

Managing Salaries Within a Salary Grade

While I recommend that the same salary structure should apply to every job and every operation in a company, the part of the salary grade used may vary for different jobs or at different locations for a number of reasons. Most importantly, individual salaries for a job should equate with performance and provide needed flexibility for making judgments within prescribed policies and guidelines. There should be no other basis for varying the salary of individuals on the same job. This means to me that where all workers on a job are performing to the same quantity and quality standards, they should each receive the same salary. If there are step progressions with time, these must be based on proven and accepted performance differences with time.

Only when there is a performance pay system should there be distinctions in individual pay. In this case, there is need for latitude or informality because performance measures are seldom factual and measurable. Furthermore, higher levels of performance are achieved a bit at a time over a period of time, and therefore time is a part of the decision making.

With respect to different salaries for the same job, I think the burden of proof should be on the manager who makes the distinctions. Presume that everyone performs equivalently. Then work on systems to support the determination of differences in individual salaries within grades that are based upon differences in performance.

It is worth some work to determine information-based guidelines with respect to performance spread in at least a section or sample of your jobs. Data and information about some jobs already exist in an organization, and information is obtainable for many others.

Recognize that if even a significant number of employers vary individual salaries based on performance, the company that does not do this will be uncompetitive. If your competitors reward performance significantly more than you do, then you are uncompetitive for high performers but you overpay for below-average performance.

Other Salary Actions

There are various other types of salary actions for individuals in addition to within-grade increases. These include promotional increases and demotional decreases and adjustments for transfers, upgrading, and downgrading. In addition, certain special situations must sometimes be considered.

Promotions

Promotions can be defined in two ways. One is the traditional promotion, which involves a move from one job to a different job in a higher salary grade. The other is the administrative promotion. In this situation, the employee stays in the same job, but with additional duties and responsibilities. These additional duties and responsibilities place the job in a higher salary grade and represent a promotion just as much as a move to another job in a higher salary grade.

It is logical and important that employees receive a pay increase with a promotion. Otherwise, they will be doing more without receiving more. It is equally important that employees experience better pay progress because of a promotion than if they had stayed in their former jobs and received either automatic or merit increases.

Occasionally, companies want to defer a promotional increase until the employee has proven himself in a new job. Such a practice is inequitable, since it would not apply to an employee recruited from outside the company. Furthermore, it is illogical, because the company has better opportunities for screening inside personnel than for evaluating outside candidates. Finally, deferment of the increase may cause the employee to doubt his ability to perform the new job and in some instances may result in employees declining a promotion.

In determining the amount of a promotional increase, supervisors must consider a number of factors, including the magnitude of the promotion and the employee's salary position within the range in the new job. Promotional increases should also take into account the progress the employee might reasonably have achieved through merit increases if he had not been promoted.

The ground rules for promotional increases that I have recommended for many years are as follows:

- Generally speaking, salary progress for a promoted employee should be greater than it would have been without the promotion.
- The salary of a promoted employee should be raised at least to the minimum of the salary grade of the new position, whatever that amount might be.
- The promotional increase should never be smaller than 10 percent.
- When a promotion of more than one salary grade is involved, the minimum promotional increase should be 5 percent per salary grade.
- Promotional increases should generally not exceed 20 percent.

With an administrative promotion, the promotion itself usually does not occur at a specific time. Rather, emerging job duties or a series of additional assignments over time result in an administrative promotion.

None of these new duties in itself may warrant a change in level; it is the cumulative effect of such actions that results in the job being properly assigned to a higher salary grade.

In these situations, most companies handle salary increases for administrative promotions through their normal salary review system. When this is the case, be certain that the salary progress is greater than it would have been if there had not been an administrative promotion.

The issue of upward mobility is critically important. For the employer, career progress can assure a reservoir of qualified, motivated talent, with knowledge of the company, and for competitive payroll costs. For the employee, upward mobility means a chance to get ahead, fulfillment, a better living standard for his family, and just plain fairness.

Upward mobility is mostly an issue for the manpower management professional specialist. * Compensation practices generally and promotion pay policies specifically are a critical part of assuring upward mobility. Make sure your promotion pay practices are sound and that the practices are properly utilized.

Demotions

Demotions are, of course, the opposite of promotions. They involve a move to a job in a lower salary grade or a reduction of duties and responsibilities over time. A demotion may occur because the employee's job has been eliminated or substantially changed and there are no other jobs available at the current pay level for which the employee is qualified. Or a demotion may occur because an employee has failed to perform properly and is assigned to a lower-level position where it is thought the employee can perform effectively.

Demotions involve broad personnel issues as well as compensation questions. Employees whose job levels have been reduced without prejudice should logically be selected for demotion. Demotions also involve manpower planning and outplacement questions.

Company pay practices vary greatly with respect to employees who are demoted without prejudice. Some companies continue to pay a demoted employee at the former salary level. However, this can create inequities if a demoted employee receives more money than others who are performing as well or even better in the same job. Other companies follow the practice of reducing the employee's pay so that it is in the same relative position in the lower salary grade as it was in the former pay grade. A third alternative is to develop the same kind of guideline rules for demotions as were illustrated for promotions.

---

*Note that effective manpower management requires as a first step a model to track upward mobility. This can't be done very well, if at all, without a single salary structure.

When an employee is demoted because of unsatisfactory performance, a different situation exists. Normally, disciplinary demotions call for cutting an employee's salary so that it fits into the proper range position in the new lower salary grade. This may be done by reducing pay in a single action. If undue hardship would result, some companies withhold salary increases over a period of time. In disciplinary cases, many companies follow the practice of terminating an employee rather than demoting him, on the grounds that, in the long run, discharge is in the best interest of both the employee and the company.

Reevaluation and Inequity Increases

Jobs may be upgraded or downgraded; that is, reassigned to either a higher or a lower pay grade. This may be done simply because reevaluation of the job indicated that this would be appropriate. Frequently, such changes are due to the fact that market pay relationships change.

The normal pay practice with respect to upgrading and downgrading is simply to continue to administer pay in the normal salary increase system. In this way, the employee's pay would be handled in the normal course of the salary review system. If reevaluated to a lower salary grade, incumbents would probably get smaller increases in the future; if reevaluated to a higher salary grade, the increases probably would get larger.

Companies must also give individual salary increases because of inequities or special situations. For example, when an employee is transferred, a pay increase is sometimes appropriate, either because of resulting salary relationships with employees in the new unit or to get the employee to accept the transfer. The latter is particularly the case when geographic relocation is involved.

There are, of course, many other circumstances that may have to be considered. A supervisor may decide that an employee should get a special adjustment because of pay relationships with other people in the unit. In the practical world of work, it may be necessary from time to time to give some employees an increase simply to keep them from quitting when a replacement is not available.

Career Pay

Employees are frequently not interested in the labels for individual pay actions. They are not always concerned about the logic of pay increases. But what they always care about is the amount of their salary increases: They want more.

They want salary increases that are at least as great as increases in their personal living costs because they do not want to see their real pay eroded. They want more than the cost of living because they want their families' living standards to increase. They frequently aspire to have a sufficient amount of real income to advance a "salary class" and enable their families to enjoy a better life style.

Surprisingly little is known about actual career pay patterns for employees. Only recently have some companies developed such information, and they have been surprised by some of the results.

It has long been known, for instance, that in some careers, starting pay is higher than in others. In some of these, however, the rate of increase in pay with time is significantly lower than in other types of work. Sales persons and engineers, for instance, tend to start with high salaries. During their first few years, pay progress is generally very rapid. But after that, their rate of progress in salary increases tends to slow down. In many cases, the rate of salary increases will, at some point, become lower than the annual increases typical for administrative or operations workers.

Special Cases

Out in the operations, compensation specialists are often asked about special cases. The number and variety of cases that are special can be great over a period of time. My basic answer to questions about special cases is that if there is more than one in twenty cases, that's too many special situations, but if there is less than one in a hundred, then that probably isn't enough.

In any operation, there will be a variety of special cases—to the point where you can't really categorize all of them. But professionals should support management in dealing with these special cases within established policies and guidelines.

Deal with special cases forthrightly. Sometimes there are weird aberrations resulting from tortured attempts by companies to deal with special cases in a way that gives the illusion that corporate management policy is still dictating every decision. I know a chemical company, for example, that has a salary structure that is 15 percent between every grade except one, which is 6.7 percent between grades. That was a corporate mutant that resulted from long struggles to deal with a special case in a way that seemed to preserve corporate systems rather than deal directly with one special case.

There are some special cases that are extremely important. First on this list are those persons of extraordinary talent. A company is not blessed with many of these. Hopefully, you will have some in most professional areas and in each of the major components of the operations. The true superstars in any company do not number more than one in every one hundred persons. Consider exempting them from the salary system altogether. Look at them much as you would price a business or in much the same way that the networks value and pay entertainers—the superstars of the networks.

There are also special cases that require exception because the employee is in need. From time to time, employees will experience severe illness or a personal tragedy. In these periods of time, their performance may not equate with their pay within range. Forget it.

A special case of commitment, I think, is to employees who are not making it. As a company, you brought these people in; you screened them with your professional recruiting methods. For some reason, they are not making it. You may find that they are not doing well because of company-generated problems. Doesn't the company have a special obligation to do everything it can to help each person be reasonably successful? Until you find out why the employee is having difficulty and conclude that he won't be successful, why not make a special exception and exempt him temporarily from your pay systems?

There is one other special case that I have always been fond of but have rarely convinced others of its merit. I believe that people who work for an organization for a significant period of time, who consistently commit themselves to excellence, always support the company, even when it is not consistent with their personal desires, and do consistently good work deserve some special reward. One of them, it seems to me, should be a special form of retirement opportunity. In fact, I think there is merit in considering that retirement is an earned right and not an actuarial calculation. But certainly, people who have contributed for many years and in great amounts should deserve some special consideration at some point. For those who have made extraordinary special contributions, the special reward should be very special.

Administrative Support

Over the years when I was giving many talks to management groups, my favorite talk was based upon questions submitted beforehand by those in attendance. I was always impressed by the nature of those questions and how the priorities of operating managers differed from the personnel needs identified by corporate professionals. Never was I more impressed than by the fact that more than one-third of all the requests were simply for better information support, particularly with respect to matters involving salary increases. That always seemed like such an obvious and reasonable request—it was always surprising that the professionals could not or would not provide that type of administrative support.

There are a number of ways in which compensation professionals and personnel generalists can provide the necessary administrative support to management in making individual salary decisions. Most of all, however, they should be available to answer questions and provide advice. The advice must always be professionally correct, but it must also be usable in a practical operating way. Provide guidelines to managers for making decisions, and provide them with information. Have a minimum number of rules.

Among the information that can be provided as administrative support with respect to salary increases for individuals is the experience of your company and the experience of others. For example, you should be able to provide information about the length of time it takes an individual to move from the bottom to the top of the range under various circumstances. This information is useful to managers, not only for making decisions but for answering questions from employees. You should also be able to provide information on salary increase comparisons of all types. You should be able to provide comparisons of pay with wage inflation and the cost of living.

The job of supporting managers in making individual salary decisions is as important as anything else the compensation professional might do. Those in compensation work should focus part of their time to meet this need. They should nurture this work and build confidence in their ability to support managers in this area, mostly by providing useful information in a timely manner.

I don't think it's sufficient to be capable of answering questions and having your phone number in the company's directory. The compensation professional must have an affirmative action activity and an effective network.

One reason you may not get many calls is because managers may not know what some of the questions are—they may not know what they don't know. You need to be accessible in this role; you need to be user-friendly.

Another reason you may not get many questions is because you were always busy when managers called you before, or more likely you were in a meeting when they called. Each of us must set priorities. My view is that many compensation professionals must set a much higher priority on servicing operating managers in basic ways, like providing information and answering questions about individual salary questions.

Chapter Nine

Pay for Performance

When employee effort and talent can affect work output, reward for performance is a critical element of compensation management. Just as general increases keep pay for a job in line with wage inflation, performance pay increases in addition to general increases reward individuals for how well that job is done. Performance increases should be intended only to reward improved performance. There are many who think that failure to reward excellence properly is the single most important problem in the field of compensation in many companies today.

Performance, Productivity, and Business Results

It is elementary logic that improved performance should result in greater employee productivity, which in turn should result in improved business results. If that logic is correct, there is then a dollar business return for improvement in employee performance. Each percent of improvement in performance should produce some equivalent improvement in business results. If each percent of improved performance is rewarded by an equal percent increase in pay, then performance pay increases involve no company expense.

More likely, in fact, each percent improvement in performance produces more dollars of improved business results than were expended in the pay increase. This would be true because more work would be done by fewer people, requiring less physical resources and support personnel. Then there is an investment yield to the company from improved performance that can be very great—often over 100 percent.

Remember that pay increases for improved performance are investment spending. There are few investment opportunities a company will ever have where the yield is higher and the risk is lower. Rarely, however, do you ever hear this idea discussed, let alone considered for implementation as a strategy for business improvement as well as a sound compensation practice.

The idea is clearly correct. For management, however, this tends to be a profit source taken as a given and assumed somehow to be inherent in operations. Make sure your company doesn't lose the built-in profit improvement factor in performance pay increases. Make sure you have a competitive advantage by managing performance increases better than business competitors; those in your labor market and those who are product competitors who are not necessarily in your labor market.

Many managers have doubts about a company's ability to apply the principles of investment return from performance improvement salary increases. The history of business provides many reasons for such doubts. The biggest problem of performance management, however, is in accounting measures. The measures of business improvement from performance improvement are not precise and usually won't show in this year's results.

The general relationship between employee performance, productivity, and business profits can be established for each enterprise. The human resources information systems' measures of yield from performance increases can be developed to provide useful information in this area. A model can be developed for a company that will illustrate and forecast the impact of improved employee performance on business results. Every model would clearly show that performance increases matched by equivalent salary increases yield a considerable return to the company.

In practice, the prophecy of greater performance resulting in increased productivity, which produces better business results, is not always fulfilled. This is largely because pay increases for "merit" are frequently for something other than improved performance. Too often, "merit increase" mean "merited" for reasons unrelated to job performance.

Another problem with the merit approach is that many extraneous elements are considered when performance is judged and performance pay increases are granted. Personal traits may be considered as meriting a pay increase, whereas, in fact, that trait, however pleasant or desirable, has no impact on the effectiveness of work. Define performance clearly in all your human resources management work. It should mean greater output per hour of work.

There are also some discontinuities between the concepts of performance and employee productivity. Increased productivity does not always correlate with better business results. Productivity, for example, may come from new machines, materials, or methods, while employee effectiveness does not change. In fact, employee performance under the new conditions may actually be lower, at least for some time, while productivity goes up.

Figure 9–1 illustrates the relationship between employee performance and business results. The capital used and methods of work affect employee productivity as well as performance. Greater employee productivity will mean greater business success, but in the long run and in relation to productivity trends in competitor companies.

The schematic in Figure 9–1 is a basic model of productivity management work. Increased productivity cannot happen over strategic periods

Figure 9-1. Performance, Productivity, and Business Results.

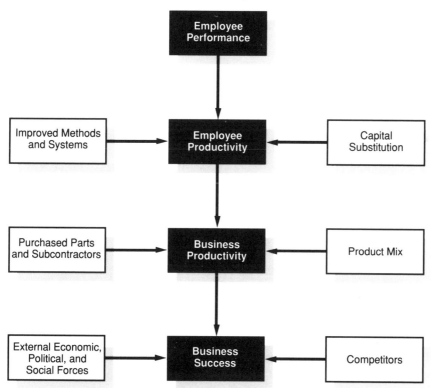

Note: Other things being equal, an increase in pay for improved performance costs nothing. This exhibit illustrates the factors affecting business results and why performance by an employee or a group of employees must impact business results but not necessarily in any direct or automatic manner.

without improved employee performance. Improved employee performance is not likely to happen without financial reward for improved performance.

If you think employee performance is as high as it can be, you are almost certain to be wrong. But even if employee performance were as high as it could be, such high levels of performance are a wasting asset, and productivity management must be an ongoing effort to sustain high levels of worker effectiveness.

A practical problem involves measuring improvement in business results from greater performance. Improved business results are usually due to a number of factors, and it is difficult to isolate the impact of any one of them, including productivity. There are methods of judging the contribution of increased employee productivity to business results over time, but they are not very accurate.

In fact, however, both performance and productivity can be measured in every company and in every unit of an enterprise. Measures of productivity in units often lack precision, but they are better than nothing, and they are usable. One way they are usable is in procedures relating to pay for performance.

Performance Reward Systems in Business

Business has done a good job of developing financial reward systems for employees for more effective work. This accomplishment by business has contributed considerably to the vitality of our business system and the success of businesses in creating jobs and wealth. In the management of personnel generally and in managing performance reward pay systems particularly, it is important to understand what these pay reward systems are and the importance of each of them.

Types of Performance Rewards

First, we know that rewards are both monetary and nonmonetary. We must never underestimate the importance of nonfinancial rewards. As far as financial rewards are concerned, it is extremely important never to forget that there are three distinctly different types of financial reward systems in business. These are merit salary increase systems, incentive pay, and promotions. Each of these is identified, with comments, in Figure 9–2.

For all employees throughout business, promotion is by far the most important financial element of reward, affecting the most people and involving the most dollars of increased compensation for individuals. Incentive pay is the second most important element of reward, both in terms of the number of people meaningfully affected and the dollars involved. Merit

Figure 9-2. Financial Reward Systems in Business.

Type of Work	Form of Reward (Comments relate to extent and importance of reward system)		
	Merit Salary	Incentive Pay	Promotion
Executive and senior management	"Merit salary" not applicable. Differences in salary make small differences in total pay.	Bonus, long-term income and special benefits represent *the* reward system.	Applies to few.
Middle-level	Extremely important for "career-peaked" employees.	Applies to few: rewards are moderate.	Most important reward system for majority.
Operations	Mixed: many employees on flat rate; many others receive increases automatically with time.	Only one of five persons covered by incentive plan, but rewards are substantial for some.	Most important reward system for majority.

salary increases, while important, are third in importance in business financial reward systems.

Salaried pay for performance, as shown in Figure 9–2, has varying importance in operations jobs. Many operations-level employees are paid a single fixed rate or get increases automatically with time. For them, salaried pay for performance is not applicable. Merit increase plans have not worked well historically in many other operations-level jobs. There have been problems with supervisors' judgments of "merit" where output and quality are, at least in part, not measurable. In addition, the spread in pay from "standard" to "maximum" is rather small in many operations-level jobs.

For some factory workers, production incentive plans are important rewards, but less than one-third of all operations workers in this country are now covered by such pay plans. Such plans need to be reviewed constantly; primarily because of a tendency for performance standards to erode.

Nine of ten production workers and office workers get at least one promotion in their working lives. For many of them, the promotion is significant, in that their pay is improved more by promotion than by either incentive pay plans or merit salary programs.

Among middle-level people, promotion is by far the number one financial reward. At any given point in time in a company, four of five middle-level people still have the potential for at least one future promotion. Almost all middle-level people receive at least three promotions during their careers, so promotions affect the most people and involve the most dollars.

Incentive pay plans cover relatively few middle-level people. The reward systems that exist do not involve much money, and such payments are often highly discretionary. Almost all middle-level people are salaried and in jobs where there is a salary range; and they should be the eligible for merit salary increases.

Promotional opportunities are rare among executives and senior managers; many of them have career-peaked. Salary increases based upon "merit" are not generally a part of salary practices for high-level managers. Therefore, all the reward systems for their jobs are in the form of incentive pay. For people who reach senior management levels, income from incentive pay systems can exceed salary.

Performance Range

If performance increases are to reward effectiveness, the question of "performance range" is crucial. Performance range means the percentage difference in output between the work of an individual who is doing the job as well as it can be done and the work of a person doing an acceptable job. Acceptable work may be below standard but would at least meet minimum requirements.

There is a considerable amount of data available to tell us what the performance range is for various types of jobs. Much of this information is from industrial engineering work and has been around for a long time. Similar but less specific results for higher-level positions have been developed over the past dozen years.

In the lowest-paid operations jobs, the range of performance difference between outstanding and acceptable performance is usually 10 to 15 percent. This is illustrated in Figure 9–3, where the salary class at about $10,000 shows a range between acceptable and outstanding work of about 12.5 percent. These data are based upon dozens of cases, including studies of assemblers, housekeepers, testers, and operations employees in the office, such as copy typists.

In skilled operations work and administrative jobs, which in 1990 dollars are in a salary class averaging $23,000, the performance spread for jobs is about 25 percent. Thus, as pay doubles, so does the performance range.

The data for class 2 job performance spread are based on a number of cases. Each case yielded somewhat different data but essentially the same conclusions. The studies covered employees as varied as skilled machinists, maintenance people, insurance claims adjustors, draftsmen, and technicians.

Figure 9-3. Performance and Productivity.

Salary Class*	Approximate Salary Level	Range from "Acceptable" to "Optimum" Productivity
1	$ 10,500	12.5%
2	23,000	25
3	53,000	50
4	125,000	100

*See Figure 6-5.

Note: Information from various studies suggests that a salary job level should double as performance doubles.

Obviously, for still higher-level jobs, the data are even less conclusive. Nonetheless, some interesting cases covering middle-level professional, administrative, and management positions suggest again that salary level doubles at each subsequent higher salary class. These cases included CPAs, design engineers, first-level supervisors, and consultants.

The fact that performance spread increases greatly in higher salary classes is due to the different nature of the jobs, not necessarily differences in people. Lower-level operations jobs are dependent upon physical skill, strength, effort, and dexterity for differences in performance. Among qualified persons, these differences are limited. In higher-level jobs, the performance range becomes more a function of knowledge or experience. In still higher-level jobs, the ability to leverage knowledge through the organization and obtain results from decisions are the critical elements in performance.

These cases suggest that performance range doubles at each incrementally higher salary class.* A sound compensation system should be structured so that such extra performance can be properly rewarded. To do otherwise would not only be inequitable, it would be bad business and could discourage excellence.

Salary Reward for Performance

Ninety-five percent of all companies say that their policy is to increase employees' salaries on the basis of merit or performance. Some companies think that they have largely achieved the goal of paying for performance. Others believe they have a long way to go before there is

---

*Data for salary classes 5 through 8 (see Figure 6–5) are lacking. However, if the relationship that exists in the first four salary classes also exists in the next higher salary classes, the performance of an extremely effective general management executive would be five to ten times greater than the acceptable-performing executive; a relationship substantiated by strategic results among competitor companies in many industries.

appropriate salary reward for performance. Companies have spent a great deal of time and effort on developing new programs and practices to make the performance pay philosophy work. Knowledge now exists so that every enterprise can have programs and practices that reward performance properly.

Basic Principles of Performance Salary Systems

There are a number of reasons why performance pay programs fail in many companies. For instance, if percentage distinctions in "merit increases" are small, differences in pay increases do not reflect improved performance. If, for example, there is an 8 percent increase for Jones and a 7 percent increase for Smith, this cannot possibly reflect performance differences, because it is not possible to make one-percentage-point distinctions in performance.

An analysis of all salary increases may also indicate why a performance pay increase program is not working. If there is little variation around the average increases, then many increases are almost certainly not for performance. Finally, there are various cases and tests that show that supervisors had something very difference from performance in mind when they granted increases.

The manager may be considering other valid business situations, such as worker shortages. In addition, there will always be human errors and a tendency to have bias and personal preferences in pay increases or to reward friends and supporters. Regardless of the reasons, if significant numbers of increases are not based on performance, then pay for performance is diluted, partly because available funds are used for other purposes.

Conceptually, it is simple to translate the idea of performance pay increases into a pay system that works. Those who perform better get paid better. The pay for different people performing the same job will be differentiated by performance.

Translating these objectives into a salary system means that the salary of each individual should reflect how well he does his work. This is illustrated in Figure 9–4. Those who do their work so well that it is difficult to see how it could be done better either should be paid at or near the maximum of the salary range or their salary increases should be large enough to move them rapidly to this position. Those who are qualified but new to the job and inexperienced should be paid near or at the bottom of the range. The bottom of the range should also be reserved for more experienced persons whose work is demonstrably unsatisfactory. Those who perform to standard should be paid at or about the midpoint of the range, which is, by definition, the company's competitive level.

The company's salary administration program should also be flexible enough to take care of special performance situations. This is also illus-

Figure 9-4. Use of Salary Range as a Guide For Performance Pay.

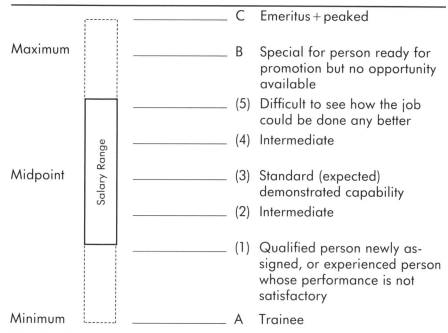

	C	Emeritus + peaked
Maximum	B	Special for person ready for promotion but no opportunity available
	(5)	Difficult to see how the job could be done any better
	(4)	Intermediate
Midpoint	(3)	Standard (expected) demonstrated capability
	(2)	Intermediate
	(1)	Qualified person newly assigned, or experienced person whose performance is not satisfactory
Minimum	A	Trainee

Note: The objective is to pay in the range in relation to performance.

trated in Figure 9–4. For instance, since trainees are sometimes not even qualified for the work, they could logically be paid something below the minimum of the range.

There are also those who have consistently performed the work as well as it can be done and who are ready for a promotion, which is not available at the moment. There is some logic to the view that they should not suffer financially at the company's convenience by receiving lower pay than they would get if that promotion were available. Furthermore, such a salary increase might encourage a good person to stay with the company until a promotion is available. These are reasons for paying such people a salary above the range.

There are also some whose work is outstanding and whose careers have peaked, but who set a good example and instruct others. Less experienced employees or those who have not yet mastered the job benefit from their guidance and suggestions. Such persons might also be paid well above the range. These cases are two examples of situations deserving special salary awards for exceptional and unusual performance.

Recognize that this concept equates salary *level* with performance, *given enough time*. This creates two issues. One issue relates to the time factor. If a person is now performing better, why not raise his salary immediately to the proper level in the range? You should do that provided there is a high level of confidence in the judgments about performance. Even then consider two or three increments of increases at short intervals when there is a great difference between performance level and salary level. Otherwise, you may be pointing out an error the company made in the past and may get a person to expect a rate of increase that will not be possible in the future.

A more troublesome issue is the performance of people and the size of the increase. If an outstanding performer is already high in the range, salary increases would just match inflation. Then those who are less effective would likely be getting bigger *increases* (but pay level would still be lower). The logical answer is that pay for performance is geared to salary level, and you can make a reasonable case on that basis with reasonable people.

The level-versus-amount problem is not simple, and those who talk technically about the logic and reasonableness of the policy of equating pay level with performance must recognize that the perceptions of a less-effective worker getting a larger increase than more-effective workers doesn't seem logical to some. Be particularly sensitive about the perceptions of the high performer.

In implementing the pay for performance logic, be sure that any assumptions managers make about top-performers are indeed correct, beyond any reasonable doubt. For example, be sure that the top performers have indeed career peaked when that is assumed. If that is not correct or if there is a reasonable doubt, then you should be looking for ways to get their next promotion or to redesign their jobs so that pay increases can come with upgrading. It is also wise to make certain that top performers receive recognition for their unique status in other ways and that they receive that recognition often.

Rating Performance

The key to rewarding performance is to make correct judgments about it. Without reasonably accurate judgments about the performance of each individual, it would never be possible to achieve the goal of relating salary to performance. A company would then not be able to reward excellence.

As far as compensation administration is concerned, it doesn't matter exactly how performance is rated; any system of performance appraisal will do as long as it gets valid performance rating conclusions. If the company's current system of performance appraisal or merit rating results in valid and reliable performance judgments, then it should continue to be used. However, this is rarely true. It is usually necessary to develop a system that will result in valid performance ratings, even if it is used only in salary administration.

Figure 9-5. Five-gradient System for Rating Employee's Performance.

Name—Subordinates	1	2	3	4	5
Lynn	——	——	——	——	——
Hollister	——	——	——	——	——
McClary	——	——	——	——	——
Overton	——	——	——	——	——
Haigh	——	——	——	——	——
McDonald	——	——	——	——	——
Gottesmann	——	——	——	——	——
Knipe	——	——	——	——	——
Name—Others					
Thurston	——	——	——	——	——
Brinckerhoff	——	——	——	——	——
Dirks	——	——	——	——	——

Performance—Gradient Definitions

1. Performance of a well-qualified person newly assigned or an experienced person whose performance must be improved to be acceptable
2. Intermediate
3. Standard
4. Intermediate
5. Difficult to see how job could be done any better

Note: Here is one system of performance appraisal that gets valid performance ratings. This system can be used for the purposes of compensation and performance systems that result in valid written performance conclusions.

One process for implementing performance rating, used successfully by many companies in the past few years, has a five-gradient rating system. This system is illustrated in Figure 9–5. Each manager or supervisor is given a list of employees. The list includes all those who report directly to that supervisor; people with whom that manager works on a regular basis; and other employees whom the manager has an opportunity to observe at work. Next to each person's name, the manager has to make performance judgments on a five-gradient system. This is best done with a member of the personnel department who can ask questions that will help the manager make appropriate performance judgments.

The definitions in the five-gradient system are important. Those used in Figure 9–5 describe the lowest rating as the level of performance expected of a well-qualified person new to the position. It would, of course, also be used for an experienced person whose work is unsatisfactory. The highest rating reflects work that is as good as can be expected. It is difficult to see how a person could be better than one who is performing at a rating of 5. The median or third gradient is the most difficult to define. It is usually described as the degree to which the individual's work meets standards of performance for the job. There are no definitions for the second and fourth gradients, which are simply labeled "intermediate." In effect, if a person's performance cannot be judged as fitting the definition of either the first or the third gradient, for example, the rating should be in the second gradient.

This process collects information about the performance of individual employees that is already well known in the organization. Tests of the system indicate that the performance rating is correct 90 percent of the time. There is a second test of such a process. Employees are, of course, rated by more than one individual. Experience shows that four of five ratings are in the identical gradient; the fifth rarely differs by more than one gradient. This merely reflects the fact that, generally speaking, managers of personnel throughout the organization are very aware of the performance levels of different employees. Thus, as long as performance ratings are limited to a five-gradient scale, the results can be extremely accurate and reliable.

It is important to tell managers how the information from performance ratings is to be used. They must know that it will be considered in salary increases. Supervisors must be required to use performance ratings as a primary consideration in their salary decisions, and they should also know that the performance rating may be used for other important personnel management purposes. For instance, it can be a key piece of information in a human resources information system.

Unfortunately, traditional merit rating and performance appraisal systems have not worked well. They do not result in reliable performance ratings, and rarely do they accomplish other important objectives. Even when great effort has been expended in developing very sophisticated and elaborate forms, they have failed.

There are three reasons for the failure of traditional merit rating and performance appraisal systems. One, they are designed to serve multiple objectives, some of which conflict. Two, they are structured for corporate purposes that are not clear to the managers who must do the ratings. Finally, many performance appraisal and merit rating systems are too complicated and time-consuming for the individual manager.

Note that the performance rating process outlined seeks only to rate performance results. It simply asks how well individuals are doing their current jobs and has nothing to do with evaluative appraisal. The objective of evaluative appraisal is to determine actions that will improve performance or to develop individuals for foreseeable future positions.

Performance rating inevitably means that some people will be rated low as well as high. Proficiency in rating performance is a job that is essential to the enterprise. If supervisors cannot do it, then they cannot manage people.

Translating Performance to Pay

If work excellence is to be rewarded, then pay differentials must mirror performance differences. If a person earning about $25,000 a year is performing in an outstanding manner, that performance is about 25 percent greater than that of a person whose work is completely acceptable. The total cash pay of that outstanding person should then be approximately 25 percent higher than the pay received by those working at acceptable levels.

The important objective of rewarding excellence can be achieved only if the salaries of different employees on the same job truly reflect performance differences and if the salary range for making such distinctions is utilized. Furthermore, for higher-level jobs, both incentive compensation and long-term income payments must reflect performance achievement if total pay is to reward success.

In fact, the potential performance reward spread from all reward systems is sufficient to match the performance spread using available compensation systems; and in management jobs, the pay spread far exceeds the performance spread. Thus plans are available that will do the job. So if a company has problems with pay for performance, compensation programs that are available are not being used or they weren't designed correctly.

If salary increases are to recognize performance, the amount of such increases must be significant. They must mirror observable performance differences. Psychological studies and practical experience suggest that to be observable, performance differences must be at least 7 to 8 percent. Since significantly smaller increments of performance differences simply cannot be observed, they cannot be rewarded. This suggests that performance increases should be at least 7 or 8 percent, in addition to amounts given for wage inflation.

Opinions differ as to whether performance pay increases should be granted at the same time as general increases. The question is not so much one of procedure; rather, it involves the basic issue of whether performance pay increases should be separate from general increases so the issues are not commingled and communications confused.

In a given company, there may be some administrative or historic reason for timing general increases and performance increases differently or for granting the two together. However, the advantages of one way or another are minor. What is important is that a performance salary increase must genuinely reflect an employee's change in performance level. To grant an employee a 7 percent increase and label it a merit increase when market inflation is 5 percent is neither factual nor honest. It is also not believable to employees.

There is also some question as to whether rewards for excellence are motivational. The question is interesting, because to argue that rewards for excellence are not motivational would be to state the employees do not care about receiving more pay. It would suggest that employees do not expect more if they perform better. We need no psychological or personnel studies to tell us that people do expect to be paid more when they contribute more and that they do indeed aspire for more.

In fact, the entire free-choice economic system is based on certain building blocks. One is that those who are effective succeed and are rewarded by the system. Those who believe in our free-choice system should apply this thinking to the individual as well as to the enterprise. Another of the building blocks of the free-choice economic system is that people as individuals and as a group strive for self-enrichment.

Usually, in fact, studies that have raised questions about the relationship between reward for excellence and motivation are based on observations of irrelevant experiences or on unrealistic expectations. For instance, some studies that concluded that reward for excellence was not motivational examined only pay systems with no performance increases. One interesting study made the conclusion that incentive bonuses were not motivational, using as the case study a company that had no bonus plan.

Some studies have also erred by looking for significant changes in behavior. Reward for excellence will not make a lazy person energetic, turn dishonest people into virtuous workers, or make a stupid person brilliant. Rather, reward for excellence—whether in the form of performance salary increases, incentive compensation awards, or promotions—motivates people to improve incrementally. Pay for excellence tends to get people to put their priorities more in line with the needs of the enterprise or the unit. Rewards for excellence provide that extra reason for people to take the initiative, consider better ways of getting the job done, and occasionally put forth some very special effort that is needed. Although these may seem to be small differences, they are actually very large; spread throughout the organization, they can make an enormous difference in employee productiveness and business results.

Performance Salary Increase Guidelines

Various guidelines and practices can assist managers in making salary increase decisions that equate pay to performance. One of these is illustrated in Figure 9–6. In this case, various suggested percentage increases

Figure 9-6. Merit Increase Guide: Suggested Percentage Increases Based on Performance and Position of Pay Within Range.

Performance Level	Band Position Within Range*				
	0–20%	20–40%	40–60%	60–80%	80–100%
Outstanding: fully qualified by knowledge and experience; meets all performance standards of position	12%	10%	8%	6%	4%†
Intermediate	14	12	10	8	6
Average: generally performs good work; meets or comes close to most performance standards	12	10	8	6	4†
Intermediate	10	8	6	4†	0
Acceptable: new to position or requires more knowledge and experience; a performer at minimum levels	8	6	4†	0	0

* $\dfrac{\text{Actual Salary} - \text{Salary Range Minimum}}{\text{Maximum of Range} - \text{Salary Range Minimum}}$

†It is preferable to give larger increases than 4 percent at longer intervals.

Note: The figures for average performance and 40 to 60 percent band position should change each planning period, depending upon market competition and wage inflation.

are established on the basis of employee performance and the position of the current salary of the employee within the salary range.

The logic of using these criteria is that at a given level of performance, employees should receive pay at approximately the same position in the range, or they should be moving rapidly to that position in their salary range. If an employee is performing at about the same level as other employees who are receiving much higher pay, then that employee should receive higher percentage increases until such time as his salary moves to the appropriate level within the salary range.

It should be noted that there is an implicit budget in this salary increase guideline. If, for instance, all the employees in a given department were at 50 percent of band position, or the midpoint of the range, then the merit increase guide in Figure 9–6 would call for a merit increase budget of 8 percent of that department's payroll.

With many supervisors making salary increase recommendations or decisions, some types of salary guidelines are important. They assist supervisors in making judgments and provide an element of consistency in salary decisions. They should not be rigid, however, but only guides.

Economic Performance Increase Systems

To reinforce reward for excellence, some companies have devised alternate systems for awarding salary increases that are geared more directly to performance. One of these is the economic performance increase approach. In its simplest form, an economic performance increase program represents a combination of a general increase plus an additional performance increase, with the performance increase representing solely a recognition of improved performance.

In this type of performance increase plan, economic factors are considered from time to time, usually once a year. The structure is adjusted to incorporate these factors, particularly labor market inflation. Salary increases for employees approximately equal to increases in the salary structure are granted to all employees at the same time.

These programs can leave room for exceptions. Some employees may not get increases because their performance has declined. In these cases, however, the withholding of the general increase must be justified in writing.

In addition to these economic increases, managers may recommend performance increases. Generally, the amounts of such increases must be significant—at least 7 percent *in addition to* the economic increase. Furthermore, increases must be in 7 percent increments. Thus in addition to the economic increase, an employee may receive a performance increase of 7 percent, or 14 percent, or 21 percent, but in no other increments.

Performance increases are paid in every case when earned. Of course, performance typically improves over time, but the increase is granted when performance improvement is measurable.

Performance increases must be justified. In some companies, this justification must be in writing. Thus the process of reviewing recommendations for performance increases is a crucial part of a performance increase system.

Obviously, the economic performance increase system requires great care to assure that amounts granted in addition to economic increases are for genuine performance improvement. Here are some actions that companies have adopted to assure the appropriateness of performance pay increases:

- Field interviews are conducted by the personnel staff.
- More specific criteria are developed regarding performance improvement.

- Personal presentations are made to high-level management of all performance increase recommendations.
- Employees who receive performance increases for possible promotion lists are earmarked.

In practice, the most effective control in this type of performance pay increase system is the required minimum 7 percent increase. Operating managers couldn't grant many 7 percent increases in addition to general increases based on inflation and meet their budget requirements at the same time unless the performance pay increases were genuinely based on improved effectiveness of work.

There should be no limit on the number of performance increases that may be granted. No organization can have too much talent and such high productivity that it cannot use all the increased performance it can get. Nor are there any direct accounting or salary increase budget controls restricting performance increases. Rather, control is exercised through the review of recommendations, which must demonstrate clearly that an employee's performance has improved.

The review system is critical or there would likely be a tendency for payroll costs to escalate. However, the reviews must assure that performance pay increases are for improved effective work only.

Financial budgets also represent controls in an economic performance pay increase system. Increases that do not reflect improved performance will cause budget overruns.

In economic performance increase systems, it is expected that if the performance of individuals in a unit improves, the performance of the unit will improve. Otherwise, it is inferred that the caliber of the supervision is unsatisfactory or deteriorating.

There are many reasons for considering an economic performance pay increase system.* When economic increases are granted to everyone (with justified exceptions) and special case salary increases are permitted, the pay system recognizes and rewards performance improvement most dramatically. The purpose of increased pay is made more clear, and performance pay increases cost nothing.

Operating Problems of Performance Pay Increases

The primary problem in any performance pay increase system is the appropriate determination of performance. It is a matter that requires con-

---

*In my work, I label this system simply a ''performance pay increase system'' and identify the more traditional approach of commingling economic and performance increases by ''merit pay increase system.''

stant care and effort. Companies will never achieve perfection, but they must strive for excellence. Various techniques are available, such as the use of the five-gradient rating system outlined, that will help to achieve excellence in performance rating.

Start by dealing with the problem of defining performance. Many define the word very differently. Even those who agree on the definition make decisions that reflect very different meanings of the word.

The dictionary defines performance simply as the execution or accomplishment of work. Top management will generally think of performance in terms of profit—this year's profit or this quarter's profit. Many in human resources management define performance, at least in part, by how well individuals or groups work together; a business version of tranquility, not effectiveness.

I have always paid attention to the basic issue of what we mean by performance. I would often have work sessions for operating managers using examples of what performance means as a method to get everybody thinking about performance in a consistent manner. It was always worthwhile.

I always define performance as worker-controlled productivity. I always reason that performance pay increase rewards are only for measurable or observable improvement of productivity, with equipment and systems then being used.

For performance pay increase programs to be successful, there must also be a commitment by top management to a policy of pay for performance. The success of a performance increase system requires effort and the allocation of resources, particularly at the introduction of the program. Furthermore, an effective performance salary increase program that genuinely rewards excellence requires a number of substantive practices that may be different from practices in the past. Typically there is resistance to change, which usually can be overcome only by the support and commitment of top management.

Employees, too, are affected by the adoption of or movement toward a performance pay increase system. Pay for performance favors high performers and disadvantages low performers. During the transition to a performance pay increase system, this may mean that a substantial number of good-performing employees receive moderate increases for some period of time.

Another problem of performance pay increase programs is the resistance of some managers of personnel. Some may not want to reward for performance. There are some who do not personally agree with the idea that high performers should be paid more. Others agree with the idea but define performance differently. Some may think that a performance pay increase is unnecessary and that withholding such an increase would help meet budget, and that is more important than performance pay increases.

Sometimes supervisors resist performance pay increase systems for less acceptable reasons. The more traditional approaches to salary increases give managers considerable latitude. Sometimes, consciously or not, that latitude has been used to reward friends. It has been used as a very effective method of exercising personal power.

Finally, despite overwhelming logic and the commitment of management, a performance pay increase system has the problem that increases cannot derive from performance and economic factors alone. In the real world of work, supervisors must occasionally consider other factors. The interrelationship between performance ratings and actual salary increases is illustrated in Figure 9–7. Certainly, performance should be the dominant consideration in granting increases above economic market inflation. But there are times when internal pay relationships and other factors must also

Figure 9-7. Relationship Between Performance Review and Compensation Review.

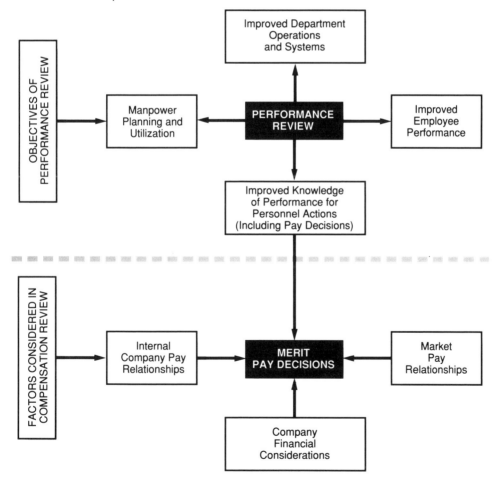

be considered. There are even occasions when illogical, but practically important, matters must be considered. For example, a supervisor may grudgingly grant an increase to an employee who does not deserve it simply to avoid losing that employee at a critical time.

Administration and review of performance salary increase systems must reflect these realities. Those who control and monitor systems should make sure that performance is a major determinant. The system will have achieved its objective if, in most cases, performance is the consideration in performance pay increases. Ultimately, the objective has been achieved if, over a period of time, performance ratings correlate closely with salary positions within salary ranges.

If you are going to pay for superior performance, then you must also manage pay correctly for low performance. Obviously, this must be so if you are also going to manage compensation costs effectively.

Granting undeserved increases to low performers—the cost of placation—is a serious problem of pay for performance programs. The funds used for placation of marginal performers reduces funds available for high performers who earned the money.

Companies talk to a fault about pay for high performers. There must be management of salary levels and salary increases for marginal performers.

Managing pay for the marginal worker is not easy. For one thing, it means smaller increases than are often expected. It requires more years of zero increases for some people than a supervisor feels comfortable about.

If your pay is generally geared to market average, then the actual salary paid to individuals who are marginal performers should be less than market average, which technically translates into the lower part of the salary range—clearly below midpoint.

Effective communication is absolutely vital in matters of pay for the marginal performer. It's easy to communicate a big salary increase to the high performer. It's extremely difficult to communicate a zero increase or a low increase.

If performance pay is managed well, sooner or later the high-performing individual will be at a salary level that reflects excellent performance and then will have to be told that future increases will be dependent only on inflation. How do you communicate this and at the same time maintain the enthusiasm and effectiveness of the person? Only the truth and a lot of personal relations skills will deal with this problem of performance pay.

Pay for Performance Is Essential

Whenever employee talent can affect work output and quality, it seems compelling to pay more to those employees who do better work. Therefore, while companies should pay market average for jobs, there should always be a variation of pay based upon how well the work is performed by each person.

A business and those who work in the business gain from pay for performance. It is both fair to employees and good business for the employer to have pay spread match performance spread.

There are three basic ways in which performance is rewarded in business. Briefly, higher performance by workers can be rewarded by promotion, by higher salary or pay rate geared to output, or by performance bonus plans. In order to reward for performance, always use all these methods as much as possible.

Many companies need to do a far better job in their reward systems. There is a particular need to improve salary or pay rate differentials based on performance. It isn't difficult to have effective salary reward pay systems. It's been done for many years in many cases, so proven performance pay systems are available, and there are many experienced persons who will help a company implement such programs.

Recognize, however, that there are also many reasons why pay for performance isn't done as well as it can be. Some of the reasons why merit pay is not done are technical. But failures of pay for performance are often human failures.

Remember the reasons why many managers don't want to pay for performance or why they may not want to pay for performance all the time. For example, higher pay for performance may mean lower pay for poor performers whose work may still be satisfactory. Pay for performance involves difficult communications with poor performers. Merit pay might identify the best performers and result in their transfer or promotion out of the manager's unit. Managers don't always see the value of pay for performance or understand its importance to the business and employees; remember that many of these are the same managers who think people are liabilities and expenses. Note particularly those managers who may not support pay for performance because they are personally not rated (or rewarded) highly, based on performance.

Human resources management professionals know of many techniques and systems that support and guide pay for performance systems. Each can be of value. They should all be considered. However, like many business practices, each pay for performance support system has drawbacks. Too often the improper use of techniques designed to support and assist implementation of pay for performance systems actually detracts from the effectiveness of work. In so many companies, the way techniques to support pay for performance are applied is the principal reason for their failure.

Three examples should suffice; each example is a pay for performance compensation technique. The cases are: salary increase budgets, control points, and distribution curves.

Salary increase budgets can be very helpful. The budgets can be geared to market salary increases and help assure the fairness of increases and the continued competitiveness of salary levels. The trouble with salary increase budgets is that they are generally misused. For example, salary increase budgets are set without consideration of performance levels. Salary increase budgets also assume that every unit of the company is improving performance at an equal pace and that the company overall is increasing performance only at the rate of the economy. These assumptions are seldom correct, and if the company's performance or the performance of any unit is greater than typical, then salary increase budgets can work to discourage pay for performance increases.

Control points, such as compa-ratios and band position controls, attempt to keep salaries paid to individuals, on average, at the midpoint of the salary range. It's thought that this will keep pay competitive and control costs. In fact, such methods are too rigid, because they leave out of the equation for competitive costs the number of people and the effectiveness of work. Control points assume that the company wants average work performance, whereas it should strive for excellence of work.

Forced distribution curves can be counterproductive. The most used salary distribution curve is a normal distribution of salary amounts around midpoints of ranges. But there is no "normal" distribution of performance and, therefore, forced distribution curves are likely to cause inequities.

Pay for performance is now also a fairness issue. For a long time, equal treatment has meant equal pay for equal work. Equal treatment has meant fairness in pay without regard to race, sex, and color, and it still does. Now equal treatment also means pay for work accomplished: pay for performance.

It is important that there are no artificial limitations on performance improvement. Extra pay for performance above standard involves zero cost. The investment return on pay for performance can be substantial. With respect to pay for performance, the more money spent, the better.

Chapter Ten

Planning, Control, and Administration

There must be effective management of salaries. This is true of all elements of compensation. This includes effectively planning salary increases, controlling salaries, and a variety of administrative tasks. The techniques and practices for planning, controlling, and administering salaries are quite different from those applicable to bonuses, long-term awards, benefits, or perquisites. Material on the effective management of the elements of compensation other than salaries will be discussed in later chapters.

The management of salaries involves many activities. It begins with the proper design of plans and programs and includes proper classification of jobs into salary grades, individual salary actions, salary rewards for excellence, and other practices that have been described.

Equally important in the management of salaries is the planning of salary increases and the planning processes that are used. Regardless of the excellence of management and the wisdom of planning, resulting increases and actions must be monitored or controlled in some way. Finally, with respect to salaries, as with respect to all facets of compensation, there are miscellaneous administrative matters that cumulatively are important to the success of the program.

PLANNING

There must be some elements of planning in every salary administration system. Salary planning includes input into operational and strategic plans. Similarly, the compensation manager must participate in translating operational and strategic plans into specific actions to accomplish these plans. The planning of salaries also involves budgeting, the development of salary increase guides, and other practices that assist managers in making sound salary increase decisions and support the company in its efforts to manage payroll costs in a fair manner.

Operational and Strategic Plans

Almost all companies engage in operational planning. Most have some aspects of strategic planning, although most have little strategic planning in human resources management. The personnel staff and each of the functional areas within the field of personnel, including compensation, should provide inputs for both operational and strategic plans. Compensation professionals must always structure their actions so as to play whatever role is appropriate to make such contributions to the basic plans of the business.

Strategic planning is, of course, the more exotic of the two types of basic company planning activities. In the past, it has been rare for compensation professionals to make a substantive contribution to these plans. In fact, it is still the exception that the personnel function overall makes any meaningful input or is in any way visible in the strategic plans of most companies.

Yet the effective management of human resources in the future will increasingly be a key element in achieving the plans of the business. Recognition of this has led some leadership companies to make regular use of personnel input, such as information about knowledge, skills, and experience of people in the companies, for developing the strategic plans of the business.

We now know how to do strategic planning in human resources management planning. Human resources management planning isn't perfect, but it is as good as the planning in most areas of business.

The basis of effective human resources management planning is the identification of current trends and developments. These are observable trends that are happening now in many companies. At any point, there are usually three to four dozen current trends and developments in human resources management. Personnel professionals must know this planning information; it is required knowledge.

Effective strategic human resources management planning essentially involves forecasting current trends and developments. Resulting predictions are descriptive illustrations of what will most likely occur. These strategic personnel planning items must be monitored each year. If the current trends change with time, the predictions must change also, and they almost always do. Eventually, what were once strategic items of planning become current trends.

In some ways, most operating plans have compensation input. They at least forecast information on payroll, which in part forecasts salaries and payroll costs. Increasingly, companies are doing a better qualitative job of this forecasting. They are also, in their operational plans, identifying key issues facing the business that require compensation actions.

Another aspect of planning for compensation is concerned with specific ways to implement operational and strategic plans. Many companies have developed this process into a fine art. Essentially, this process involves identifying the elements of a business plan—either the operating plan or the strategic plan—that involve human resources matters. The compensation professional must then work on those items that have a direct impact on compensation and also those that affect other functional areas in such a way that there will be a derivative effect on compensation administration. Then specific actions must be planned by compensation professionals to help implement the operational and strategic plans of the business.

Finally, the compensation department must do its own planning. This involves more than identifying what to do, when to do it, and who should do it. Increasingly, companies recognize the advantage of developing an overall plan of compensation and identifying the type of plans in existence for each group and in each location. In this way, top management as well as compensation professionals can see the overall compensation picture and understand how different elements of compensation interact and interrelate. Management can see the overall pay elements and the cost to the company.

Also consider a long-term plan on the part of the compensation department. This would identify how different elements of the compensation program should be changed in the future, the basic objectives of such changes, and a timetable for accomplishing changes.

This describes a far more orderly system than can be achieved. There is now too often just a reaction to each situation or problem; an endless series of crises. The planning approach is a more orderly and more businesslike approach to compensation and provides valuable inputs for dealing with each crisis that occurs.

Budgets

Part of the operational planning process involves the development of budgets. It is important to remember that there are different types of pay budgets and that each type should be considered, well understood, and properly utilized. The budget for *salary increases by position* reflects salary increases for all employees who were in the same position throughout the budgeting period. This figure is most useful in developing salary increase budgets. The budget for *salary increases for employees* reflects the salary increases of all persons who were on the payroll throughout the budgeting period, even though some changed positions, and includes promotions and organizational changes. There is also a budget that is used to indicate the average increase for those who will receive increases. This is the figure that is most useful to individual managers in planning increases for eligible employees. Finally, there is a budget for payroll. This reflects the increase in total dollars paid to those on the payroll.

In planning, you can forecast general increase amounts for the portion of pay increases reflecting general labor market inflation a year in advance. You can't really forecast improved performance, and, therefore, you can't forecast performance pay increase amounts very well. Any overall pay increase is, therefore, an estimate of what should be granted if it includes both performance pay increases and inflation increases. All too often, this estimate becomes a requirement of what *must* be spent on payroll increases, regardless of what performance-justified pay increases turn out to be.

The estimating process for salary increase budgets is the job of the compensation professional. The process for doing this has been covered in Chapters 6 and 8. The need for excellence in this professional work should be emphasized, particularly because the planned increases—the budget—often become the money expected to be spent.

In fact, when economic circumstances change, budgets also change, including salary increase budgets. Actual increase amounts should be compared with budgets historically. It is a way of sharpening the budgeting process, and valuable operating management lessons can often be learned from the reasons that caused actual salary increase amounts to differ significantly from those budgeted.

Companies have experienced serious problems with salary increase budgeting. The problem is often the budgeting process itself, which really involves another matter. Compensation professionals have to play by the rules of the budgeting game, whatever they are in their own company. Recognize, however, that for many companies the budgeting process itself has become a major obstacle to effective work and, in some companies, one of the last-ditch efforts to maintain programmatic management.

The process of setting the salary increase budget is often artificial, resulting in a percentage that is unrealistic. Even when the budget for salary increases for the company overall is realistic, that same percentage is not appropriate for each unit. Yet in most organizations, the salary increase budget for the company overall is applied to each unit.

Salary increase budgets often represent numbers that cannot be exceeded but which must be spent. Managers need more flexibility than that. The argument against flexibility is that managers aren't qualified or can't be trusted for even minor variations from budget. That is a hard notion to accept when the same managers are assigned major accountabilities for expenditures and for the utilization of assets.

Perhaps as much as anything, salary increase budgets are just superfluous. As a guideline or information input, a salary increase budget might be helpful, but as a requirement, it is obsolete, in my opinion, and another leftover practice from the era of programmatic management.

Also recognize that there are two basically different budgets in compensation. One is the specific salary increase budget. However, in financial budgeting, salary figures are included, and these, indirectly or directly, involve salary increase budgets also. These two budgets must be compatible.

Salary Planning

The number and complexity of the things that must be considered in making individual salary decisions require some organized approach to granting salary increases. One method is to adopt a formal salary planning system. Even when there is no official company salary planning system, many managers have, in fact, developed their own systems of salary planning. Planning salary increases for all employees throughout the year at one time gives supervisors the opportunity to consider relevant information and treat all employees at the same time in a consistent and equitable manner.

A formal salary increase planning process should provide background information about the salary level and salary increase history of each employee so that the manager has a factual basis for considering increases. The process should also involve preplanning by the supervisor, both as to the amount and the timing of increases for all employees within the unit during the budget period. Salary planning is best done when managers also have staff specialists available for counsel and advice on this process.

The type of information required for salary planning depends on the type of jobs that are being considered. Basically, the information should include a salary history for each employee over at least a three-year period. The manager should also have facts relating to the salary relationships of people in the unit and information about performance ratings of each person. Such information can be prepared on salary planning sheets such as that illustrated in Figure 10–1. This may be supplemented by special data and exhibits.

Using the planning work sheet, the supervisor can record the time and

Figure 10-1. Salary Planning Worksheet.

Department: Data Processing								Supervisor: I. Johnson			Budget: 8%	$17,914
Position	Name	Current Salary	Pay Grade	Percentage Band Position	Total Percentage Increase from 1/1/83	Amount	Percentage	Date	Performance Rating	Amount	Percentage	Date
Manager, Systems	N. Bos	$42,254	IX	45	48	$1,160	8	3/12/88	3	$2,960	7	3/15/89
Manager, Operations	L. Jones	41,200	VIII	57	64	1,600	12	7/02/88	4	4,120	10	7/01/89
Programmer	J. Smith	37,551	VI	55	36	810	7	2/05/88	2	2,250	6	2/01/89
Programmer	T. Gray	34,555	VI	11	(a)				4	5,180	15	9/01/89
Computer Operator	S. Lee	25,137	V	67	30	510	5	2/05/88	4	0	0	—
Computer Operator	C. Thomas	23,916	IV	45	46	550	6	5/14/88	3	1,675	7	5/15/89
Computer Operator	H. Cook	22,311	IV	17	34	0	0	—	3	2,230	10	2/01/89

Total preplanning $18,415

Total after

Average preplanning $2,631

Average after

Total increase 8.2%

Variance

(a) Hired 9/14/88

amount of each planned increase. The total increases planned can then be compared against authorized budgets to make sure that the total amounts are within the limits set by the company.

This type of formal approach to salary planning has a number of distinct advantages:

- Preplanning brings consistency and objectivity to the manager's salary increase decisions.
- Salary planning is the most effective way of considering all relevant information. Otherwise, the manager would have to organize and review a great deal of data concerning an employee each time a salary increase came due.
- Planning at one time for the year enables managers to predict the impact of salary increases on operating costs.
- Preplanning is more likely to ensure equal treatment of all employees, regardless of the time of year their salary increases are due. Unless this is done, some employees may suffer because of operating circumstances or other conditions that affect management's willingness to grant increases at a particular time.
- Preplanning of salary increases by all supervisors within a company or an operating unit ensures that employees as a group are being treated in a manner that is consistent with other groups.
- Salary planning can make possible greater delegation of authority for salary increase decisions and also facilitates the approval process.

In general, salary planning is effective because basic personnel qualities do not change dramatically during the budgeting period. There may be occasional cases where an employee's work changes significantly within the planning period so that his actual work at the time a salary increase is due is different than it was at the time of planning. The salary planning process must always be flexible enough to make it possible for the supervisor to change his decision if circumstances change.

The worksheet in Figure 10–1 relates only to salary planning. Some companies use this same system for organized one-time planning of other important personnel actions, including bonus awards, promotions, transfers, recognition, terminations, and reorganization of duties.

CONTROL

The best "control" is by affirmative management and by the assurance of appropriate compensation through the implementation of sound policies, programs, and practices. Excellence always means doing things correctly the first time. However, to rely on excellence of compensation programs and administration alone is an imprudent risk. Therefore, some controls and monitoring, mostly on the part of corporate compensation professionals, are appropriate in any compensation program.

Controls should be imposed only to the extent that they are needed. Avoid controls that anticipate problems or situations that may or may not develop. Controls should essentially be installed to meet needs, problems, or errors as they happen and where they exist, and they must be geared to the nature of the problem. It follows, therefore, that the best types of controls are probably selective and that the best controls would vary in different companies, in different divisions within a company, and, to some extent, for different managers within a unit.

Recognize that the move is toward delegation of decision making. Under a delegative management style, there is greater need for quality assurance. With more people making more decisions, monitoring and control systems become even more essential.

There are a number of practical methods of monitoring and controlling compensation actions. The principal methods most often applied are identified here. Keep in mind, however, that above all else, controls must be fashioned to each company and should be as much a part of the overall management control system as is practical.

Information

Inherent to any control system is information. In fact, sufficient information may itself be the most useful and least costly control system in compensation.

To be effective, the information must be accessible. Above all else, this means that there must be a general personnel data base for computerized data. With state-of-the-art management information sciences, every company should have a general personnel data base, but it certainly does not need to be part of an overall company information system.

With a broad variety of data accessible for monitoring and control, a diagnostic approach to using information in monitoring compensation actions can be utilized. Identify first those decisions that are most critical. Identify those that are symptoms of appropriate or inappropriate actions. When you find something through diagnostic analysis that suggests an issue or problem, then the general data base can be used to dig further and, if necessary, to deal with the issues of what, if, and why.

Have your management information systems experts design special-purpose software to monitor compensation actions. Make sure that the software they design provides you the opportunity to test or randomly sample compensation decisions quickly.

A broad variety of comparisons can be made to verify control and audit areas of special interests. For example, job classification results can be monitored by a variety of methods of cross evaluation and multiple evaluation. The computer system can do its own paired ranking work and indicate possible issues. The computer can store prior case experiences and flag new cases with similar characteristics.

The number of monitoring methods is impressive and certainly more than adequate. The information monitoring can be done quickly and at a very low cost.

Have a sampling method developed that will give you a sense of what is happening with a one percent sample. Sampling methodology with respect to compensation control information as well as compensation survey information is greatly needed in the field of compensation. We need to work to get the same results, or even better results, with smaller samples of information.

The use of this information through computer networks is necessarily something that must be conducted by key professionals. An experienced compensation professional would best understand the implications and relevance of sample data and diagnostic information. That person must then communicate the essence of what he has found to executive management in plain English, with understandable data, and, when appropriate, recommend corrective actions.

Control Curves

Salary increase control curves indicate a dollar amount of salary increase for each person and also provide a total dollar salary increase for each operating unit. The control curves can be used in any department, regardless of performance ratings, like a band position. Salary control curves should mirror salary increase guidelines, such as salary increase budgets.

To construct a salary control curve, three points must be determined. These are labeled points X, Y, and Z in Figure 10–2. Point X is fixed in the sense that if the maximums of salary ranges are to be enforced, the increase budget should be zero when the average band position is 100 percent. Point Y is also fixed and represents the average band position for the entire business unit.

The determination of point Z, the average percentage salary increase contemplated for all employees, is more difficult and requires some analysis and decision on the part of management. This percentage is, in effect, the general increase portion of increases granted to employees.

Figure 10-2. Salary-Increase-Budget Control Curves.

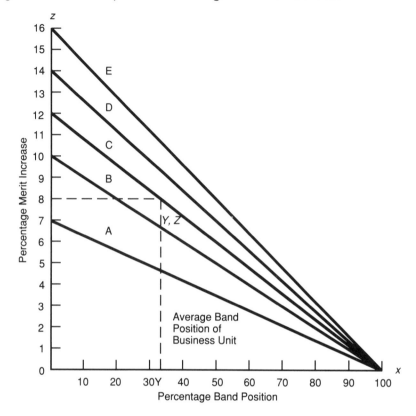

Once these three points are established, a control curve can be drawn. This can then be used to determine the appropriate total salary increase amounts for every unit simply by calculating each unit's band position and reading the average salary increase percentage indicated. This is then multiplied by the payroll of the unit for the actual dollar increase budget.

As illustrated in Figure 10–2, management can recognize performance differences among different units with different control curves (curves A through D). This means that if a group performs significantly higher than typical or in excess of standard, then the average band position of salaries and employees in that unit should be higher than the midpoint.

Unless you have multiple salary control curve guidelines, you are penalizing performance in some units and rewarding mediocrity in others. To argue otherwise would be to assume that all units in your firm just happen to have the same level of performance.

It is sometimes difficult to get a multiple business to apply different control curves to different whole businesses. It is even more difficult to have different control curves in different units within businesses.

Clearly, to have control curves for each unit based upon band position and performance, there must be judgments of unit performance. These must be business measures based upon business considerations and not, for example, the summation of individual performance ratings.

Review and Approval

Another method of control is through review and approval by higher-level managers. In some companies, even though salary increases have gone through a process of budgeting and planning, they are reviewed and approved by a number of levels of management. The theory is that such reviews not only keep higher-level managers informed but assure that salary increases are appropriate.

Approval requirements rarely provide adequate control; nor do they result in better increase decisions. In fact, in many types of personnel reviews, including salary increases, the involvement of more than two organizational levels is not management but meddling. This is because the higher-level manager would find it difficult to approve, disapprove, or modify salary decisions without knowing the facts surrounding each individual situation. Only the immediate supervisor has information about such crucial questions as employee performance, the possibility of quitting, relationships within the group, the potential of the individual employee, the criticalness of the employee's particular work at that time, and other factors that are so important in making appropriate salary decisions.

One higher level of management review may be helpful to make sure that all relevant factors have been considered and that the immediate supervisor has done a thoughtful job in reaching decisions. It is also usually helpful for the person responsible for making salary increase decisions to discuss salary changes with personnel representatives. In this way, he can be sure that he understands the program and has all the facts and information available. Skilled personnel people may also provide helpful advice.

In fact, approval requirements frequently become obstacle courses. What is worse, when considering salary increases, individual supervisors may base their decisions on what they perceive to be the expectations of higher-level managers and what will likely be approved rather than on the merits of the case or the requirements of the operation.

Figure 10–3 illustrates one company's practice in reviewing pay recommendations. As the exhibit shows, the immediate supervisor is accountable for thinking through each salary situation and for making recommendations in line with established policies and guidelines in light of relevant circumstances in each individual case. Salary recommendations for individuals are approved by the next higher-level manager. Beyond that, reviews are made only to ensure compliance with company policies,

Figure 10-3. One Company's Policy On Reviewing Salary Recommendations.

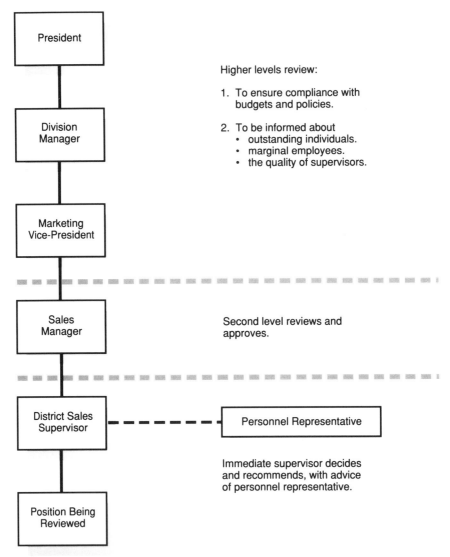

President

Higher levels review:

1. To ensure compliance with budgets and policies.

Division Manager

2. To be informed about
   • outstanding individuals.
   • marginal employees.
   • the quality of supervisors.

Marketing Vice-President

Sales Manager

Second level reviews and approves.

District Sales Supervisor

Personnel Representative

Immediate supervisor decides and recommends, with advice of personnel representative.

Position Being Reviewed

to obtain information on individual employees, and to assess the performance of supervisors.

Distribution Controls

Many companies have experienced difficulties because all or many employees are rated high or because employees' salaries automatically tend to go to the maximum of the salary range regardless of levels of performance. In these situations, there is little distinction in salary increases recommended for different employees. These circumstances tend to develop particularly during inflationary periods or where people have been on the job for a long time.

This type of situation represents a serious problem, because the company is failing to reward excellence. It reflects a breakdown in the implementation of company policies and objectives. Most important, such situations may reflect the fact that supervisors are experiencing some problems in implementing company programs and objectives.

To deal with such problems, some companies have attempted "forced distribution." Under this approach, a preset percentage of employees must be rated at various performance levels or a preset salary increase must be given on a predetermined distribution. This usually includes some required number of zero increases. These forced-distribution requirements surely cure the problem of inadequate distinctions between employees but usually create far greater problems in turn.

Like government pay controls, these company versions of internal controls on pay increases force dislocations in pay relationships. They force lower-than appropriate increases for some high-performing employees. They may discourage improved effectiveness of work because of discrimination and induce some valued employees to leave. On the other hand, forced distribution may force some increases for employees that are more than appropriate or sufficient.

One problem of normal distribution curves is that there isn't anything normal about such curves in business and in the field of compensation. In fact, a company should seek a distribution of salary levels within range that is skewed to the right of average or midpoint of band. Companies work hard to build better-than-average or expected performance, and this should be reflected in the control curves (see Figure 10–4). The appropriate distribution in a unit will be a function of performance levels, the nature of the work, and the work of the group.

There isn't one desired distribution curve to the exclusion of all others in all circumstances. You can develop expected distribution curves for your business. These are distributions of pay based upon such sources as business unit performance data and performance appraisals. You may also have an ideal distribution curve: a realistic goal for every manager of personnel to strive for.

Monitoring Results

The most benign form of salary control is the monitoring of results by compensation professionals. Personnel generalists, supported by com-

Figure 10-4. Normal and Expected Distributions.

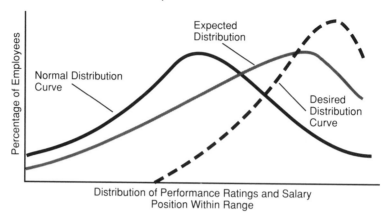

Distribution of Performance Ratings and Salary
Position Within Range

pensation professionals, who keep informed about the program by reviewing, at least on a sample basis, decisions that are made can get a clear view of how well the program is being administered in various parts of the company. When the personnel staff sees a problem or feels it needs to work with some manager or groups of managers, it can take constructive action to improve decisions under the program. Monitoring results is, therefore, also the most constructive and positive type of control.

Control by monitoring is supportive rather than authoritarian. It focuses on the solution of problems and the improvement of the administration of the program rather than on corrections or a set of actions and decisions that fit some preconceived mold. Control by monitoring provides opportunities to deal with real problems and real situations. Actions resulting from monitoring also tend to be developmental experiences for supervisors, and therefore, a system of control by monitoring, when properly applied, is not only a control system but a development technique.

When a program is controlled by proper guidelines and practices in the first instance, and by direct monitoring to improve results in the second, then the whole concept of control is designed to improve administration and make compensation more effective.

To be effective, this ideal set of controls requires sound policies, programs, and practices. It requires experienced, senior managers not only to make reasonably good decisions in the first place, but to accept rather than resist suggestions and actions that result from monitoring activities.

Monitoring compensation should be ongoing and in three steps. For one thing, there should be continuous sample monitoring of data. This monitoring should be from computer data. This work should be done by compensation professionals. And the work must be considered diagnostic and is intended only to identify matters that should be looked at in more detail.

At the other extreme, there should be personnel audits. Companies should audit the use of human resources management just as surely as they audit financial resources, although the methods can be different. Human resources management audits need to be conducted formally no more than once every two years and no less than once every five years. Personnel audits cover every facet of the field, including compensation. These audits should be conducted by experienced persons whose views are objective. This is ideal work to assign to truly qualified consultants.

Ninety percent of all monitoring should be done in the normal course of work. This should be done by managers of personnel and personnel professionals. Because this work is part of managing, there is no incremental work.

Human resources management people should be doing a lot of their work out in the operations. In the course of doing their work, they should monitor various areas of personnel. Compensation professionals should be asking about compensation issues and monitoring first-hand how well the program is working. Ask the managers of personnel about their problems and experiences. Ask employees for their opinions. Give cases or examples so they can give multiple-choice answers. Do this in a rather structured way so the feedback has greater relevance.

ADMINISTRATION

Much of compensation administration really happens in the day-to-day operations of the enterprise. These involve continuous individual questions or problems and sometimes crises. They are reflected by recurring "fire drills." To a great extent, administration is, in fact, a reaction to events: employee actions or reactions, or some problem in the operations that requires a quick and responsive reaction from compensation professionals.

Daily Chores

Basic administration is an endless chronology of unglamorous events. They are the types of actions and activities that are never discussed at a meeting of the American Compensation Association, are rarely even referred to in published articles, and are dealt with here only on a random basis for illustration.

These administrative matters are the events that occupy a majority of the compensation professional's time. Rarely are any of these events noteworthy. Cumulatively, however, they are largely the compensation program of the enterprise as it is experienced by those in the business.

Administrative activities involve implementing the program, dealing with the "hardware" issues, keeping records, answering questions, constantly modifying and changing practices, and assuring that what is done in compensation is properly interrelated with other functional activities of personnel.

In a delegative management style, fewer daily administrative chores are handled by compensation professionals. They are handled by the managers of personnel who have been delegated such matters. Only special cases get to the compensation professionals.

Increasingly, there will be fewer special cases that will be referred to compensation professionals. More and more managers of personnel will access expert knowledge directly through computerized expert systems.

Implementation Work

The task of carrying on the compensation program is never-ending, time-consuming, difficult, and sometimes aggravating. Jobs do not get classified unless someone does it or sees to it that it is done. Key issues won't get communicated without someone taking the initiative. Decisions won't necessarily be made in a timely manner, let alone an appropriate manner, unless someone is on top of the program all the time. This is the implementation of the program.

Compensation programs are not dormant. Every manager has to make compensation decisions periodically about every subordinate. People, at unpredictable times, have problems or questions about pay. Rarely do these events occur at convenient times. In fact, implementing the compensation program is like cutting grass in Florida; it is necessary all year long.

Administration work requirements do not come in equal increments, fifty-two times a year, five times a week, or seven times a day. In compensation administration, this necessarily means some crisis work and some flexible time. Somehow the work done in flexible or discretionary time periods often quickly becomes recurring crisis work and required work.

Many of these activities involved in implementation not only come up suddenly but must be dealt with quickly. Therefore, there is pressure to get things done immediately. Despite such pressure, work must always be done carefully; in technical matters, remember that the compensation professional can never make mistakes.

Mistakes are costly, and each case can become a precedent for other mistakes. Therefore, even though each case may not involve serious amounts of money, cumulatively these daily administrative chores can have a most important impact on the company. Furthermore, precedents tend to be long term if not permanent. For instance, you cannot take away what has been given, and it is always a struggle to reduce pay, even by holding back further improvements.

Compliance and Comparable Worth

Compliance work has become a major area of work in compensation. This subject was not mentioned in the 1974 edition, and only a brief paragraph was devoted to it in the 1981 edition. I think the specific matter of compliance and the vague issues of comparable worth are still to be treated briefly—they can still be dealt with in a few paragraphs. But I'm a consultant, not an attorney.

With respect to compliance matters, employers must, of course, comply with the letter of the law, and I would always urge management to be in compliance with the full spirit of the law. Companies should initiate affirmative actions* to assure that all persons are treated the same with respect to pay and without regard for age, race, creed, sex, or color.

Make sure that your compensation policies are without bias and that there are no procedures or practices that would be biased against any group. Compensation should be completely sexless and colorless. Monitor and audit your compensation programs to assure that neither color nor sex has any impact on job worth and that the individual pay system is biased only in favor of performance.

Having done those things and having done them well, you are in full compliance. When the compliance examiner comes around, be cooperative—be as helpful as you can. If he has issues or questions, welcome them—perhaps he has noticed something that you missed. Perhaps the compliance authorities will have suggestions about how you can do better what you set out to do in the first place.

However, never let anything, including representatives of the federal government, change your system to be biased against high performers. If suggestions are made that would result in bias against performance, then just say no.

In all legal matters, it seems clear that a company should obey the letter and the spirit of the law. But, of course, it isn't that simple. There are cases where right and wrong aren't clear, and there is no way of knowing what is legal either. Furthermore, a company doesn't want lawsuits, no matter how frivolous they may be. Finally, judges and juries are unpredictable.

In this environment, it is prudent, as well as right, to err consistently in the direction of overcompliance. But be careful that you don't move toward a zero-risk management mentality.

Base your judgments upon business considerations, your company's policies, and what you think is fair. Then if there is any question, check

---

*Make sure that affirmative actions remove discriminatory practices and are not themselves discriminatory, requiring more affirmative actions sometime in the future.

the legal merits of what you have concluded. If there is reasonable doubt, then be more legal, but go no further.

Never run compensation matters past the legal department unless there is a legal question. And never ask the legal department an open-ended question: Tell them your conclusions, and ask for any legal "why nots."

Questions and Complaints

Handling employee questions and complaints is one of the essentials of human resources management. In fact, in presentations on the basics of personnel management, I include questions and complaints as one of the six most essential personnel practices.* I believe every operation needs a formal system for answering questions and complaints—in the sense that there is some way that is known to all employees that is an ensured method for having questions answered by someone else if the immediate manager will not or cannot handle the matter to the reasonable satisfaction of the employee.

Some think that a "grievance system" is appropriate in a union group but not in a normal work group. I argue that a formal system of handling questions and complaints is particularly important in regular work situations (and, in fact, I have serious questions about grievance systems in union situations).

There are a number of specific methods that will work. Consider having one of them. Recognize that the principal question area will be compensation. A survey of questions submitted in a dozen formal question and grievance systems over a five-year period in nonunion situations in the area of compensation found that the following question areas were also raised:

- Pay progress
- Competitive pay
- Health and benefit claims
- All other issues combined

Hardware Issues

Effective administration and implementation also means answering a variety of bread-and-butter questions on a recurring basis. Many of these, of course, are local or unique to a company. The hardware questions will also vary from time to time.

Recruiting-pay questions occur as often as any and must always be

---

*The six essentials of personnel management that I emphasize are: Ensure excellence of recruiting; prepare and distribute to all employees a written personnel policy manual; establish competitive pay for all jobs; have effective communications with employees; have effective performance appraisal; and have a grievance system.

answered immediately, because the job is open and very often the perfect candidate has just been found but has two other job offers. The questions that come up most often, however, when I'm sitting in the office of someone who works in compensation involve questions from senior managers about the pay increase for some subordinate. For some reason, these must always be answered right away.

There are also recurring problems of relocation. These are becoming increasingly complex and costly. They usually require a complicated set of guidelines, and there seem to be as many exceptions as there are cases.

There are questions about how often employee salaries should be reviewed for increases. Generally, the answer is simple: once a year. But the frequency of review is also a function of the size of the increase. For example, if a person is entitled to a very large increase, such as 20 percent, then it may be prudent to give two 10 percent increases, but at much shorter intervals. Also, the frequency of review should be a function of the rate of inflation and the rate of personal growth of those who are being reviewed.

There are always new issues that come up and, even more often, old issues that resurface. I have often heard it said by people in the field that there really isn't anything new in personnel. My experience in personnel generally and in the specific area of compensation is that there have been a lot of new issues, practices, programs, and ideas but that none of these ever seems to go away permanently; they resurface from time to time.

The Effective Administrator

Those who do compensation work must be effective in planning, administering, and controlling compensation work. Those who work in compensation must be effective in managing their own work. They must be effective administrators.

One reason why I pursued a career in consulting and not in business is because I am not an effective administrator. Therefore, I'm really not the one to give advice to anyone about how to be a good administrator. In fact, in the companies I ran, I always had somebody else be the business administrator and managed to keep my hands out of that pot. Perhaps for some, that's the key to being an effective administrator.

It's always impressive to watch the effective administrator at work. The effective administrator is not the same thing as the effective manager. The effective administrator is one who handles a lot of information and deals with processes involving many people and many points of view and somehow gets through all of that and has something implemented that somehow works and somehow pleases everybody. That kind of activity is very important, and you need good people to do it. You need effective administrators doing compensation work.

Chapter Eleven

Extra Pay Plans

Salaried pay is current cash for current work. Salaried pay has been the subject of Chapters 4 through 10. There are other methods of cash payments. These are not fixed amounts like salaries; they vary in amount. When earned, these payments are paid periodically, but the periods of payment may be as frequent as salaries or at longer intervals.

These extra pay plans would include bonus plans of various types, including factory incentive and sales commission plans. These kinds of plans are covered in Chapters 14 through 18, where special compensation plans for operations, sales, middle-level, professional, and management employees are described.

In addition to special bonus plans for different groups or types of work, there are also extra pay plans that are applied to all employees or to a broad class of employees, such as nonunion employees. These plans are described in this chapter. They include variable pay plans, success sharing plans, thrift plans, contingent compensation plans, and stock ownership plans.

Needs and Objectives—Extra Pay Plans

From the employer's point of view, the need for extra pay plans is seldom compelling and the objectives may seem to be somewhat unclear. From the employer's view, the emphasis is often on the potential value to the business in terms of general employee morale and attitude. Therefore, there is usually no compelling need for the employer to have such plans in order to attract, retain, and motivate. The objectives of extra pay plans are more related to fairness than to competitiveness.

It is important to note, however, that extra pay plans usually involve variable costs. Therefore, from the employer's point of view, expenditures under extra pay plans are contingent costs in the form of investment spending. Because the costs are generally both variable and moderate, extra pay plans are appropriate in many cases even though the business objective may not be clear and compelling.

Extra pay plans can also have derivative advantages for an employer. For example, there may be cash flow and financing advantages. When stock is involved, payments under such plans represent a form of stock purchase and, therefore, assist in financing the business. Extra pay plans also serve as a more prudent and less risky method of partially meeting the retirement needs of the workers.

Because of these considerations, more and more companies have some form of an extra pay plan. Three-fourths of all companies that publish reports about such matters have extra pay plans. Most of these plans include an accrual system that is based upon a sharing of profits above a reasonable profit base. Thus extra pay plans truly represent extra income to employees when business results are favorable. Part of the reward under an extra pay plan is sometimes paid in the form of company stock, and there is likely a closer identity of interests between the employees and the employer.

Consider the values of designing extra pay plans so that those employees who create the wealth share in the profits of the company. It is sometimes hard to provide tangible proof, but it has always seemed to many in the field that sharing the profits with those who create the wealth will always contribute to employees having a greater consciousness of employer welfare and a greater commitment to excellence of work. Employees gain a stronger feeling of identification with their employer when extra pay plans are designed properly. They feel that they are stakeholders in the company, and if stock ownership is involved, they are indeed stockholders.

Employees always value extra pay plans, provided they believe that the payments are in addition to full competitive salaries and that their individual salaries fairly relate pay to performance. Few employees and even fewer lower-paid employees would choose to have their money at risk. They would not want some of their income dependent upon company results, even if their total earnings were greater in favorable times and their earnings were substantially more over a period of time. Employees almost always only want extra pay plans that represent extra income.

Every study of employee opinions on compensation suggests that employees, on their own, would not request an extra pay plan or value such plans very highly unless the employees were assured that these plans would provide significant amounts of money over a period of time and unless they thought the amounts were clearly in addition to fully competitive and fair salaries.

Normally, most levels of employees want cash now. It's not until you get above income class 3, where employees have sufficient amounts of income to meet their ongoing expenses, that you find a high degree of interest in estate plans.

For employees in class 4 and 5, extra pay plans may be prized because they provide an opportunity to acquire capital that might be difficult to accrue otherwise. Extra pay plans may provide important estate needs, such as educating children or providing care for parents. Extra pay plans may make the impossible dream a reality or give promise that it could happen.

Employees will also realize the advantage of a unique opportunity to save. Even if extra pay plans are composed largely of their own money, they will be valued as long as the plans truly represent an opportunity to save on a favorable basis, provided there is no risk of loss and values in the extra pay plans are truly extra pay. Employees must be assured that the money they save under an extra pay plan has a high degree of security and that the funds are professionally managed.

Variable Pay Plans

Variable pay plans have existed for many years. However, in the past few years, there has been a renewed interest in this type of extra pay plan. In fact, some suggest that variable pay plans should represent an important facet of compensation. Thus variable pay plans should be considered.

Under a variable pay plan, salary levels are set lower than they would be otherwise. Most often, the thought is to set salary levels generally at 10 percent below market average. Then variable payments are made, provided business standards are achieved. As a result, *total* cash pay may be higher than competitive levels for everyone or it may be lower.

Thus under these variable pay plans, the compensation of employees covered by such programs will be higher under certain conditions and lower under other conditions. Some of the competitive salary of employees is, in effect, at risk. This contrasts with bonus plans and success-sharing plans, where salary levels are fixed at competitive levels and then extra payments under the extra pay plan are additional amounts based upon success measures of various types.

Note that it isn't practical to have a variable pay plan if there is an incentive bonus plan. Also note that a variable pay plan is a variation of profit sharing, except that base salaries are lower, so employees may get more or they may get less.

Variable pay plans evolved from payroll cost containment efforts and reflect a management desire to control and manage payroll costs more effectively. Variable pay plans are cost-oriented plans, designed specifically to shift some of the downside business risks from company profits to lower compensation for employees.

If you consider a variable pay plan, there are a number of factors that must be analyzed and evaluated. Here are some critical issues to be explored:

- What is the basis for variability? In most variable pay plans that have been proposed, pay varies with corporate profits. Consider unit business result measures at least as the basis for payments up to competitive pay levels.

- What are the standards of business performance that will determine variable pay? These must be formalized; there can be no discretion in variable pay plans. Yet we know the risks of pay plan formulas and that these plans become obsolete very quickly.

- How much of a downside risk should there be? There obviously must be enough of a downsize compensation take-away in order to make a significant impact upon overall company costs. However, there must be some realistic limitation on what employees can afford or what employees (particularly high-performance employees) will accept.

- Consider carefully the effect of pay take-aways from high-talent, high-performance employees.

- Calculate specifically for your firm the effect of different levels of profitability on compensation levels.

- How much should the upside opportunity be? In variable pay plans, it is difficult to put any cap on extra payments, and this runs the risk of runaway payout formulas.

- Be sure you consider the perceptions of employees. Except in cases where loss of jobs seems imminent, employees are not likely to think well of any variable pay plan, at least in years they think they are paid below competitive levels, or in any period where they receive less than they did in a prior period.

- Determine the experience of companies like yours with plans like this. What you will likely find out is that very few companies have adopted variable pay plans, although many have considered them. You will find that companies that did adopt variable pay plans are modifying them or abandoning them.

The advantages of variable pay plans are obvious. They help companies relieve compensation cost pressures. Variable pay plans shift some of the risks of the business to employees.

Some see variable pay plans as a way of maintaining top management *control*. It is top management that sets the variable pay levels and the business standards. For some, variable pay plans have been a return to programmatic management.

The difficulties are very serious. They must be weighed heavily in the design of any variable pay program.

Variable pay is a form of give-back or take-back in the nonunion worker area. It is a way of avoiding risks by the company and shifting business risks to employees.

There are many problems in communicating these plans to employees. In fact, if the company tells the truth, I don't think a variable pay plan can be communicated to employees in a way that will gain employee acceptance.

Don't think that higher than average pay in good years will be a selling feature. Employees will accept that, as they would payments under a profit-sharing plan. Employees won't accept the take-away from competitive pay in not so good years; particularly if executives continue to get bonus payments in those years.

If the variable pay results in levels of compensation that are uncompetitive, then difficulties in recruiting and retention may be experienced. Even short-term reductions in pay under a variable pay plan may affect competitiveness.

If you believe that your firm can be competitive with lower fixed salary levels contemplated by a variable pay plan, then you have another issue to consider: Why not reduce salaries to the lower levels now without adopting a variable pay plan? After consideration, you must support one salary level or the other. If your conclusion is that you doubt the competitiveness of the lower salary level, then you should not consider a variable pay plan.

In weighing the competitiveness of a variable pay plan, consider two related issues: upward mobility and emerging labor scarcity. Even intermittent labor uncompetitiveness can do serious harm to business competitiveness, making it more difficult for the business to compete for effective people in good years and in bad years. This in turn may detract later from the firm's ability to develop people for future promotions and make it more difficult for the firm to meet future manpower needs.

Isn't it imprudent to take the risk of becoming less competitive by adopting a variable pay plan if a company is now experiencing or thinks it will experience labor scarcity problems? You don't deal effectively with labor scarcity by raising pay, but it is equally true that it is unsound to aggravate a situation of labor scarcity by paying lower than competitive salaries.

Finally, we must consider the impact of a variable pay plan on the living standards of employees, particularly lower-paid employees. Try to write out a script that will be honest and convincing to employees. If you think the resulting message is convincing, try it on a sample of low-paid employees before proceeding with your variable pay plan.

In the past few years, I have been asked a number of times to consider variable pay plans that were being developed by clients. In each case, I worked as hard as I could and as open-mindedly as I could in considering the plans, mostly because the companies were predisposed to implement these plans. However, in every case, the conclusion was that a variable pay plan should not be implemented. The result of my work was that I strongly recommended against the implementation of a variable pay plan or any variation of a variable pay plan.

To be responsible and as constructive as possible in response to requests for help in developing variable pay plans, I developed a model variable pay plan. This identifies what I consider to be the essentials for an effective and reasonably fair variable pay plan.

The model variable pay plan uses unit performance measures for determining both below competitive pay and full competitive pay. Under a model variable pay plan, business performance standards above competitive levels use a grid of both unit performance and corporate profitability.

Payments above competitive levels are in part deferred—preferably in company stock. These payments vest serially every five years. The values may be used to buy retirement annuities. Then the variable pay plan has substantial holding power and is part of the retirement pay system.

This model variable pay plan most importantly calls first for variable salary reduction. The variable salary reduction involves some complications, but essentially:

- There is no salary reduction for the lowest four salary grades (see Figure 6–1).
- There is a 5 percent reduction in salaries for grades 5 through 12.
- There is a 10 percent reduction in salaries for grades 13 through 20.
- There is a 15 percent reduction in salaries for grades 21 through 28.
- There is a 20 percent reduction in salaries for grades 29 and above.

I have a very persuasive presentation to convince the decision-makers of the rightness of this salary reduction schedule under a variable pay plan. There are also different performance standards for payments to competitive levels and for extra payments above competitive levels for each of these groups, so it all works out fairly.

Success Sharing

Fair pay means comparable pay. Fair pay means reward for performance, whether by promotion, incentive bonus payments, salary increases, or by all these methods. In addition to this, you can also make a case that those who create the wealth should share in the wealth. Then employees who collectively make profits would share in the profits. Success-sharing plans are based upon this type of thinking.

Success-sharing plans should always be structured so they represent extra compensation for business results above standard or expected results. Companies must pay fairly for the job and reward fairly for achievement. But the owners should also get a reasonable return on their investment. There should be no payments to employees under success-sharing plans until reasonable business target levels, such as reasonable financial return on capital, are achieved. Thus success-sharing plans should be designed to make payments that are extra pay for employees when employees as a group have performed in such a way that the company exceeds reasonable enterprise goals.

In this sense, success-sharing plans are always investment return spending. Success-sharing payments cost the employer nothing in relative terms; such spending is an investment yield after the return is received.

There are many specific types of success-sharing plans. For example, they may be simple lump-sum cash payments to employees beyond a prescribed level of enterprise results. The success-sharing plan may be a qualified retirement plan. The plan may be used to finance the purchase of company stock. In spite of the variations, all success-sharing plans have these characteristics:

- There are no downside risks for employees; salaries are competitive and not dependent in any way on provisions of the plan.
- There is a threshold of business performance below which no payments to employees would accrue.
- Above the threshold, there is a formal method of accruing funds for payments to employees.
- Payments are made in a formal and fixed manner in some proportion to the salary of those who are eligible.

In commercial businesses, success-sharing plans almost always mean extra compensation based upon the sharing of profits—profit-sharing plans. In a hospital, success sharing might mean extra compensation paid in a lump sum based upon measures of patient care and hospital cost containment. In a school district, payments under success-sharing plans might be partially geared to students' SAT scores and grade point averages. In all success-sharing plans, reasonable enterprise success must be achieved before any payments are made. Then above that threshold, payments are made.

Any enterprise can have a success-sharing plan. Success-sharing plans have been devised for private as well as public companies, small as well as large companies. You can have success-sharing plans for schools, cities, hospitals, and penal institutions. The key is that there must be a mathematic, though not necessarily accounting, method for measuring enterprise results.

Success-sharing plans don't represent direct incentives to work more effectively; they are not incentive bonus plans. These plans won't visibly change behavior or provide an incentive for people to improve their work effectiveness directly.

Success-sharing plans are what the name suggests: a sharing of success. Sharing success is not likely to create strong incentives for broad groups of employees. Such plans will reinforce a commitment by employees to the organization and to work excellence. Over time, this attitude will almost certainly improve the quality and effectiveness of the organization.

The dollar value of success-sharing plans is usually not very much in a single year. There may be some years in which there will be no payments at all because enterprise goals were not achieved. Over a number of years, however, payments from success-sharing plans can accrue into substantial funds. In the working life of an average employee, the accumulated funds could represent a fortune.

The data in Figure 11–1 shows a typical case of funds accrued in a success-sharing plan. In this case, it was a profit-sharing plan. The num-

Figure 11-1. Values From Success-Sharing Plans ($000).

Years in Plan	Salary That Year +2% Inflation	Amount to Fund That Year at 6%	Cumulative Cash Amount With 9% Interest	Stock Values +2% Inflation
1	$15.0	$ 900	$ 900	$ 900
5	16.2	972	7,266	8,022
10	17.7	1,062	16,524	20,165
15	19.7	1,182	32,795	44,109
20	21.7	1,302	54,149	80,411
25	24.7	1,482	92,339	151,436

bers are based upon actual cases. These companies successfully improved profits during the period of study at a rate that was greater than the increase in the rate of inflation.

Calculations of the values of funds accrued in profit-sharing plans are complex because there are so many variables, none of which can be predicted with precision. It is necessary to make assumptions about inflation, pay increases, and future company profitability. The firm can build a computer model to get a number for each of the most likely predictions of future values.

Most of all, in making assumptions in designing success-sharing plans, there is the issue of business success. If the success of the company is reasonably great, then employees can accumulate a sufficient amount of money from a success-sharing plan to meet estate needs and goals. In the case of a very successful company, a career employee can educate three children and, at age sixty-five, use the capital to retire at a full-salaried lifestyle from the profit-sharing plan alone.

Payments from success-sharing plans can be important to employees well beyond their dollar values, even though the dollar values may be substantial. Funds accumulated from success-sharing plans can make practical for workers the achievement of financial goals that would otherwise be impossible dreams. Success sharing gives the average worker hope for reasonable financial security. The whole idea of success-sharing plans makes enterprise success seem more important to those who work in the companies and more important to those who create company profits. Such plans also make worker-voters more inclined to support an economic system they are part of.

The effect on the attitudes of employee stockholders is always impressive. There is a consciousness about the company's welfare in companies that have success-sharing plans. There is more effectiveness and quality and more concern about costs. In many small ways, work is done somewhat better; different enough cumulatively, from many cases over a period of time, to cause better results.

Success-sharing plans often defer awards and require continued employment. Then they represent an additional reason for employees to stay with the company. I always recommend that some part of the success-sharing payments should be serially deferred, most likely on a five-year cycle. If possible, put the money in company stock; but in some way always use the funds not yet vested to finance your business. Also permit withdrawals, as provided by the plan, so employees can use these funds to meet genuine estate needs. Even if these features mean that the plan cannot be qualified, the company is still better off, and deferrals are not a penalty for employees who stay with the company.

Success-sharing plans might also represent unique forms of financing the business. For example, funds accumulated in a profit-sharing plan can be sufficient to buy a controlling interest in a company.

I always enjoy communicating success-sharing plans to employees. It is particularly nice to see some faces light up when I describe how this plan might make possible the financing of their children's education.

Communicating success-sharing plans is very easy. Everyone gains. You don't really have to say much. Just tell the truth, describe the plan, and give a few illustrations.

The difficult part about success-sharing plans is company success. Success-sharing plans only work in successful companies. Be sure to tell employees that also.

There are so many advantages of success-sharing plans that it's surprising that every company doesn't have such plans. Some have been discouraged by cases where success-sharing plans have failed. However, every case of failure that I know of was because the plan was poorly designed, often because the plan was structured too much for tax and accounting considerations, or because the company failed.

Thrift Plans

Another type of extra pay plan is a thrift plan. In these plans, employees contribute a percentage of their pay, and the employer usually matches employees' savings in some proportion.

The employee's contribution may be in any amount. Most plans permit up to 10 percent of pay. The employer's contribution may be in any amount and in any proportion, although there are limitations on each if the plan is to be qualified. In most plans, the employer's contribution is 50 to 100 percent of the amount saved by the employee.

These plans can be qualified, and the contributions are then tax-deferred. However, the plan must meet certain IRS regulations; for example, all employees must contribute equally and the prescribed portion of lower-paid persons must choose to enroll in the plan.

Employee contributions are not tax-deferred. The employee pays taxes on any funds contributed to a thrift plan. Thus the employee is saving after-tax dollars.

Employee contributions are usually put into a fixed-value, high-grade investment fund. The employer's contribution is often in whole or in part in company stock. In many plans, the employee has a choice as to which funds either his own or the employer's contributions may be put into. This doesn't mean much to employees who lack know-how about investments.

Thrift plan matching may be fixed or the employer's contributions may be geared to business results. If the employer's contributions are geared to business results, then that portion of the thrift plan is similar to success-sharing plans. Where operations lack confidence in measures of enterprise success, such as in public school systems, then the fixed employee contribution is preferred. If the employer doesn't care about enterprise results in the usual sense of measurements or doesn't have concerns about funding such plans, then fixed contributions by the employer are also preferable. This would be the case of government operations.

Thrift plans are contributory, and that is a significant advantage of this type of extra pay plan. Some think that employee contributions to any extra pay plan, insured benefit, or retirement program are of great value because of employee interest and commitment. In the case of extra pay plans, which largely serve employees' estate-building needs, it seems particularly important to some that employees' savings contribute to building employees' estates. The employees' contributions must also result in larger estates.

The biggest problem with thrift plans is that employees must contribute to be eligible. Those who don't contribute their own savings get no matching employer contribution. Usually those who don't contribute are the lowest-paid employees, who may need the thrift plan values the most. But the need for current income is so important to lower-paid persons that they do not think they are able to participate in such programs.

To get enough lower-paid employees to participate in order to qualify such plans, employers may increase the amount of their contributions. If the company's contributions are high enough, most employees will participate. This can be very costly, and a company must weigh the values and the costs of qualification and consider alternate plans.

Contingent Compensation

Contingent compensation is compensation to be paid at a future time and is dependent upon a person's continued employment with the company. It is commonly called golden handcuffs. Contingent compensation is money that an employee has a right to receive, but payment will be deferred and is contingent upon specified conditions, such as continued employment. Contingent payments can only be attached to some form of an extra pay plan.

Golden handcuffs were an important part of compensation packages not many years ago. Pensions were unvested for twenty to twenty-five years, and that represented a considerable amount of holding power. Accrued benefits were often geared to length of service, and executives had to wait at least five years before they could exercise options.

Vesting is now five years in pensions, and options start vesting almost immediately in most plans. Compensation values at risk or contingent are not a factor in many compensation plans and are a minor factor in others.

While contingent compensation was declining as a practice, the need for golden handcuffs was increasing. Back when golden handcuffs were common in compensation programs, there was also a great deal of company loyalty—an inclination for people to stay with one company as a matter of obligation. Many people felt a deep loyalty to the company they worked for. For many, the goal was to work all their careers in one company and then retire from that company. To leave one's company was thought by many to be an act of disloyalty. Much has happened since then, and company loyalty has eroded to the point where today the attitudes toward employers are clearly very shallow. Thus holding power, as a practice in compensation, is used less at the very period of time when it is needed more.

The case for golden handcuffs is compelling. Golden handcuffs don't prevent employees from leaving, but the sums involved can be large enough to discourage impulse turnover and quits because recruiting offers have been made for more money for about the same level of job.

To meet the needs of extra pay and retention, a new type of compensation plan is evolving, which, until labeled more dramatically, can be generically called contingent compensation plans. There are many types of specific plans that are being developed and implemented, usually designed to deal with turnover of targeted persons.

In my strategic planning reports, I predict the emergence of these plans. In fact, I predict that 10 percent of large firms may have some form of a contingent compensation plan by the year 1990 and more than half of all firms will have such plans by the year 2000.

I predict that contingent compensation plans will have the following characteristics:

- Salaries will be competitive but could be somewhat less than the statistical average.
- Some payments will be made on a cycle of less than one year.
- Part of the performance measurement system will be unit or location performance.
- Payments will be moderate compared to current bonus plans—most comparable to the level of awards paid in profit-sharing plans—and payments will be open-ended.
- Individual awards will be based only partially on salary levels.
- Payments, at least in part, will be deferred and contingent upon continued employment. There will often be other contingency requirements.

• Deferred values will increase or decrease, based upon long-term measures of enterprise success; for example, stock prices.

The most unique feature of these plans is that they will only be applied to some employees. Labor-scarce jobs, jobs requiring long learning periods, and high-performance persons will be targeted.

Employee Stock Ownership

Stock ownership by employees may be an important part of any attempt to develop a work environment that is more appropriate to today's social and political environment. Stock ownership is also a proven method of contributing to a greater identity of interests between employees and employers. Stock ownership alone will not create a more favorable work environment or a greater work commitment. However, stock ownership is a tangible act that makes employees part of the company. Stock ownership by employees must create more interest on their part for the welfare of the company and a greater commitment to excellence of work, because employees are among the owners of the company.

For many years, managers recognized the value of stock ownership by employees. The first stock ownership plans were introduced in industry in the 1920s. Unfortunately, these plans were designed so that employees used their after-tax savings in order to buy the stock. As long as the stock market went up, such plans were popular, but when the market went down (particularly in the 1920s and 1930s), then employees lost savings.

Logically, one could argue that employees who buy stock under stock ownership plans are investors and take their chances like anyone else. However, employees are not sophisticated investors. Many assume that stock purchase plans were recommended by the company because they were beneficial to employees. Then if the stock goes up, the company has already gotten the credit, but if the stock goes down, employees blame the company for their losses. And many employees, particularly lower-paid employees, simply cannot afford to lose savings.

In recent years, companies have attempted to reestablish employee stock ownership plans (ESOP) by adopting various types of advantageous purchase arrangements for employees. These special purchase arrangements were designed to reduce the downside risks of stock purchases. One method of doing this was to sell employee stock below market price. Other companies have tried to establish plans that have a safety net: a minimum value below which the stock could not go without being redeemed by the company.

All these plans tend to become far too complicated. They also involve potentially high costs for employers. These costs would most likely impact the company in years of poor earnings, which is when they can least afford them.

Employee stock ownership plans are another method of getting stock into the hands of employees. Under an ESOP, the cost of stock grants is offset by tax credits. In effect, the government is partially paying for your company's stock grants. The amount of stock is quite limited under ESOPs, but cumulatively can represent a significant degree of employee ownership.

For some time, I have urged companies to consider employee stock ownership plans that utilize a separate class of employee stock. The employee stock would be traded only between the employees and the company. The company would sell the stock to employees for cash, perhaps through payroll deductions. There would have to be a "formula" basis for valuing the stock. For example, the stock might be transacted at book value.

Employee class stock would have prescribed voting rights and other specified stockholder rights, which might be different than the rights of common stockholders. Employee class stock would not pay dividends in the normal sense. The company could, however, make bonus payments to owners of employee class stock on a profit-sharing basis.

Whenever an employee left the company, he would be required to redeem the stock. In the event of a change in control, employee-class stock would also be redeemed, either at the formula price or at the market price of common stock, whichever was higher.

It should be noted that for many companies employee stock ownership plans would deal effectively with problems of declining stock values. Employee class stock values would decline only if the company lost money, and to the extent of the losses each year.

Employees could purchase employee class stock or be granted the stock as a payment under an extra pay plan or option plan. The funds from employee class stock could be a major source of low-cost equity financing on the part of the company.

When it comes to employee stock ownership, I tend to be an evangelist rather than just a consultant. I strongly believe that employees should be owners of the company's stock. All regular and full-time employees should own some company stock and as a group should own at least one-third of the company's stock.

It isn't difficult to convince top executives and the board that employees should own stock. The advantages are easily identified, and they are very substantial. The problem is in convincing executives and directors that employee stock transactions should be different than market-traded stock and in some ways more favorable.

Employee stockholders will always face risks. They should view their money in stock as money at risk. But employees usually can't handle the risks of the stock market *and* the risks of layoffs, downgrading, and pay-roll freezes, which often come with the poor business conditions that cause declining stock prices. They need to buy and sell company stock on some basis other than as a trader. Employee class stock was designed to do that.

It's surprising that executives don't always support a more favorable stock ownership arrangement for all employees in view of the fact that stock options are a favored stock transaction exclusively for managers. Furthermore, options and executive-supported plans soften the downside risks of stock ownership by executives by stock appreciation rights plus option cancellation and reissue. The special features and beneficial conditions of employee class stock are basically no more favorable than the beneficial conditions of stock options.

Don't look to Congress for some special plan. Congress may have to pass legislation to permit employee class stock or specific provisions regarding employee class stock ownership as it did with stock options. But we don't need tax shelters for employees in employee class stock.

You can have employee ownership in your organization today. This is possible (though difficult) even if you are a nonprofit or privately-owned company. It's worth thinking about. For whatever it's worth, after thirty years as a consultant in human resources management, I think employee stock ownership is as important as anything else.

Company Strategy Regarding Extra Pay Plans

Too often extra pay plans have been adopted because the tax was less, which is like saving money by buying things you don't need at a sale. Extra pay plans also sometimes become fads in business, and the Joneses have cost some firms a lot of money.

Extra pay plans *are* extra, or in the case of variable pay plans, they are sometimes extra and sometimes less. Extra pay plans are in addition to salary, bonus, pay for performance, appropriate benefits, and retirement payment plans. Of course, some pay, bonus, benefits, and retirement pay may be considered as extra pay also, in the sense that payments are more than appropriate. But in the case of extra pay plans, the amounts are *designed* to be extra. This means that values are not always clear, and costs must be variable or moderate or both variable and moderate.

In any compensation plan, you start by determining needs and objectives. With extra pay plans, the needs are rarely compelling. For example, there is rarely a compelling competitive need for extra pay plans. These plans are not major factors in attracting talent and are a factor in retaining people only if retention features are designed into the plan. Thus the reason to consider extra pay plans is related more to fairness and worker commitment to excellence, plus any special purposes that are built into the plan, such as financing the business.

For employees, these plans represent extra payments also. Employees will always accept those extra payments unless they have to take from their own savings in order to participate in the plan. They may also object if they come to think that what they are getting in deferred pay is in lieu of current income.

Too often, extra pay plans have really been designed for the benefit of high-paid persons. Then they are extended downward, either for egalitarian reasons or more likely so that they can become qualified under Internal Revenue Service (IRS) regulations.

Keep in mind that extra pay plans (and pension plans) often serve the interests of third parties. There are always people who are knocking on company doors and aggressively selling some extra pay plan, some special benefit like executive life insurance, or some special pension plan that only they can provide. Always keep in mind that they are selling their programs for the good of *their* business.

Bottom-line management would be hard to sell on the basis of fairness and workers' attitudes alone. So the objective of fairness must be paired with plans that encourage work excellence, involve retention, and ideally have other business values at well. Combine these values with moderate levels of opportunity costs.

For employers, the hard values of extra pay plans are in sharing profits, stock ownership, and retention. Sharing profits above a reasonable threshold return on capital *is* investment spending.

The fairness of sharing profits with those who create the profits seems compelling. A good argument can be made with some hard evidence that profit sharing does, in some ways, get greater worker attention and attentiveness to the welfare of the business and, therefore, does have a value in terms of enhancing the long-term success of the company. But even if that isn't true, it is just fair to share profits with all those who work in the organization, particularly where payments represent opportunity costs.

An equally strong case can be made for employee stock ownership as long as that doesn't cost much and as long as employees don't buy stock subject to stock market swings with their after-tax savings. This argues for at least partial payments of profit-sharing values in stock. Consider making those payments in employee class stock that is convertible to common stock if there is an unfriendly takeover.

There is also value in contingent pay—golden handcuffs. Extra pay plans are the place to make payments contingent upon staying with the company. Specific contingent pay plans are now available.

Developing extra pay plans is difficult in privately-held companies where there are substantial reasons why owners will not divulge basic financial data. In effect, the owners must describe their criteria for making contributions into the plan but the payments must be made on a discretionary basis or based upon the judgments and declarations of a third party.

In enterprises that serve noncommercial business goals, such as health care units and educational facilities, the criteria for success must, of course, be related to that organization's objectives, not necessarily cost alone. Both near-term and long-term goals can then be described in a meaningful manner in any type of enterprise. In extra pay plans, keep in mind that payments in any one year are designed to be moderate, so there is little risk of "overpayment" or excessive costs. Extra pay plans are designed to be extra compensation to be paid in years of better-than-average enterprise success.

Be sure you include calculations and values for extra pay plans when you consider the design of your retirement plans. Under some circumstances, extra pay plans can serve as a retirement income plan or as an integral part of a retirement income strategy.

Chapter Twelve

Employee Benefits

Benefits are payments made by an employer for programs that are advantageous to employees and accrue to employees by reason of employment. Benefits are a form of compensation that is of value to employees in a way or ways in which more pay would not, and for some reason, there is an inference in benefits that the payment has more value than its cash equivalent. There is also frequently an inference that benefits are something extra beyond compensation, which is perhaps why they were once called fringe benefits.

Types of Benefits

There are many types of benefits. Each serves somewhat different purposes or exists for somewhat different reasons. Some benefits are very complex. In combination, the issues of benefits are difficult and costly.

Start by identifying the different types of benefits that are now part of your compensation program. Be sure you also know the benefit items that exist and that are not in effect in your organization. Make sure that you analyze these and identify why your company does not have some benefits as well as reasons why your firm has benefits that you do have. Have an outline of all benefit programs that identifies the basic features and objectives of each benefit. To help get the process started, here is a list of a dozen principal benefits, or benefit categories, with a brief description of each:

1. Health care benefits
2. Disability and sickness insurance
3. Life insurance
4. Legally required payments
5. Vacations
6. Holidays
7. Employee services
8. Prepaid legal services
9. Education
10. Financial assistance
11. Outplacement
12. The unique company benefit

Health Care Benefits

Almost all companies have hospitalization and surgical benefits, including major medical provisions. Plans cover employees and often their dependents as well. The employer typically pays most of the cost of the coverage for the employee.

These benefits are extremely valuable to employees. Such plans provide protection against the expense of illness, which many workers simply cannot afford, and they provide payments for escalating hospital bills. Such benefits are tax-sheltered; that is, the expense of such coverage is a tax deduction for the employer but is not taxable income for employees.

Health care costs have been escalating rapidly. Company benefits in these areas are valuable, but they also face great unknowns in the future. The special problems of health care have become a major human resources management issue. These special matters are dealt with in a separate section in this chapter.

Disability and Sickness Insurance

Disability and sickness insurance are insured benefits paid for prolonged disabilities. They provide income for permanently disabled employees for the balance of their lives. Many plans also include programs for rehabilitation; the objective is to help the disabled employee become a productive worker again.

Benefits for sickness are in two parts. Many companies have sick-leave plans. These continue the salary, or a percentage of the salary, of people with short-term illnesses. Some companies have problems preventing the abuse of this benefit. Workers sometimes see sick leave as extra paid vacation time. Even if they are not sick, some employees want to use their sick days for vacations or personal leisure.

In addition, each state requires sickness insurance, and companies have what amounts to temporary disability programs. These insured benefits provide payments directly to the employee to offset part of the loss of income due to sickness or accidents after sick leave benefits terminate.

Life Insurance

Most companies have some amount of life insurance available for all employees. This is usually put into effect for all employees after a minimum length of service.

Life insurance benefits are frequently geared to annual earnings. A typical provision would be life insurance values of two to four times annual salary. Life insurance programs will often have larger payments for accidental death and disability provisions that will pay the cost of premiums until retirement.

Employers often pay the entire cost of life insurance. If employees make contributions, they are modest. Note also that the government prescribes maximums of insurance coverage, above which the premium value of the life insurance would be charged as taxable income to the employee.

Legally Required Payments

Employers are required to pay both worker's compensation and unemployment insurance. Worker's compensation payments involve both medical expense reimbursement and direct payments to those injured on the job. Benefits are also provided for survivors of those who are killed.

Unemployment insurance, of course, provides payments by the state to people who are laid off because of lack of work or who are terminated through no fault of their own. The amount and duration of these benefits vary considerably among the states. The employer pays the cost of these benefits, and these amounts are, therefore, part of employee remuneration.

Vacations

An important principle is involved in vacation payments. This involves the question of whether vacation benefits are an earned right or a paid rest from work. If they are regarded as an earned right, then an employee who voluntarily leaves the company is entitled to vacation benefits that have been accrued but not used. The other view is that an employee needs a rest from work, and this is of value to the employer. Where this philosophy exists, employees become eligible for one or two weeks of vacation immediately upon employment. However, if they voluntarily leave the company, they have no rights to accrued but unused vacation days.

Some companies permit employees to accrue unused vacations to future years. In this case, if an employee doesn't take vacations, or doesn't take all his entitled vacation time, the unused portion is accumulated for future use, which could be to retirement. When this happens, the employee does not get a rest from work, and such a provision clearly reflects an entitlement view of pay for time not worked.

Today, the most typical provision is two weeks of vacation after one year of service, three weeks after five years of service, and four or more weeks after ten years of service. Individual company plans obviously vary a great deal.

Holidays

All companies provide for some paid holidays. Today, the typical practice is to grant from eight to fourteen paid holidays. If a holiday falls on a Saturday or Sunday, then employees are given an alternate day off.

The exact number of holidays is typically geared to local practice. Different communities and areas of the country observe different holidays. Companies often have a number of set holidays and then give employees choices for others. This is particularly important when families have more than one working member.

The competition for holiday designation is quite strong. Christmas and Easter are the only religious holidays. New Year's Day is a tradition. Then there are the patriot days, although our pride in America seems to be stronger on Mondays and Fridays. The competition for holidays for famous persons is intense. The favorite of many employees is becoming the floating holiday, which represents more vacation days.

Employee Services

A broad variety of services are provided by companies. Some of these are quite overt, and others are very subtle. Some of the services are for all employees or for a broad class of employees, whereas others are granted very selectively.

Services such as resident health-care activities have been a part of compensation for a long time. These have mostly been related to the company's dispensary and to safety or meeting legal requirements. Many companies have extended those health-care facilities to provide minor treatment during working hours, for health education, and for protective health activities, such as X-rays and blood pressure tests.

Many company location have food service operations, which are almost always subsidized by the company. The cost and value can be significant. For lower-paid employees, the company cafeteria can provide needed nourishment, and for higher-paid executives, the company cafeteria—or the private dining room attached to the company cafeteria—can be yet another item of extra pay.

Preschool child-care facilities have become a wide-spread practice in the eight years since the fourth edition of *Compensation* was published. These started in labor-scarce areas. But companies now feel pressure to provide these facilities in all locations and under all conditions. For the few who benefit, these have substantial value for a period of time. For example, the cost to the employer for child-care facilities will be at least 10 percent of the employee's pay.

Prepaid Legal Services

Some well-known companies have adopted annual prepaid legal fees at all their locations. Some provide legal services more selectively and on a limited basis by in-house council or from their outside law firms. Usually, these kinds of legal services are provided only to high-paid persons or for employees who are involved in work that is closely related to the company's legal matters.

Education

Recently, some companies in intercity locations have started teaching centers. Their job is to teach employees to read and write and to do simple math. These centers were started because the operations of the companies could not find a sufficient number of functionally literate workers in the labor market. The teaching centers are costly, and operations raise a fundamental issue about an employer's obligation to provide such basic community services as public education.

Many companies provide expense reimbursement to employees for courses they take on their own time that support their work or assist in their career development. Usually, courses that are reimbursed must be approved by the employer. These evolved to help develop employees, as an extension of company training efforts. If they serve that purpose, then they are truly investment spending and not expensed compensation dollars.

Many companies have also provided matching grants. When an employee contributes to the college of his choice, then the company will match that donation. These matching grants can involve significant costs, and the degree to which they support education is open to question.

Financial Assistance

It's rare that companies provide loans directly to employees, but companies have provided subsidies to loan facilities for many years. For example, they permit unions and other loan institutions on the company's premises at no cost or at a low cost and in other ways subsidize the operation of these lending institutions.

Companies are also starting to be concerned about home equity by employees. There are new home equity loans or equity participation programs where the company provides financial backing for purchasing homes. In this case, the company need is selective, but it does relate directly to golden handcuffs.

Outplacement

As a standard part of compensation, outplacement started in the middle 1970s. It began when business acquisitions started and friendly takeovers occurred. The acquiring company had surplus persons, some with long service with the acquired company. It was an embarrassment to the acquiring company to get rid of these people and was thought to be harmful to the morale of the survivors. So the acquiring company adopted what became known as outplacement. Since these modest beginnings, outplacement has been extended to those outplaced because of downsizing and in some cases to those who were earmarked for termination for cause.

Outplacement, essentially, is a termination plan plus assistance in finding another job. At first, the assistance was simply advice in job hunting techniques, resume writing, and interviewing skills. Then some consultants got into the business. Now, for very large companies, outplacement can also mean an office with secretarial services, telephone answering services, and varying degrees of psychiatric help.

Recognize that outplacement costs of all types are not really compensation because the people affected are no longer employees. Therefore, outplacement cannot be considered an employee benefit unless the company is saying to current employees that they may be next.

The Unique Company Benefit

A number of companies have had considerable success in adopting a "unique company benefit" for employees. The idea of the unique benefit is simple. A company provides competitive benefits overall and, in addition, some special benefits that are not available to those who work for other companies.

The unique benefit is not a new idea. Many long-standing cases illustrate not only the idea but the value of the unique benefit. Employees in the airline industry, of course, travel free, and they consider this to be of great value. Those who work in travel agencies travel free or at a low cost. Hospitals provide free medical services of various types at no cost to their employees. Department stores permit their employees to buy merchandise at a discount. All these are unique benefits. Some companies are now searching for unique benefits for their employees for the sole purpose of enhancing employees' perceptions of the fairness and appropriateness of compensation in their company.

Unique benefits can have a financial and psychological value that is totally out of proportion to their cost. Although it is difficult to prove that the unique benefit in any company either helped to retain or motivate any employees, companies with unique benefits feel that the benefits have a very special value; dollar for dollar, they are well worth the cost involved.

Designing the Employee Benefit Program

Employee benefit programs must be designed with great care. Considerable amounts of money are involved in employee benefits, and they are items of great importance to employees. Many items are complex and have technical features that are extremely difficult for the layman to understand.

Each employee benefit has a value, and the values are important to employees. It is difficult to argue against the social merits of many benefit proposals. There is, therefore, a tendency to add to benefits. But unless the company has unlimited resources, the company as well as its employees must understand that extra benefits of "fringe" value mean less than some other form of compensation, such as current cash.

Designing employee benefits is a matter of human resources management. The key considerations in the design of a benefit program must be personnel considerations. Too often, actuaries or benefit technicians have had far too much influence on the design of benefit programs. Their expertise is critical, but they should not determine the *design* of the program.

The objective is not to have benefits that are better than any other employer or to design an elaborate or clever benefit package. Rather, the objective is to have benefits that best meet the needs of employees; which represent the maximum value to employees for each dollar of compensation cost; and which are the best balance between cash income and benefits.

Employers are regularly approached by insurance specialists or consultants who are selling various programs and thus are expert salespersons. These salespersons frequently give the impression that benefits offered by their programs will be of great value at little or no cost, which is never the case. When approached by such salespersons, a company must find out what question or problem the program answers. Remember that consideration of any compensation program starts with identifiable and provable needs.

Purchase considerations should not dominate the design of employee fringe benefit programs. The buyers of insurance benefits are frequently in the financial department, because when a company buys many types of insurance, it seems logical that all insurance, including employee insurance, should be purchased by the same person. The buying agent's job, however, is to make the best purchase agreement for the benefit package that has been designed, with employee relations considerations dominant in the design.

The benefit practices of other companies are of importance in the design of the employee benefit package, but less in importance than levels of pay in other companies. For one thing, it is extremely difficult to get information on benefit provisions in other firms. It is only possible to get rough estimates of competitive values and competitive costs. There is such a wide range of practices that getting some sense of what the competition is doing is extremely difficult.

Employee benefits have little effect on a company's ability to attract and retain employees. Rarely does a company have an offer rejected because of inadequacies in its benefit program, and very few employees will quit because of inadequacies in the benefit program.

In designing the employee benefit package, therefore, it is the needs of employees that must dominate. Basically, employees should need each item in the benefit package. The relationship of benefits overall to cash, as well as the priority given to different benefits, should essentially be determined by the nature of the work force and the preferences of employees.

In the design of benefits, always consider employee preferences. These are benefits for employees in lieu of cash. If they are to benefit employees, then the employees' preferences should be important factors to consider.

Some argue for flexible benefits. Sometimes flexible benefits cover all types of benefits and sometimes insured benefits only. In the early 1970s, I did a great deal of developmental work for clients in this area; it seemed to be such a reasonable thing to do. In the early work, the IRS represented a major obstacle, but it also became clear that there were major problems with flexible benefits.

For one thing, there really isn't any way to have comparative costing. More importantly, employees cannot make informed choices. Finally, the cost of administration and communication is a burden. Flexible benefits violate the principles of insurance anyway, which is to provide protection on a prudent basis for a variety of risks for a group, at a reasonable cost for each member of the group.

Here are some other points to consider in the design of a benefit package:

- A model should be designed, and the elements of the plan that is to be adopted or revised should be examined against this model. The model should be the ideal benefit package.
- Various aspects of coverage should be considered in terms of the impact of current trends in the company and in the economy. This

is particularly important in areas such as pensions and health insurance.

- The effectiveness of various types of benefit plans in achieving basic company objectives and employee aspirations must be analyzed.
- Companies should always seek ways to take advantage of lower costs resulting from more effective buying practices.
- Benefits must be monitored, not only in terms of their current costs but in terms of future costs, taking into account inflation, increasing pay, and long-term social and political trends.
- Overlapping coverage should be avoided, and each benefit item that is of value to only a few employees or that is of marginal value to many employees should be earmarked for review and possible discontinuance.

Administering the Benefit Program

The administration of employee benefits is an extremely time-consuming but critical activity. To a large extent, employee perceptions of benefits are based upon their own experiences. Therefore, ongoing administration, informing employees about benefits, and monitoring the program to prevent abuses are all critical elements of effective administration.

Ongoing administration requires a considerable amount of work. This is particularly true for some items of insured benefits, such as health insurance. In these cases, claims must be examined, processed, and paid, all of which is time-consuming and costly.

How ongoing administration is handled is also vital to the success of the employee benefit program. Handling a heavy load of claims is anything but routine. Interpretations of cases to determine whether a claim is covered are regularly required. Those who process claims must make sure they are only paying claims that are justified. They must also make sure that employees receive what they are entitled to, even if through some administrative error they do not make a claim for the benefit payment.

To a large extent, what is paid, how it is paid, and how the payments are communicated are how the benefit program is perceived by employees. When employees have an illness, for instance, and they submit a claim, that is when they understand the kind of benefit protection they have. How well the claim is handled and sometimes how timely it is processed can have a great impact upon the employee's perception of benefits.

Information about the benefit program may be communicated in a number of ways. Most companies prepare booklets describing key benefit items, particularly insured benefits, which are distributed to all employees. Employee benefit booklets must be written in the language of the reader, not in technical language that is incomprehensible to most employees. At the other extreme, some companies have tried to make comic books out of their employee benefit handbooks. This approach does not help effective communication either, and it may create the impression that the company is talking down to the people who work in the company.

Many companies also give their employees annual benefit statements. These are often prepared by a computer. They itemize in detail the value of each element of benefit to the employee at that time. This tends to put dollar values on the benefits in the package.

However, putting information in writing does not ensure that it is communicated. Employees may or may not read the handbook. Even if they read it, the information will not be retained for very long, as many studies have shown.

Companies frequently have meetings in which members of the personnel department explain benefits. They may make special announcements about changes in employee benefits or important developments or precedents in employee benefit cases. Some companies provide periodic briefings for managers so they can keep employees informed. Still other companies make sure that employees can contact the benefits department directly for answers to their questions.

Communicating the benefit program is also largely dependent on what happens when a benefit claim is submitted. A single claim that is handled poorly or in an unfair manner becomes known to everyone. Proper and timely handling of these matters and questions that may occur when specific cases are raised or issues presented will tend to create a general understanding of and a good attitude toward the employee benefit program, even though most employees would still not know specific details about all aspects of the program.

Communicating employee benefits is a continuing process. It is best handled in the normal procedures for communicating with all employees in the company.

In communications, generally, the employer must function above all as a quick responder and an accurate transponder. When an employee has a question, he has a reasonable right to know the answer, and the answer should be given quickly and accurately.

With computer communications technology, companies can build expert systems with respect to hundreds of technical issues of benefits. Personnel generalists in every company location can have access to this information, and then personnel generalists can become benefit experts.

There will always be some people who try to abuse employee benefits. They will try to take advantage of benefit provisions, and some may even submit false claims. It is the basic objective of the administrators who process the claims to make sure they are no improper claims. These simply add to the cost and, therefore, detract from future benefit provisions for all employees.

There are some benefit items that are particularly subject to abuse. One example is sick leave. As noted, some employees tend to think that sick-leave days represent an earned right, and they take time off whether they are sick or not. However, this issue is like tardiness or absenteeism. It is a matter of company discipline. Discipline may seem like a harsh notion. The fact of the matter is, however, that those who abuse provisions such as sick leave are taking away from others. If there were no abuse of sick-leave days, then more sick-leave days could be granted—days that might be needed by those who are actually sick.

Thus those who abuse the provisions of a benefit program are really doing so at a cost to their fellow workers. All employees understand this. They also know who is abusing such benefits. Under the proper circumstances, peer pressure can be part of the overall control of the employee benefit program.

Health Care Cost Containment

Starting in the late 1970s, it became clear that health care costs were escalating faster than payroll costs. This was partly due to increased operating costs in the health care industry, especially the compensation costs in hospitals. Also, however, the quality of medical care was improving rapidly, so some of the increase in costs for health care was for better health care. Much of the advances in medical care, in turn, required more expensive medical research, and more expensive facilities and equipment were required.

By 1980, the rate of health care costs was increasing at twice the rate of salary costs. If nothing was done, health care costs would exceed salary payroll costs before the 21st century. Something was done: Many companies worked hard on benefit cost containment.

In a period of about ten years, a dozen health care cost containment actions had been evolved, and each had been implemented in some companies. Here are the dozen health care cost containment areas that may be considered:*

1. *Benefit reductions.* Companies are looking particularly at benefits that are applied to a few; where the services provided are nonessential; and where there is a high cost for benefits received.

2. *Involve employees in the selection process.* This approach assumes that if employees are involved in the selection of the benefits they will value more the benefits received and be more inclined to take initia-

---

*These are reported only for consideration and information. Some doubt whether some of these items really represent cost containment, and I am one of the doubters.

tives to control costs when they can. The involvement in the selection process might be as informal as inputs from location personnel people to formal focus opinion surveys.

3. *Flexible benefits.* Those who have adopted flexible benefit programs claim that their experience shows substantially better control of costs and somewhat reduced benefit costs.

4. *Employee contributions.* Some companies that have never required employee contributions to benefits have instituted them. Others have increased the level of employee contributions. Financially, of course, this act directly represents a benefit cost containment action. However, the thinking is also that if employees pay part of the cost of the benefits, they will exercise restraints in the use of benefits and exercise cost containment when they can. Some employers have focused employee contributions on benefits for dependents; a course of action I favor highly.

5. *Limitation of employer contribution.* An example here would be where a company freezes the amount of benefits as a percentage of current salary. The freeze is usually at the current level. Benefit costs will not be allowed to rise above that proportion of salary.

6. *Deductibles.* In 1980, about one in ten health care plans had front-end deductibles, and today two-thirds of all plans have them. This means that employees pay some of the up-front cost, and this represents another shifting of the cost of health care to the employee.

7. *Establish two-tier benefit programs.* There are two approaches that have been used here. One is to establish a core plan and a high-level plan. The core plan might be the current plan. The higher- level plan might be somewhat more generous, but it would also require employee contributions. A second approach is to maintain the benefit plan in existence for current employees but adopt a less generous benefit program for new hires.

8. *More effective management of providers.* Companies do this through supporting hospitals with lower costs; by preferred physician lists; and by supporting various new delivery systems in medicine, such as the storefront medical practice.

9. *More effective buying habits.* Some companies have reported substantial opportunities, including pressure on current providers or shopping for lower prices.

10. *Share cost savings with employees.* There are a number of ways in which companies are doing this. One is to have a policy of a higher employee contribution for benefits where there is preapproved hospitalization. In this case, emergencies are considered to be preapproved. There is also greater employer contribution when the employees purchase generic drugs or when they use outpatient care instead of hospital care.

11. *Affirmative support of legislative actions to control costs.* Companies feel that this should be on a low-key basis. They recognize, however, that future costs of benefits are influenced by the level of benefits to

be provided. Limitations on malpractice suits would also tend to be a legislative action that would reduce benefit costs in the future. Licensing paramedics or permitting nurses to perform certain medical services that they are fully qualified to do would be another legislative act that would lower benefit costs.

12. *Wellness programs.* Companies have adopted a variety of wellness programs. Some send newsletters to employees that help them manage their family's health better. Others have established employee assistance programs where, for example, there is an 800 number to help employees deal with problems such as alcohol and drugs. Some have refunded money spent by employees for specific programs; for example, to stop smoking. Others have included self-help articles in their company periodicals.

While that seems like an impressive list, at least 90 percent of all cost savings have been achieved so far by employers shifting costs to employees: by greater deductibles and by greater employee contributions. Some of the balance of cost containment involves management people in medical decisions, and that is cause for major concern.

If it were not for cost-containment measures that have been implemented, premiums in 1990 would be eight times what they were in 1975, the last full year before any benefit cost-containment actions were developed. Nevertheless, the employer's premium is still about four times the 1975 figure. Net of inflation, health care costs almost doubled in the past 15 years, although much of that was for better health care, and a significant part of the rest was because health care payees must pay for nonpayees.

Most of the containment of the employer's health care cost has been by getting employees to pay more and by reducing services. Most of the potential in these areas has been achieved. Now, future health care cost containment must come from plan redesign; withholding or allocating health care, particularly from nonpayees, and some system of rationing high-cost medical treatment. These will be very difficult cost-containment methods.

It may no longer be sufficient just to "contain" benefits. Health care costs in large companies now average close to 15 percent of payroll. Benefit costs have escalated to the point in many companies where there is also a need to reduce benefit costs.

If your company considers benefit cost reduction, recognize that you face some difficult issues. Here are some guidelines to follow. You won't do all these things, but you should consider all of them.

• With respect to benefits of all types, make sure that coverage involves matters of absolute need in terms of insured benefits and that it reflects strong employee preferences. If companies are having difficulties containing health care and retirement costs or managing the risks of these costs, then surely one way to do it is to restrict benefits to the *essentials*. Eliminate the frill benefits, such as routine dental work and eye care. Eliminate benefits such as legal aid, psychiatric care, and cosmetic surgery.

• All employee benefits with a dollar cost expenditure should involve employee contributions. Employees should contribute to every insured benefit. It should be known up-front that the same fixed proportion of costs between the employer and the employee will be continued, as it is with respect to employer-employee contributions to Social Security. The fixed proportion may vary, of course, with different insured benefits.

• Consider a much higher employee contribution for dependent coverage; or have employees pay the full cost of this coverage. Let employees know that the overall costs for health care must be limited and that company-paid dependent coverage is preferenced treatment for some employees and discrimination against others.

• Never design a benefit or any provision of a benefit to take advantage of legal provisions or accounting rules. Benefits involve costly expenditures and compensation items that are in place not to save taxes or to meet accounting rules but to provide values to employees. The goals are fairness to employees and competitiveness for the employer. Furthermore, tax laws change regularly, and accounting rules are just a method of counting.

Much of the health care costs borne by employers are due to the fact that their expenditures are tax deductible, and many benefits would not exist if these expenditures were not treated favorably from a tax point of view.

• There should be absolute equivalency of benefits at all levels and in all jobs. No benefit or perquisite of any kind should be extended to one group of employees unless it is necessary because of clear and compelling competitive needs or because it plainly contributes to more effective work by those in that group. The test of the competitive need should be the labor market, not necessarily what other companies do. A test of fairness should also be its perception by employees.

• Consider two-tier health plans. One plan would be typical of generous health coverage plans in industry today. The second should be a bare-bones health care plan with large deductions.

Determination of the benefit package should first be based upon employee preference. If an employee chooses the lower-tiered plan, that's what he should participate in, regardless of any employer criteria for selection. Many employees will chose the lower tiered plan because they contribute to the cost of the plan.

Employer criteria for selection should simply state that those who are in the top-tier health care plan should be good health risks and meet *all* the following requirements:

- They should be nonsmokers.
- They should be within plus or minus 20 percent of their normal weight.
- They should be only social drinkers.
- They should not use drugs.

With respect to each of these items, persons should sign an affidavit expressing a willingness to be tested in any of these areas. This should involve a physical examination. It should include random drug testing.

- There is need for some basic thinking in attitudes about benefits. It's not clear why the cost of health care alone from among all personal expenses was determined to be tax deductible by the government, and why health care has been a matter of special concern by employers. Employers don't have house-purchase plans or food-purchase plans for employees. Sometimes the assumption is that the purchase of health care insurance is an entitlement.

- Benefits should exclude payments of any kind that are traceable directly to an individual's lifestyle preference or when the activity that causes illness is illegal. Examine such illnesses carefully, and then seek other ways to eliminate health care costs caused voluntarily because of personal habits or personal lifestyle preferences.

- The benefit system should be as simple as possible. Major efforts should be made to simplify benefit systems for the purpose of understanding as well as cost reduction.

- Never provide choices for employees in benefit packages of any kind unless the employees themselves are qualified to make the choices, and have information available to help them make informed judgments.

- Develop better information with respect to various benefit systems. For example, with computer technology, it should be practical to develop models that show values and costs of alternate insured benefit systems.

- Be sure you have an accurate and quick-response communication system. Cut back to an absolute minimum the communication about benefits. But make sure that when an employee has a question, it is answered accurately and immediately.

You should have a total benefit cost control approach, not just health care cost containment. If you do this, then you consider the cost and value of all benefits. If basic health care benefits are better, because of improved medical practices, and health care costs increase for various reasons, then perhaps a company should reduce dental coverage or eliminate legal counseling.

You can't compare total pay with other companies for reasons outlined earlier in this book, but a company can measure its own total pay and track total pay over a period of time. The mix will vary, but one goal of any company should be to maintain total payroll costs as a portion of total costs and as a portion of revenues. When you view benefit costs in this way, the trend of the past 20 years has not been bad in most companies.

Some Basic Thinking About Benefits

The past two years have required many who work in human resources management to allocate far more time on employee benefits and the management of employee benefits. My agenda was filled with this work, and the work was often done in sessions for a number of employers to get required work done with a reasonable use of my time. There was so much interest in this work that it had to be done, and it often had to be done in groups.

I was especially well-suited for this work because I am not an actuary, don't sell insurance, and am not a technical benefits person. Therefore, my thinking was directed at substantive issues, and I had nothing to defend. That's important today because management must forget the technical trivia and ignore the plain vanilla answers. Health care particularly, but benefits generally, requires some substantive policy reviews.

The time has passed for thinking that benefit problems will go away. The time has come to recognize that there were many reasons why benefits were added until they got out of control. There are many who contributed to the benefit mess, including unions and health care institutions. Much of the blame, however, must be placed on the managers of big companies and those who did employee benefit consulting.

For many years, large companies had a competitive advantage in the labor marketplace. They often paid more; for many years it was fashionable to pay at the 75th percentile. But the big companies almost always provided big benefits. Now the big companies must scale back their benefits; and, in fact, most of the benefit cost containment work has had to be done in the big companies.

The government has not scaled back benefits. In fact, benefits and pensions for government employees are much higher than is typical in business, and there has been no cost containment in health care costs of government workers. It's time to start benefit cost containment in the government.

I have no suggestions to offer with respect to curbing the enthusiasm of consultant-salespersons. However, the problem is particularly acute where there is legally-required actuarial work to do and the people who do it also recommend benefit plan design. Then the difference between what is legally required and what is right is often unclear.

One thing seems to be very clear; managers must change their mind-set. Benefits are definitely not fringes. They can no longer be thought of as something extra that employees would like and that won't cost the company very much.

Benefits must now be viewed as an alternate form of compensation. If you're thinking of adding a benefit that costs ten cents an hour, then you are deciding that you will not increase salaries by ten cents an hour. Similarly, if you save money by benefit cost reduction, then you should be thinking about using that money to increase salaries.

We must also change our definition of benefits. There are now seven definitions of benefits in my dictionary, and I would like to add an eighth:

> Employee benefits are a part of compensation, paid for work done, and designed to provide income or expense reimbursement in cases of major personal crises or difficulties that would not be available on a reasonable basis to an individual person.

Companies must stop regulating the breakdown of pay for those who work in the company and substituting unnecessarily the judgment of management or experts as to what employees should want as contrasted to what employees do want. In some respects, companies are playing the same bureaucratic, centralist role for employees in things like type of benefit coverage as the federal government. Above all, employers must stop favoring some employees over other employees. Obviously, they should be particularly alert to making decisions that might be perceived as favoring themselves. Company plans must stop all favoritism in benefit plan design.

Recognize that cash compensation is the ultimate benefit. Cash compensation is the totally flexible benefit. A dollar of cash can be used for health care, sick leave, maternity benefits, retirement, or to meet current income needs. If there has ever been any inclination in the minds of managers to do good things for employees, stop it. Give them the cash and let them do good things for themselves.

I urge benefit cost reductions. I urge dramatic benefit cost reductions. My purpose, however, is not cost savings. My purpose is to straighten out the benefit mess, and I always urge companies to take the savings and put them into salaries. In the long run, that will represent cost savings because salaries are escalating less rapidly than health care costs.

Employers must recognize that company health care benefits have created a preferred class of citizen in this country. Many politicians and others find it an unacceptable situation that some big corporate employees have every benefit and those who are in other areas of employment are barred from having certain types of benefits at all. The days of preferential benefits must end. In fact, it may be too late already; national health insurance in some manner seems to be inevitable, mostly because of the unfairness of the present system.

Expect that benefits will continue to increase for some time in the future. The increase in health care costs is a part of the basic changes that are occurring in our society.

Our economy is moving from one of agriculture and industry to one of agriculture, industry, and personal care. The personal care business includes a broad variety of specific areas relating to taking better care of one's self and having a good time. This new business area includes health care, education, entertainment, recreation, travel, and leisure.

Health care costs will increase because health care will get better. We want to live longer and feel better. That costs more money. In my planning model, I predict that health care costs alone will grow to 25 percent of compensation and will then level off; and that noncash compensation will reach almost 50 percent by the 21st century.

Chapter Thirteen

Retirement Plans

Retirement plans have become a major issue during the same period of time that health care cost containment became an issue and for some of the same reasons. Thousands of pension plans have been cancelled since 1980. Many millions of workers have found that the pensions they thought they had no longer exist or the value of their retirement benefits is far less. For some, the pension dream has become a nightmare. It is time for many companies to rethink the issues of retirement pay plans.

The Superannuation Problem

The purpose of retirement plans is to provide a stream of income to employees when they are too old to continue to work. The purpose of retirement income is to provide income to the superannuated employee.

The problem of the superannuated employee has existed since the beginning of time. People have always aged, and with increasing age, their economic productivity—their ability to produce—has declined. As that productivity declined to the point where they consume more than they produce, the superannuation problem came into existence.

What should we do with the superannuated worker? That is the question that employers or, in the case of the self-employed, friends and relatives have always asked. The answers that have evolved from varying situations have taken various forms. In general, however, these solutions have taken the following four basic alternative forms:

1. The worker is permitted to continue on active employment, in spite of the fact that he produces less than he earns.
2. He is abandoned to shift for himself as best as he can.
3. He is supported by a formal plan.
4. He is supported by an informal plan.

As applied to the modern business situation, this means that the worker is retained on the payroll, is discharged after his useful life has passed, or is retired, either on an informal basis or under a formal retirement plan.

Actually, then, it has never been a question of whether to meet the problem of the superannuated employee but how. The first two ''solutions'' noted above are, in fact, no solutions at all, but rather represent attempts to avoid completely the responsibility of meeting the problem. While the discharge of workers whose economic usefulness has declined below their income is still practiced in some places in our modern society, it is certainly not condoned either as a proper social attitude or as a profitable personnel policy.

Keeping employees on the company's active payroll is also an unsatisfactory situation. When the worker's ability to produce declines, as it surely will in later years, the problem must be met. Either the employer reduces the worker's pay in relation to declining productivity or he pays the worker more than he produces. The former procedure has obvious handicaps and would certainly produce more personnel problems than it would solve. Employee dissatisfaction throughout the company is bound to result in any attempt to reduce the worker's pay as he reaches old age. An alternative solution that is sometimes tried is equally unsatisfactory. This procedure involves transferring the older worker to an easier and lower-paying job. If there are enough such easy jobs available throughout the company, the system is little if any better than merely reducing the worker's salary and is certainly a more complex procedure.

Informal retirement systems were a step in the right direction when first adopted many years ago, but, of course, they represent no assured basis for retirement. The informal system was often highly selective and, therefore, arbitrary, personal, and discretionary.

Formal retirement programs emerged at the beginning of the 20th century. Of course, there was a great impetus to the development of these plans with the passage of the Social Security Act, which is itself a formal retirement plan.

Sources of Retirement Income

There has been a three-tiered philosophy regarding retirement income in this country since the 1930s. This is illustrated in Figure 13–1 by the

Figure 13-1. Sources of Retirement Income.

The retirement triangle

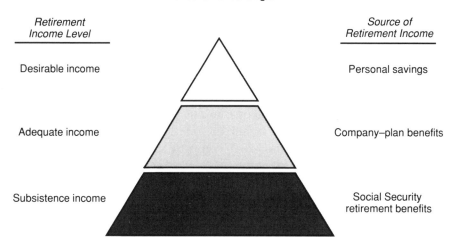

Retirement Income Level		Source of Retirement Income
Desirable income		Personal savings
Adequate income		Company–plan benefits
Subsistence income		Social Security retirement benefits

The concept of retirement income that emerged in the 1930s was a three-tiered system, illustrated in this exhibit.

''retirement triangle.'' Social Security or other government-supported systems were available for most workers and were designed to provide income at retirement to provide for minimum living standards; for example, a poverty threshold for retired persons. The second tier was to come from company retirement programs. Company retirement benefits, when combined with Social Security benefits, were designed to be sufficient to provide an income at retirement that would be sufficient for living in decency and comfort. Companies aimed at combined benefits of about 50 percent of salary at the time of retirement from their company retirement programs and Social Security. Then it was thought that workers themselves, through their savings, would add whatever income was possible to achieve the style of retirement living they chose and could afford.

All three elements of this three-tiered retirement philosophy have problems. Social Security problems have been greatly publicized and need more attention. It's also common knowledge, particularly among our young people, that it is increasingly difficult to save: many find it impossible even to acquire the capital to make their first home purchase. Private retirement plans are now also in deep trouble in many companies.

Not everyone agrees on the proper role of these three sources of retirement income. Some think that it is the responsibility of the federal government to assume the entire burden of retirement income; others feel that employer-sponsored pension plans are the proper source of retirement income; and there are still many who believe that it is the responsibility of the individual and that individual's family to provide for future retirement needs.

With changing conditions and changing values, it is necessary for compensation professionals to understand the history of pensions and the source of retirement income. Company pension issues need to be evaluated in the context of this three-tier retirement strategy, which has dominated pension thinking and pension plan design for over 50 years. In strategizing about retirement income issues, it's necessary to recognize the existence of three sources of retirement income in this country and that each of the sources of retirement income, including your company's plan, is vulnerable to great change. Therefore, your company's retirement plan must be evaluated in the context of the future of Social Security and the likelihood of employees having funds for retirement income supplements. There are major issues and questions about all three sources of retirement income.

Social Security Issues

We can all be certain that Social Security will be in effect for some time, certainly as long as the current political environment is maintained. You can count on Social Security existing, and you can count on Social Security providing a portion of retirement income for all covered employees. However, there are some major problems and questions about future retirement payments from Social Security.

Some call it Social Security insurance, but it isn't insurance at all. Social Security isn't insured; nor is it trusteed. Money is essentially paid out of the current national output with payments from current workers made into the system. In some years, payments to retirees exceed payments from current workers, and then money must be drawn from a reserve fund. In other years, payments from workers exceed those paid to retirees, and money goes into the reserve fund. The reserve fund is small compared to payments made each year. Therefore, the basic financing of retirement income from Social Security is on a pay-as-you-go basis, and payments are made by those currently working. There is nothing assured for the future except the promises of politicians.

Payments made into Social Security by current workers for the benefit of retired workers are a tax. Social Security "contributions" are a legally required tax on current workers for the retirement income of those not working, and current workers far outnumber the voting constituency of the retired. That always leaves retirement benefits in a vulnerable position.

Social Security is a compulsory system. No one can choose to be in Social Security or not to be in Social Security. You are in Social Security or you are in jail.

One reason why Social Security payments must be compulsory is that few of the working people who pay the cost of the program would choose to be in the program. Some say that working people wouldn't choose to be in Social Security because they are irresponsible; they would take the cash now in favor of possible future pensions. When you are in income classes 1 and 2, there are great pressures to meet current needs. Those families earning below the national average of $26,000 a year have difficulty deferring payments for future needs. For them, the future is now.

The fact is that a logical person who works all his life would not be in the program simply because he would know, if informed, that if he put in half the after-tax money he had actually contributed to Social Security, he would get far more money out,* and the payments would be insured, payable to himself upon retirement or, in the event of death before retirement, to his survivors and heirs.

Social Security retirement payments are highly favorable to some persons and, therefore, necessarily highly unfavorable to others. Benefit payments are not geared to pay and total years of service. The Social Security payment formula discriminates against those who work full time for their entire adult working lives.

Social Security retirement funds are ample at the current time (1989), but there have been periods in recent history where there was concern that the fund would run out of money and additional funds would have to come from general taxation. I predict that before the 21st century the Social Security reserve fund will face depletion again and there will again be a need to raise the employee and employer contributions significantly, or increase the earnings base that is taxed, or take money out of general tax revenues.

The Social Security system is far more than retirement income. It was designed to provide retirement benefits, but now funds are used for many purposes. There isn't any reason to think that they may not be used for additional purposes in the future. It is now a broad social payments system. Retirement income may be the driving force of the system, but there are other objectives that are becoming more important.

Finally, we have an aging population. With improved health care and greater wellness, every projection shows a continued aging population. The average life expectancy of those born in 1990 will be about 75, and sometime in the 21st century, the average life expectancy will be 100. By that time, each working head of a household will likely pay for at least one-half the Social Security benefits of a retired person, and the working taxpayer may not be willing to do this. Actually, early in the 21st century,

---

*A middle-level income worker (income class 2) who worked full time starting at age 20 could retire at fully salary at age 55 if contributions went into a private pension fund instead of Social Security.

each two working people will support their own families plus a nonworker and the nonworker's family, and many of the nonworkers will be drawing Social Security.

Workers versus nonworkers will be a major problem of the next decade and will have to be resolved early in the 21st century. It's hard to see how it can be resolved without Social Security cost containment. If that happens, the primary point of containment will be to keep increases in retirement benefits less than wage inflation.

Private Retirement Plans

The substantive and technical issues of company pension plans will be covered later in this chapter. But note that private companies' pension systems are now based upon tax shelters. Ninety-nine percent of all pension plans are tax sheltered; which means that employees covered pay taxes only at retirement and the employer deducts such costs as business expenses. This means, in turn, that all working people subsidize the costs of private pension plans, whether or not they are covered by a private pension plan themselves.

It's not likely that the majority of voters, who subsidize those who are the beneficiaries of tax-advantaged pensions, will cause political pressure to eliminate private pensions. What is likely is that tax subsidization of the private pensions of others will become a major fairness issue. This would likely lead to a continuing erosion in the values of private pension plans, mostly by regulatory actions, more plan cancellations, and further reductions in the number of persons covered by private pension plans.

Personal Savings

Personal savings are a source of retirement income, but that also has changed since the original concept of three-tiered retirement income evolved in the 1930s. Most importantly, both the income and net worth of the American people has been polarizing.

The number of people who are in high-paid jobs has been increasing, but similarly the number of those who are in low-paid jobs has also been increasing. Obviously, middle-income positions have been relatively declining. Partly because of this, there is a greater disparity in the capacity of workers at different levels to save money for retirement purposes. There are increasing numbers of high-paid persons who can save for their own retirement needs without help from company retirement plans or Social Security. There are also increasing numbers of low-paid persons who can't save at all; and most aren't covered by any private pension plan.

There is a new generation of adults, many of whom are workers with inherited wealth. One-quarter of all working families stands to inherit estates in excess of $100,000. At the other extreme, there are those with no net worth at all. Thus, while the average American family has a net worth of something over $35,000, there are great differences in this amount—many having a great deal and many having nothing.

In an oversimplified manner, the result is that there are increasing numbers of employees who simply don't need company retirement plans or Social Security retirement benefits to provide them with retirement income. At the same time, there is a large portion of the working population that has no private retirement plan and no savings.

Finally, the government has institutionalized private pension plans through Keoghs and Individual Retirement Accounts (IRAs). Under these plans, even the self-employed and those who work for companies without private pensions can have tax-deferred contributions to funds for retirement; and there are many investment firms that will handle these accounts. These IRAs and Keoghs aren't likely to be canceled or disqualified in the future. They're popular with voters. They also ease the burden on private retirement plans.

Essential Features of Private Retirement Plans

There are many types of private plans, and most of them are complex. If you get into the technical aspects of pensions, you could write a book.*

For compensation professionals and human resources management generalists, the essential part of pension plans involves the basis for payment of retirement benefits, other benefits paid to retirees from accumulated funds, and methods of funding. Payment methods are particularly vital because the compensation professional should be the expert on this subject.

Essentially, there are deferred contribution plans and defined benefit plans. With respect to defined benefit plans, the method of accruing pension benefits may be prescribed by a flat amount of benefits for each year of covered service or a percentage of earnings for each year of service. The percentage of earnings plans, in turn, can be based on every year of service or on a prescribed number of years, such as the average earnings of the last five years prior to retirement.

With inflation, the flat rate of pensions is usually increased from time to time. Then flat benefit pension plans are not greatly different from a defined benefit plan based upon career earnings. A final pay plan will provide higher benefits in a period of inflation, assuming the same accrual rate. Over the past thirty years, assuming the same accrual rate, employ-

---

*In fact, I did write such a book in 1953: *A Survey of Pension Planning,* Commerce Clearing House, Chicago, Illinois.

ees, on average, would have received twice as much in pension benefits from a final five-year fixed benefit plan than from a career pay based plan. High-paid persons and upwardly mobile employees would have done much better under final pay retirement plans than under career pay defined benefit plans.

In the flat payment defined benefit plan, all employees are treated equally. Under career earnings defined benefit plans, retirement income pay relationships are about the same as pay relationships of earned income during a working life. In final pay defined benefit plans, the rate of pay increases during working careers is a major determinant of pension costs. In all cases, length of service is a proportional determinant of pension benefits.

Flat benefit plans provide a specific benefit and a known cost. The benefit and cost are the same for all employees.

In defined benefit plans based on career earnings, the same percentage of earnings rather than amount of benefits accrues to all employees each year of service. Benefits and costs are proportional to earnings.

A defined benefit plan geared to final pay assures a retirement income standard at retirement for employees with equal years of service. However, the cost of the plan is open-ended. Essentially, defined contribution plans control costs each year in a prescribed manner. Then the benefits an employee will receive will not be known, although they can be estimated.

Financial persons usually have direct accountability for the method of financing and the management of funds. In pensions, however, fund management and demographics of the work force as well as plan design affect costs. Human resources management professionals should have an interest in and some accountability for these broad management matters.

Problems With Private Retirement Plans

There are many problems of private retirement plans that have emerged over the years. There wasn't any single circumstance or any one event that caused the problems of private pension plans. There were many factors that occurred over a long period of time. The result for some employees is a serious problem. Every company should review its private pension plan and monitor that plan closely in future years. Outlined below are some of the principal issues of private pension plans.

Imprudent Risks

Some types of private retirement plans involve risks that are not acceptable for the prudent employer. Final pay based fixed benefits plans represent an unacceptable risk.

In final pay benefit pension formulas, future inflation must be applied retroactively to all the years of employment. In a period of double-digit inflation, the funds required to finance retirement benefits could double every five years. In periods of high inflation and a declining stock market, the pension payment obligation could have a devastating impact on company profits or losses.

It is likely that there will be periods of high inflation or much higher inflation. It's possible that there will be double-digit inflation again as there was in 1974, 1979, 1980, and 1981. Calculate the financial impact of 11.7 percent compounded inflation (the average of 1978–1981) for five years and for ten years on your company's pension obligations. Under such conditions, a final pay plan could wipe out profits altogether, and in many cases could put a firm into bankruptcy. That seems to be an imprudent risk.

Remember that it is the upwardly mobile person and senior managers who alone benefit from final pay plans. For all others, the benefit formula could be adjusted from time to time, considering pay inflation, financial conditions, and pension objectives.

Fixed-contribution retirement plans limit financial risks to the amount contributed each year, and there is enough flexibility in the funding requirements to pay more in years of high profits and less in poor years, or none at all. Fixed-contribution plans do a great deal for the problem of financial management, but they have no clear value in retirement benefits. Of course, the future is uncertain for any person, and this inability to put a future specific retirement income number on a piece of paper never was of great value.

Vesting

During the 1980s, vesting of private plans was reduced twice by legislation. Until 1983, the matter of vesting was an issue of plan design without limitation. In fact, most plans required at least twenty-five years of continuous service before any employee had the right to start collecting pension benefits at the prescribed retirement age (which was almost always age 65). Now, vesting is five years. This has been a major change in pension plans.

Shorter vesting increases the cost of pensions, because unvested amounts contributed for employees who leave the employment of the firm remain in the funds of the pension plan. Reduction of vesting from twenty-five to five years will often increase the cost of pensions by 50 percent.

Short vesting also means no retention power in pension plans. One of the reasons companies incurred the cost of pensions was that they had retention value. With five-year vesting, there are no golden handcuffs in private pension plans any more.

Short vesting also means that pensions are no longer a benefit for company employees. Pensions are benefits provided by a number of employers, each of whom contributes to the retirement income of a person after he is too old to work. In the future, most persons who draw pensions from a company's pension plan will have been employees for only a few years.

There is logic for shorter vesting. When Social Security laws were first passed in the 1930s, the average employee worked for one company for about 20 years, based on sketchy data that was then available. By 1980, the average length of service had fallen to less than ten years. By 1986, that number had become six years and is still declining. This meant that unless vesting was lowered, fewer workers would collect under any pension plan.

With average tenure for any employee continuing to decline, expect full portability before many years. Full portability and the impact of inflation on final pay based fixed benefit retirement plans mean that many pension plans are simply obsolete and must be replaced.

The full impact of these factors has not been obvious in much of the 1980s because of low rates of inflation and the fact that the long-term increase in the stock market helped to increase the value of pension funds. Any future period of high inflation or a free-fall in the stock market, or both, will cause severe funding problems for many of the remaining pension plans and could cause severe financial problems for any business.

Regulatory Problems

Regulatory problems have also increased. Even if you don't take sides on the matter of the need for greater regulation, the costs of compliance are more of a factor in pension planning. The issues of regulatory reporting and compliance are particularly troublesome to smaller employers and have, in fact, led to the cancellation of thousands of pension plans, particularly by smaller companies.

There have been many reasons for regulation. With so many people involved, the temptation for theft, fraud, or misconduct is very great. Money in pension plans must be protected as much as the funds in savings and loan associations.

Some financing transactions need to be regulated. There have been takeovers of businesses just because pensions were overfunded. Companies and unions have been guilty of investing pension money in pet schemes that lacked sufficient merit so that commercial investment funds were not available.

The problem with regulation is the burden of administration. That burden is particularly onerous for small companies. The cost of compliance can equal the amount of company contributions in some plans. Either regulations must be greatly simplified or the result will lead to more cancellations of private pension plans.

Indexing Pensions for Retirees

An emerging problem of pension plans is the increasing pressure to index benefits for retirees. The need for increases in retirement income for those already retired, particularly during periods of rapid inflation, is considerable. Those companies that set out to provide private retirement benefits that, combined with Social Security, would provide retirement income of 50 percent of income found that many of their retirees were not doing nearly that well in terms of any measure of real income.

For example, if you set a pension benefit that would meet the poverty level of $10,000 a year today and inflation was only 5 percent a year, within five years your pensions would achieve only 75 percent of poverty; in ten years, it would be little less than 60 percent, and in twenty years, the retirement income would be about one-third the poverty level.

Many companies have, in fact, taken the initiative from time to time with respect to the income of retired persons and increased the benefits of their retirees. Some had a strong feeling when they did this that they were obligated to "their employees." This has been viewed by some as a precedent to require future indexing.

Social Security benefits are indexed to the consumer price index, and that establishes a precedent for increasing retirement pay under private pension plans whenever the "cost of living" increases.* There is a real probability that by the year 2000 employers will be required by law to index benefits for retirees.

If you combine the costs and risks of inflation in final pay plans, indexing of benefits, full portability, and greater regulatory costs and risks, you have many reasons for rethinking your private pension plan. It is a complex and gloomy subject. But it is an issue that cannot be avoided for much longer in any company.

An Aging Population

In addition, people are living longer, and, therefore, there are more retirees. The ratio of retired to working employees is increasing and has reached 50 percent in some companies. For companies in high-technology

---

*It is worth noting that retired persons who are drawing Social Security are the largest group of persons who have been immunized from increases in the cost of living. Under these conditions, the large and growing block of retired voters has no vested interest in controlling inflation. The nonworker component, which is retired, is privileged over workers who are paying for those benefits.

businesses with high levels of automation, it is possible that retirement payments each year will exceed payroll by the year 2000.

In the 1930s, the average life expectancy was age sixty-five, and life expectancy was about thirteen and a half years at that age. Today, those who reach age sixty-five have an average life expectancy of over twenty years. So we have more people reaching retirement age, and they live almost twice as long after retirement.

Voluntary Retirement

It is illegal to force a person to retire at any set age or date. A person is free to voluntarily retire at any time. An employee cannot be forced to retire unless his work is unsatisfactory.

Pension plans may stop accruing benefits at a specified normal retirement age. This encourages employees to retire but they cannot be forced to retire.

A person must literally be fired for ineffective work, not age alone. But as anyone over age fifty can tell you, a person doesn't get too old to work at a point in time or on a given day. So proving that a person is not able to perform rather than that he is just old is very difficult and, for a valued long-service employee, very unpleasant. Yet additional financial inducements to retirement at a planned retirement age are costly and have their own set of uncertainties and risks. So voluntary retirement is another issue of private pension plans.

Data show that significant numbers of employees are choosing to work beyond age sixty-five, although a vast majority still pick the ''normal'' retirement date, partly because more retirement benefits and higher Social Security benefits are not accrued by a person who elects to work past age sixty-five.

At the same time, however, increasing numbers of employees—particularly high-paid managerial and professional employees—are electing to retire before ''normal'' retirement age.*

The issues of voluntary retirement are often a matter of point of view. But one thing is clear: Voluntary retirement adds to the complexity of retirement pension planning. It is another reason why companies must rethink their retirement income strategies and, having done that, redo their retirement income plans. There may still be some uncertainties in the future with respect to retirement planning, but there have been enough changes already to chart a new course and set new strategies.

---

*Note that normal retirement age is usually thought to be age sixty-five. This was set as the normal retirement age because in the 1930s, when Social Security was being considered, the average life expectancy for men was age sixty-five.

The Problems

Now add up all the ways private pension plan costs and risks have increased:

- The impact of inflation on fixed benefit plans, particularly final pay based plans
- Shorter vesting
- Regulatory issues
- Pressures to index pensions
- An aging population
- Voluntary retirement

These add up to costs and risks that may be unacceptable. At the very least, these factors must be monitored. Very likely, your company must start to deal with the problems of retirement plan cost containment.

A Rethinking of Private Pension Plans

It's clear that there are plenty of serious problems with retirement plans. There are major issues and problems with all three sources of retirement income plans: Social Security, private retirement plans, and personal savings. The time has come to review and develop new pension policies and strategies.

Start a review by recognizing that some employees don't need your pension plan at all and that others don't need it very much. For many of your employees, your retirement income plan is simply superfluous. All retirees will cash their pension checks, but for many, company retirement income, like Social Security payments, just isn't needed.

Next realize that many of your employees who need your company's pension don't value it very much. It's always been true that young people value pensions less than older workers, but there was reason then to think that many younger employees intended to work with the company for many years until retirement. Now there are shallow roots at work, and few employees think of a career with one company.

One of the substantial employer values of pension plans was that they represented holding power. With five-year vesting, pensions simply do not have any holding power at all, and mandatory full portability will likely be legislated within a few years.

A retirement plan never was a major factor in recruiting employees. Pensions were a major factor in retaining employees as long as there were substantial unvested pension benefits. Now there are few labor market reasons for having a pension plan.

Recognize that a substantial amount of the total cost of pension payments will be for people who did not work for your company for many years prior to their retirement. Similarly, some of those who do work for you at retirement will have worked for your company for only a small part of their working lives. For most who draw benefits from your pension plan, the retirement income from your plan will be a moderate part of their total retirement income.

Pension payments will go mostly to those who worked for your company for a few years—too few years to be regarded as "our employees."

Clearly, retirement benefits have some value, to at least some employees. But for most companies, pensions have seriously diminished in value at the same time that pension costs and risks have escalated greatly.

Use this type of analysis in your own company among your management people. Very likely, you will at least conclude that the type of pension plans that were thought proper only a few years ago are simply not appropriate anymore. Many companies must terminate the company's pension plan in some way. That won't be so unusual; many companies have terminated pension plans.*

It is so hard to come to that conclusion, particularly because it is so out of step with recent traditions. For those who grew up in the brief period of economic history when pensions were accepted as right and necessary,† it is particularly difficult to conclude that pensions in their recent form must be discontinued. But the more the matter is examined, the more clear it is that at least some types of private retirement income plans serve no business purpose that, by any stretch of the imagination, can be justified by the costs and risks that pensions now involve.

A New Retirement Income Strategy

It is still necessary to provide income for retirees. Employers still have the superannuation problem: what to do with an employee who is too old to work. There is still logic in multiple sources of retirement income. In fact, the three-tier retirement income strategy is valid. However, each source of retirement income has changed, and a new retirement income

---

*If you consider acquisitions and business failures in your calculation of private pension plans, then two-thirds of all pension plans that existed in companies with traded stock when the first edition of this book was published do not exist today.

†Prior to 1930, less than 5 percent of all workers in this country were covered by any type of pension, and most pension plans that existed then had payments that were discretionary and financed on a pay-as-you-go basis.

strategy must be developed. There must be a rethinking of retirement income strategies.

Social Security

Social Security funds have been the source of benefits other than retirement benefits. Predictably, the system is strained financially from time to time, and the Social Security tax has to be raised again—and again. With an aging population and the desire for more benefits from Social Security, there will inevitably be financial strains on the system in the future, with more increases in taxes, again and again. The whole system involves current workers supporting former workers, and it essentially involves a political issue as well as an economic issue. All of these considerations suggest that, in the long run, retirement income from Social Security is at risk.

I have often urged that Social Security be split. Part of the new system would involve welfare payments and health-care payments for the elderly. The other would be strictly retirement benefits: a federal retirement system.

My federal retirement income system would be voluntary, although favorable tax treatment and other incentives might be appropriate to encourage savings for retirement. Every worker would be eligible for the retirement system, but no one would be compelled to join. Each person would have an individual account. The plan would be a defined contribution plan. Participants could retire at any age, but if they retired prior to normal retirement age, benefits would be reduced on an actuarial basis.

This plan would be privatized, with government controls and safeguards, but private companies would operate the system and make benefit payments. Funds would be limited to amounts that could be paid from individual accounts. But the only benefits from this system would be retirement benefits.*

My rough calculations show that an employee who worked from age twenty to age sixty-five and contributed less than 2 percent of his wages every year would get a retirement benefit from this federal retirement income program greater than the pension he would now get from Social Security.

In the foreseeable and planable future, Social Security will continue, however, and may still be regarded as the base of the retirement income system. Social Security will continue to provide a level of benefits at the

---

*When first proposed, this plan was attacked as being radical. Yet Keogh and IRA plans were authorized shortly after this plan was proposed.

poverty threshold for retirees, but it is a retirement system that is at risk in the future.

Savings

Personal savings are now the second tier of the three-tiered retirement income strategy. Savings for retirement come from personal savings, including inherited wealth. Savings for retirement also come from tax-advantaged retirement savings plans, including IRAs and Keoghs. These are available to just about every employee. They are all tax-sheltered or, more accurately, tax-deferred. If utilized at all, any of these sources of savings would likely provide a supplement to Social Security payments that would be sufficient to raise the total retirement income of workers to a level of decency and comfort. This source of retirement income is funded and ensured. But such income is not immunized against inflation after retirement by any indexing. For a substantial number of workers in the future (probably more than half), retirement income from this source will be greater than Social Security retirement payments. Then retirement income for all workers who are in class 1 through class 3 will be, at retirement, at about one-half of final pay.*

All employees above income class 1 are likely to have some form of savings for retirement, provided they are informed and make rational decisions. Then these sources can provide substantial amounts, and they are not at risk in any way, other than a national income disaster like runaway inflation.

Private Retirement Plans

Employer retirement income planning should now focus on the third tier of the retirement income triangle. Funds from private employer plans and extra personal savings provide the funds for income above comfort and decency to a desired level of retirement income. These sources provide funds for other estate needs, such as education of children or major illnesses.

Private sources of retirement income under this strategy are flexible. They provide for the needs of workers, not just retirement needs alone. They are extra funds for a variety of purposes; and they may just represent a reserve.

In this role, extra pay plans, rather than the traditional pension plan,

---

*This has been thought to be equivalent to the style of life while working on the assumption that: a retired couple would have no dependents; they would downsize their home and/ or have no house payment costs; there would be no cost of working; and that the cost of their lifestyle in retirement is somehow less than when working.

should be the company-supported source of retirement income. If there are any pension plans at all, they should be defined contribution plans, and the amounts involved should be moderate.

The Future of Private Pension Plans

In 1981 I wrote about the future of pensions in *The Sibson Report*. The essence of that report was that there was no future for pensions. It was an unpopular view at that time, and to many it is still an unpopular view. But this is only a reporting on my part, drawing reasonable conclusions from what has happened.

For many, it may be too much to abandon company pension plans altogether, in spite of reason and facts. Perhaps they are correct, and some form of retirement income should remain. However, moderate company pension plans should be used as a supplement to personal retirement savings (preferably on a contributory basis).

Many companies, particularly smaller firms and those in new business areas, have already made the transition. For some, with sound professional guidance, the change to the new retirement strategy will be natural, logical, and positive.

There are major parts of the work force for whom the transition to the needed new retirement strategy will be very painful. Government pensions are a major problem. Starting with Congress, government workers have always had a very preferred status in pensions and most government officials think there are no cost reasons for changing. For some militant unions, pensions are a religion, and change is unthinkable, even changing to something better. Of course, this resistance to change is also influenced by union control of pension funds. Big corporations are also sometimes reluctant to change to a new retirement strategy. Some who run big corporations in traditional industries find it as difficult to give up pensions as they find it to give up a central bureaucratic management style. But they have cost pressures that will bring about change.

Of the three, government pensions are the biggest issue. Corporations are changing, and unions are continuing to decline. But government gets bigger and more centralized. In this case, the entrenched government pension interests are led by Congress, which makes the rules and has shown a great appetite for high income for itself.

For more than ten years, I have been recommending that companies terminate fixed benefit plans based on any type of final pay formula. I have urged companies to freeze benefit levels in all positions related to retirement, and I have urged a shifting of funds from retirement plans to success-sharing plans. In some cases where there were substantial costs recaptured from retirement plans, money saved was used, at least in part, to finance health care costs.

Pension plans that exist in many companies do not significantly serve business needs and have little value to many employees. In such cases, companies should consider reallocating that pension money to some other purpose.

The most logical place to reallocate pension monies now earmarked for retirement plans would be in extra pay plans that now exist in your firm. Don't add any more pay plans unless necessary.

Consider actions that support employees to provide for their retirement with personal savings in tax-deferred plans. Many companies have adopted 401(k)* plans that are tax-supported individual retirement plans, and they are worth considering. I urge companies to use 401(k)s only if employee participation is broad enough so there is no risk of disqualification: only use the plan for the benefit of all employees if most employees see it as a benefit. Never enrich the plan with employer contributions to entice employees into participating.

In any plan that is adopted, the employee should contribute as a matter of principle. As in the case of health care plans, the contribution should be significant and in a fixed portion in future years with the employer's contribution. In Social Security, the contributions of the employee and the employer are fifty-fifty. It seems reasonable that the same portions of contribution should exist in any company retirement program.

A company with publicly-traded stock might also consider a phantom stock plan as a part of retirement planning. Phantom stock, redeemable only in minimum ten-year periods serially after grant each year, would provide an *opportunity* for a significant estate that among other things could provide a substantial retirement income, provided the company did very well and the stock market had as many up-years as down-years. If financed by matched purchased stock, this benefit would cost nothing other than the net cost of cash, if any.

A Sample Retirement Plan for Consideration

There are many specific plans that might be designed consistent with the features described for the retirement income opportunity plan. Here is one example.

The pension plan I would propose would consist of two parts:

1. Plan A would be a fixed percentage, defined cash contribution plan. The prescribed contributions would be made in individual accounts during

---

*Under these plans, employees defer current pay on a tax-sheltered basis. There are company matching grants that are tax deductible by the company.

each year of employment. They would go into a secure interest-producing but not fixed-value fund. Company contributions would be modest; about 2 percent of compensation. Employees would contribute 50 percent of the cost of this portion of the plan. This could be a 401(k) plan.

2. Plan B would be a fixed percentage, defined contribution phantom stock contribution plan. Stock unit grants would be modest.

Plan A would be a committed cost. But it would be a modest cost and considered mostly as a supplement to personal savings as the second tier of retirement income. A total of 4 percent of payroll each year in this part of the private company retirement plan would be sufficient and provide more income at retirement than Social Security.

For plan A, consider a nonqualified plan; even if you have to make proportionately less contributions. Then require twenty–year vesting. I think the values of an after-tax equivalent nonqualified plan with twenty–year vesting are about the same as a qualified plan with five-year vesting.

Plan B would involve no cost to the company whatsoever, except possibly for the cost of the capital. Phantom stock retirement benefits would potentially have very high benefits. Note that this plan is a nonqualified plan with serial vesting each ten years. This can result in substantial holding power. Two to 4 percent of payroll contributions to plan B would be sufficient.

Never consider indexing any pension benefit for any retiree. For practical business reasons, it is an imprudent and open-ended risk. Cost of living adjustment plans are not reasonable or logical under any circumstances, but in this case the company must also think about the impact on employee attitudes if it is granting COLAs to retired persons without extending such a provision to current workers.

Never extend health-care benefits to retirees. It is very costly. Furthermore, Medicare provides a great deal of coverage, and a variety of Medicare supplements are available. There are great risks in adopting any kind of health-care benefits for retirees; for example, such a course may lead to company-paid nursing home care. Recent accounting changes resulted in substantial charges to earnings for companies with health-care benefits for retirees; a reminder that we should never assume that either tax laws or accounting rules regarding compensation will remain the same in the future.

For many, the notion that the era of traditional pension plans as a widespread and valued element of employee compensation is over will be very hard to accept. It won't be any easier if one points out that pension plans have been a part of economic history and compensation of employees for a very short period of time. It doesn't even help many when they understand that the conditions have changed, and that if there were sound reasons for having pension plans some years ago, few of them exist today. If the questions that led to the adoption of pension plans no longer apply, then pension plans as an answer are simply not relevant.

I have been asked what will happen to people who become too old to work. This, of course, is the question that was asked back in the 1920s and the 1930s when pension plans were first widely adopted in business. It's a very real question that should be answered. Keep in mind, however, that it is a question that was never answered. Only a minority of American workers—those in a few industries and in a few levels of jobs—really benefited from the system of private company retirement plans that has been in effect for about fifty years. Private pension plans that must now be canceled never did solve the problem of superannuation for a vast majority of American workers.

Chapter Fourteen

Operations Workers

Some compensation matters are particularly important in operations-level jobs. In addition, the nature of operations jobs requires that some compensation practices be especially tailored to this group. Furthermore, there are some special issues that are particularly relevant to operations-level positions and those who fill them.

The Operations Job

Compensation policies, in principle, should be the same for all employees. All are contributors, and all should have equal rights and opportunities in work-related matters. Therefore, differences in compensation practices for any group of persons who work in the enterprise should be based only on the nature of the job being performed or competitive requirements. Otherwise, all employees should be treated equivalently with respect to pay, benefits, and conditions of work.

Operations positions do have certain unique job characteristics that require special practices and thinking. One characteristic that must be considered in compensation is that specific things are done in these jobs. Material is cut, machined, or assembled; things are maintained; material is typed; something is processed.

Work in operations is largely done by the employees who make the products or provide the services in our economy. Many employees in this grouping are the operators who do the work that results in the products or services people buy and use. Others support the work of operations people. Many operations people are, therefore, the ones who deliver, produce, or provide the products or services of the firm.

Operations work is specific and definable. Specific information as to equipment used, processes followed, and methods of work required can usually be observed, identified, and described. There is increasing technology in operations jobs as in all jobs, requiring more knowledge and skills, but generally speaking, operations jobs require less knowledge than other groups of jobs.

There is usually a relatively short training time for operations jobs. Half of all operations jobs can be learned in a month; half of the rest can be learned in one year. This attribute of operations jobs is now changing with increasing technology, and learning times are longer. But in operations jobs, the learning time is still relatively short.

Many operations jobs involve physical demands and hazards of some type. Many are repetitious in nature but require continuous care and attention. Work methods and tools (broadly defined) affect output greatly. Many operations jobs are called unskilled, but many of these increasingly require basic word and number literacy.

Basically, operations workers are mostly the lowest paid in the company's hierarchy. Most of the jobs included in the category of operations positions would fit into the bottom 12 salary grades shown in Figure 6–1. The hourly pay of operations workers in 1990 ranges from the minimum wage to $20 an hour. Not only are most operations jobs in the lowest 12 grades, but they are in the lowest four salary levels and cover only two salary classes.

It is characteristics such as these that must be considered in developing compensation policies and practices for operations jobs. Some of the unique requirements are identified in this chapter, along with the special programs and practices that meet such special circumstances.

These used to be factory and office jobs. But factories are getting smaller on average, more high-tech, cleaner, and quieter. Offices, on the other hand, are getting more machines and equipment, and the office and the factory interconnect so much that physical location can't always define the type of work or grouping of jobs.

Wage Administration

Each company may have some unusual situations that require special pay practices for their operations. There are certain characteristics, however, that are common to most operations jobs and apply to nearly all companies. Job classification, for instance, is a system that is useful in wage administration for most companies. Salary increase systems for operations jobs are usually either single-rate systems or systems with a rather narrow range of pay. Finally, there are some key issues in wage administration for operations-level workers in many companies.

Use of Market Data

In most labor market areas, a great deal of survey data are available for operations-level positions. The Bureau of Labor Statistics surveys many areas. Frequently, firms in an area exchange data on jobs, particularly those in short supply. Market data are valid and reliable at these levels, assuming survey techniques are appropriate.

In operations-level jobs, there is a considerable amount of employment experience. These are also the entry-level positions, and even in a company with relatively stable turnover, there are many hires in the lower operations positions. This provides a very good basis for pricing benchmark positions by employment experience in operations jobs.

Use of Pay Structures

Pay structures are almost always used in operations-level positions. The structure and the process of slotting jobs into it must be geared to local labor markets. Different local labor markets have not only different levels of pay but different pay relationships among positions. A typical structure for operations-level jobs is shown in Figure 14–1.

Sometimes there is less between-grade progression in operations-level jobs. This is partly because there are only a few grades to use. Also, the specific nature of the jobs makes them more measurable by market pricing and job evaluation systems, which makes possible smaller distinctions in between-grade progression. Between-grade progression in operations jobs may be as little as 7 percent.

Typically, there is also less within-grade progression. This is because differences in output from acceptable to maximum are typically less in operations-level jobs than in professional, middle-level administrative or management positions.

The maximums and minimums of pay structures in operations jobs are usually more rigorously applied than they are at other levels. The minimums are followed more closely because so many jobs are filled at these entry levels, and the employment decisions are made by many supervisors. Therefore, adherence to minimums is usually considered important in controlling hiring costs.

Maximums tend to be more closely enforced primarily because of cost considerations. If even a small percentage of operations employees were paid above the maximum, it would make a significant difference in total costs. If maximums are indeed geared to the top pay for that work in the

Figure 14-1. Pay Structure for
Operations Jobs.

Pay Grade	Hourly Rate Range		
	Minimum	Midpoint	Maximum
14	$12.62	$14.52	$16.68
13	11.47	13.20	15.16
12	10.43	12.00	13.78
11	9.48	10.91	12.53
10	8.62	9.92	11.39
9	7.84	9.02	10.35
8	7.13	8.20	9.41
7	6.48	7.45	8.55
6	5.89	6.77	7.77
5	5.35	6.15	7.06
4	4.86	5.59	6.42
3	4.42	5.08	5.84
2	4.02	4.62	5.31
1	3.65	4.20	4.83

Note: This firm's structure has a 10 percent between-grade progression and 15 percent between midpoint and minimum and midpoint and maximum. By policy, this firm's lowest rate is above the minimum wage.

marketplace, then the premium paid for excellence should be sufficient and equitable.

Use of Descriptions

Because the work is so specific, job descriptions for operations jobs can be written in a moderate amount of time and at a reasonable cost. These descriptions are used in many firms and are good for a number of purposes, such as communicating basic job duties to operations employees. This is important in some cases because of the high turnover and/or frequent job transfer or reassignment of personnel in these jobs. Descriptions can also form a concrete basis for evaluating performance. Some programs use information from descriptions as an input for training efforts. Descriptions can also be useful in productivity improvement work.

Job descriptions can have value in compensation. In operations-level work, there are many supervisors for the same job, and with transfers, an employee may have many supervisors in a pay-review period. For these reasons, jobs may be classified more centrally, with the immediate supervisors either participating in making the classifications or reviewing them. Where this is the case, the classification is done by people who really do not know the job as well, and, therefore, written job descriptions can be helpful in classification work.

Use of Job Evaluation

Job evaluation tends to be used more for operations jobs than for any other job group. Many managers are making supervisory decisions, and they may be less experienced in the management of personnel. Some also think that job evaluation helps to explain classification decisions to employees. Perhaps, as much as anything else, job evaluation has been used in some units for operations-level jobs for many years, and there is a long-standing precedent for the practice.

If job evaluation is to be used, a number of factors should be taken into account, although any or all of them can be subdivided. One essential factor would be responsibility. This can usually be described tangibly in terms of assets used, impact on product, value added, and so on. Now there is a need to consider authority or latitude of action as separate measures in a job evaluation plan for operations-level employees. These jobs often have substantial latitude with respect to work methods and, in an increasingly delegative environment, are expected to exercise latitude.

Knowledge and skills must be part of any administrative job evaluation plan for operations-level jobs. This factor should measure knowledge and skills directly rather than by proxy measures such as years of experience or years of formal education.

Another factor that must be considered is working conditions, which rarely applies to positions other than operations jobs. Safety, noise, dirt, physical demands, and the like are important in determining the value of operations jobs, and such elements are reflected by pay in the marketplace.

Pay Increase Practices

Many operations jobs pay a single rate or have step rates. In these jobs, the work is often learned very quickly or in a rather predetermined manner and time period. Job standards can be set and the work standards achieved within a few months. In these circumstances, when all employees must perform the same and produce the same, they should be paid a single rate. It is fair to have equal pay for equal work.

When there are predictable and short periods of learning on a job, step rates may be appropriate. However, the issues are the number of steps there should be and the length of time it should take to get to the maximum.

Figure 14-2. Wage Progression.

Time After Hire	Old Schedule	New Schedule
Hiring Rate	$4.00	$4.00
After 30 days		4.60
After 90 days	4.25	
After 120 days*		5.25
After 180 days—6 months	4.50	
After 1 year and 6 months	4.75	
After 2 years	5.00	
After 2 years and 6 months	5.25	

*Or when job standard is achieved, if that occurs before 120 days after hire.

An actual case, which is not unusual, is illustrated in Figure 14–2. In this case, it took two and one-half years to get from the hiring rate of $4.00 an hour to $5.25 an hour, which was the full job rate. In the work used for illustration, it takes between three weeks and three months for a person who is inexperienced when hired to produce at the top standard set for the job. The issue is, then, whether to hire people at a higher rate and raise them to the job rate in three months or when they have shown they can and will work to job standard. The company adopted the new schedule of increases shown in Figure 14–2 so that employees could reach the job rate in three months instead of two and one-half years.

The accelerated schedule costs more, but it has two advantages. First, people doing the same level of work are paid the same: equal pay for equal work. Second, the accelerated rate broadens the recruiting market, because the effective recruiting pay seemed higher—with only a thirty-day wait for $4.60 and a 120-day wait for $5.25.

Where there are wage and salary ranges, employees progress through these ranges by various methods. There are still cases where progression is automatic with time, but most companies try to relate the pay of a person to performance. In these cases, the principles described in Chapter 8 apply equally to operations—in fact, even more so, since this work can be more objectively observed and often partially measured.

To operations workers, when pay range is appropriate, the opportunity for a pay increase within range is of critical importance. Even the difference between the minimum and maximum of one salary range can change the living standards for many operations workers and their families. Because these increases are of vital importance, pay increases must genuinely reflect the level and effectiveness of their work if increases are to be based on performance.

It is also important to recognize that many supervisors make decisions about pay within range. Not all of them are experienced: Some are not highly trained or skilled. Furthermore, not all are inclined to reward for performance. Yet these decisions, or at least recommendations, must be delegated to the immediate supervisor. Therefore, it is essential to establish a particularly sound process, constant communication, supervisory training, and very careful monitoring of decisions.

Cost-of-Living Adjustments

During periods of rapid inflation, cost-of-living adjustments (COLAs)* have been applied to some groups of operations workers. Today, about one of ten firms with traded stock has cost-of-living adjustments for at least some of its operations workers. A great deal of attention is continuing to be paid to COLAs. Those on Social Security draw COLAs, and the media often refers to cost of living in relation to pay. Some even propose COLAs for public executives, judges, and members of Congress.

Unless pay does match the cost of living, real earnings decline. For operations workers, this is more than an inconvenience; it means fewer necessary items in the household budget. COLAs are a simplistic way of dealing with this problem. As the cost of living goes up, wages go up proportionately. It seems to be a fair and simple way of granting pay increases, and it assures that the living standards of operations workers do not decline.

The method also seems fair because operations-level workers do not cause inflation. Therefore, why should these workers who are most affected by increases in inflation suffer? They do not cause it; they are the ones who can least afford it.

Understandably, operations workers take a very personal view of cost of living increases and see merit in COLAs. It is not their job to manage the national economy; their concern is their own work and the welfare of their own families. Similarly, a union's job is to represent its own constituents to the best of its ability, and therefore it is concerned with the impact of the cost of living on the real earnings of its members.

Management in some companies shares this view. It is the company's responsibility to deal with company matters. Deteriorating earnings of operations workers are a company matter. As long as it can pass on those costs by price increases to customers, COLAs may not do any damage to the business or diminish the welfare of stockholders.

These views may be correct, but they are narrow and short range. In fact, each company has strong reasons to resist COLAs by all proper means

---

*The subject of COLAs and indexing is also covered in Chapter 8.

and, where possible, to eliminate COLA provisions where they now exist. Here are some of the reasons that cost-of-living adjustment formulas are not appropriate even for operations workers except in very unusual situations:

• The Consumer Price Index does not measure the cost of living for anyone. Rather, it measures the trend of prices in a market basket of goods and services. As the price of a product goes up, people may buy less of it. Generally, the Consumer Price Index goes up somewhat less than the cost of living.

• The Consumer Price Index is not relevant for anybody except a semi-skilled factory worker with a family of four who earns approximately $12,000 a year. It is this family unit that the Bureau of Labor Statistics studied to determine the "market basket"—the goods and services bought that are priced by the Consumer Price Index. For others, the pattern of expenditures may be very different. The Consumer Price Index has no relevance for jobs like judges or Congressmen. It doesn't apply equally to all operations jobs in all locations.

• If the objective is to protect people from increases in living costs, then changes, however imperfectly measured, must be matched against family income. However, many families have more than one worker in the household, and it is rare for all of those who work in a family to work for the same company. Therefore, a company cannot match pay against family living costs.

• To a large extent, cost-of-living increases for some people transfer to others the problem of declining real earnings.

• By following the philosophy of indexing the prices of goods and services that people buy, you create a self-fulfilling prophecy, and the indexing itself will contribute to more inflation.

• For a company, the use of COLAs is a form of abdication of management; it is a blank check on which somebody else fills in the numbers.

• Except for the lowest-paid person, many factors beside prices of goods determine how well a family lives. What and how much it buys influences its lifestyle. The number of children in a family, its tastes in automobiles, the way it chooses to live, the kind of vacations it selects, and many other factors influence the "cost of living." Except for the lowest-paid workers, the "cost of living" is really the amount of money spent to support a style of living.

• With time, cost-of-living increases will bring the company's pay out of line with the marketplace; Consumer Price Index trends and market pay trends do not move together, and the costs of goods and services are only one factor that impacts wage levels.

Employees are vitally concerned about changes in living costs. They want their real earnings to increase, certainly not decrease. If a company does not use COLAs, how can it deal with this critical employee problem?

For one thing, companies should get the facts on actual the movement in pay for each employee and for operations employees as a group. Almost always, over a period of time, promotional and other types of increases have caused employee pay to outpace the cost of living, even when pay rates don't.

Individuals may get performance increases for improved effectiveness, and promotions are likely as well. Individuals who earn these additional increases will have a pay progress that far outpaces trends in living costs.

A firm must also "tell it like it is" if real earnings paid for jobs have been declining. There have been periods of time when real earnings for workers have declined. Tell employees the truth and give your employees the facts.

A company should consider a commitment to increase job pay to match *market pay inflation*, without hedges or stretch-outs. It should consider making this commitment regardless of the impact of such a policy on one year's profits. But that is a commitment to matching pay increases in the market, not the government's Consumer Price Index.

A company productivity improvement program is sometimes the key to assuring that pay increases match increases in measures of inflation. If productivity increases, then the company can pay more, relative to the marketplace, preferably by extra pay plans. If employees contribute to improved productivity through more effective work, they should share in the results. This would mean market adjustments plus success-sharing payments which, together, could be greater than increases in the cost of living in one company, even if the real earnings of workers generally were declining.

Wage Incentive Plans

Many firms have wage incentive plans for operations workers, particularly those working in a factory. The plans are usually complex, and program design and implementation frequently require the assistance of specialists in the field.

Incentive pay systems represent a concept of worker pay that is different from the salary systems described earlier. The systems so far described pay employees for time spent on the job. Under the incentive system, the employee's pay is geared to the amount of production, regardless of the number of hours worked.

Bureau of Labor Statistics' surveys reveal a steady decline in the overall percentage of factory workers who are paid under wage incentive plans. About half of all factory workers were covered by incentive pay systems in the 1950s. This figure declined to less than 30 percent in the early 1960s and is now below 15 percent. The principal reason for this decline is the steady decrease in the proportion of jobs in the total work force that lend themselves to incentive pay systems.

Logic of Incentive Plans

Underlying incentive plans is the assumption that if employees' pay is based at least partly upon the number of units produced, they will produce more to earn more. Incentive plans, therefore, attempt to motivate operations workers to perform above standard by relating compensation to units produced.

Incentive plans also mean that a principal element of cost—the pay of operations workers—is variable. With increasing production under incentive plans, the unit cost of each product will decline. Thus incentive plans contribute to lower unit costs.

Workers sometimes like incentive pay systems simply because they tend to earn more. The plans also provide automatic rewards for better performance.

Elements of an Effective Wage Incentive System

Because wage incentive systems have been in effect for many years, there are many precedents and a great deal of experience to draw on in designing or administering such systems. The success of an incentive system depends on several factors. For one thing, existing pay levels and practices must be reasonable and include competitive hourly rates and fringe benefits. Problems in the administration of the basic pay structure would be magnified by an incentive program.

Furthermore, the output from operations must be measurable. The operator must be able to have a significant effect on output, and the work environment must be appropriate; for example, equipment must be effective and tools must be available.

Management must be committed to spend the time and effort necessary to maintain an incentive program effectively. The development of an appropriate incentive system is a shared responsibility of the industrial engineer and the personnel specialist.

All incentive pay programs require predetermined standards, whose degree of accuracy determines the plan's success in gearing pay directly to production. Under an incentive plan, workers can be motivated either to increase output or to reduce standards. Therefore, the system of setting standards is critical.

Standards may be established in one of three ways. The simplest is to base the standard on past performance. To do this, the company needs only to analyze production records. A more objective method of setting standards is a time and motion study that is carried out by a trained industrial engineer who observes the operation, records the time necessary to accomplish a job, and judges the worker's efficiency in performing a task. The time and motion study obviously depends on how closely the engineer observes the job and how well he estimates the worker's efficiency.

A third and still more refined method of determining work standards uses preestablished time values for every conceivable type of work or motion. These values are based on years of observation and study in many different production situations. Since worker efficiency is already built into these time values, the industrial engineer needs only to observe and record each motion and attach the established time value to it. The standard for that particular task is then set, after making proper allowances for rest time and downtime. This method not only eliminates many errors in individual judgment but also permits a more careful study of the job.

Types of Incentive Plans

Wage incentive plans have been used for many years. There is a great deal of experience with these plans. Basically, no new production incentive plans have been developed for more than thirty years. The plans most widely used are the piecework plan, the Taylor differential-piece-rate plan, the Halsey gain-share plan, the standard-hour plan, various incentive and group incentive systems, and the Scanlon plan. There are many variations and combinations of these.

Not many years ago, these plans were used, perhaps with some modification, in many companies. Over the years, however, company industrial engineering staffs have learned to customize plans for their own operations. Therefore, these have become generic terms, descriptive of basic approaches. Essentially, plans pay either per unit of production, above a standard, or on the basis of cost reduction.

Exactly which is correct for an individual operation is a highly technical matter and a subject for industrial engineering specialists. Personnel specialists should be involved, however, in making sure that the type of plan that best meets industrial engineering needs also reinforces the personnel policies and practices of the company.

Management Issues

Just as managers must play an active role in determining proper work methods, they must also control the standards that are set by industrial engineers. Managers must review standards and be accountable for their appropriateness because they are responsible for costs.

Management must also make sure that employees follow the methods that have been established. This involves training employees to do the job—a process that frequently requires not only telling them what to do but showing them how to do it. The quality of job training determines both how much work is produced and how quickly employees learn the job.

The manager also has the job of daily supervision, which includes assigning duties and correcting employees' work. People vary in their aptitude for different types of work. An employee who makes 30 percent more incentive pay on one job may have difficulty attaining standard pay in another. Assigning workers to do the jobs for which they are best suited can contribute substantially to the workers' achievement and satisfaction.

Managers must motivate workers on the job. By receiving continuous follow-up, employees know not only what is expected of them but also how well they are doing. When an employee fails to produce satisfactorily, some form of personnel action is necessary. If this is not taken, the supervisor is being unfair to those employees who do perform effectively as well as to the company and all its employees. Ideally, actions will be constructive; for instance, they may involve a transfer. But if an employee is unwilling or unable to do the work assigned, he must be transferred to another type of job or outplaced.

Finally, managers play a key role in explaining the incentive program to employees. To be motivated to increase production, workers must believe that the plan is fair and that extra effort on their parts will bring about commensurate increases in earnings. In this connection, it is the job of the supervisor to handle questions and complaints about standards and the wage incentive plan.

Collective Bargaining

When a union represents employees, there is a legal requirement for collective bargaining that sets rates of pay. A union's focus is usually different than the employer's. Union representatives want their constituency to be treated better than others in the marketplace. Union representatives may also want reasonable pay relationships within the organization, but they may take somewhat different views about what fairness is and the criteria of pay equity.

In preparation for collective bargaining, the employer may follow the normal process of pricing jobs and classifying them. This would be the company's position, which can be arrived at the same way as in a non-union operation. Thus in collective bargaining, the company's representatives can use wage administration information as a basis for persuasion and bargaining.

When a company has a nonunion operation and other jobs in the marketplace are filled with employees who are members of unions, then the union rates become simply a part of the market. The pay relationships in unionized firms, as in nonunionized firms, must be considered in pay classification.

There are some in nonunion operations who believe they have to copy both the pay levels and pay relationships established in unionized organizations in order to stay nonunion. Copying union practices never prevented an organization from becoming unionized. Employees may think that if a union has such a great effect on company actions, the union could do a great deal more for them if they joined it. A company should follow a competitive system that establishes fair pay relationships and which it believes is in the best interest of its employees. This should be as good as union practices, and perhaps better.

Collective bargaining is regulated pay. It is the opposite of free choice in the marketplace. In fact, it is the stated goal of unions to get more than market pay for their members; which necessarily means denying free choice for other operations workers.

Regulated pay will always tend to become different than market pay, both with respect to salary levels and salary relationships. This is true whether the regulation is by the employer in administered pay programs such as job evaluation or by an employer and a union in collective bargaining. In collective bargaining, might makes right. Fairness in collective bargaining is a matter of economic strength.

You can easily start a heated debate about the role of unions, but some things are plain. First, collective bargaining over wages, benefits, and conditions is a contest. Unions try to get more; the employer's representatives try to give less. Winning becomes the goal of collective bargaining, not competitiveness or fairness. The basic attitudes in collective bargaining are adversarial. Thus the system does not directly relate to competitiveness and fairness.

When an entire industry is regulated by collective bargaining agreements, then there can be the appearance that negotiated contracts have changed the market—they have, in fact, become the market. That has never been true, because the illusion was created by comparisons within the industry, without recognition that the market is a continuum. The machinists might bargain more for their members throughout the airline industry; but those persons represent less than one percent of all machinists in all industries and in all areas.

No doubt, in regulated situations, union members get more for a time—and sometimes much more. History may show, however, that the advantage of union workers was always temporary. In many smokestack industries, for example, the much higher pay for jobs led eventually to many cases where the work was farmed out or transferred to foreign producers—or foreign competitors captured the market. Certainly, one reason was higher labor costs—higher by far. Most jobs that have been exported were union jobs.

In some regulated industries, pay was fixed by the employer, the company, *and* government regulators. When these industries, such as airlines, became deregulated, the resulting pay situation was chaotic—and there were major strikes when employers attempted to set pay and hire workers closer to market average.

Union-negotiated pay was once a major factor in compensation management, and it still is in some industries. But for thirty years, union membership has been declining in terms of the share of the work force and in absolute numbers. A small portion of the work force now has the privilege of favored treatment under regulated pay agreements with unions.

Special Questions and Considerations

There are a number of special compensation matters that apply particularly to operations-level jobs. Some matters are related to unique company or industry operational characteristics. Some relate to legal issues. Most, however, involve questions relating to the low skill and low status of many of the operations jobs.

Hourly Pay Status

Most factory operations workers are paid on an hourly basis. The hours worked as well as the rate of pay affect the income of workers. Payment on an hourly basis is also sometimes a matter of status.

Many companies have been rethinking the question of why operations workers are paid on an hourly basis while middle-level persons and many office workers are paid a salary. Differences in sick pay and paid days off between hourly and salaried jobs have narrowed greatly over the past thirty years. Why should there be any difference at all in the method of payment?

For those who are paid on an hourly basis, there are some important differences. If nothing else, there is a class distinction. In addition, even where conditions net out to the same rate of pay, there is the appearance of lower annual income and the risk of lower earnings because of work schedule cutbacks for those paid on an hourly basis.

For purposes of cost accounting and cost control, it may be desirable to keep records on the number of hours worked. Time records for time management are important in many jobs, including high-paid professional positions. This can be done whether a person is paid on an hourly basis or is paid a salary.

For many years I have urged companies to eliminate classes of workers wherever possible. My recommendations were based on fairness, worker perceptions, and one method of creating an environment that is more likely to promote higher effectiveness of work and more of a commitment to quality and excellence. Now there is another reason. With increasing technology in many jobs, a changing mix of industry classifications, and greater mechanization of offices, the old distinctions between hourly and salaried status is very blurred.

Make all workers either hourly or salaried. Don't have artificial differences or different classes of workers.

There are two cases where hourly status is appropriate. Unionized workers should be hourly; even if they are highly paid persons, like teachers or engineers. Contract workers should also be hourly whenever there is flexibility in hours of work.

Overtime

Most operations workers are paid overtime by law. This requires pay at time-and-a-half for work in excess of forty hours a week. In fact, companies typically pay overtime at time-and-a-half for hours in excess of seven a day and for work on Saturdays and Sundays, regardless of total hours worked. Most operations workers are also paid double time when they work on holidays or during scheduled vacations. For those who work overtime, these payments result in an increase in their *effective rate of pay*. A person, for instance, who works six hours overtime a week for only fifteen weeks a year increases his rate of pay by 4 percent.

There is a maximum amount of overtime that people want to work. This depends not only on the type of work and individual choice, but also on how long the overtime work continues. However, most people are eager for a considerable amount of overtime, because it does increase the effective rate. In fact, equal distribution of overtime is a critical issue among operations workers.

The economics of overtime pay and employee preferences are important business matters. Now the use of contract workers is part of the business issue of how much work and what kind of workers are appropriate. These are important issues, and compensation professionals should be expert in these areas.

Undertime also affects the effective rate paid. A person who is laid off four weeks a year, without pay, perhaps because of a model change or inclement weather, would have a decline of 8 percent in his effective rate of pay. The production worker who is laid off six months every six years also suffers a cut in his effective rate of about 8 percent. Thus factors in undertime as well as overtime are a compensation consideration.

Net Pay

The employer calculates hours of work by the time a person spends on the job. The employee, however, will tend to think of hours away from home. If an employee commutes three-quarters of an hour each way each day, the effective rate, counting travel time, is lowered. Furthermore, if a worker has to drive one and one-half hours each day, the cost of travel represents another significant deduction from his effective rate of pay. Travel and meals are two important items in the cost of working.

The concepts of net pay and total work hours are very important and practical issues. Managers calculate wages paid and hours of work. Those are the numbers accountants and human resources management people put on paper. For an operations worker, this would mean that a full-time worker earning $12,000 a year would earn $231 a week or $5.77 an hour. But if the cost of work and the cost of taxes and all other deductions are 25 percent of gross pay (a conservative figure) and commuting time is three-quarters of an hour each way, the net pay of that worker is $9,600 a year or $3.64 an hour.

Workers look at the amounts on their checks, not the amounts on their pay statements. Workers think of time spent because of work, not just the hours at work. Workers can only spend what is left after taxes, after deductions, and after the cost of work. Net pay is almost always one-third less than gross pay and may be as little as one-half.

Compression

A great deal has been said and written about the compression of pay from one level to another. This is an issue at every level in a company and is a particularly serious problem for operations workers.

In its most elementary form, the pay-level compression problem for operations workers involves the nonworker versus the unskilled worker and the unskilled versus the skilled worker. After taxes and after the cost of work, the median-paid unskilled worker takes home little more than the nonworker who is on welfare and receiving food stamps. This represents little reward for working.

On the other hand, the difference between the highest-paid unskilled worker and the lower levels of journeymen skilled workers is only 20 to 30 percent. This is reward for years of study, apprenticeship, successful work, and experience. These differences do not even represent more than one salary class difference between the highest-skilled operations worker and the average unskilled worker.

With respect to differentials in pay between jobs, it is the labor market that determines the differences. The market makes significant differences between levels of jobs in job families. In other cases, the market may not create the same differences a person expects. But free choice makes differences that exist in the market fair. The perceptions of workers, however, may still be a problem. Communication about the realities of labor markets helps. Reward for performance through upward mobility and pay for performance is essential.

Conditions

Operations employees are no different from others. They want more, and they want more of those items they have the least.

For many reasons, there are six conditions of work that are particularly important to operations employees:

1. Fair pay
2. Reasonable benefits
3. Job security
4. Treatment on the job
5. Opportunity to get ahead
6. Proper handling of questions and grievances

Fair pay means pay that is reasonably competitive. It means pay increases that at least match market inflation and hopefully will maintain or increase the real earnings of workers. Fair pay also means pay actions that are reasonable, equitable among all employees, and impartially administered. Fair pay means pay for performance when differences are possible. Fair pay means equal pay for equal work. These are matters that have been discussed under wage administration.

Benefits are particularly important to operations employees. They form a large proportion of their total income. Also, some of the benefit items are not available to operations employees except through their employer. Finally, these are the people who can least afford the major expenses covered by insured benefits.

Operations workers are the first to be let go when business turns bad. Many operations employees accept periodic layoffs as part of the world in which they work. They do not expect to be guaranteed jobs, and most recognize that the possibility of layoffs is the price that must be paid for their right to change jobs. However, they do expect layoffs to be handled fairly. This includes, among other things, consideration of seniority.

Everybody wants to be treated fairly and with dignity. It is particularly important to operations workers, who fill the lowest-level jobs in the company. Because they do not always have the range of job choices available to professionals, managers, or salespersons, they are sometimes forced to stay even if they feel they are not treated fairly and with dignity.

No one wants to start his career at pay level one and retire at pay level one. Everyone wants a chance to get ahead. It means not only more money but personal accomplishment. Operations workers want a fair chance to know about job operations and to be considered for better jobs. They want the selection process to be free of discrimination or personal prejudice.

Operations workers have questions and sometimes grievances. They want to be able to ask their questions and get reasonable answers. If they have a complaint, they want it handled, with their point of view represented.

Safety

An elevator construction worker, a miner, or a steel mill worker knows his job is hazardous. But whether the job is hazardous or relatively safe, operations workers want employers to do what is reasonable to protect their safety. They do not want to hear that the company can't afford necessary safety equipment. They don't like to think that the money for such equipment is valued more than their lives or welfare.

People are increasingly becoming aware of environmental problems. Not surprisingly, they want environmental protection in the work place. That is an important condition of work, a part of compensation in the broadest sense of the word.

Safety takes on a new meaning in the work place. It is more than injuries; more than hard hats and safety glasses. People expect adequate lighting and clean air. Many want a smoke-free environment. Workers are increasingly demanding a drug-free work place.

Fairness

All workers want fairness in the work place. Fairness is now a major issue of our time, and it is an important issue in the work place. Operations workers are particularly sensitive to fairness because they fill the lowest levels of jobs and are the lowest-paid persons. Ask them, and you will find that operations-level workers are particularly sensitive to the issue of fairness because more than any other group they have been treated unfairly.

I made my arguments for fairness at work as eloquently as possible in 1985.* At the time, many thought it was radical to argue for fairness, but now it is an expectation.

---

*Sibson, Robert E. *The Management of Personnel,* "Personal Values in Personnel Work," Chapter 18. Hilton Head, SC: R. B. Keck & Company, Inc., 1985.

My view then and now is that employers should have personal values in their personnel policies and practices because it is good business and because it is right to do so. Some thought that I was preaching, but I only urged the following:

- Employers should always tell the truth to employees.
- Executives and managers should show respect for everyone who works in the firm and believe that every person is equally trustworthy.
- There should be equivalency of treatment for every person in the firm.
- The company must make a commitment to the work success of every employee.
- We should all have concern for every other person at work; requiring the best but recognizing that personal circumstances vary and one's very best is not always equally good.
- Make sure there is justice in all policies and rules; and the reason for which it is applied.
- Accept every employee as a stakeholder and view them all as human beings who are income-producing assets.

I think these personal values should guide everything that is done in the field of human resources management. Each basic fairness issue is particularly important in matters of compensation. Fairness in compensation is particularly needed with respect to the compensation of operations workers.

Chapter Fifteen

Sales Compensation

In all businesses, distribution is a key part of company operations, and the success of distribution depends in large measure on the effectiveness of the sales force. When a company has its own field sales force, good personnel management of salespersons is critical to business success. These salespersons interact with customers and are a key source of business intelligence. Furthermore, a major portion of sales expense is personnel. Thus, from the viewpoints of both effectiveness and costs, the compensation of salespersons is a vital concern to management.

The Sales Job

In the broadest sense, everyone who affects the quality of the product, the service rendered, the image of the company, or relationships with customers is involved in sales. Many employees, in fact, perform professional, technical, or administrative work in support of the company's sales effort. Some actually have direct selling responsibility even though their primary job may be professional or managerial. Such employees, however, would not likely be defined as salespersons for the purpose of personnel administration or compensation.

Strictly speaking, a salesperson is someone who works with buyers to procure orders. The bulk of a salesperson's time is devoted to this task, and it constitutes the main activity for which he is paid.

Sales positions usually involve a variety of duties. Most field sales jobs involve the actual solicitation of orders. To understand this critical aspect of the job, it is necessary to know the products or services of the selling firm, the business of the customers, the nature of the sales transaction, the way in which buying decisions are made, and similar information about the sales activity.

Many sales jobs have important servicing responsibilities. In fact, it is sometimes difficult to distinguish between a solicitation call and a servicing or missionary call. Part of the sales job may also involve prospecting—ferreting out potential users of the company's goods or services. The salesperson may be expected to undertake promotions or merchandising, or to train customer personnel in the use of products or services.

Every sales job requires the accumulation of information about the customer, the business of the customer, people within the customer's organization, and potential customers in the area. The salesperson may also send information to headquarters about markets, customers' requirements, forecasts, competitors' products, and new sales possibilities. Frequently, salespersons provide inputs that form the basis for sales forecasts.

Some people in the field organization spend a great deal of their time carrying out management responsibilities. They may manage other salespersons, office personnel,* or storage facilities. In addition, salespersons sometimes make management decisions involving credit, pricing, and product adaptation or modification.

Thus the sales job has many facets. The job of the salesperson varies with different organizations. Similarly, the backgrounds and experience of people who fill the jobs will differ. The differences among sales jobs are just as disparate as those in operations-level positions.

There are two characteristics of most sales positions which require different compensation practices. First, salespersons are the ones who interact with the customers, know people in customer organizations, and build customer relationships. The salespersons possess this knowledge, and their personal working relationships are important assets to the company. Second, the salespersons in the field are located away from headquarters, frequently at considerable distances. Because salespersons are on their own much of the time, they have a great deal of latitude of action and self-management.

Elements of Sales Compensation

Since the basic objectives of compensation are the same for salespersons as for any other group of employees, essentially the same elements

---

*In many field sales organizations, there are administrative personnel in the field offices. These may be rather large groups. They are operations-level employees, and the principles, practices, and problems covered in the last chapter would apply to these jobs and individuals.

of compensation administration apply. First, it is necessary to understand the jobs involved. Second, there must be a method for determining relative job worth, with respect to both other sales jobs and other positions within the organization. Third, the compensation of sales personnel must be related to the compensation of comparable jobs outside the company. Fourth, individual achievement must be rewarded. Finally, policies, guidelines, and procedures must be established for administering pay. For sales positions, as for other jobs, the unique features of a compensation plan lie in its application of methods, not in its basic requirements or objectives.

In sales compensation, the primary emphasis is on giving salespersons an incentive to achieve the sales goals of the company. These goals range from improved service to clients, to optimization of profits, to maximum increase of sales volume. The methods of creating the incentive also vary from straight salary (used primarily where the emphasis is on the service to clients), through various combinations of salary, bonus, and commission plans, to straight commission (where the emphasis of the sales effort is on volume).

The personality traits that lead people into the sales field are often entrepreneurial. Thus salespersons are often willing to assume a certain financial risk in order to reap the large financial rewards that go with high achievement in sales. Therefore, incentive compensation can be a major factor in the motivation of salespersons.

Since a high percentage of a salesperson's pay is often in the form of incentive compensation, the compensation program must take into account such factors as market characteristics, allocation of districts, and assignment of personnel. All these variables have a significant effect on a salesperson's performance level and, therefore, on his income. In fact, to be sure that these essentially administrative matters are handled competently and equitably, most companies assign the administration of sales compensation to sales management instead of personnel management.

When the sales effort is performed by a group of people rather than by a single salesperson, the compensation plan must provide for a method to reward the group and distribute the reward equitably within the group. The sales "group" may be a series of task forces, each with a different membership. The sales transaction may result from the sequential work of a number of persons, some not even in the sales organization. Then a sales incentive plan must somehow isolate the work of the salespersons.

The overwhelming variety of sales jobs and, for many companies, the constant change in marketing make sales compensation complex. New products are introduced, customers move, and there is variation in the allocation of advertising dollars, to mention only some of the changes that materially affect sales transactions. Such factors require constant change in compensation programs for salespersons. There are, therefore, a great number and diversity of sales compensation plans. In fact, few sales compensation programs remain unchanged for more than five years.

Generally speaking, companies favor some form of incentive compensation for salespersons. Incentive pay is most practical when the following conditions exist:

- The sales function involves individual sales rather than a joint effort.
- The buyer's decisions are influenced by the salesperson's presentation more than by other factors, such as availability or technical specifications.
- Sales volume per se is critical to the success of the business.
- There is little product differentiation.
- The salesperson is required to develop potential customers as well as sell.
- Intangibles such as personal relationships and persuasiveness are critical.
- The product is not highly technical.
- Preselling through advertising or promotions is not a significant factor in the sales transaction.

Pricing Sales Jobs

The level of total compensation for salespersons is determined primarily by internal pay relationships, competitive market conditions, and the economics of the business. Internal comparisons may be made with sales management positions, administrative sales positions, and other positions that have a supportive relationship to the sales activity. Actually, of course, the sales job is the pivotal job. Therefore, it is more logical to compare support jobs to sales jobs than vice versa. Finally, external pay relationships are critical in determining the level of sales compensation, salespersons' pay relationships, and the type of sales pay plan.

Market competitiveness is vital for sales positions because salespersons can be highly mobile. Many are motivated, perhaps more than those in other jobs, by the prospect of more money. Therefore, they would be inclined to leave the company unless the pay was competitive. Out in the field, they have opportunities to hear about and explore job opportunities in other firms. For all these reasons, external pay relationships are critical.

Surveying the pay of sales positions is sometimes difficult because there are a number of factors that determine the reported level of pay for salespersons. These include:

- The industry: Average pay levels for salespersons vary considerably from industry to industry.
- The job: Product mix, territorial assignments, and other job-oriented factors affect actual earnings of salespersons.
- The product: Where the salespersons have a unique product that is highly in demand, their earnings may be extremely high, at least for some time.
- The supply situation: If the product being sold is in short supply, earnings can also be very high. However, this may be offset by lower prices and lower salespersons' earnings when the supply situation adjusts and the supply exceeds the demand.
- The form of compensation: Generally speaking, the higher the proportion of incentive compensation to total compensation, the higher the level of total pay.
- The person: Nowhere is pay more dependent on individual performance than in sales positions. A salesperson's effectiveness, the customer following developed by the salesperson, and other attributes determine the level of pay to a considerable degree.

The dispersion of pay of individuals around the reported average or median pay is frequently very great for sales positions. The range of reported pay from lowest to highest in a group of two dozen sales positions was greater than 300 percent. With such dispersion, a company has more latitude in positioning the pay of its salespersons to the market.

Determining Base Salaries

When salespersons receive all or most of their compensation in the form of salary, the considerations outlined in earlier chapters are generally applicable for determining base salary. The only variations will be in format and techniques to reflect the unique nature of sales positions. When a large part of the total compensation depends on incentive earnings, broader measures and more simplified techniques of determining base salary or draw may be used.

Use of Job Descriptions

Whether a company should use job descriptions for salespersons depends primarily on how many sales positions exist, how complex the positions are, and how much is known about them by the people who make job classification decisions. Various studies indicate that, today, fewer than one in thirty companies uses job descriptions for sales positions.

The format for sales job descriptions, if they are to be used, frequently differs from that of production or office positions. The information needed involves more than the job responsibilities; it might include the number of customers, volume of sales, identification of products sold, geographic areas covered, and other information. If all sales positions have the same basic responsibilities, only such extra data will make it possible to distinguish among sales jobs.

Use of Job Evaluation

Some companies still use some form of job evaluation when base salary is all or a major part of a salesperson's total compensation. More often than not, the plan used to classify administrative, supervisory, and middle-level management persons will be used for sales positions too. When the basic responsibilities of all sales positions are similar and variations occur only in the number of customers, sales volume, or other objective criteria, simplified techniques can be used to establish appropriate levels. Figure 15–1 illustrates such a program. This company used the simplified system to relate the five levels of sales positions to salary grades.

Sales positions very often had to be exempted from job evaluation because when company policy required the use of the same job evaluation system throughout the company, the company plan did not yield results compatible with labor market experience in the sales department. The old point factor comparison plans, in fact, were not designed to value sales positions. Now job evaluation, if used at all, is not a requirement but is in the category of an available guideline. If used in sales, the "factors" of such a guideline plan should be practical sales criteria, like sales volume, number of customers, and service requirements.

Figure 15-1. Simplified Position Evaluation for Sales Jobs.

Job Title	Salary Level	Sales Volume	Number of Lines	Persons Supervised	
				Sales	Other
Salesman III	8	Under $500,000	1–3	0	0
Salesman II	10	$500,000 to $2,500,000	3–7	0–1	0
Salesman I	12	$2,500,000 to $5,000,000	All	1–2	0–1
District Mgr.	14	Over $5,000,000	All	3–10	1–5
Regional Mgr.	17	Over $20,000,000	All	Over 10	Over 5

Salary Classification

For sales jobs, it is far more practical to use salary levels rather than salary grades. Levels that cover three salary grades are usually appropriate. In retail and in most consumer sales positions, the entry salary level is level 2—with annual total pay (base plus commission) averaging $15,000 in 1990 dollars. In technical sales, level 3 with total pay of $22,000 in 1990 dollars is more typical as the entry level.

Nonmanagement sales will cover at least two salary levels, and in most cases, there are three career salary levels. Total pay usually starts higher than average for sales positions, but after the first few years, the pay progress is less in sales than in production, administrative, or technical work.

Salary Increases

The key to an effective salary program for the field salesperson is performance salary increases. Salary grade ranges for salespersons are frequently quite broad, reflecting the broad performance range that is typical in sales positions. Salary ranges may be anywhere between 50 percent and 100 percent from minimum to maximum.

If you use salary levels and broad ranges, there is a great deal of performance pay money available for salespersons. This is illustrated in Figure 15–2. In this illustration, there are four levels of nonmanagement sales work. Salary levels may be salary draw against quotas and goals. The performance payments are lump-sum, based on any form of sales incentive. While the exhibit shows a maximum pay, the sales incentive plan's formula or system would be determining.

Figure 15-2. Sales Salary Level Structure and Career Progression.

Salary Level	Salary-Salary Draw			Performance Range	
	Training	Qualified	Standard	Target	Planned Maximum
2	$11,000(A)	$13,500(B)	$15,500(C)	$ +3,875	$ +7,750
3	16,300	19,500(D)	22,500(E)	+5,625	+11,250
4	N.A.	28,800	33,000	+8,250	+16,500
5	N.A.	42,000	48,000	+12,000	+24,000

Note: N.A. means not applicable: no trainees at these levels.

Letters indicate typical progression. By point (E), a career decision must be made as to whether the person will continue up the sales-career-path ladder or move to the management ladder.

Performance range payments are extra pay each year when earned.

Performance must be carefully defined for salespersons. It will frequently include such factors as people the salesperson knows, the quality of sales relationships, and demonstrated sales skills. Some rather quantifiable factors would also be considered in evaluating performance, such as information on sales volume, the mix of sales, and the number of customer calls.

A typical progression of a salesperson is indicated by the letters in Figure 15–2. All those without experience are hired at the minimum of the extended level 2, point A in Figure 15–2. As their effectiveness increases, they may be promoted to level 3 and move to points B and C. At this point, most are promoted to the next level. Others move into sales management.

Companies should expend considerable effort to identify salespersons with supervisory and sales management potential. Candidates for sales management are typically selected for the first level of supervision when they are candidates for promotion to the highest level of nonsupervisory salesperson. At this point (point E in Figure 15–2), there is a fundamental career decision to be made. Will the person continue in nonsupervisory sales work, eventually reaching or exceeding the maximum of salary level 5, or will that individual make a career-path move to management?

Note that when those who are selected for supervisory positions reach level 4, they become eligible for the company's management bonus plan, and when they reach the highest level of sales management, they will also become eligible for the company's stock-option program. These extra pay plans assure proper pay relationships between the highest-paid nonmanagement salesperson and various levels of supervisory and management salespersons.

The salary system described has much to recommend it and has been often used successfully in different formats. It is not presented here as a recommendation for any company, but because this system embodies the essentials of a successful sales compensation plan. It allows people to progress through various levels of nonmanagement sales work and, through early identification, opens opportunities for selection to sales management positions. The range of pay from starting salary to maximum in nonsupervisory sales work is sufficient to reward capability and performance. Sales compensation must also provide for some direct extra payment for achievement, and this plan does that. In fact, the use of a lump-sum performance payment range permits flexibility with respect to criteria of payments and time of payments.

Promotion is a critical part of pay for performance in sales positions, with some special considerations. For example, a form of job redesign may be a promotion method in sales positions. A salesperson's district may be extended or his line supplemented, and this could represent a substantial promotion. With respect to promotion into sales management, it is critical to use early identification in sales jobs and to select those for career moves into management before they move into top-pay sales-producing jobs.

In sales, the best producer is not necessarily the best candidate for selection for a management position. On the other hand, very often there will be many nonsupervisory salespersons who earn far more than management—often more than their own supervisory managers.

Ground Rules and Special Problems

One special problem of salary administration for salespersons concerns moving them to different geographic locations. Many companies move salespersons frequently, to fill manpower needs in different areas, to broaden the experience of salespersons, or because of promotional opportunities. In such cases, special pay adjustments may be necessary, either to assure proper salary relationships in the new location or to match potential changes in the salespersons's earnings.

Increasingly, companies are finding that the cost of relocation is rising while people's inclination to relocate is declining. The disinclination to relocate is particularly strong among the more successful salespersons. Relocation is costly and causes family disruption. For the field salesperson, a transfer or relocation means exploring a new territory and may mean building new relationships, which he is not inclined to do without substantial financial rewards.

Expense control is another special problem with salespersons. Of course, all sales expenses must be business-related, but there is a considerable amount of discretion. It is true that many transactions are conducted on the golf course or at dinner. Proper entertainment of various sorts may be expected and may be necessary in order to succeed. Some may not think that this is right, but it may be necessary: Congress makes the rules.

Company rules and IRS regulations cannot alone be relied upon to control expenses and, at the same time, meet the varied needs of the salesperson. The expenses of salespersons represent a substantial part of sales costs, which, to a large extent, must be managed in the field by first-level sales supervisors or by the salespersons themselves.

Company management achieves greatest control over the work of the sales force by paying either all or a large portion of total income in the form of salary. Salespersons can be assigned a great deal of work in developmental activities and research, customer servicing, or prospecting, without risking loss of income. On the other hand, incentive plans provide greater financial motivation to achieve sales goals and more tangible rewards for success.

There are two very special problems in sales compensation. One involves pay and hours of work; the other involves burnout.

You see it in the classified ads every day—big pay for salespersons with little experience required. And the claims are true—at least in a few cases. Some of those few cases are the true sales all-stars: usually in work like automobile sales, retail brokerage, and life insurance. Sometimes they are cases of luck—a few persons who just had a hot product at the right time. There are even cases of created luck—manufactured success cases to recruit more salespersons. But the big earners in sales are mostly the result of people spending very long hours at work.

The long hours and the pressures of the job (including those built into incentive pay plans) cause many to burnout, physically and emotionally unable to continue the work at the pace required. Simple burnout is the greatest cause of turnover of nonsupervisory salespersons. Some companies know that four of five of their successful salespersons will not last in the job for more than five years.

Sales Incentive Compensation Plans

Since sales incentive plans must be tailored to the company's products, organization, and operating circumstances, there are many different programs. Most of these, however, fall into four categories: commission plans, quota systems, bonus systems, and planned compensation programs. Combinations of these basic approaches are also used.

Commission Plans

Commission plans are those that, in one way or another, relate the salesperson's pay directly to the volume of sales produced. In its simplest form, it means that the salesperson is paid X percent of each dollar of sales booked or shipped. That commission rate may vary from a fraction of one percent to as much as 25 percent. The rate may increase, remain constant, or decrease with increasing sales. Frequently, the sales commission rate percentage will vary with the product line.

Commission plans give the salesperson the greatest incentive to sell the largest volume, and this single feature accounts for most of the advantages and disadvantages of commission plans. On the one hand, the commission system creates the maximum incentive for sales volume. Commission plans also provide fixed unit costs of sales, and they also provide salespersons with a maximum opportunity for optimum income.

Studies indicate that, on the average, commissioned salespersons earn about 20 percent more in gross pay than those in comparable jobs paid by other pay systems. This focus on sales volume makes it difficult to control the product mix or the nonsales responsibility of the field sales force. Salespersons tend to push items that provide the greatest commission. In addition, commissioned salespersons tend to be more independent, more money-oriented, and less company- or customer-oriented. This can erode customer relationships.

There is also a traditional mind-set by management in some businesses, such as automobile agencies, that sales don't cost anything, because the salesmen are on commission. Just try to talk your automobile dealer into any other system of sales pay, and he won't do it—not even if compensation costs were less under a new system. This is because his thinking is that the pay of salespersons is actually a contingent sales expense and not a payroll cost at all. Recognize that some of that thinking is part of the sales management mind-set in many businesses.

Quota Systems

Quota plans are similar to commission plans, except that the salespersons are usually paid a salary for a minimum level of sales and then receive a percentage of sales over that quota. Thus in return for salary, the company can require a variety of activities other than direct sales. These other activities might involve customer relations, missionary work, and gathering information. The commission then provides incentive to exceed the quota.

The success of these plans depends partly on the soundness of the quotas established. Setting quotas requires a thorough knowledge of markets, precise estimates of sales potential, and other important statistical analyses. Quota plans are frequently geared to a district, with the money for extra compensation accumulated on a district basis. This money is then allocated either on a pro rata basis among all salespersons or allocated to individual salespersons on the basis of their contribution to overall results.

Quota systems may try to achieve multiple goals and accomplish none of them. For example, if a system is based partly on prescribed duties, such as customer service, and partly on production volume, there is an inherent conflict of goals.

Bonus Plans

Insofar as bonus plans are geared to the sales a person makes above a given quota, they are very similar to the quota system. Generally, however, bonus plans also consider such factors as the penetration of the market, profit results, and expense control.

Bonus funds are usually accumulated on a group basis and allocated according to individual contributions. Bonus payment decisions take into account more of the variables of the sales job and duties than commission or quota plans do. However, the methods of rewarding individual salespersons are less direct.

When using bonus plans for salespersons, companies should consider integrating them with bonus pay systems for other middle-level positions, using the same bonus pay standards whenever possible. Should performance measures be used to determine actual payments, they would necessarily be tailored to the sales jobs, as they would for each middle-level group.

Bonus rewards for any group of employees are always a good idea for achieving organizational goals. The issues are the amount of the bonus and the performance standards. Bonus plans for salespersons are no different than any other bonus plans and have the same issues.

Planned Compensation

Some companies follow an approach of planned compensation. They consider competitive levels of pay and career compensation patterns. Under this system, standards are set for judging what employee compensation should be. These are matched against expectations with respect to sales targets. Salary decisions and bonus judgments are based upon analysis of such considerations.

Planned compensation systems are interesting for a number of reasons. They consider potential as much as current performance, reflecting a long-term view of salespersons. Frequently, the compensation planned is purposely higher than market during the early years of work, primarily to reduce turnover, and lower in later years, on the logic that pay has been advanced and people are less likely to quit. Whatever the mechanics, this compensation approach is highly discretionary.

Planned compensation systems, by nature, tend to design the performance standards to conform to predetermined ideas as to how much salespersons should earn. That seems to be illogical and unfair business thinking. Many incentive and quota plans in sales, however, have the same characteristics and elements of planned compensation.

Combination Plans

About one-third of all companies today use some combination of the basic plans described for salespersons or several different plans tailored to divisions or subsidiary operations. Such plans can be designed as salary plus commission, salary plus bonus or quota, salary plus commission plus bonus, or almost any other possible combination.

There are several advantages to using combination plans. The company can retain a degree of control over sales activities and, at the same time, encourage sales volume. Salespersons have the potential for high income, but they also have a base salary as a floor below which their earnings will not fall.

The disadvantage of combination plans centers on their complexity. They are far more difficult to understand and administer than other plans, and many companies find it necessary to alter them periodically. However, the flexibility of combination plans has led to the development of literally hundreds of different incentive programs, almost as many as there are companies that use them.

Total Pay of Salespersons

In some companies, the level of income of salespersons is thought to be a problem. Many who sell life insurance, for example, earn more than $1 million a year, and earnings of hundreds of thousands of dollars a year are common in fields such as automobile sales, residential real estate, and retail security sales. Such earnings are usually well known in the company and the community and are occasionally publicized in the media.

High earnings are not necessarily bad, whether they go to salespersons, executives, or baseball players. But nonmanagement salespersons are company employees with backgrounds similar to those of middle-group employees who earn far less. Salespersons with big earnings work hard and are highly effective, but factory superintendents may work equally hard and effectively and earn far less. It's this type of comparison that presents a problem.

With respect to the high total compensation of salespersons, there is also a question of sufficiency and the proper management of costs. These high earnings figures represent high costs. They are payments to a few, partially at the expense of many. And companies wonder, with reason, whether far less income might not attract and retain equally effective persons and provide sufficient motivation.

In most cases where total compensation of salespersons is perceived to be a problem, there was a fixed rate of commission or bonus that was correct and reasonable at some time. As conditions changed, that rate produced very high income, frequently for no better results. For example, the great inflation in real estate values, particularly in some geographic areas, has escalated the income of real estate salespersons far more than wage inflation generally. In rapidly growing areas, this produces high earnings for no more work.

In many cases of high compensation, employers feel helpless, because if they cut the rate or change the method of pay, they stand to lose their best producers to competitors that continue to pay the traditional rate. And usually the producer takes customers with him.

These situations evolved over time, and there was no precise moment when either necessity or logic called for action or even a study. Perhaps, for example, as real estate market values inflated, the real estate commission should have been cut from 2 percent of the sales price to 1.95 percent, and so on. But that would not have been practical.

There is an inclination to explain, excuse, or justify super earnings by citing similar earnings figures in other fields. The individuals used as precedents, however, are usually in sports or entertainment. They are, in fact, businesses, not employees. The successful syndicated columnist, for instance, actually has a staff and, therefore, a payroll of his own. There is logic in basing the pay of such individuals on their business value.

Some sales personnel are quite similar. They have such a following or such special sales skills that they might be regarded as a business. Then an entrepreneurial pay plan may be the thing to meet these needs.

In this era of cost containment, subcontracting work, and downsizing the staff, it is timely to review sales compensation. At least develop the proper sales compensation plans for contemporary conditions. It may be necessary to grandfather some persons, but at least stop creating more problems by applying outdated sales compensation plans to new salespersons.

The same principles apply to sales employees that apply to any other. Their pay should be competitive, and it should be fair.

Designing the Sales Compensation Program

The process of designing a sales compensation program is no different from that of designing any other program: determining needs, setting objectives, determining compensation levels and conditions, considering past practices, considering available alternates, and the actual design. What's often different about sales compensation is the special need to customize the plans, the frequency of modification, and responsibilities for developing and administering the program.

The basic methods of incentive pay for salespersons outlined earlier have all been used for many years, and there hasn't been any new basic technology of compensation in this area for a very long time. Most of the improved technology is in marketing knowledge, information management expertise, and the implementation of the basic approaches. Market information and criteria, not personnel expertise, are the key to the tailoring of any of the basic sales plans.

Thus what is "new" in the design of sales compensation programs is increased skill and experience in applying marketing knowledge. Although one still hears of "new" programs for sales compensation, examination shows them to be old programs with new labels or long-standing ideas told with youthful enthusiasm.

It is vital to sales compensation to monitor programs. This includes making revisions and, when required, basic changes. Elements of the marketing compensation program must also adapt to the changes in marketing. The marketing changes are not always dramatic, like a new product introduction. But market changes are constant and they accumulate, usually in a few years to the point where change or modification of salespersons' compensation is required.

The important technologies in the development of a sales compensation program derive from marketing. Personnel considerations tend to be either essentially the same as those affecting other employees or related to relatively simple compensation concepts. In fact, personnel has added little of value or anything fundamentally new to sales compensation for a very long time.

Salespersons are company personnel. Basic principles, policies, and practices that contribute to the effective work of all employees in the company will generally apply to sales personnel as well. Therefore, the personnel organization must participate in the human resources management of the company, including personnel aspects of sales management. This necessarily involves a form of matrix organization in the management of sales personnel. The essential responsibilities for developing new programs must rest with the marketing organization of the company or be assigned to outside consultants who have marketing experience in the company's lines or in similar sales activities. Human resources policies and know-how must be part of all such project work.

Once a sales compensation plan has been designed, it is very important to test that plan before implementing it. It should be checked against actual sales figures for the last few years to determine what each person would have earned under the new system. More important, it must be tested against the future. This may involve complex modeling and the use of computer technology to determine the income and the costs of sales under various possible business developments.

Inevitably, this type of testing will indicate potential problems in the new sales program, which call for adjustments and then further testing—which, in turn, may require further refinements. This fine-tuning system can entail considerable amounts of time and analysis.

Sales Compensation Issues and Trends

Studies suggest that for some time there has been a distinct trend away from commission plans to straight salary and quota plans. This trend reflects the changing nature of sales jobs and the increasing number of sales positions where customer service, missionary work, and information inputs are critical to long-term success. Better market research techniques and computer technology have also facilitated this trend to straight salary and quota systems of compensating salespersons.

There has also been a great deal of fundamental rethinking in sales compensation over the past few years. Much of this has involved a basic analysis of the business aspects of marketing and their implications on sales compensation. As a result, a considerable amount of time and money has been invested in attempts to develop new plans and approaches that are built primarily on marketing technology. There have been some interesting results from all this work but few successes. While probably correct in basing sales compensation plans more on marketing technology than on plan design, the plans have all been too complicated and too programmatic.

One positive result of development work in sales compensation during the past dozen years is that some companies have successfully instituted plans and programs in which regions and districts are considered as separate business units. They have paralleled their organization along the lines of "distributor" businesses. The company puts up the capital and exercises various controls, but district managers have considerable latitude in marketing, including the specifics of sales compensation.

Some form of entrepreneurial pay in direct sales work should always be considered. The pay of a distributor organization is one approach. Various commission plans are entrepreneurial pay. If a firm ever considers research and development (R&D) activities in human resources management, the development of more entrepreneurial pay plans, particularly for the sales organization, would seem to be a very promising subject.

Looking back, it is fair to conclude that sales pay plans generally have reflected too much the ultimate of programmatic management. Great effort was put into them, and elaborate testing was undertaken to make sure that the top sales management persons, aided by the best professional advice available, came up with the perfect plan that would reward individuals in the correct way for achieving the specific goals of the sales organization in every respect. All the strings were then to be manipulated in the central sales office. The program and the string manipulators would orchestrate the organization—the sales plan would do the management.

Sales pay plans have never worked like that. The promise of the ultimate programmatic system in pay that would manage the sales force and direct the behavior of salespersons never did work. Many tried it. But if you want a measure of how badly it worked, go back in history and see how often those magic sales compensation plans were changed.

Incentive pay plans do affect behavior and thinking wherever significant amounts of money are involved. However, they may affect behavior in ways you did not anticipate and management does not want. For example, the incentive pay plan in the sales organization, just like in the factory, may cause some to scale back their work or control output.

Chapter Sixteen

Compensation of Professional Personnel

Personnel policies and practices, including those involving compensation, have a number of unique applications for professionals. This is not because people doing professional work are different but rather because their jobs are different.

In an increasingly technological work place, there are more jobs that have the basic characteristics of professional work. If you use a broad definition of professional work, then today there are more professional workers than factory hourly workers and more professional workers than union members.

Thus if manufacturing operations and office work were the models for developing compensation in 1960, when the first edition of this book was written, professional jobs would be the model in the 1990s. Therefore, much of what was used as a primary reference for the material in Chapters 1 through 14 of this edition was largely influenced by professional work and the increasing technology in jobs. In addition, there are some compensation matters that are largely unique to truly professional jobs.

Professional Jobs

If you are going to do human resources management work in professional job categories, it is important to understand the essential characteristics of that type of work. Differences in practices for any group of jobs should only be based on competitive essentials or unique requirements to do work effectively.

In its broadest sense, professional work involves the application of learned knowledge to the solution of enterprise problems and the achievement of enterprise goals. A professional may engage in a variety of tasks, but the essence of his work is the application of learned knowledge. The knowledge of the professional may be in areas of recognized academic disciplines such as law, economics, medicine, one of the physical sciences, or in one of the recognized business disciplines. In any case, the knowledge applied has been acquired through prolonged periods of formal study.

Those who work in personnel should have little difficulty understanding professional work. Most of the work done by those in the field is professional work.

The key to successful personnel practices for professionals is understanding the unique characteristics of professional work. Some of these are:

• Essentially, the enterprise is using the knowledge of the professional. It does not pay the professional for his time or his physical output, but rather for the level and relevance of his knowledge. It is the job of management to use this knowledge effectively.

• The knowledge of the professional represents the assets of the group, which, in turn, are important assets of the enterprise.

• The professional job involves many choices of what to do as well as how to proceed. Such work decisions must often be made by the professional doing the work.

• Since the user of professional services is frequently a layman who cannot really judge the appropriateness of professional work, the user is, to a large extent, buying on confidence. This is true whether the provider is in the company or an outside person.

• The professional has multiple goals. One is the financial well-being of the company, but there is also the secondary objective of achieving a high caliber of professional work.

Such characteristics as these not only identify professional work but they determine to a great extent the effective management of personnel and appropriate compensation programs and practices. Understanding the job is the key to the effective management of professional work. For the compensation specialist, knowledge of the characteristics of professional work is essential for developing policies and practices that assist in attracting, retaining, and motivating professional employees.

The Management of Professional Work

Because of the special characteristics of professional work, the effective management of professional operations has some unique features. This suggests that there needs to be some differences in compensation management practices as applied to professional work. The key to effective human resources management of professionals in all areas involves an understanding of the professional job and key areas of activity in professional work.

Effective management of people in general has changed significantly over the past decade and will be substantially different in the future. Many of these emerging management practices are, in effect, a result of the increasing technology of work. The changes have come about and will continue to evolve partly because of the increasing number of professionals and the growing complexity of technology. Much of what must be learned about more effective management of people in general, therefore, will probably evolve from lessons learned from the management of professional enterprises and professional groups within product and service enterprises.

Professional work must be directed to the needs of the enterprise. Scientists, for example, must develop new products with commercial value. Management must assure not only that appropriate knowledge exists but that knowledge is used to deal with company problems and opportunities.

Professional knowledge is an asset. To have value, the asset must be usable—it must have relevance to the company. As important as anything else is the use of knowledge and intelligence. The use of knowledge is a special skill. The use of knowledge is a special input to productivity and an area of work effectiveness we must learn far more about.

The professional tends to use the knowledge he has and the areas of knowledge in which he has the greatest personal interest; the manager must see to it that the knowledge used is most relevant to the company. The professional must be redirected from doing work that is of interest to himself to focusing on company priorities. A professional in personnel, for example, cannot be working on "matrix management" if what the company requires is more effective recruiting.

Those who exercise general management responsibilities over professional work must have a broad business perspective and an understanding of the professional areas involved. Managers must understand the capacities of professional work like other managers must understand the capability of equipment. Managers must direct the application of that capability to serve customers and otherwise achieve enterprise goals.

Managers of professional work must be skilled in managing interdisciplinary professional areas. For example, the successful R&D activity in a pharmaceutical firm must involve the management of biologists, chemists, mathematicians, doctors, and others with widely different professional knowledge and skills. Such different knowledge and professional disciplines must be brought together in a way that enables each to contribute optimally his particular knowledge to the achievement of some specific enterprise goal.

There are also unique characteristics of operational management in professional work. Only a professional can direct the operational work of other professionals. Only an attorney can direct the professional aspects of the work of a law firm. Only a professional can review the technical appropriateness of work in any professional discipline.

In professional work, much is done in project groups, and at different times each professional may be working for different managers. There must then be networking between managers to understand the work excellence of each professional.

There are limits to the levels that can be managed and reviewed in an operational sense even within a professional discipline. For example, the management information system (MIS) manager rarely understands in detail what is being done by specialists within the MIS department. At best, the head of that department can recognize people's capabilities and know how to use them, but he must trust intermediate levels of management to see that the technical work is proceeding effectively and with excellence.

Delegative management, therefore, is essential to the successful management of professional work. In fact, the concepts of delegative management emerged from professional work, where the successful practices of this management style were learned.

There are some particular skills of managing people in professional work, and these also have relevance in the appropriate compensation of both the managers of professional work and the professional worker. Here are some of the key skills of managing professional work:

- The manager of knowledge workers adds a great deal to the results of those workers by bringing a special expertise to all of them with respect to the work process; how to proceed in a variety of situations.
- The manager must have very special skills in performance appraisals, in part because the performance of professional work can rarely be measured quantitatively.
- A key part of the management of professionals is manpower management: the determination of the correct amount of manpower necessary to accomplish assigned missions.
- A manager of knowledge workers must be quality-minded. In professional work, quality is the correct work and the relevant work. Quality management in professional work requires knowledge of what might have been done as well as what was done.
- Management of knowledge necessarily means excellence in the management of interdisciplinary skills.

- Management also means effective accessing of knowledge from other persons, inside and outside the company.
- Finally, management of professional work means facilitating administrative support; and that often means relieving professionals of administrative chores.

Even this brief sketch of some of the elements of managing professional operations illustrates the uniqueness of management practices and work in a professional organization. An understanding of these basic aspects of professional work, of the management of professional work, and of the limitations of management is crucial to the development and administration of an effective compensation program for professional employees.

Compensation programs must match the quality of management. In my opinion, there has been excellence in the management of professional work, particularly in corporate engineering departments and in professional businesses. In those two categories of work, compensation practices have worked well. Compensation systems that are appropriate for professional work are available and experience proven, and these must be applied.

Salary Administration for Professionals

The focus of salary administration for professionals is career pay progress geared to professional growth. Many of the techniques of salary administration described in Chapters 1 through 5 apply to professional jobs, but this general approach must be modified to meet this key requirement of effective salary administration for professional work.

Use of Job Descriptions

Traditional job descriptions are rarely used for professional jobs, because it is extremely difficult to describe professional duties in a specific way. If job descriptions are used at all, one of three systems is used in professional work: modified functional descriptions, generic descriptions, or work-sample descriptions. Even these descriptions are used mostly for employment and surveying.

Modified functional descriptions identify the various tasks performed by the professional, but they are intended only to illustrate the functions performed. They are written to help differentiate among levels of professional work.

Generic descriptions of professional jobs do not attempt to describe job duties or work performed but rather seek to define, in very broad terms, the level of professional work involved. The generic descriptions are rather simple and brief. However, the writer must know the field and understand what constitutes various levels of professional competence.

There are also work-sample descriptions. Some may involve a listing of assignments completed by an individual. Others emphasize the highest level of professional work the individual has demonstrated he is capable of performing. These work-sample descriptions outline, in effect, the value of the work that can be done. Thus a work-sample description for a lawyer might list clients served and samples of the most advanced legal work the employee has performed.

Job Evaluation

Rarely are traditional methods of job evaluation used for professional jobs. It is simply not possible to identify factors and degrees of factors that meaningfully differentiate among the values of professional work.

Most companies use the market classification system in evaluating professional jobs. They price professional jobs in the marketplace to the best of their ability to establish values for benchmark jobs, which are slotted into a structure. This is essentially the same basic approach of market-position evaluation described earlier.

Market-position classification has many advantages for any group of employees. It is particularly useful for professionals, because job evaluation systems are not applicable. In addition, since so many professional people are active in the labor market and identify more with their field than with their industry or employer, companies have found that ensuring competitiveness and classifying jobs directly in the marketplace are more understandable and acceptable to employees.

Market-pricing systems usually result in each professional discipline having four to six generic levels of jobs. This necessarily requires quite broad salary ranges. But the generic levels indicate different levels of professional attainment or different levels of professional work that might be done in the firm.

Salary Structures for Professional Positions

Salary structures for professionals may take the traditional form of pay minimums and maximums. Using salary grades for professional jobs is not practical. Salary levels should be used, usually overlapping three salary grades. This reflects the fact that there are four to six levels of nonmanagement professional work. These levels can be related to the salary grade system used for other areas of work and the salary level system used for salespersons, such as that described for sales compensation.

Figure 16–1 illustrates how one company adapted its salary structure for professional employees. Five professional levels were established for

Figure 16-1. Salary Ranges for Nonmanagement Professional Positions.

Company Salary Structure ($000)				Engineering Levels ($000)				Staff Levels ($000)			
Grade	Minimum	Midpoint	Maximum	Level	Generic Title	Minimum	Maximum	Level	Generic Title	Minimum	Maximum
22	$56.2	$64.6	$74.3	I	Scientist	$42.2	$67.5	A	Consultant	$42.2	$74.3
21	51.1	58.7	67.5								
20	46.4	53.4	61.4								
19	42.2	48.5	55.8								
18	38.4	44.1	50.8	II	Staff Engineer	31.7	50.8	B	Director	28.8	50.8
17	34.9	40.1	46.1								
16	31.7	36.5	41.9								
15	28.8	33.2	38.1	III	Senior Engineer	23.8	38.1				
14	26.2	30.1	34.7								
13	23.8	27.4	31.5					C	Manager	17.9	31.5
12	21.7	24.9	28.6	IV	Engineer	17.9	28.6				
11	19.7	22.6	26.0								
10	17.9	20.6	23.7								
9	16.3	18.7	21.5	V	Associate Engineer	13.5	21.5	D	Analyst	12.2	21.5
8	14.8	17.0	19.6								
7	13.5	15.5	17.8								
6	12.2	14.1	16.2								

Salary levels are more useful than salary grades in professional work. Levels cover two to five grades. These levels also represent professional career ladders.

engineering positions and four levels for staff positions. Each engineering level encompasses three salary grades and has a spread of 60 percent from minimum to maximum. The four staff levels have a total range of 76 percent, and each staff level covers four salary grades. Note that these cover only nonmanagement positions.

Pricing Professional Positions

Slotting benchmark positions into the proper level involves special problems for professional jobs. For one thing, there are a number of professional markets for most companies, and survey methods are particularly difficult.

Selecting the appropriate companies and the right jobs for pricing is more difficult for professional positions than for most other jobs. This is because the professional tends to identify more closely with his field of work than with a particular employee or industry. Many different types of companies in many different geographic areas are competitors for professional talent, and frequently potential competitors for professional talent are very diverse. Therefore, considerable effort and cost are required to ensure competitiveness of salary levels, even generic salary levels.

Professional organizations spend relatively more time on pricing professional jobs. For many years, professional groups have priced jobs by employment experience. And many special groups in professional business fields are engaged in pricing jobs.

Because of the special difficulties of surveying professional positions, it is frequently necessary to use supplemental methods of determining competitive pay. This may involve a number of innovative or hybrid survey techniques, including:

- Establishing college hiring rates for the lowest levels of professional management, then determining intermediate levels by career progress.
- Making more intensive use of employment experience as a source of market salary data.
- Establishing link-ratio information with positions priced in available surveys.
- Conducting intensive surveys for a few key professional positions to serve as benchmarks.
- Using information-based surveys.

Recognize that in many cases the pay of professionals is a prime determinant of the price of the professional organization's product. Part of the special care in pricing jobs is to ensure competitiveness and fairness of pay for professional persons, and part of the special effort is to ensure that the prices of products and services are competitive.

Managing Salary Increases

Managing salary increases is the primary focus of compensation administration for professionals because salary ranges are very broad. Furthermore, professionals tend to advance through at least a few levels with time and experience. Therefore, for most professionals, there is one range from the college hiring rate to somewhere in the salary range for the senior professional. This is a total effective range of about 300 percent. Obviously, it places a great emphasis on salary increase management.

Furthermore, a number of persons must often contribute to making effective decisions for salary increases for each professional. One is, obviously, the immediate supervisor, who has the responsibility for making decisions and recommendations. In professional work, however, each individual will often perform in different project groups under a number of supervisors. Therefore, supervisors must exchange experiences, observations, and judgments on the effectiveness of the work and the professional abilities of each individual before salary increase decisions can be made.

The persons receiving increases are very bright and usually also read about professional pay in professional journals. Professionals often think they know about market trends. They can calculate market and cost-of-living trends and their own pay progress. They ask questions—usually very intelligent and searching questions. Professionals will likely assess answers carefully. They are a difficult audience.

The career-curve approach is a method specifically designed for professional jobs, particularly engineering positions. In essence, it assumes that, after completing their education, professional employees with different capabilities will progress within their discipline at some standard rate as a result of their experience in the field. This assumed progress is usually described as a curve, constructed by plotting average earnings against the number of years since the employee received his professional degree.

Under the career-curve approach, determining salaries is largely a matter of first determining professional capabilities, then looking up the number of years since the employee received his degree, and then reading the salary indicated by the curve. A number of curves are drawn, representing different levels or ratings of employee proficiency. This is illustrated in the graph shown in Figure 16–2. Managers must judge the professional level of the employee before determining an appropriate salary level.

Career curves are similar to grades or levels, except that years since

Figure 16-2. Career Curves for Professional Positions.

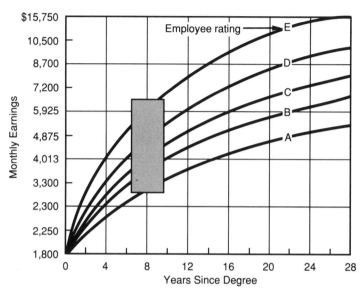

graduation are substituted for judgments of job difficulty or importance. Note in Figure 16–2 that there is a range of pay for those with eight years of experience (boxed area). Judgments of an individual's performance determine where he fits in that range.

The greatest advantage of the career-curve approach is that it concentrates managers' thinking on individual progress and contribution. This process is less complicated and less costly than standard job evaluation and classification systems, which won't work anyway. In addition, career curves frequently represent a mathematically-oriented technique for professional managers, which is more in line with their way of thinking.

In summary, the career-curve approach, with a number of embellishments, has proven to be a practical, though far from perfect, method of administering salary increases in large professional organizations. Although this approach is probably not sufficient to serve as the only salary increase guide for professionals, it can be a useful technique for pay decisions.

The salary planning systems described in Chapter 11 are very effective in salary increase management in professional work. There are other special techniques for managing salary increases for professional persons. However, particularly in professional work, the key is, first, delegation and, second, that salary increase work is a management activity that is done by managers.

Extra Compensation

Studies of the unique characteristics of successful professional organizations indicate that some form of incentive pay is used in many of them. This suggests that incentive pay plans for professional employees are feasible and even critical elements of successful compensation administration for professionals.

Case studies in the pharmaceutical, chemical, and aerospace industries, for example, identified operating characteristics common to successful R&D groups and generally lacking in ineffective R&D operations. The success elements vary somewhat by industry. Common to all, however, is an incentive pay plan for professionals.

Incentive pay plans for professionals are difficult to develop and administer. Don't undertake work on incentive plans for professionals unless your firm is willing to make a substantial commitment. Experience has shown that they should have several characteristics. All of these are vital if the professional bonus plan is to be successful.

The first essential step is to identify performance criteria. Multiple criteria are often needed for incentive pay plans for professionals. The criteria must be related directly to what the professionals contribute. This frequently includes the dollar profits generated by new products, services, or processes that are developed by the professional group.

Second, most bonus plans for professional work must include a conservative relationship between bonus and salary. Bonus standards in professional bonus plans range from 15 to 20 percent of salary a year. This reflects in part the difficulty of administering these plans and, therefore, the tendency to have smaller portions of total current pay in the form of a bonus.

Third, the time cycle of an incentive pay program for professionals must typically be longer than one year. Professional bonus plans should run three to five years before payout. As an alternate to long-cycle bonus plans, companies have tried using milestones for measuring progress toward success as a basis for partial payments on an annual basis.

There are also a number of nonsalary items in professional compensation that represent real costs to the company and real value to employees. Many of these items are nonfinancial and relate to work achievement. For the professional, they may all be thought of as some form of incentive pay. Examples would be the equipment used, the facilities made available, a supportive management style, and resulting high-level professional work. Other items with costs and/or income values include:

- Patent recognition.
- Encouragement, support, and compensation for publication in professional journals.

- Special bonuses for inventions, important research, or solutions to major company problems.
- Company-paid memberships in professional organizations or attendance at meetings.
- Encouragement, time off, and financial support for additional education.
- Greater flexibility in hours and location of work.

There are some types of compensation plans that I urge all professional organizations to consider, even though work on the plan proves to be impractical for a given firm at a point in time. They are worth considering anyway. Remember that one of my urgings was that all marketing organizations should move, to the extent possible, toward a "distributor" form of compensation plan. In addition, every professional organization should try to develop a "contract pay plan" in its professional businesses. Contract pay plans may vary greatly, but they are all a form of group entrepreneurial pay for professional units. Like distributor pay plans, these simulate the payments of contract professional firms; and specifically have extra pay geared to the commercial usefulness of the professional work of the group.

Also consider contingent compensation plans. Payments under bonus pay plans or contract compensation plans should also have contingent pay features. Professional work often has a long-term business impact, and contingent pay seems appropriate. The golden handcuffs features of contingent pay also seem appropriate in an era of scarcity of knowledge workers.

Consider stock ownership plans for at least the top three levels of nonsupervisory professional workers and for all managers of professional work. This can be done through option plans or by special stock purchase plans.

Career Development and Career Ladders

Career development is part of the overall personnel management of the firm. In professional jobs, however, it is also an integral part of compensation administration. To a very large extent, career development involves the improvement of professional qualifications, which in turn means advancement in professional work and a potential for greater earnings.

Pay programs for professionals should reward progress in professional competence and for more ability to handle higher levels of professional work. The various activities that are a part of career development facilitate professional development and therefore have a direct impact on pay progress. In this way, career development is an integral part of compensation administration.

In essence, this thinking reflects a philosophy of pay for capability. Management is paying, in part, for assets (knowledge, in this case) and must recognize that it is then a management job to utilize capabilities. This isn't really much different than pay for time where management has the task of using workers' time well.

To the professional employee, this aspect of pay administration represents not only an opportunity for higher income but a means of building personal *assets*—assets that may be sold elsewhere if not used by the current employer. The development enhances the professional's image and esteem among his peers as well as his value in the marketplace. Moreover, because career development programs can lead to more productive professional work, their cost is really an investment.

Reeducation must be part of career development. Methods of updating formal education (reeducation) in the physical sciences have been used for many years. Similarly, reeducation must be extended to other professional areas, including professional work in knowledge areas that are not recognized academic disciplines, such as human resources management. With computers and communication technology, new methods of reeducation will be available.

With more effective reeducation, careers will be extended, career development will become proportionately of greater importance, and career compensation plans and practices will be more important in the compensation of professional persons. The span of effective nonsupervisory professional work has been relatively few years in some professional disciplines and rarely more than twenty years. With effective reeducation, the span of work in professional categories can be extended greatly.

Career ladders are important, and with longer careers, they will be even more important in professional work. The engineering and staff levels shown in Figure 16–1 are career ladders. These are nonmanagement career ladders; and they should be parallel to management career ladders.

The time to move from one rung of a ladder to the next is an important variable. The time in the lowest levels of professional ladders will vary from two to five years. The time in each subsequent step in a career ladder will be roughly 50 percent longer.

Rewards for moving up the ladder are also progressive, partly because of extra compensation at higher levels. The first step will typically be about 35 percent, including promotion but net of inflation; then each subsequent step up the ladder will roughly amount to one-third more pay. Using median numbers, Figure 16–3 illustrates career ladders. Over a thirty-year work career, total pay increases will range from about 4 percent a year net of inflation for those who progress two steps in a career compen-

Figure 16-3. Career Ladders.

Salary Ladder Level	Illustrative Time in Ladder Step	Average Increase per Year Net of Inflation
1	3 years	12%
2	5	7
3	7	5
4	9	3
5	12 or balance of career	2 or less

Data shows time and median yearly increase in each step of a career ladder. The actual number will vary with individuals, of course, and also by professional discipline. Competitive labor markets and individual perceptions of fairness are the forces behind such variations.

sation ladder to as much as 7 percent a year net of inflation for those who go to the top levels of nonmanagement professional work.

Career ladders represent an important compensation tool in professional compensation and should be constantly reviewed and fine-tuned wherever they exist. Career ladders should be considered in professional work areas where they don't exist. I personally urge career ladder compensation for teachers and for human resources management professionals in particular.

The Management of Compensation for Professionals

Salary management systems applied to professional jobs must be designed to facilitate a highly delegative managerial style. Knowledge of jobs and the work of individuals are known only by the immediate higher-level manager of professional work. Even one level above that, managers can only review very generally.

Centralized programmatic methods of compensation management will not work well in any type of professional work, and that includes job evaluation and the management of salary increases. The special need for delegative management skills in a professional work area requires the highest levels of excellence in the management of personnel. On three different occasions, I was the general manager of professional businesses, although all were consulting firms and the largest had only 150 professionals. So I have considerable operating experience as well as human resources management know-how on this subject.

In professional operations, people are clearly and directly the assets.

General management is, therefore, likely to deal directly and personally with human resources management activities. In fact, the manager of professional work will likely delegate to others "business matters" and "administrative matters"—which usually means everything except the management of personnel. To professional management, the management of personnel *is* management.

As a result, in professional work the general manager is his own personnel manager. Therefore, compensation is a matter for general management in professional businesses and not professional specialists. The operating managers throughout the organization will not only accept delegative management but they will think that it is the only relevant style of management.

There are certain salary administration practices that must be applied to every area of a company, including professional organizations. For example, the company's salary structure must be used, and the policy of classification by market pricing must apply to professional organizations as well as any other. Beyond a few such requirements, however, the compensation professional should approach the professional organization with a consultant's mind-set.

In professional work operations, recognize that people are the product. There is no other product. Marketing is done by the professionals, and professionals develop the product. There is professional specialization in the same professional businesses, and some personnel focus mostly on marketing, for example, but in professional work, it is the professional person who designs, produces, and sells the products or services.

In any kind of work, I argue that people are the only assets of the operation. In professional work, this is indisputably true. It can't be surprising then that in professional operations the operating managers themselves do personnel management work, and the personnel department focuses on administrative, facilitating, and consultative activities.

If you want reference models for the compensation of professionals, look at pay practices in professional businesses. There are many professional businesses, including those in legal, accounting, and consulting companies. More people work for professional businesses today than there are workers in unionized factory operations.

In professional businesses, each professional is a business unit, in much the same manner as an individual contributor-professional in the arts, entertainment, and sports. In most of these companies, the time of the professional is billed, and the billing rate is directly linked to pay. As one example, when I ran Sibson & Company, Inc., any consultant could request that his salary be raised, and it would be done without approvals required. The higher salary rate meant a higher billing rate, and the clients, in effect, approved or disapproved the level of billing rates when they did or did not hire the consultant for more work. Also, billing rates at Sibson

& Company were used to set the billing goals and business development goals of each consultant—and those goals determined bonuses for each person in a formal manner. This is one example of a contract pay plan, which is an entrepreneurial pay plan in professional work areas.

Special Pay Issues for Professionals

On average, entry-level salaries in professional work are significantly higher than for most other college graduates. Salary progress is very rapid during the first ten years of work in most professional disciplines. However, progress slows down materially, and in many areas of professional work, the pay progress of nonmanagement professionals barely matches inflation after as few as fifteen years. This obsolescence of professional career manpower management involves difficulties in capping increases for senior professionals, who in effect career peak when they are in their forties. Reeducation is one answer to professional obsolescence.

In most professional disciplines, there is intense competition for individual contributors until they are out of school for ten to fifteen years. The market demand for nonmanagement professionals at graduation is intense. Recruiting pay is therefore a critical matter, and excellence in recruiting is a critical skill.

In professional work, there is also a period, sometimes after five to eight years of experience, when many professionals get restless and want to change. I call this the seven-year itch, and it is sometimes repeated at about fifteen years of experience. It has to do mostly with more earnings, professional development, and a change in work assignments. The time of the seven-year itch-cycle is not the time to be conservative with salary increases. In fact, some companies have special lump-sum ''stay'' bonus plans to deal with this tendency of restlessness every seven years in professional work.

After about fifteen years, many professionals move into a ''second career'' involving project direction or supervision. They are leveraging knowledge and experience through the work of others. Others find their second careers in administration or related areas such as marketing, where professional knowledge is essential to effective work. Increasingly, some seek a different though related professional assignment.

Multiple careers were thought to be a unique practice of professionals, but two factors have changed that situation. For one thing (partly because of increased technology), the obsolescence rate of professional knowledge and the resulting need for second careers in many areas of business require multiple career planning. There are far greater job and career changes due to such considerations as mandatory retirement, decreasing company loyalty, and an increasing portion of the work force who can afford second careers. Multiple careers are typical in professional work today. This must be considered in manpower management, and it must also be considered in salary administration.

There is labor scarcity in many areas of professional work. Companies cannot deal with labor scarcity with more pay alone, but selected uses of higher pay and accelerated pay progress must be considered in professional areas of particular strategic importance where there is labor scarcity.

The ultimate answer to labor scarcity in professional work lies in better and broader education—producing more qualified professionals. That is the job of the education community, but there are activities that individual companies can take to support better education.

Reeducation may extend the professional working life of a nonsupervisory professional a great deal. In theory, with formal reeducation, the maximum productive life of a professional might be extended to retirement. Expert systems will also extend the period of productive work by the professional as well as provide access to more specific knowledge when needed. In fact, some formal reeducation can be accomplished by expert systems.

Pay decisions regarding professional employees involve some difficult questions. One concerns the relationship between money and motivation for professionals. Although money is certainly not unimportant to professionals, it is probably true for many that, during most of their careers, money is less important than it is for employees in other work groups. This is partly because the pay is good to start with but also because of an identity with professional work and professional accomplishments.

Professionals generally strive to produce high-caliber work and to advance in their careers. Professionals expect pay progress and equitable treatment and can become dissatisfied if they feel they are being treated unfairly. As a practical matter, the theories of pay as a "dissatisfier" are probably more applicable to professionals than to any other group.

There is probably an artificial cap on the pay of nonmanagement professionals in many disciplines. Maximum pay levels are partly limited by the ability to measure value in professional work. Salaries of top-level nonmanagement professionals have also been limited by their managers. The top-level scientist, however, receives no technical direction from his manager, who is more like a homeroom teacher. In professional work, where the outstanding individual contributors have such great latitude of action, some individuals may properly be paid as much or more than their managers. In fact, it seems logical that an outstanding scientist might receive more pay than the chief executive officer, just as some salespersons in some businesses earn more than their chief executive officer.

Except for those who are clearly aiming for management of professional work and, eventually, general management positions, super-high income expectations are not realistic for most professionals. Many professionals, in fact, advance only three salary levels, or one salary class. This means that they are only three salary *classes* above unskilled operations workers. Most people who enter professional work as employees of a company do so knowing their income limitations. Their value systems must derive partly from the gratification of the work itself, the pride of advanced knowledge, and other attributes of professional work.

Typically in professional work, employees will be involved in a number of project groups. These different project groups often report to different managers. This means that in making decisions the supervising manager must rely on the inputs and evaluations from a number of managers of personnel. This focus of matrix decision making is inefficient and therefore costly. Managing in this environment requires very special skills and appropriate systems—including appropriate compensation systems.

Appropriate distribution of salary increases is dependent upon assessment of performance. In professional jobs, performance needs to be somewhat specifically defined. Professionals must first have greater professional knowledge, and then do the right things efficiently and correctly. This broader concept of performance, labeled *competence,* is difficult to rate. Work has shown, however, that competence ratings on a five-gradient system, such as that described for performance ratings in Chapter 10, can be done by other professionals. The key is to recognize the need for rating the broader concept.

In regulated industries, such as education and airlines, professional unions evolved. How this could happen and what to do about unions of professional employees and resulting strikes (sometimes against the public) is another matter. Compensation administration for these professionals, however, is a matter of collective bargaining. Compensation for professionals is complex enough, but the addition of an element of power and might makes this already complex matter almost impossible to handle on a reasonable basis.

In the past few years, there has been a great deal of talk about pay for knowledge. The theory is that a company pays for knowledge possessed, not time on the job or the output of a person. Those who urge consideration of the approach argue with correctness that knowledge is the critical resource in this increasingly technological world. Then they incorrectly conclude that an employee should be paid for knowledge.

Recognize first that no company has successfully implemented a pay-for-knowledge salary system. So far there have only been some thoughts, some words, and some pilot programs. There have been some cases when substantial efforts and costs have been expended, but I know of no success cases.

Pay-for-knowledge salary systems will never work for two reasons. First, the market will never value jobs by knowledge possessed, and no administered program will change the market. The market—millions of decision makers—knows that it is *usable knowledge* that matters, not just knowledge possessed. Second, it is not possible to *measure* the knowledge of professionals in all or many disciplines.

You can make the subject of compensation for professionals intolerably complicated if you like, but the practices don't have to be any more difficult than they are for any other group. Some matters, in fact, are more complex in compensation work for professionals, and others are less complex. The key to successful management of compensation for professional organizations is, first, to maintain a business view and recognize that a highly delegative style is essential because of the technology involved and because management of personnel *is* management. Second, recognize that to a large extent in determining pay for professionals, you are setting prices for their services.

Chapter Seventeen

Compensation for the Middle Group

Effective compensation administration for middle-level positions is a particularly difficult and important subject in many firms. Many compensation practices applied to middle-level positions were designed for office or factory positions and simply extended upward. Others were designed for management positions and extended downward to middle-level positions. In either case, compensation practices have rarely worked well for middle-level jobs, primarily because they were not designed for these positions.

The Middle Group

Middle-level employees are those who are neither operational workers nor in the management group. Middle-group employees would include salespersons and professionals, and special compensation practices for these groups have already been covered. The middle group also includes a disparate group of supervisory, administrative, and technical positions. In 1990 dollars, the supervisory, administrative, and technical positions would generally include salaried personnel earning between $15,000 and $50,000 a year. The compensation practices for these groups are the focus of this chapter.

Characteristics of the Middle Group

Although very different, supervisory, technical, and administrative jobs have one thing in common: They are all intermediate-level positions. Supervisory employees are intermediate between management and nonsupervisory personnel; administrative employees fall between office and top-level staff positions; and technical employees occupy a place between skilled production workers and professionals.

The people who fill these job categories are also disparate. Some are young college-trained persons who are on their way up to management or professional positions. Supervisory, administrative, and technical positions are also filled by people who have many years of experience, are very senior, and will spend the remainder of their careers in these types of positions.

In enterprises generally, the middle group represents about 15 percent of the total personnel and 20 percent of payroll costs. This represents a significant portion of enterprise costs. Therefore, administration of salaries for middle-level employees is important simply from the cost view.

The effectiveness of the work of supervisory, administrative, and technical employees is important in any company and is critical to the success of many. Effective personnel management for these middle-group persons is, therefore, important to all companies and vital to many. Yet to a large extent, personnel practices, including compensation policies and programs now used, have not been designed for these middle-level persons, and some need to be redesigned to meet the specific needs of middle-level people.

Various productivity studies have shown that work effectiveness is lower in supervisory, administrative, and technical positions than in any other group in the work force. Attitude studies always show more discontent on the part of people in these middle-level positions than in any other group, except unionized workers. Productivity tends to be low, therefore, and discontent high in a group of employees who perform important duties.

Some believe that improved personnel practices for supervisory, administrative, and technical positions are particularly important because of special problems of managing these positions. Many of these middle-level positions involve technologies and practices that are not well-known by general management and are not easily manageable. Marshalling the talents of such people toward the achievement of business goals is difficult.

These positions often have a significant impact on the effectiveness of the work of others. The effectiveness of supervisors, for example, affects the work of subordinates. The work of administrative and technical people influences the effectiveness of the work of operations workers and management. Therefore, how well these positions are managed has a ripple effect on the productivity of others. Under such conditions, excellence of compensation practices for these positions may be particularly critical to many companies.

A Compensation Framework

The approach to effective compensation administration for supervisory, administrative, and technical positions involves first the establishment of a compensation framework. This, in turn, involves the establishment of policies and general procedures. Then guidelines can be developed that represent corporate requirements for compensation administration. Within these guidelines, local operations and divisions should then have considerable flexibility in designing and implementing specific compensation practices that meet the needs of supervisory, administrative, and technical positions in their units.

A corporate compensation framework for all administrative, supervisory, and technical employees is essential because many of these people who are in different business units will work in the same building or in the same work area, and comparisons are inevitable. Furthermore, companies find it desirable occasionally to transfer employees from one unit or area to another; for example, from administrative to technical or to the third floor from the second. 'With such disparate jobs, a framework is likely necessary to ensure competitiveness. Also, from the point of view of fairness, companies want to make sure that there is reasonable consistency in the treatment of different groups and individuals within these groups.

Exactly which salary administration framework is suitable for a given enterprise depends upon many factors. But in any system, at least three elements are essential. First, a single salary structure must be established for all supervisory, administrative, and technical positions. Second, a survey system must be developed that allows slotting a sample number of positions into the salary structure. Each benchmark job must be priced in its own relevant labor market. A final requirement is that methods of salary increase administration must be similar for all supervisory, technical, and administrative jobs in each operation and in each location. For instance, if a performance increase system is applied to supervisors, then a consistent method for granting increases should be used for other middle-level groups.

These three guidelines should constitute corporate requirements for compensation systems covering supervisory, administrative, and technical positions, and they must be followed in every operating unit and at every location. The guidelines assure competitiveness, equity, and sound practices. It is adherence to these requirements that makes it possible to have differences in other specific practices in business units and location, geared to local needs and objectives and to the needs of each subgroup. This approach reflects a delegative management style, in tune with trends in modern practices of managing people.

Recognize that what has been briefly described is the essence of delegative management. The techniques and practices of true delegative management evolved from work with middle-level groups and professionals.

Salary Classification and Surveying

One system that is useful in salary administration for middle-level jobs is a market benchmark classification system. What is described here as the benchmark system is quite similar to the market-classification system described in Chapter 4. In middle-level jobs, however, many of the corporate-required classification jobs are determined internally or administratively partly because of a shortage of qualified survey data but also to meet internal needs, such as job transfers and career pathing.

A key to a tailored market benchmark salary administration system for supervisory, administrative, and technical positions is the determination of as many market-priced jobs as possible. This is a particularly important facet of the middle-level salary administration system, because of the diversity of jobs and the fact that there may be a number of labor markets.

Companies have experienced problems in pricing supervisory, administrative, and technical positions. The result has been that there was difficulty in finding a sufficient number of jobs priced to get a cross-section of benchmark positions. This required the development of supplementary job pricing methods.

One way to expand the pricing data produced by traditional survey systems is for the company to conduct its own surveys. Company-conducted surveys are very costly. It is prudent, therefore, to conduct surveys for only a few crucial positions in the supervisory, administrative, and technical areas.

Other economical survey techniques can be used to price additional jobs. One method is the information-based survey. Employment experience is another supplementary source that can be very effective with supervisory, administrative, and technical positions. There can be internal pricing. For some key middle-group positions, the labor market is the company itself, because these positions are often filled internally by operations-level employees.

Some middle-level operations positions must be priced by internal benchmarking because they are truly unique to the enterprise. If these salary relationships have existed for a long time, they are frequently well-established and accepted. They are also frequently immune from normal market pressures. Therefore, they can be priced by historic relationships and then used as part of the benchmarking system.

A related method of internalizing the benchmarking system uses established career paths within companies. For each basic area of supervisory, administrative, and technical work, there are sometimes well-established progressions that people follow as they grow in their careers. Each position prepares an individual for the next. That, by definition, is a career path. This being the case, all career-path jobs can be priced if any one of them can be priced by any of the methods described.

Benchmarking Salaries and Use of a Salary Structure

To establish the benchmark classification system, a company must slot the benchmarked positions into a salary structure. Benchmarked positions then form the basis upon which all other positions are classified. To make the benchmark classification system work, there must be a firm company policy that the grade assigned to market-priced positions cannot be changed for any reason. Reclassification of benchmarked jobs would be justified only if subsequent pricing showed clearly that over a period of time the relative value of a benchmark position had changed in the marketplace.

A structure for supervisory, administrative, and technical persons that is compatible with that shown in Figure 6–1 is shown in Figure 17–1. The basic minimums and maximums are the same as in the companywide structure. In the supervisory, administrative, and technical levels, however, there

Figure 17-1. Salary Structure: Supervisory, Administrative, and Technical Positions.

Salary Grade	Salary Amount ($000)			
	Training	Minimum	Maximum	Special Maximum
18	$33.4	$38.4	$50.8	$58.4
17	30.3	34.9	46.1	53.0
16	27.6	31.7	41.9	48.2
15	25.0	28.8	38.1	43.8
14	22.8	26.2	34.7	39.9
13	20.7	23.8	31.5	36.2
12	18.9	21.7	28.6	32.9
11	17.1	19.7	26.0	29.9
10	*	17.9	23.7	27.3
9	*	16.3	21.5	24.7
8	*	14.8	19.6	22.5
7	*	13.4	17.8	20.5

*Generally not used.

is an extra level below the minimum to provide for those in training status and levels above the maximum to be used for emeritus employees. The training range provides opportunities for pay for high-potential persons passing through jobs for developmental purposes. The training range also accommodates internal placement and except at entry levels, very few supervisory, administrative, and technical persons should be recruited from the outside.

The special maximum is for the effective, long-service employee who has career peaked. This extra range is not recognition, but pay for performance. In this case, it is for the special usable knowledge from long experience and the potential for teaching others.

The classification of benchmark jobs (those not market-priced) is done essentially by comparisons against benchmark jobs in each unit and division. There is generally latitude for each location or unit to use whatever supplementary system it finds useful in pricing and classifying nonbenchmark positions in each location or unit within the company. The actual system that is found to be most useful will vary a great deal, depending upon the size of the organization, the experience of the supervisors, and the mix of supervisory, administrative, and technical positions.

Job evaluation systems, particularly the point-factor system, are still being used by some companies for middle-level positions. This is partly because the labor market is really the company for so many of these jobs. Most of these jobs can also be described sufficiently for central job evaluation decisions.

This is illustrative of the types of guideline systems that are so critical in compensation for supervisory, administrative, and technical people. There are specific corporate requirements—everyone must use one structure, follow the benchmarking pricing system, and use prescribed methods for pricing jobs. All are required to compare nonbenchmark jobs against benchmark jobs. Beyond that there is considerable latitude at locations to develop those systems and techniques of classification that are specifically useful in getting the job done. Local management is supported and assisted in this work by the central staff.

Salary Increase Systems

The basic systems for salary increases that have been described apply well to supervisory, administrative, and technical positions. Frequently, there must be special emphasis with respect to specific practices, but the basic principles described earlier apply.

Special consideration, for instance, may be necessary in rating performance. For example, to a large degree, the level of performance of a supervisor is reflected in the performance of those supervised. For technical people, the level of performance is not just a matter of the effectiveness of the technical person's work but how that person's work supports and increases the effectiveness of professional people. Similarly, the performance of some administrative employees is measured partly by how well they support senior staff or general management.

There is a rather narrow range of career pay for the supervisory, administrative, or technical person. In professional work, the total range of pay from the lowest-level professional job to the highest-level nonsupervisory position can be a 500 percent spread. In nonmanagement sales work, the range can be 1,000 percent. But for supervisory, administrative, and technical people, the range is considerably smaller—300 percent or less.

Those promoted from operations-level jobs to this middle group would have a broader range from entry-level job to career peak, as would employees who enter work in middle-group jobs but get promoted to professional or management positions. But those who enter the work force at the supervisory, administrative, or technical-group level and spend their careers in middle-group jobs have the range of salary opportunity shown in Figure 17–1. Typically, the person who spends a career in middle-level jobs is promoted only two or three times in his entire working career. This means that annual pay increases, in excess of inflation, may average only 3 percent a year, including promotional increases.

There may be different effective ranges in middle-group jobs. The spread from minimum to maximum may be greater in some, covering an entire salary level or only part of a grade. In other middle-level jobs, there may be a flat salary, a few steps, or a very narrow range.

Incentive Pay Plans

Middle-level employees would not be part of the corporate management incentive compensation program and should have special incentive bonus plans. There is interest in many companies in the development and implementation of incentive compensation plans for middle-level employees, including supervisory, administrative, and technical people.

Policy Issues

Incentive compensation plans for middle-group employees have been explored a great deal, and there have been some successful installations. The starting point is an examination of policy issues.

Companies need to examine what problems such plans would solve and what opportunities they might exploit. They must ask specific questions, such as whether the plan is designed to increase productivity, to make total pay reasonable and more competitive, to reduce manpower, or to reduce turnover. They must ask whether there are other objectives that are less quantifiable, such as increasing the quality of work.

Unless specific objectives emerge from this type of rigorous examination, a middle-level incentive plan is probably not appropriate, regardless of its surface appeal. Furthermore, only by answering such questions can basic plan concepts be identified. Finally, policy objectives are essential in evaluating the progress in the development of the plan and the results of the program once it is installed.

Actually, many employees in this category are now covered by incentive plans. Many factory supervisors, for instance, are part of factory incentive plans related to costs. Sales personnel are frequently covered by an incentive plan or some overriding pay plan. A significant number of professional people are also covered by incentive plans. For some companies, therefore, it has become a matter of simple equity. If significant numbers of middle-group people are already covered by incentive bonus plans, then isn't there a compelling reason to develop a plan that would cover all middle-group jobs? Such an overall incentive approach for middle-level employees may also bring greater equity in administration and payment levels.

Principles of Incentive Compensation for Middle-Level Positions

Experience with middle-level incentive plans has indicated certain basic principles that seem to be appropriate for most if not all situations. These should guide the development and management of such plans.

For one thing, bonus payments should never be a substitute for appropriate salary. Too often bonus plans for middle-level jobs have been established because salary structures, actual salary levels, or salary progress were not satisfactory or were not thought to be satisfactory. Variations of variable pay plans have been used in middle-level jobs for many years.

Similarly, bonus payments should not be a method of paying more to employees when a salary level is inappropriate or when a permissible salary increase is inadequate. In fact, there have been cases where, at least in some section of a company, bonuses were paid to people because salary increases were not permitted by the system or because the supervisor felt the system did not allow salary increases he thought were appropriate. In middle-level positions, incentive awards should always be in addition to salary.

Bonus guidelines for supervisory, administrative, and technical positions not covered by any other plan are shown in Figure 17–2. Note that awards are paid only for exceeding target results, which are budgeted amounts and goals established in operational planning.

In developing incentive compensation for middle-level employees, it

Figure 17-2. Bonus Standards for
Incentive Pay Plan for
Supervisory, Administrative,
and Technical Positions.

Salary Grade	Salary Midpoint ($000)	Bonus as Percentage of Salary		
		Target Results	P1	P2
15	$33.5	0%	15%	27%
14	31.1	0	14	25
13	27.4	0	13	23
12	24.9	0	12	21
11	22.6	0	11	19
10	20.6	0	10	17
9	18.7	0	9	15
8	17.0	0	8	13
7	15.5	0	7	11

Note: P1 and P2 are performance standards set by budgets and objectives built into operational plans.

is important to base the award system first of all on the achievements of the unit and then consider the contributions of individuals. Plans that attempt to relate middle-level awards directly to individual performance have been extremely complex and cumbersome, poorly understood, and frequently misinterpreted, and they have always failed.

All participants in the unit generally share proportionately, on the basis of unit performance. Then individuals may be credited or debited, depending on their contributions or failures. However, these individual adjustments should generally be in increments of not less than plus or minus 20 percent of any adjusted standard bonus and should net out.

The key to middle-level incentive compensation plans is sound unit performance measures. The development of unit performance measures is very complex, frequently imprecise, and almost always dependent upon detailed knowledge about operations within each unit. Therefore, managers of the unit must at least participate in the development of such performance measures.

Because business performance criteria and standards must be customized to many different types of work and, therefore, set by managers who know the operation, there must be some system for monitoring and reviewing the basis for bonus payments. Unit performance standards are reviewed in part by the periodic operational planning and budgeting system, but additional monitoring is required if middle-level bonus payments are linked to budgets. This is best done by reviewing results obtained and awards paid. There is an expected pattern of award payments over time. If that pattern does not appear in a unit, a review can be made to see if this is due to actual performance achievement levels or defects in either the performance criteria or the standards.

Problems of Bonus Plans for Middle-Group Jobs

Developing bonus plans for middle-group positions not already covered by some incentive system can be time-consuming and costly. There are all the elements of design and implementation of such plans that exist in any case—and there are usually dozens of them. Furthermore, as the enterprise grows and changes, plans must be modified and new plans developed. The amount of work is considerable.

Much of that work must be done in the organization by managers of units, with the support of the local personnel staff. Typically, such people are less experienced in this work than is the case with developing management, sales, or operations workers' incentive pay plans, and the results cannot be as good as when the work is done by high-level managers and corporate compensation professionals. The number of people involved in this work is considerable, and this also poses a quality problem.

Regardless of how well the work is done, in many units the performance standards are not as apparent as they are at division or corporate organization levels. Nor are accounting or statistical measures as precise or reliable at the unit level. Therefore, some imprecision is inherent in unit bonus plans for supervisory, administrative, and technical employees.

Finally, because of imprecision in middle-level bonus systems and the number of people involved, the chance of human error of various types is very great. In particular, there is a danger that some will make arbitrary judgments, resulting in unfairness, dissatisfaction, or both. These are the types of problems that must be weighed against the value of objectives identified for the implementation of bonus plans for supervisory, administrative, and technical employees.

Unit Variable Pay Plans

In the past few years, a new form of industrial engineering or methods engineering practice has emerged. These allege, as did method time measurement (MTM) specialists in factories, that they can analyze middle-group administrative jobs, develop the best methods, and then set correct work standards. Then as a basis for incentive bonuses, the standards are used to set performance standards for individual jobs, categories of jobs, or units. Often, base rates are set lower than market, and the unit incentive plan then becomes a variable pay plan.

These plans have been applied in some financial institutions. Companies in traditional transportation and manufacturing businesses, where MTM and time studies were widely practiced, have had a particular interest in the unit variable pay plan system because they are accustomed to the approach. Some consulting companies have made these plans a major part of their businesses and have launched major marketing efforts. The plans have been much discussed at personnel meetings.

We should always applaud innovation and wait to see how these plans work out. There are some cases of original increases in output, but this always happens in new plans with much fanfare, and in many cases these plans have been applied where the effectiveness of work was known to have been low in the first place.

I urge that great caution be used in these plans and think that within a few years they will be history. The use of variable pay plans has already started to decline, and the unit variable pay plans will almost certainly do the same—most likely starting by 1991.

If there are known inefficiencies in middle-level positions, first question why that low productivity exists. Why not address the matter directly, immediately, and simply, by expecting operating managers to correct the situation right away?

In the cases I've seen, managers didn't and couldn't get better effectiveness of work because they weren't managers. The consultants sold top management on using their programs and keeping the nonmanagers. It seems better to structure the business so there are managers, expect them to do management jobs, and give them training and support necessary to do their jobs.

That answer seems so obvious and so simple, but we must ask why companies would do anything else. The consultants obviously have a reason for having something else—it's good business for them. In some cases, top management is using these unit variable pay plans as a way of preserving centralized programmatic management, but they will hold back that tide and more delegative styles of management are inevitable.

The methods work systems used to set performance systems and standards can't set the "best method"—and even if they could, it would be the best method for a short period of time in this changing world. Those methods work systems are mostly management engineering techniques applied to the office, and they are no better. Management engineering methods can be helpful, but my main argument would then be why not use such techniques to help managers manage and workers in the units develop better ways of getting the work done.

If these consultants have something of value, then use it. But first structure real management jobs, and be sure managers are capable of doing these jobs. Have information and advice for doing the work more effectively available to the manager and employees.

Special Compensation Problems for Supervisory Employees

Special compensation problems relating to supervisory personnel have long been examined in business. Some of the key issues are unique to individual companies, but a number are common to many firms. Many of them have been around for a long time, and companies still find that they reoccur from time to time.

Many companies have worked hard, for example, at developing a salary increase system for supervisors that gears salary within range to performance on the job. Each effort reflects a general management policy of rewarding for excellence of performance. Experience has demonstrated, however, that a performance increase program for supervisors can be successful only if two conditions are met. First, supervisory jobs must be structured so that individual performance can have a meaningful impact on the results of the unit supervised. Second, there must be sufficient authority and scope of responsibility built into the supervisory job. Thus job structuring and organizational structuring are two key conditions for a successful salary performance increase system for supervisors.

These are the supervisory jobs in the traditional sense of getting work done through other people. It is for this reason that supervisors' performance should be judged largely by how their subordinates perform. Yet it is rarely as simple as translating the performance of individuals or the group into the performance measures of the supervisor, because the performance of subordinates is affected by other factors, such as the availability of equipment and the training and supervision they received in prior work assignments.

The most publicized salary compensation problem for supervisors is the salary relationship between the supervisor and those supervised. In many cases, it was found that the real problem was one of job structure and company organization: The supervisory jobs did not have sufficient scope of responsibility to justify a greater difference between the appropriate job pay for the supervisor and the job pay of the highest-paid employees supervised. In effect, "supervisors" frequently direct only some aspects of work. They are called supervisors but are often not permitted to make decisions in labor relations, quality control, scheduling, maintenance, and other important areas of the work. Therefore, it is a very diluted supervisory job, perhaps more accurately described as group leader. When viewed in the context of the way the job is structured and performed, what seemed to be inadequate differentials are often appropriate and adequate.

Where there are to be real supervisory management jobs, there must be reasonable differentials, and proper job-pricing methods always result in adequate supervisory-supervised pay differentials. It is particularly necessary to assure proper supervisory pay differentials where the primary labor market for supervisory employees is those in operations jobs. Unless there are reasonable differentials in these instances, the best qualified operations employees may not be induced to accept the promotion.

There have been long-standing rules of thumb to help judge what constitutes satisfactory differentials between supervisors and those supervised. Usually, no single one of these guidelines is adequate, and certainly none should be followed without judgment and discretion. The following are five general criteria for adequate differentials between supervisors and those supervised.

1. The supervisor's salary grade should be at least two grades higher than the grade of the highest-rated person supervised. In practice, the supervisor is usually three to four salary levels higher.
2. The supervisor's base salary should be at least 15 percent higher than the straight-time earnings of the highest-paid subordinate.
3. The supervisor's gross pay (including bonus and any overtime compensation) should be at least 10 percent higher than the gross pay (including overtime) of the highest-paid subordinate.
4. The gross pay of the supervisor should be at least 25 percent higher than the average gross pay of all subordinates.
5. The gross pay of the supervisor should be no more than 75 percent higher than the average gross pay of all subordinates.

When operations workers are required to work significant amounts of overtime, their gross earnings will obviously increase substantially. This can narrow the differential between supervisors and those supervised even though the supervisors themselves must usually work just as much overtime. In such situations, there is the recurring question of whether supervisors should be paid overtime.

Many organizations are reluctant to pay supervisors overtime for fear that this will lead supervisors to work their departments unnecessarily long hours to get extra pay. Others are concerned about the administrative problems that might arise from giving supervisors overtime pay. Some are also concerned that the status of the supervisor's job would be diminished if he were paid for overtime work.

While some companies pay supervisors full premium rates of pay for overtime work, most follow a middle course. This approach allows some extra compensation, but at less than premium rates and only under prescribed conditions. For example, a company may not pay supervisors any extra compensation for intermittent overtime or for overtime that does not bring the total to more than forty-five hours a week. Beyond the forty-five hours a week, a company may pay straight time for extra hours worked by supervisors rather than premium rates.

Usually, when there are long hours of overtime work, the company is busy; and when the company is busy, there are frequently profits or the unit is successful by other financial or statistical measures. For this reason, many companies have adopted the practice of paying bonuses to supervisory personnel when long overtime hours are required. These may be based upon extra hours worked, actual profits, reduced costs, extra production, or some combination of such factors.

Always consider a bonus plan for supervisors instead of overtime pay. The number of hours worked should never be a consideration in the pay of managers of personnel at any level. Achieving objectives, higher profits, and lower costs should be the performance criteria in the bonus plan. Rewards for achievement help to maintain gross pay relationships and yet avoid treating managers as hourly workers.

An important part of the supervisor's job is to explain the salary administration program to nonsupervisory personnel and to administer that program. How supervisors apply the program and how they explain it is essentially how operations workers understand the program. By the same token, however, salary administration is applied to supervisors. How well they understand the salary program, what it means to them, and how they view their own treatment will influence how they administer and explain the program to their subordinates.

Thus part of the problem of inadequate or inappropriate communication of salary administration to operations workers is sometimes due to supervisors' dissatisfaction with the program or their misunderstanding of the program. Therefore, excellence in communicating the salary administration program to supervisors is of great importance.

Special Compensation Problems for Technical Employees

Technical employees occupy a position between professional workers and skilled operations workers. These employees perform mechanical duties, do administrative work, and engage in activities to support the work of professional employees. Their specific jobs vary greatly in different technical areas. For instance, in economics the technician might be a statistician; in engineering he may be a draftsman; in personnel, a survey specialist; in finance, an accountant; in medicine, a nurse.

This variety presents special problems in pricing technical jobs. Furthermore, the labor market for technical employees is quite diverse and at times unclear. Many technical employees are recruited from technical schools. Others are promoted from skilled operations work. Still others are recruited from other companies. Finally, many are transferred from other areas of technical work and trained to do new technical assignments.

These circumstances make it very difficult to price a sufficient number of technical jobs. Furthermore, pricing some families of technical jobs is of little help for a benchmark comparison for others. Drafting positions, for instance, can usually be priced, but they provide little help in establishing the proper salary grade for a metallurgical laboratory technician.

The category of technicians comprises many families of jobs, each quite different from the others. There may be few jobs and few people filling the jobs in each family. It may then be difficult to price some technical jobs, and internal comparisons may be the only method of job classification.

This diversity of types of jobs and roles performed by technicians also creates a considerable problem in judging performance. As in professional jobs, performance must be judged, to some extent, by those familiar with the technical work—either more senior technical people or professional employees. In addition, performance is only partly a matter of how well the technicians do their work; it is also a question of how well they support the professionals. If, by their work, the effectiveness of the professional's work is increased, that may be more important than increasing the effectiveness of what the technicians do themselves.

In some technical jobs there is a very narrow range from the pay of the beginner to that of the highest-paid technician in that job family. There are few levels of drafting work, for example. Typically, a family of technical jobs will cover only six salary grades. There isn't much upward mobility or promotional opportunity. Yet persons who fill these jobs often have high intelligence and considerable talent. In such cases, explore two possibilities. One would be movement to a management career ladder. More likely would be education and training to permit these persons to qualify for lower levels of professional work.

These cases indicate the need for a framework salary system for middle-group jobs. Within the guidelines, there must be broad latitude for using practices that reflect the situations of each job family.

There are also problems of overtime compensation for technical people. The key issue is the control of overtime. Frequently, technicians work in small groups and are closely involved with the work of professional employees. Professionals who are not paid overtime may work long hours for any number of reasons. If it is necessary to have technicians work with them, however, the overtime work of technical personnel can be substantial.

At one time, there was a rather broad distinction between professional work and technical work. In many fields, however, these distinctions have become far less clear. A form of paraprofessional job is continuing to emerge in business, and this will likely continue because of labor scarcity in technological work. So far, it seems practical to handle compensation administration for these paraprofessionals in the same way as for technicians rather than treating them as professionals. But this new category of technical-professional work, plus the increasing number and complexity of technical jobs in business, requires constant attention by compensation professionals.

Special Compensation Problems for Administrative Employees

The only characteristic shared by administrative jobs is that they do not fit into any other category. They are not management, supervisory, professional, sales, technical, or operations jobs. They usually fall within the two top salary grades of nonexempt jobs and within the lowest five salary grades of the exempt positions. Except for this, there are more dissimilarities than similarities among administrative positions. Thus there are no guidelines that fit all the employees who fall into this category. It is best to describe only particular administrative jobs and the special problems associated with each.

Executive secretaries represent one special group of administrative employees. Their relationship to managers is much like that of the technician to the professional, for although they perform various mechanical duties, their primary function is to conserve the manager's time and help managers perform their jobs better. This suggests that salary treatment for executive secretaries should be similar to that for technicians.

Another case would be trainees being groomed for higher-level managerial or professional responsibilities. Here the problem is that the position the trainee currently performs may have little relationship to the salary paid. Frequently, trainees are rotated in jobs so that they can gain diversity of experience, and the fact that they are given trainee assignments means that their responsibilities are somewhat limited. By any measure, therefore, their value does not match their pay. Salary administration in this case should follow a planned compensation approach, from required starting salaries to proper levels of pay when the trainee status is over and these people are finally assigned work that they are expected to perform to standard.

There are also senior clerks in this category of administrative employees. They are long-service employees who have come up through operations such as accounting and statistics. Because of their extensive and sometimes detailed knowledge of administrative matters, they have assumed high levels of responsibility. Their careers have peaked, but they are highly valued. It is in these cases that the special range maximum shown in Figure 17–1 can be very useful. It is not just a reward but recognizes a value that is difficult to assess or measure. So much of what they do is unknown by others. Much of what they do is also highly supportive of others in the organization.

Administrative jobs are typically very difficult to price, even if all the supplemental pricing techniques in addition to surveying are used. Generally, titles tell little about the job that is done. There are typically very few job matches in the marketplace. There is, however, little movement into the labor market from these jobs or into these jobs. Thus the jobs can be classified almost exclusively by internal comparisons.

Usually, salary increases can be handled effectively by the systems described in Chapters 8 and 9. There are cases where administrative persons have a close and integral working relationship with a senior person, and that individual's judgment of value is the basis of performance conclusions. Such cases often seem to yield unsatisfactory results, but there are few such cases. Do the best you can, but recognize that there will be exceptions.

These are but a few illustrations of the different types of administrative positions and the special situations involved in salary administration. A comprehensive list would include dozens of special cases, each requiring some general administrative practice if salary administration is to be appropriate and sound.

Chapter Eighteen

Management Compensation

Management jobs are those in which the incumbents' decisions and judgments make a significant impact on business profitability and the success of organizational units. The management group, on average, represents about one percent of total company employment. This percentage tends to be higher in small enterprises, in highly decentralized companies, in people-intensive organizations, and in companies with a rapid growth rate. Within the management group are executives, who, by the nature of their positions, make decisions and judgments that affect the long-term results of the business. Generally, they represent one-tenth of one percent of the total employment.

Management compensation is paid in four different forms: salary, bonus, long-term income, and benefits. Each represents an important component of total management pay, each of which must be handled properly.

Management Salaries

Salary payments represent from two-thirds of total income of lower-level managers to one-third of total pay for some top executives in large corporations. Salary levels and salary administration practices are still important, however, for every management and executive job. The salary managers receive sets their style of life because annual bonus awards and long-term awards are (or should be) money at risk. Furthermore, the salary amounts, although only a portion of total pay, are still substantial. In addition, salary levels can affect the amount of bonus awards, long-term income, and benefits.

Market Pricing

The cornerstone of effective management pay is information. This includes knowledge of the many alternate management pay programs and practices. More basic is the information on amounts paid and access to data for market pricing of management salaries.

Many sources of data of management salaries are now available. There are well-known surveys that are sold on a subscription or fee basis by many of the specialist compensation consulting firms. There are also annual management pay surveys by industry groups, and there are broad-based surveys by functional area, such as finance, engineering, and law. You can get management pay information from required reporting, such as proxy statements. Finally, some periodicals publish useful pay information. For instance, *Forbes* and *Business Week* now publish annually pay information on top executives in hundreds of companies.

Salaries paid chief executive officers and top general management executives are key data to use in management salary administration, and a great deal of data is available. Figure 18–1 provides salary guideline data for top general management positions, as of January 1990. The data reflects industry in general, adjusted for time spans in actual reports and market samples from different surveys.

Always recognize that survey averages represent an averaging of widely different salaries paid. In management salary surveys, the dispersion from the lowest salary to the highest salary in any size category is usually more than 100 percent.

Figure 18–1 relates salary to size of company or division, the usual practice in management salary survey reporting. Size (measured by sales volume in Figure 18–1) remains the factor that correlates most strongly with salaries of general management executives; the bigger the business, the higher the salary of the executive in charge. Other factors affecting the level of senior management and executive salaries include:

- The industry itself; some industries simply pay higher salaries than others, primarily because of pay levels of jobs throughout the business.
- The level of bonus standards and the mix of executive pay; some companies place more weight on nonsalary compensation.
- The rate of growth of the firm.

In determining the appropriateness of salaries of your key executives and senior management positions, first consider salaries paid for similar

Figure 18-1. Salary Guidelines: General Management Positions.

Sales Volume ($millions)	Chief Executive Officers	Average Salary ($000) Paid to		
		General Mgrs. Operating Cos.	General Mgrs. Business Units	General Mgrs. Operating Units
$ 5	$112	$107	$ 96	$ 78
10	127	119	107	87
20	145	134	123	99
35	168	154	143	111
65	206	187	169	133
125	250	225	200	160
250	302	269	238	190
500	360	321	293	234
1,000	433	381	334	—
2,000	500	—	—	—
4,000	586	—	—	—
8,000	657	—	—	—

"Division" definitions used as follows:

OPERATING COMPANIES: Complete businesses or subsidiaries that are not dependent on other operating units; they have their own staff and have delegated a high degree of independent action to the head of the unit.

BUSINESS UNITS: Complete businesses that have their own manufacturing, product development, and marketing operation. They are also profit and loss (P&L) centers. Typically, however, some key decisions are made either at the corporate level or in other units of the organization. Also, there is typically close overview and direction in staff areas, such as finance, personnel, and planning.

OPERATING UNITS: These are typically operating units that have either manufacturing, distribution, or product development activities, but never all three. Frequently, they are simply a manufacturing operation or a marketing division. They are not P&L centers.

Source: The Twenty-Fifth Annual Management Compensation Study, written entirely or in part each year for the past twenty-five years by the author.

positions in peer-group companies—companies that are most like your own company. Obviously, no company is exactly like another. There are, however, many companies that will likely have similar economic and operating characteristics. If you look hard, you will be able to identify at least twenty peer-group companies.

From these companies you should get detailed and specific information on salary levels, bonuses, and pay practices. Continue to track the same companies year after year. Only then can you understand such important data as the mix of management pay. In making judgments about management pay, it is far better to get detailed, specific, and useful data from a limited number of peer-group companies than large samples of data that may include information about many companies that are not relevant to your own.

Salaries paid to key functional managers are useful inputs to management salary administration. Figure 18–2 shows this data for principal func-

Figure 18-2. Salary Guidelines: Functional Positions.

Sales Volume ($millions)	Average Salary ($000) Paid to Top Functional Executive*				
	Marketing	Finance	Manufacturing	Engineering	Personnel
$ 5	$ 87	—	$ 65	—	$ 47
10	91	51	71	—	55
20	98	61	81	—	60
35	108	76	86	81	64
65	118	97	94	96	75
125	125	120	107	108	88
250	133	142	130	125	100
500	155	169	147	145	119
1,000	182	228	165	167	143
2,000	210	266	—	190	177
4,000	234	329	—	229	227
8,000	262	396	—	269	263

*Where the position reports directly to the chief executive officer or to the chief operating officer. When there are blanks, the position is rarely found or there was insufficient information to present a guideline figure.

Source: The Twenty-Fifth Annual Management Compensation Study.

tional positions at the corporate level adjusted to January 1990. Obviously, comparability of job content is critical in establishing appropriate salary levels for functional management positions. Rarely are functional management jobs in your company matched perfectly with jobs in survey sources. Therefore, you must weight your job's content against jobs that have been surveyed in the market.

Data for pricing other management jobs come mostly from purchased surveys. A number of these are good enough to use for pricing. At the third organizational level, the company will likely have significant employment experience, and at those levels it is possible to get data from employment experience.

Use of Slope Data

There is need to maintain reasonable salary differentials at various management levels. The salary of the chief executive officer must be high enough, for example, or that salary will tend to depress a number of levels of management jobs below the chief executive officer. Similarly, if salaries of division managers are too low, this will tend to make salaries of a

Figure 18-3. Slope Guidelines.

Rank in Level of Salary	Salary as a Percentage of CEO's Salary			
	Large Firms(a)	Intermediate-Size Firms(b)	Moderate-Size Firms(c)	Small Firms(d)
CEO	100%	100%	100%	100%
2nd	70	65	60	55
5th	40	42	45	40
10th	25	28	35	N.A.
50th	21	24	N.A.	N.A.
100th	18	20	N.A.	N.A.
Median: All Managers	14%	17%	17%	22%

(a) Over $1 billion in sales
(b) $250 million to $1 billion in sales
(c) $75 million to $250 million in sales
(d) Under $75 million in sales
N.A. Not applicable

number of levels of managers within that division too low.* Thus salary relationships between each level in the manager group are affected by the salary amounts of higher-level managers.

The relationship of salaries paid to subordinates of a key executive manager is referred to as "slope." Slope refers specifically to the percentage relationship between the salary of a position and that of a designated position that is more senior.

The most frequently used slope data is the salary relationship between the ten highest paid executives and the chief executive officer. Such slope data is shown in Figure 18–3. The most usable figures are for the fifth highest paid executive's salary and the tenth highest paid executive's salary.

The organization of the company affects appropriate management pay. Steep organizations—those with a low ratio of supervised people per supervisor—depress salary relationships. This forces up the salary of the chief executive officer and/or depresses the salaries of very key subordinate executive managers.

Reasonable organizational ratios can be another way of using slope data. Identifiably different organizational levels of management should have a certain prescribed salary relationship with that of the chief executive

---

*Low salaries for these apex jobs cause compression, but very high salaries for these apex jobs have less of a tendency to pull subordinate managers' salaries higher.

officer. Rather than a single slope percentage, however, a range of data can be used as a guideline.

You can also use salary levels as a guide to management salary administration. Salary levels (approximately three salary grades), as defined, are appropriate differences between organizational and job career levels; and, therefore, different levels of management. All companies start with first-level management in level 4 (salary grade 13 through 16—see Figure 6–1 and Figure 6–4). Then each subsequently higher level of management should be one salary level higher, right up to the chief executive officer. Try that in your own company.

Fair Salaries

Fair salaries for managers should mean the same as fair salaries for any other employee of the company. Fair salaries for managers should mean the statistical average paid in the market.

The problem with applying the same criteria to high-level management jobs is that there is no salaried labor market for some executive management jobs. You don't attract a senior executive because of more salary, when salary may be less than half of total pay. In these circumstances, a 30 percent salary increase might amount to less than an 8 percent of total pay increase. Executives move for big dollars and much of that up-front.*

When you make comparisons of salaries paid for comparable executive jobs in other companies, that is done as a matter of interest and fairness. The chances that your company would ever recruit any of those persons who are reported in executive salary surveys are very small.

A company can still apply the same standards of competitiveness and fairness to executives and executive-level persons as it does to all others. Look down the organization until you get to the level where there is labor market data in the real world sense of attract and retain. Then use organizational slope data to identify a fair and proper salary for executive jobs.

Salary Structure and Job Classification

Almost all firms use salary structures in the administration of salaries for management-level positions. Sometimes the salary structure covering management positions has somewhat broader within-grade progressions than the model shown in Figure 6–1. This is usually done because people spend

---

*Of course, the ultimate solution is promotion from within. For a big corporation to *ever* recruit general management executives from outside is a symptom of a potentially serious human resources problem.

longer periods of time in management jobs and also because the performance spread is broader in management-level jobs.

Salary structures are now primarily part of the company's information system. The need for human resources information applies at management levels as well as at any other level. The use of structures in some way at management levels also has merit because of equivalency of treatment.

Almost all companies use some form of benchmarking as the basic system for classifying management positions into the salary structure. Market data are available for a high percentage of management positions. Therefore, the use of a complex and costly administrative system to determine the proper salary grade of such positions is unnecessary. Even companies that "officially" work with job evaluation plans for management positions use such plans as a secondary tool or for cosmetic appearances.

As a practical matter, job evaluation was never very effective in classifying management positions. The complexity and diversity of management positions made evaluation by any job evaluation system not only extremely time-consuming and difficult but yielded questionable results. More important, during the past few years market data and multifactor analysis have proved that there is a very imperfect correlation between the factors used in job evaluation plans and those that operate in the marketplace or in the minds of most top executives who make decisions about salary levels for managers.

The cost of job evaluation for management positions has also always been extremely high. Furthermore, administrative job evaluation usually takes an inordinate amount of top management's time, which is required for other matters. Now that there are ample market data to set management level salaries, job evaluation has become an administrative practice of the past.

Salary Increase Practices

The salary planning techniques outlined in Chapter 9 could apply to management-level positions. At management levels, such salary planning processes require greater amounts of information because of the nature of work done. Also, the information is prepared and used by high-level persons so there is need for special excellence in support information work.

There needs to be some special focus in salary increase administration for management positions. For example, salary increases must always maintain proper salary relationships. Probably the most influential factor in determining salary increases for managers is the salary increase budgets for other employees within the organization. One constant objective in granting salary increases to managers is to maintain reasonable salary differentials.

Companies also consider what other companies are doing in the way of salary increases for managers. Mostly to be fair, they want to keep their management salaries abreast of market inflation in the management labor market.

Salary inflation in the management labor market has been rather constant over the years. Managers tend to get roughly the same salary increases in good years and bad, and in years of high and low inflation. It must be noted, of course, that this only relates to management salaries. Management pay, including bonus and long-term income amounts, varies with good and bad business years.

One special issue is that, in business generally, salary increases for executive managers have been a higher percentage than salary increases for any other employee group each year for the past fifteen years—from 1975 through 1989. Over that period of time, executive salary increases have been 35 percentage points more than nonmanagement salaried persons received and 20 percentage points more than nonexecutive managers received. The technical reasons for why this has been happening are plain; the result is one reason why many think executives are overpaid. There is reason to think that the same reasons that have been used in the past for giving executives bigger salary increases than any others will continue to be factors considered in the future.

Within companies, the dispersion of salary increases to managers is typically rather moderate. Except for promotions or situations where management jobs have been substantially redesigned, most managers in a group tend to get about the same salary increases in a year.

Companies often tend to pay all managers of the same level exactly the same salary to avoid small distinctions in salary levels. They try to avoid paying one manager $50,500 and another one $50,000. Such small differences can neither be justified nor explained. Companies want to avoid such small irritants.

Companies want to reward excellence in management jobs, but they recognize that, in management positions, this is done primarily through payments under annual bonus plans and long-term income plans. Top management and directors should think of a broader concept of salary value when applied to people at a managerial level. This is the concept of managerial *capability*. It includes effectiveness on the job, but also considers the flexibility of the manager and his ability and willingness to take on special tasks or new responsibilities as needed by the company. Capability also takes into account the ability to interrelate effectively with other managers in the company for the common good of the company. Capability covers how well a person contributes to issues that cut across several areas.

Annual Bonus Award Plans

Annual bonuses are an important element of management compensation. "Bonus" is a generic term referring to extra compensation paid periodically, usually once each year. About 80 percent of all nongovernment, profit-oriented, public corporations have some form of bonus program for managers.

All managers in a company should be eligible for bonus awards. Over the years, an increasing number have been covered by bonus award plans. Today, one-third more managers are eligible for bonus awards than even ten years ago. Usually, one percent of all persons employed are eligible for bonus plans.

Types of Bonus Plans

A number of different types of annual bonus plans are used for management positions. These include:

• Profit-Sharing Plans: Under these plans, an amount of money is made available from a prescribed formula. A threshold of earnings is usually required before any amounts are accrued for payment, and above that threshold some fixed percentage of profits goes into a fund for payment to managers. All participants generally share proportionately, usually in a fixed relationship to their salary.

• Discretionary Awards: Under these plans, funds may or may not be accrued by a formula plan approved by stockholders or by some other formula that earmarks a percentage of profits for bonus awards. Payments are usually decided in a thoughtful way, but the criteria for making these judgments are unknown to participants.

• Incentive Awards: The basic difference between incentive awards and discretionary awards is that participants know the basis for making awards, and awards are geared directly to the achievement of preset goals or criteria. These plans may or may not be covered by an umbrella corporate plan approved by stockholders.

Almost 90 percent of all companies that have bonus plans for managers have stockholder approval for these payments. It must be understood, however, that these stockholder-approved plans usually only cover bonus plans for officers of the firm. Furthermore, the stockholder-approved plans generally reproduced in proxy statements do not necessarily describe the basis upon which bonuses are paid or the amounts that will be paid but rather the limits of payments and procedures for making payments. Participants in the corporate plan represent only about two-tenths of one percent of all employment and about 10 to 20 percent of all managers covered by annual bonus awards systems.

Figure 18-4. Management Bonus Payment Standards.

	Bonuses as Percentage of Salary in:	
Salary Level ($000)	General Management	Other Management
$ 40	28%	20%
50	30	24
60	34	29
75	38	37
100	42	42
150	50	50
250	65	65
500	80	—
750	90	—

Note: Data based on a sample of bonus plans where details of the plans and payments from the plans were known. Standards are bonus paid over ten years to salary paid in those ten years. Data are heavily weighted by corporate jobs. Published survey data often show somewhat flatter progression and top percentage of 60 percent or 70 percent. The data in this exhibit, in the opinion of the author, best reflect actual current bonus standards.

Incentive Pay Standards

Directly or implicitly, most management bonus plans have incentive pay standards that prescribe the amounts of bonuses intended to be paid when expected or targeted business results are achieved. The actual amounts paid would be smaller if business results are disappointing or there would be no bonus at all. Payments may be greater if business targets are exceeded, generally up to two times the standard bonus.

Typical bonus standards under management bonus plans are shown in Figure 18–4. It is important to note that the data in this exhibit are for bonus standards, the amounts intended to be paid when company targets are achieved. They are not the actual bonus amounts paid.

Note also that the percentage of bonus to salary in bonus standards increases by percent as well as amount in higher-level positions. The logic of this relationship is that since higher-level managers have a greater effect on the results of the business, a higher percentage of their total pay should be dependent upon business results. Other reasons for increasing percentage bonus standards are tax considerations and attempts to match performance spread with pay spread.

Types of Incentive Compensation Plans

There are essentially two types of management incentive compensation plans. One is a goal-oriented plan. The other type involves the use of multiple goals or criteria.

Figure 18-5. Illustration of Goal-Oriented Management Incentive Compensation System.

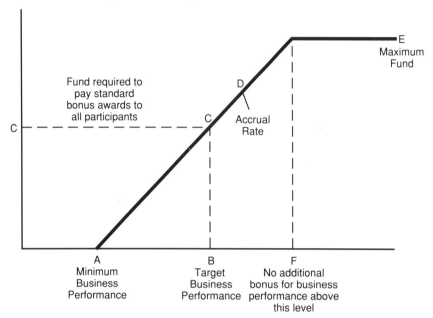

Under goal-oriented plans, a single business goal (usually profits) is set each year, preferably on the basis of business forecasts. This number should be profits forecasted in the operating budget. A goal is set for the company overall (the corporate incentive compensation plan) and for each operating unit (the business incentive compensation plans).

The system of accrual and payment is illustrated in Figure 18–5. There is usually a minimum business performance goal, below which no bonus would be paid. There is also a target for that year. When it is reached, sufficient funds would be accrued to pay standard bonuses to all plan participants. Then there is a maximum performance goal, above which no additional bonuses would be paid. This maximum bonus accrual would be an amount equal to the sum of all the maximum standards for participants.

Note that under these types of plans the goal varies each year. If economic forecasts suggest a difficult year, then a lower profit target would be established and, typically, a lower threshold accepted. In this way, companies set an equivalent task for managers in each unit and for the corporation each year. This plan provides optimum financial incentives for achievement in all businesses in good and bad years, regardless of circumstances.

Criteria plans are similar except that there is more than one goal. This is illustrated in Figure 18–6. In this case, the company used three criteria

Figure 18-6. Criteria and Standards: Example of Annual Management Incentive Compensation Plan.

Levels of Business Achievement— Awards Paid	Criteria with Respect to:		
	Return on Assets	Earnings Growth	Sales Change Against Peer Group
Minimum: No awards made below this level	Exceeds company's average return on assets during past five years. (20%)	Prior year's earnings, adjusted for inflation. (15%)	30th percentile in peer-group rating. (15%)
Target: Business performance level at which competitive awards are made.	ROA which reflects recent performance actually achieved by the company. (40%)	Strategic earnings goals; currently 4% compounded annual improvement in excess of inflation. (30%)	50th percentile in peer-group rating. (30%)
Maximum: Levels above which no additional awards are made.	Top 35% ROA in publishing business. (80%)	Earnings improvement compounded 8% in excess of inflation. (60%)	80th percentile in peer-group rating. (60%)

of managerial performance: return on assets, earnings growth, and sales change. Under each criterion, written standards were established for target or expected performance; the maximum standard above which no additional bonus would be accrued; and the minimum standard below which no funds would be accrued. The criteria and standards were weighted.

Criteria plans were developed for those companies that have great difficulty in setting budgets with precision. Many companies also consider them to be a better system, because they incorporate a number of principal quantifiable measures of managerial achievement and because standards are unchanged from year to year.

Important Principles of Management Incentive Compensation Plans

Industry has had almost thirty years of experience with management incentive plans. The lessons learned from this experience reflect principles to guide the development and administration of management incentive compensation plans. These principles include the following:

- A management incentive compensation plan can never be a substitute for sound management.
- At its worst, a management incentive plan will detract from some important elements of management. For instance, such plans may lead a manager to achieve short-term success at the expense of long-term results.
- If the company is involved in different businesses, a management incentive plan must be developed for each.
- Where there are multiple incentive plans, it is necessary to develop guidelines for eligibility in each and a set of incentive compensation standards that would apply to all.
- When business goals are achieved, awards under the plan must be significant for participants but still only a small portion of incrementally greater profits.
- Never create a management bonus plan because management salaries are inadequate.
- In a well-conceived management incentive plan, zero bonus awards are inevitable in some years.
- If individual differences and individual contributions to business results are to be recognized in incentive award systems, then it is important to develop the rewards for the overall group first and then make adjustments for individual contributions.
- ''Golden handcuffs'' have no place in an annual incentive plan.
- Usually, the most time-consuming, complex, and difficult part of developing and managing a management incentive plan is establishing the business performance standards. This is a job of general management, not a task of compensation.
- Business performance criteria or goals for each unit must reflect reasonable expectations for that group.
- Bonus plans never reward business achievement perfectly, nor can any plan anticipate or account for every significant circumstance that may occur.
- Participants must know in advance that they are eligible for the plan and what the potential incentive award levels are.
- Top managers must be only equivalent participants in the plan.
- Incentive plans must always provide for the possibility of changes in the business, such as acquisitions or divestitures, basic changes in accounting practices, and extraordinary profit or loss items.
- Annual incentive plans can motivate managers, and performance goals must always mirror reasonable business goals.
- Annual award plans rarely contribute to individual or business development.

- It must be recognized that in a dynamic environment and in a changing company, it will be necessary to make changes in plans and concepts from time to time; and one of the most critical and difficult decisions is when to change a plan, particularly a plan that has worked well.

The value of management incentive compensation plans has been amply demonstrated by both empirical studies and the experience of many individual firms. These sources indicate that management incentive plans contribute to business success. In addition, close observation of management behavior under these plans suggests that incentive plans encourage managers to reorder their priorities and to refocus their attention on the company's goals and objectives.

These changes in management behavior may not be great. They may range from a 2 percent to a 5 percent increase in the effectiveness of top-level managers and perhaps a 10 percent to a 25 percent increase in that of lower-level managers. Furthermore, changes in effectiveness occur gradually. But even slight improvements in managerial effectiveness over time can have an enormous impact on the achievement of business objectives.

Management Bonus Plan Issues

A great deal of good work has been done in the area of management bonus plans—particularly at division levels. Many problems have been faced and resolved. New issues always seem to come up, but there always seems to be the capability to find solutions. However, there are four major issues relating to management bonus plans that have existed for a number of years and which are still unresolved in most firms. These are:

1. The increasing percentage in bonus standards
2. The mix of management pay
3. Corporate staff bonuses
4. Corporate executive bonuses

Increasing Percentage in Bonus Standards. The bonus standards reported in Figure 18–4 are representative of those in most companies in this country today. They show an increasing percentage in higher-salaried jobs. The issue is why there should be progressive bonus standards at all, and if so, how progressive they should be.

There was a time when highly-progressive tax rates were one reason for highly-progressive bonus standards, but that doesn't apply anymore. Some urge progressive levels of accountability as the reason for progressive bonus standards, but executive accountability is mostly for long-term issues, and a good case could be made for the fact that, proportionately, operating managers have as much accountability for this year's results as executives do. With flat percentage bonus standards, bonus dollar standards would be higher for higher-level persons, because the same percentage is applied to more dollars. Increasingly, there are experts who think that flat percentage bonus standards are logical and fair (see Figure 18–7).

Mix of Management Pay. One consequence of highly-progressive bonus pay standards is that a high proportion of executive management pay is for this year's results. Executive responsibility is for long-term results; in fact, a definition of the executive job is that these are jobs where decisions and judgments are made which impact the long-term success of the company. It's hard for executives to do that when so much of their pay is for short-term results. Even if the executives do make decisions consistent with the long-term interests of the company, so much pay for this year's business results raises questions.

Figure 18–7 shows the mix of management pay that is typical in large companies today. In high-level executive positions, as much as three-quarters of pay and sometimes as much as 90 percent of total compensation is paid annually. Furthermore, most executives consider the bonus portion of their pay ''more assured'' and their long-term pay ''more at risk.''

A firm can convert to the alternate mix of management pay shown in Figure 18–7 and use flat or moderately progressive bonus standards by using a bonus pay adjustment plan. Under these plans, standard bonus dollar *amounts* are frozen. They remain the same in terms of dollar amounts until the percentage of bonus to salary reaches new target levels. The difference in standard amounts between new and old standards would be calculated before the plan was initiated. This would be based upon forecasted increases in salary amounts. The total amount over the elapsed time to get to the new standard bonus percentages would be calculated and the amount of time required to do so determined.

Those total amounts for each executive would be put into an individual fund account at the beginning of the plan. The fund amounts would draw interest, and this interest could vary, depending upon business results. When the new bonus standards become applicable, then the total fund—the original amount plus accrued interest—would be paid to the executive, assuming, of course, he is still with the company.

Corporate Staff Bonuses. Another subject of high interest at senior levels in many companies relates to the method of paying corporate staff bonuses. This issue has persisted for a long time, and various solutions have been suggested. One that seems to deal with the issues the most effectively pays bonuses to corporate staff persons based upon three components. One component is based upon corporate profit performance. The second is related to the achievement of business results in the different divisions and sections of the company. The third fraction is focused on the professional capabilities of the staff unit.

Figure 18-7. Mix of Management Pay ($000).

	Current Mix of Management Pay						Alternate Mix of Management Pay					
Salary Level	Bonus Standard		Long-Term		Standard Total Pay	Approximate Percent Received This Year	Bonus Standard		Long-Term		Standard Total Pay	Approximate Percent Received This Year
	Percent	Amount	Percent	Amount			Percent*	Amount	Percent	Amount		
$750	90%	$675	80%	$600	$2,025	70%	25%	$187	145%	$1,088	$2,025	44%
500	80	400	70	350	1,250	72	25	125	125	625	1,250	50
250	65	162	60	150	562	73	25	62	100	250	562	56
150	50	75	40	60	285	79	25	38	65	97	285	66
75	38	29	25	19	123	85	25	19	38	29	123	76

*For those who see merit in "progressive" bonus standards, consider no less than 20 percent of salary and no more than 40 percent.

The fraction based on corporate performance would reflect the same percentage bonus standards that are applied to senior executives. Similarly, the business unit portions would be linked to division incentive standards. The third portion would vary with the professional field and the nature of the professional work.

Corporate Executive Bonus Payments. Bonus payments for executives in some companies are a big problem. In 1988 and again in 1989, dozens of corporate executives received bonus payment amounts in a single year that were ten times more than the average employee in their companies earned in a lifetime. There seems to be no rationale for such bonus payments, and there has been no explanation. For many, there also seems to be no upper limit or cap on how much cash may be paid to senior executives in some big corporations.

Too often, bonus plans for executives are discretionary. This provides a number of ways in which executives can justify large payments to themselves. In other cases, formulas have been devised, usually by the executives themselves or under their supervision, which start out with a base year in which the company did poorly.

Corporate executive bonuses should be based on formal plans—preferably formulas. These should be determined independently by the board of directors and approved in detail by stockholders. Such plans should pay nothing until earnings cover the cost of capital by some formal measure and should require improvement in earnings greater than the rate of increase of price inflation in that company, using a reasonable base year.

Long-Term Income Plans

Commercial companies with publicly-reported results usually have long-term income plans for management. These plans provide extra compensation paid over a long period. Usually, about one percent of total employment, or the manager group, is also eligible for long-term income awards.

Long-Term Income Standards

In long-term income plans, as in annual-award plans, there are either actual or implicit long-term awards standards. These are the awards that are intended to be paid to executives over a set period if the long-term business objectives of the company are achieved. Long-term income standards are difficult to determine in industry. A number of studies suggest, however, that the data shown in Figure 18–8 reflect general industry practice. Also shown are long-term income goals I would recommend if companies reduced bonus standards for executives (see Figure 18–7).

If for some reason, such as in the case of a company that has no

Figure 18-8. Long-Term Income Standards: All Industries.

| Salary Level ($000) | Annualized Income Potential From Options | | | |
| | Current | | If Bonus Payments Reduced | |
	% of Salary	Amount	% of Salary	Amount
$750	80%	$600	145%	$1,088
500	70	350	125	625
250	60	150	100	250
150	40	60	65	97
75	25	19	38	29

traded stock, some long-term plan other than options must be used, then income targets should be much less than shown in Figure 18–8. In performance improvement award plans, the income goals should probably be one-half the values shown, and in grant plans, the income values should be much less than that.

Note that in these long-term income standards (as is the case with bonus standards in annual plans) both the amounts of awards and the percentage of salary are substantially larger in higher-level jobs. The logic again is that people in higher-level positions have a greater impact on results and should, therefore, have a higher proportion of total pay dependent upon these results. In the case of long-term income plans, progressive percentage income standards seem reasonable. It is the senior executives who are accountable for long-term results.

These are long-term income standards. In years of depressed business conditions, when earnings decline and stock market prices tumble, long-term income awards are zero. This should happen in long-term income plans. In years of very good business conditions, when earnings increase dramatically and the stock market surges upward, the income values can be very high.

There are also important issues and questions involved in the proper reporting of long-term awards. Values accrued under options, for instance, should be reported when they vest. Unfortunately, they are reported when exercised and appear in leading publications as income earned in that year even though the award may have accumulated over a number of years.

Nevertheless, in successful businesses, long-term income awards can be very substantial. They offer a way for a business person in a highly successful concern to become very rich. This is the way the plans are designed; to simulate the income of the owner-manager and create an entrepreneurial attitude among executives of the company.

Figure 18-9. Alternative Long-Term Income Plans.

A. Options

  1. Stock options
  2. Options on securities other than common stock
  3. Stock appreciation rights
  4. Alternate options

B. Restricted Stock

  1. Stock incentive plans
  2. Guidelines grants

C. Stock Ownership Plans

  1. Management stock ownership plans
  2. Stock grants

D. Long-Term Bonus Plans

  1. Performance unit plans
  2. Performance improvement award plans
  3. Long-term incentive plans
  4. Phantom stock plans
  5. Linkage plans

E. Combination Plans

  1. Multiple plans
  2. Combination incentives
  3. Linkage plans
  4. Tandem options

Alternative Long-Term Income Plans

There are many types of long-term income plans. New plans seem to be reported monthly, although many of them are simply variations of existing programs. Seventeen different types of long-term income award plans are listed in Figure 18–9.

An option is simply a right to buy stock at a specified price. Non-qualified options must be granted at market price and exercised within ten years. Under most plans, options start vesting (become exercisable) in part within one year and are fully exercisable within three years.

The market value of shares granted in a five-year period typically varies from an amount equivalent to salary for a $50,000 salaried manager to eight times salary for managers with salaries in excess of $500,000. There is no legal limit on the number of shares that may be granted to any single executive, but it isn't difficult to show that any grant or grants covering a five-year period should not involve a total number of shares whose market value at the time of grant exceeds ten times the amount of a top executive's salary.

An alternate stock option generally calls for the granting of far more shares but with more restrictive conditions. Two to four times as many shares will be granted under an alternate stock option, but the option price will be above market, frequently requires indexing upward with inflation, and vesting will be much longer.

Eighty percent of all companies still use nonqualified options on common stock as at least a part of their long-term income plan for managers. A few have also used options on securities other than company stock, particularly preferred stock and warrants.

Stock appreciation rights would logically be extended only to insiders. Under this provision, when options become exercisable, the company may, at its discretion, pay the spread in value for some or all of the shares under option in cash. This provision was adopted to protect against unreasonable tax consequences under laws that existed a number of years ago. The provisions became popular with executives and are now used broadly.

Under the stock incentive plan, some part of the annual-award payment earned is paid in restricted stock. The amount of restricted stock is usually linked to bonus amounts earned. The length and conditions of the restrictions are important features to be considered in designing these plans.

Under restricted stock grants, the executive is actually given stock, which is usually restricted for up to five years. If he is still with the company at the end of the period of restriction, he owns the stock without restriction. The difficulty with these plans is that, even if business results are disappointing and stock prices go down, managers may still receive large awards.

There are a number of types of management stock ownership plans. Typically, these plans permit managers to buy stock under favored conditions. Under the "executive stock ownership plan," for example, executives may buy a prescribed number of shares at market price. The company lends money to the managers to buy the stock. These are full-recourse loans with interest. A long-term bonus plan is part of the program. The awards are usually geared to improvement in company earnings. Part of the payments from the long-term bonus plan automatically goes to the repayment of the loan that was granted to purchase the stock.

Under performance unit plans, managers are granted units that have a specified value at the time of grant. These units and their values vest with time (usually three to five years).

Performance improvement plans grant units that have no value at the time of grant. The value of each unit is tied to some profit performance measure. These were designed to remove the stock market as an element of executive pay. However, one problem with the plans is that inevitably executive income and changes in shareholder value may be very different.

Long-term incentive plans typically mirror an annual bonus award plan, whether it is a goal-oriented or criteria plan. The difference is that long-term incentive plans have performance standards that must be met over a three- to five-year period.

A phantom stock plan is a long-term bonus plan in which the performance measure is the price of the company stock rather than earnings improvement. Managers receive cash payments from time to time on the basis of the appreciated value of company stock.

Long-term bonus plans are often based on formulas only loosely related to the firm's strategic financial objectives. The ''linkage plan'' presents a way to assure that this relationship is strong and direct.

Primarily because of disappointments in the performance of stock option plans and other stock-related long-term income plans, companies in the early 1970s initiated combination long-term income plans. These usually involved a nonqualified option plan and some type of performance award plan. The combined values from the two plans were designed to be equivalent to values that had existed under the nonqualified option plan alone. The purpose was to base part of the long-term income award on earnings improvement and part on stock appreciation.

More recently, companies have put in multiple long-term income plans. These usually represent two plans and occasionally three, each of which has inherent values equivalent to those that existed in the nonqualified option plan alone. This practice, plus some increases in long-term income standards, has resulted in a substantial increase in long-term income values for executives.

Issues With Respect to Long-Term Income

There are a few key issues with respect to long-term income plans that have persisted. Most of all is the fact that there are no long-term income plans anymore, *none at all* that I can find.

The long-term or strategic period in most companies is more than three years and often five years or more. Yet all long-term income plans start vesting in a year or two and are completely vested by five years. That's why there aren't any long-term income plans anymore—they are all bonus supplements.

A second critical issue is performance measures in these bonus supplement plans. For many years, it has been broadly agreed that the values in these plans should be geared to shareholder values. But shareholder values are measured by stock price appreciation and dividends. This rules out any long-term income plan other than options and stock ownership plans. If shareholder values are the proper performance measure in a long-term income plan, then all long-term bonus plans are necessarily questionable.

The third serious issue involves the matter of incentive and performance reward. Why should executives be immunized from declining stock prices? If a policy answer is that they shouldn't, then options should never be canceled and reissued. Stock appreciation rights should never be used except for their original purpose, which was to hedge against a major tax exposure for insiders. There should never be "catch-up" because the so-called long-term income plan didn't pay off.

The fourth question involves performance rewards also. If these plans were long-term incentive plans, the logical conclusion would be that executives in successful companies would do far better than executives in a business with a record of mediocrity. In fact, executives in top-performing companies do only slightly better than companies with average performance and not that much better than executives in companies that fail. Executive pay in too many companies has been designed to reward mediocrity almost as well as success.

Finally, there is the simple question of how much is enough. If an executive is granted enough shares in options, then the rewards can be millions for performance that wasn't very great or because the stock market went up. Also, adding one long-term income plan on top of another seems to be more than fair—and more than sufficient.

Special Management Benefits

There continues to be considerable interest in special benefits for executives, and there is now a very long list of such benefits that are exclusively or primarily for executives and senior managers. Here is a sample list:

- Pension supplements, usually adopted to permit payment of benefits prescribed by the company's pension plan but not permitted by the Employee Retirement Income Security Act (ERISA) to be paid from a qualified plan
- Special life insurance contracts, usually designed to preserve capital against the impact of estate taxes
- Family income assurance plans, which can be designed to provide income supplements for the first of a number of possible events, such as termination, permanent disability, or premature death
- Post-retirement employment contracts, which may prescribe consulting or other work, but the payments far exceed any services that may be performed

- Employment contracts that guarantee employment or payments upon termination
- Staff support for conducting personal affairs
- Supplemental medical benefits not paid for by the company's medical plan
- Use of company cars or company planes
- Membership in clubs
- Special eating privileges at the company's expense
- Trips to company locations or to conferences that are only partially for business purposes
- Company-paid medical health programs, including annual physicals, preventive health programs, and executive exercise rooms
- Use of company facilities, such as company retreats, partially for social or personal reasons
- Company loans for personal use, either directly or through the friendly bank
- Special casualty insurance
- Membership on outside boards, or other second-income opportunities
- Purchase of company products at discount
- Special perquisites, such as titles and offices
- Extended vacations or paid sabbaticals
- Limousine service
- Use of company apartments, for personal use or for use by friends
- Counseling services of various types, including financial and psychological
- Travel expenses for spouse
- Outside services, such as legal services, billed to the company's account

Recognize that all these special benefits are legal. Companies are playing by the rules. In that sense, they are all proper. Nevertheless, special benefits for executives have become a very special problem. Part of the problem is an increasingly widespread perception, correct or not, that executives in many companies are overpaid. Part of the problem is due to the publicity about such benefits for executives while the pay, benefits, and conditions of work for other workers have been reduced.

I recommend to companies that they do three things with respect to special benefits for executives. First, identify all the special benefits and perquisites for executives that now exist in your company. Don't underestimate the magnitude of this job. Unless your company is different than most, there are a lot of them. Of course, there will be no record of some of them. You may also find that some executives have "acquired" special benefits or perquisites that are unknown to the company.

Obviously, this is a time-consuming, difficult, and sensitive undertaking. But it is an essential first step. You cannot deal intelligently or in a business-like manner with this subject unless you start by knowing what exists.

Second, list the business purposes or advantages of every special benefit and perquisite now in effect in your company. Put down every reason you hear, regardless of how frivolous or unrealistic it may seem. Sometimes you develop an understanding just by what you do hear. If nothing else, you'll learn what some think constitutes a "business purpose;" although, of course, they may not really be serious.

Next, identify the cost to the company and the value to managers of every special benefit or perquisite. Cost and value will not always be the same. You will face some technical difficulties here. The determination of some costs is very complex, such as deferred compensation funded in part by life insurance. Other items may have no acceptable or standard basis for determining cost or value. When you have technical problems, go to the "experts" in your company. When there is no basis for determining cost or value, establish one. Remember that well-accepted costing of some benefits is also imperfect; just elaborate.

A Model Management Compensation Program

There has been a great deal of comment and criticism about management pay, and it seems to becoming more frequent and more intense. Rather than emphasizing what may be wrong, I prefer to suggest answers. Here, in a brief outline, is a model management compensation program that can be used as a guide in reviewing a company's compensation programs and practices.

Guidelines With Respect to Management Salaries

If management salary levels are anywhere within a range of plus or minus 15 percent statistical average, they are fully competitive in the labor market; being neither an advantage nor a problem with respect to attracting and retaining management persons. At these levels, management salaries can be presumed to be reasonable.

Just where management salaries are positioned relative to the market (plus or minus 15 percent) depends on the following considerations:

- The rate of growth of the firm
- The organizational structure of the firm and resultant salary level compression

- Requirements of salary progress
- The general "capability" of the executive manager group

Individual salary compared to company standards should be determined primarily by considering each manager's "capability," which includes consideration of:

- Proven ability
- Nature and diversity of experience
- Flexibility in jobs that can be done and the willingness to do different jobs when needed

Performance, in the sense of achievement, is rewarded by extra pay plans. Use market pricing at the levels of management where there is salary competition, on an attract and retain basis. This will generally be in salary levels 3, 4, and 5 (salary grades 9 through 20 in Figure 6–1). For higher-level managers, use slope data; one salary level differential for each genuine organizational level.*

Guidelines for Management Bonus Plans

In bonus plans, the threshold would be tied either to a defined cost of capital or a defined alternate use of capital. Exceptions may be made with respect to divisions that have not met such standards in recent years, provided they establish a strategic plan that would exceed such standards and demonstrate progress toward achieving such goals, or establish an ability to generate cash for the development of other businesses, or have an approved plan for disposition of the division.

The target for the accrual of funds in the annual awards plan would be based upon a top-down target, which would preferably be related to budgets. This budget amount would be determined by the corporate office (with the participation of division persons and perhaps the use of outside consultants) and based upon such considerations as:

- Historic profit achievement
- Achievement of peer-group companies
- Achievement of other divisions
- The threshold
- And, as much as anything, corporate analysis of the business

---

*If this indicates lower salaries for executives than those that exist, which will be the case in many companies, consider a system of buyout. Cash funds would be created equal to the difference between the lower new salary and the existing salary times the number of years remaining until retirement. These would pay interest and would be payable at a designated retirement age.

Bonus standards, as a percentage of salary, would be a flat percent. In plans that meet corporate profit-goal yardsticks, bonus standards would be 30 percent. In other cases, the bonus standards would be 20 percent or less.

The corporate executive plan would be a formal plan, which would require profit improvement in excess of price inflation, although not necessarily improvement each year over the prior year.

There would be no maximum on payments under the bonus plan. If payments for achievement made to some top executives might cause problems in reported earnings in proxy statements, those persons might, at the discretion of the board, have some part of their award deferred on favorable terms.

Guidelines for Long-Term Income Plans

Executives should own a significant amount of company stock. The minimum amount owned should be at least two times annual salary. If a person does not own this amount of stock when appointed to an executive position, he would be able to purchase that amount of stock under a special executive stock purchase plan.

Stock options would be used. These option plans would have the following features:

- The number of shares granted would be generous by industry-comparison standards.
- Option prices would be at "fair market value." Fair market value would be determined by the board of directors within guidelines set by the board. Such guidelines would prescribe the following: option prices would never be below book value, and option prices would be adjusted upward for inflation.
- Options would be granted each year, and the number of shares granted might vary from year to year, based upon the price/earnings (P/E) ratio at the time.
- Except for reasons of potential tax liability, stock appreciation rights (SARs) would never be used and there would never be cancellation and reissuing of options.

Special Benefits

There would never be special benefits or perquisites, such as supplemental health plans or extra life insurance for executives, unless they supported productive work done by the executive and were common practice.

Are Executives Overpaid?

For a number of years, there has been a growing belief that many executives of large corporations are overpaid. Some say that there is insanity in executive pay; many feel that executive pay is running out of control.

The intensity of feelings about executive pay excesses has become very great. Even in the conferences I hold with top-level personnel executives, I find there is an intense feeling about the fact that their own executives are overpaid. The intensity of feelings about the unfairness of executive pay on the part of working people at operations levels throughout the country is widespread and very great.

In connection with the publication of *The Twenty-Fifth Annual Management Study* in 1989, I had reason to compare executive pay today with that in effect in 1965.

Of course, it is difficult to compare executive pay then and now. You need to take into account inflation and changes in business. There is room for a lot of error. Nevertheless, based on in-depth studies for *The Twentieth Annual Management Study* that were updated for this edition of *Compensation,* I would conclude that the following statements are true for comparable-sized firms and net of inflation:

• Executive salaries are 50 percent higher in 1990 than in 1965, net of inflation. This is less than 2 percent a year compounded. From 1965 through 1980, executive salaries increased less than one percent more than inflation; but since 1983, the rate of salary increases for executives has been more than 3 percent in excess of inflation.

• Executive bonus standards have increased fourfold in this twenty-five-year period. Bonuses paid have gone from around 100 percent of standard, on average, each year to almost 120 percent of standard.

• Long-term income values have more than doubled. This has happened mostly by adding a second long-term income plan in many firms and by increasing the potential for income gains; for example, more option shares.

• Executive benefits and perquisites are about the same; mostly because the IRS disallowed many executive benefits that were popular in 1965.

Overall executive pay for comparable jobs has almost doubled, *net of inflation.* Real income of other salaried workers in the same period has increased about 25 percent.

Today, in large and moderate-sized public corporations, the average chief executive officer's total compensation is about one hundred times larger than the average compensation of all employees in their company. It was about twenty-five times higher than the average employee's compensation in 1965.

In the twenty-five years from 1965 through 1990, salary increases for executives have been higher than salary increases for nonmanagement employees in nineteen years, including the last consecutive eleven years. Executive salary increases have been about the same as the salary increases of others in six of the twenty-five years.

Today, there are a thousand executives who earned more in 1989 than the average employee in their company will earn in his working lifetime.

There are many other comparisons that companies might make. Such facts as these have led many to think that something must be done about executive pay. Action must be taken by the board of directors or Congress will inevitably adopt more controls on executive pay—and they have many options to consider.

The board's job to contain executive compensation is not easy. The material is often complex. Matters of great sensitivity are obviously involved when executives make recommendations regarding executive pay. It's extremely hard not to go along, particularly when the company seems to be doing rather well.

Chapter Nineteen

Special Cases

Every operation is unique in some way, and compensation programs and practices must reflect this. In effect, a special chapter about compensation could be written for each operation. Compensation professionals must "write" these chapters for the operations in their own company. However, there are some cases or categories that apply to many companies, and just about every firm would reflect two or more of the cases covered in this chapter.

Small Companies

A small company could be described as one that does less than $5 million in sales and/or has fewer than a hundred employees. Add to those criteria the fact that such businesses are too small to have their own functional specialists, for any purpose, and that particularly means that there is no in-house know-how with respect to compensation.

Two-thirds of all workers in this country are employed by companies with less than a hundred employees. Small businesses are the most rapidly growing in our economy. For the past twenty years, these small companies have provided all the net new jobs for a growing work force. In terms of profits, the small company may be losing money or it may be yielding profits that can be as high as ten times more than the profit earnings rates reported by any large, publicly-owned company.

Few small firms have formal compensation programs as they have been described. Most do things in compensation that many compensation professionals would regard as improper or inadequate. Small companies don't have compensation experts, and they haven't had access to compensation consultants. Nevertheless, many of these businesses are doing very well.

We shouldn't conclude that informal compensation practices contribute to business success. Small companies as well as large companies could probably improve compensation programs and practices, and that improvement would likely contribute to far greater enterprise success. But the fact that many small companies are often so successful without any type of formal compensation program or without what compensation professionals consider sound compensation practices must have some significance, and we can all draw our own conclusions.

If someone made an extensive and elaborate study of human resources management practices in successful small companies, here's what I think the study would show with respect to matters relating directly to compensation:

- The successful small company always has good skills in recruiting.

- In that recruiting activity, the successful small company always has a keen sense of market pay for jobs; and rarely loses the people it wants to hire because of money. This isn't because the pay is high but because the overall effectiveness in recruiting is good in successful small operations.

- Most successful small companies pay salaries that are average or somewhat below average, but they always do vertical recruiting. These companies also often do transference recruiting, which means they recruit vertically from businesses in related areas of work, preferably those that typically have lower rates of pay.

- In successful small companies, the chief executive officer or a close associate will be the one who has direct accountability for human resources management work, whatever that is, and will supervise rather closely the management of personnel throughout the organization. There are many critical accounts in business literature about chief executive officers in some small companies who keep pay data private. But there is a bright side to such practices because at least such practices show that compensation is a direct function of the chief executive officer.

- Small isn't necessarily beautiful, but it is always quick. In successful small companies, pay decisions of all types are made quickly. These decisions may not be any better than those made in large companies, but they are made in a more timely manner.

- Chief executive officers in successful small companies have developed a level of trust among employees that has a great value in compensation matters.

• Employees don't deal with programs or rules but mostly with people and almost always with top-management people.

Small companies have some special problems in the area of compensation. Most of all, they don't have expertise in the field. They have access to some of the same books and articles as any manager in any size company, but they're less qualified to identify what is proper, sound, and valuable.

Consulting work in compensation for small companies has been terrible and often provided by people without knowledge of human resources management or compensation. Most specifically, those who have rendered professional advice in the area of compensation have frequently been accountants, actuaries, or attorneys—and lower-level people in these other functional fields as well. Quality consultants, at affordable fees, simply have not yet been available to the small company.

I always advise executives of small companies to look at the good experiences with respect to compensation by successful small companies in the past, already briefly outlined. Be sure these things are done well. In addition, I recommend:

• Have one person (who may be the chief executive officer) with knowledge responsibility for human resources management, including compensation. Small companies particularly suffer from too much advice from amateurs. By concentrating the knowledge responsibility in personnel and compensation with one person, that individual may not be an expert to start with, but he will accumulate knowledge and become more expert than all other managers in the organization.

• Have a salary structure. The structure in Figure 6–1 will do just fine.

• Slot jobs in the structure by labor-market pricing. Make sure that the market-pricing system is based largely on employment experience—although small companies have almost as much access as anyone to professional association data, government data, and industry association data.

• Rank jobs that can't be priced against market-priced jobs. Never use job evaluation.

• Be attentive to performance judgments, and make certain that better performance translates visibly into higher pay.

• Keep benefits conservative, and always have employee contributions to every benefit. Have no retirement plan at all, and have as few perquisites as possible.

• Have a success-sharing extra pay plan.

• Seek out a human resources management consultant. Get a person who is capable of giving useful advice in many areas of personnel, not just compensation alone. Never hire a compensation specialist from a large consulting company who has a product to sell. To make sure that your consultant is available, a local person is preferable. You don't need much information and advice from a consultant. Usually, two hours a month in all areas of human resources management are enough.

If a small company does these basics well, it can have an excellent compensation program. In addition, decisions can be quick.

The excellence of human resources management and compensation management in small firms is a matter of importance to every small company. It is also important to many large firms. Remember all the reasons why compensation practices must be tailored to each company. These are some of the same reasons why compensation practices need to be tailored to each operation in a large organization and to each location. Use these practices in small, geographically separated operations. Don't smother small operations with big company ways.

Privately-Owned Companies

Many small companies are also privately owned, and some very large companies are also owned privately. These businesses have unique compensation issues.

For example, you often cannot separate the thinking of the owner or owners from the management practices of the company. Thus what should be done may not be done if it conflicts with the views or the values of the owners of a private company. The thinking and the culture of the owners are often like laws governing the conduct of the company and limiting what can practically be done.

The culture of the owners is not necessarily good or bad. In a privately-owned company, the culture, thinking, style, and values of the owners are all part of reality. Many managers and other persons have experienced great frustration and failure for not recognizing this simple and obvious truth. In some private companies, it is said that one requirement for getting into management is marriage.

The views and thinking of owners of privately-owned businesses may reflect themselves in many ways. Certainly, the training, experience, and know-how of the owner will necessarily be reflected in the practices of all managers. For example, if you have an engineer who is highly technical in his thinking and detailed in his ways, that must be part of the culture of the organization, because it is the culture of the individual owner.

Privately-owned companies may be foreign-owned. Foreign-owned companies bring people with the culture of their own nation and the traditions of their own people, and this then becomes a factor that affects every facet of the business, including compensation. For example, the Japanese way is certainly a different way from the American way. Japanese traditions and ways of doing things, their point of view and their culture, are all different from American history and traditions. In Japanese-owned operations in the United States, the Japanese way has impact, regardless of how irrational that may be.

The national views and traditions of foreign-owned companies dominate the culture of a foreign-owned company as much as the individual views of owners in a privately-owned company. Foreign-owned companies with private owners are a particular breed, as I have learned from working for them.

Foreign owners of operations in this country, like American owners of businesses overseas, know that they must accommodate local ways. But it is human nature to think that your own way is better—and it is the way you know. To get into management of foreign-owned companies may often require a change in citizenship or something just as dramatic.

Private often means that records are confidential. That, in turn, rules out many types of compensation plans. For example, you can't have profit-sharing plans without reported profits unless the plan is based on categories of profitability or certification.

Large privately-owned companies with resources and available expertise have developed a broad range of extra pay plans. These represent mostly estate-building plans. The fact that some privately-owned companies actually have extra pay plans means that any privately-owned companies can have such plans. In fact, all privately-owned companies should have some estate-building plan, preferably geared to company growth—stock value or net worth.

For most privately-owned companies, the key is to keep compensation simple, pay mostly in cash, and have a success-sharing extra pay plan. Ideally, the success-sharing should involve moderate employee investments.

I have never had much difficulty with private companies owned by Americans. You recognize that the owners are part of the culture. They may not be perfect, but they are always interested because it is their money. Emphasize that at every opportunity.

I have stopped trying to be helpful to foreign-owned companies that have operations in this country. If they have the investor view and American management (or Americanized management), then they are no different than publicly-owned businesses with American ownership. If not, I have concluded that the foreign manager's long-term future in operating in this country is bleak, no matter how much money is pumped into the operation.

Just because your company is publicly-owned, don't think that none of this description about privately-owned companies applies. Top executives of large, publicly-owned companies sometimes get to think that they are the company, or at least that they are the owners. To the extent this happens, then the special issues of privately-owned companies have relevance.

Government Organizations and Nonprofit Enterprises

Perhaps the most significant characteristic of compensation in many public operations (like government and educational institutions) is the "funding" of compensation, as a local politician likes to call it. In our Indian River County School District, for example, compensation starts with property taxes—the millage and the assessed rates. Then the next step in determining the compensation of teachers and others who work in our school district happens in Tallahassee, which collects all our taxes and sends some back (about half comes back in our district). How much is sent back is obviously an important factor in the compensation of the people who work in our educational institutions.

Thus the school board, the voters, and state officials make decisions that importantly affect the compensation of all those who work in schools. This represents one of the principal causes of educational deficiency. This, unfortunately, is a reality in the compensation of employees in public organizations.

Somewhat the same process happens in nonprofit organizations that are dependent in whole or in large part on government grants. Those who depend mostly on fund raising are closer to commercial businesses that depend upon sales.

When compensation is based upon funding from the government, you can budget whatever the government grants, and that includes budgeting for compensation. But those who provide the funds are not your customers, so factors like the excellence of the work of your people may have nothing to do directly with what is available for compensation.

Recognize that this funding process of compensation is a two-edged sword. It may result in uncompetitively low pay, which is unfair. But, on the other hand, taxes or other revenues may provide more payroll than is necessary. When this happens, then salaries are set at a premium, regardless of performance or the value of services; there are usually more people on the payroll than necessary; there are usually wonderful benefits and retirement plans; and low productivity becomes a cultural goal of the enterprise in order to spend appropriated money.

More people work for government organizations than for model A types of businesses (the smokestack industrial company that resembles General Electric). There are far more government nonunion workers than union workers in and out of government. Yet there is little model G (government) information or guidelines for effective compensation. Few compensation plans and programs have been designed specifically for these types of organizations.

In government organizations, it is difficult to have pay reward for performance when the process of budget setting described determines funds available. In addition, it is often difficult to define performance for the operation. This makes salary reward for performance difficult and performance-based extra compensation plans virtually impossible. Incentive bonus plans aren't practical in government operations either. The nature of government operations—and most nonprofit operations—makes reward for performance more difficult. However, there can be promotions, and there can be genuine salary merit increases for performance.

Compensation in government operations is complicated by low employment standards, set deliberately in the federal government and in every state, county, and local government I know. You can get a lot of arguments about how much lower government employment standards are than they are in private business and many explanations as to why that exists. We needn't deal with these issues here.* The level of employment standards affects pay levels, and if performance expectations are lower than in nongovernment operations, then it would be reasonable to expect government salaries to be lower also. In fact, government salaries are fully competitive at every level.

Don't think the absence of bonus plans is a reason for having average salaries in government. The absence of bonuses in government work is more than offset by excellent health-care benefits and superior pensions.

The essential starting point for sound management—and the sound management of compensation—in model G organizations is management objectives and accountability. You can't have good management without clear objectives and specific accountability to meet the objectives. If you can't have these things, you can't have sound compensation. There cannot be effectiveness of work and a judicious use of funds, including compensation dollars, unless there is accountability. All these factors suggest that in government operations there must be massive reform plus as much deregulation and privatization as possible.

An enormous amount of money has been spent on compensation studies in government operations and some nonprofit operations, and these organizations have proportionately as many human resources management persons and compensation specialists as any other organization. Very often, the caliber of human resources management professionals and compensa-

---

*I am ducking these issues not only because they are not central to the scope of this book but also because my experience suggests that the matters involved are very complex and not "right or wrong"—"good or bad."

tion experts is not up to business standards, and even more often, either the wrong questions in the compensation studies are asked or sound answers are prohibited by law for political or other reasons.

Too often, the solution to every pay problem, in governmental organizations and in government-funded nonprofit organizations, is simply more payroll money. For example, some say it was necessary to pay Congress 50 percent more when, in fact, many seek the office and 99 percent of those in Congress seek reelection, unless they retire. More pay is not the answer to Congressional problems, and yet within two months after the overwhelming majority of people in this country openly opposed pay increases for Congress, another effort was launched to get big raises for key government employees, including Congress.

Conditions are very often a problem of pay in many government operations. It's not just getting paid for a job but the difficulty of doing the job that keeps many qualified persons from choosing work in these types of operations.

Is there any reason to think that equivalent excellence in human resources management generally and in compensation specifically cannot be achieved in government? Why can't compensation in government be every bit as good as it is in the best-managed privately-owned company? I think there can be excellence in compensation in government even though I haven't made the substantial paid-for study. Let's at least start with these actions, which we know are needed:

- End compensation by appropriation. If government can't do this by acting responsibly, then perhaps Messrs. Gramm and Rudman will show them how.
- Market-price jobs by comparisons with comparable jobs in private firms.
- End tenure.
- Take the politics out of employment and promotion.
- Establish a reasonable system for setting the pay of the president, cabinet officers, congress persons, judges, and key public executives. Like any big organization, pay must be appropriate at the top.

The same recommendations should be enacted in every state organization and local government.

That seems like a reasonable agenda for a year or two. During that period, make the substantial paid-for study, at least on how compensation in government could be managed.

Starting now, accelerate the trend toward deregulation and privatization in government. Operations spun off from the government will be nonprofit government-funded operations. These can and basically are managed by the government in a delegative manner.

These recommendations on improving the management of compensation are based, of course, only on management and compensation considerations. Government is a political entity, so politics also have an impact.

Nonprofit businesses are really no different than private organizations if they are not funded by the government. Often, however, the nonprofit operation, whether funded by the government or not, does not have access to high-level information and advice. Perhaps we can privatize some government human resources management people and have a government-funded consulting firm, solely for nonprofit organizations and government operations. Then they could make the substantial studies in the future.

Fast-Growing Enterprises

A fast-growth enterprise is one that experiences sales and payroll increases that are significantly greater than inflation in a continued manner and over a period of years. The percentage increase in employment will likely be in excess of 15 percent a year for at least a five-year period in true fast-growth enterprises. This means that employment doubles in these firms each five years.

There is continuous change in these firms. Therefore, compensation systems must be simple and highly adaptable to change. Pay must be market sensitive, because there is necessarily a great deal of recruiting.

Pay for jobs in fast-growing enterprises will likely be below market average—at least 10 percent below market average. Yet salaries of individuals will be substantially higher than peers in the marketplace with similar backgrounds. All of this happens because promotion is rapid. And faster pay progress is the principal method of rewarding for performance.

Of course, the opportunities for fast growth in fast-growth companies are not equally available to all. For those who do operations work, either in the factory or in the office, fast-growth companies often represent no employment growth at all. But for many salaried people and for professional and managerial people, employment in fast-growth companies means fast growth in personal opportunities.

I have worked as a consultant for a number of companies during their periods of rapid growth and have kept some records on promotions and pay progress. Over a period of more than ten years, those on upward career paths in this type of company average one promotion about every eighteen months. Those in salaried jobs had salary increases that were almost fourfold in ten years. In the management group, pay (including stock appreciation values) increased, on average, sixfold in ten years.

Obviously, in model F (fast-growth) firms, the types of compensation systems and programs must be different than in the traditional model A firm and, for that matter, different than compensation in model G (government) and model N (nonprofit) firms. Recruiting pay must be the focus, promotion is the reward for performance, and everyone will do well with some equity participation plans.

In fast-growth companies, you don't have annual bonus plans. Performance standards would be changing frequently. Also, some plans, like management bonus plans, can be divisive in a fast-growth environment.

Mature Enterprises

A mature or nongrowth company is one that, by any measure of size, is not growing at even half the rate of inflation. In these companies there must be a matching of salaries to the market, and care in granting increases to assure fairness is critical. Fairness in pay increases is particularly important for high-performers.

Don't assume that only large companies are mature. Many small commercial enterprises never experience a growth phase and stay small. Many public and nonprofit organizations grow, if at all, with the population served—or they are limited in their growth by the population served. Most mature organizations have less than a thousand employees.

Regardless of size, the mature organization feels disadvantaged in the labor market, because it doesn't have growth opportunities and, therefore, it doesn't have fast-track pay programs for high-performers. No growth often means no change or slow change, and this tends to discourage or drive out the movers and the innovators, who really aren't needed very much anyway.

For these companies, the best advice is to first find out how much upward mobility there is for high-performers. Even in studies of companies with zero employment growth there have been opportunities for some people with high potential to move ahead rapidly. There are fast-growth persons in mature companies; just fewer of them than in a fast-growth company.

Having determined what the actual growth has been and what it will likely be in the future, then roughly equate your recruiting practices and the potential of those brought into the company with future growth opportunities. Build a sizeable safety factor into recruiting plans because you must expect turnover among high-performers.

In a nongrowth environment, good people are needed, but good is not heavily weighted by potential for growth, innovation, and challenge. This is where nonfinancial elements of compensation become more important. In this climate, golden handcuffs, rewards for long service, and human resources management practices to gain employees' commitment to excellence are important. In addition, for reasons that aren't always clear, it is the nongrowth enterprise that has an inclination to add benefits, perquisites, and the symbols of success, like titles.

It can be argued that vitality, effectiveness, and quality of work in nongrowth companies are just as important as in any enterprise, regardless of the phase of growth. I would subscribe to that view and think that the absence of qualities like vitality, effectiveness, and quality of work is sometimes the *cause* of nongrowth. But there are also more measures of enterprise success than growth, and vitality, effectiveness, and quality of work are important for the success of any type of operation.

The excellence of compensation in a mature company is not likely to be a source of growth or a major contributor to better business performance. Poor or inappropriate compensation practices may be the source of dissatisfaction and negative response. Competitive salary and fairness avoid dissatisfaction and have a neutral effect on attitude. Success sharing, pay for performance, and incentive rewards contribute to effectiveness, and for many are satisfiers that reinforce positive responses. Those whose research concluded that compensation is mostly a dissatisfier were correct, but they didn't realize that all their study cases were nongrowth enterprises where there were no appropriate extra pay plans, pay for performance was automatic, and fairness was questionable.

Thus in mature enterprises, appropriate compensation programs are those that assure competitiveness and fairness and are not sources of dissatisfaction or demotivation. Satisfaction and motivation in nongrowth companies are based more on conditions, work interaction, security, and the tranquility of predictability, success sharing, and fairness. Recruiting should recognize these factors and bring in people whose values are consistent with this work environment.

Model M businesses must then have competitive salary levels or slightly higher-than-competitive levels. There must be excellence in performance pay systems. Incentive bonus plans can be very important in motivation and retention. Benefits tend to grow naturally, so there is need for benefit cost containment. The design of pension systems is critical, and conditions must receive a lot of attention.

Two of the most important requirements for effective compensation in mature firms are noncompensation matters. One is that there always must be particularly good vertical recruiting in the company. Mature companies must also have excellence in manpower management.

Large Enterprises

It may seem that large companies need big compensation programs and that big means complicated and sophisticated. That often seems to be the case, but there is no reason for a big company or a big operation to have compensation programs and practices which are different from a small organization. Size alone should make no difference in any area of human resources management.

Big companies can economically afford experienced people and support more specialist areas. Those knowledgeable and experienced persons may want different types of compensation programs, but there isn't any organizational need in large organizations that requires compensation programs to be essentially more complicated.

A large commercial venture is often in multiple business areas. In fact, some became large from acquiring operations in different business areas. Some of these business operations are in fast-growth areas; some may be in nongrowth areas. In fact, some business wisdom says you need both: the nongrowth businesses are the cash sources for the growth businesses.

In multiple business companies, some business units are large and others are small. They may be in totally different businesses—like ethical pharmaceutical businesses and over-the-counter drugs businesses. Some may be highly capital-intensive and others may be essentially people-intensive. Keep in mind that the divisions, locations, and units differ also.

It's little wonder why large multiple businesses seem at times to have split personalities. They have, in fact, totally different cultures under the same corporate name. Each of these entities requires totally different management systems, and this includes different compensation programs and practices. Successful multibusiness companies recognize this imperative and nurture needed differences in organizational systems.

Never try to force one program into all operations for the sake of conformance or on the mistaken belief that there is one best compensation practice. Large businesses need corporate policies, a few corporate requirements, and guidelines. Then the corporate experts should support the operations in developing the practices that fit each one the best. More and more, the activities of corporate compensation professionals in large enterprises are consultative.

My compensation system for model L (large) enterprises is to have many systems, each developed in the operations. In compensation, setting salaries and determining bonus payments are at the unit level and, therefore, procedurally are very much like small companies.

Under my model L compensation system, there are policies—about a half-dozen in compensation. There are also very few requirements; for example, a single salary structure. Consultative services and compensation information are available. Mostly there is a great deal of latitude.

There is monitoring and control. The core control is some system of measuring management operations at the unit level. Unit success and individual employee success are my primary measures of sound human resources management practices in the large firm—and that includes sound compensation practices.

Models A Through Z

There are many models of different enterprises: large, small, private, public, fast growth—and there are many categories in between. Furthermore, there are businesses in different areas of work, such as steel, airlines, school districts, and accounting firms. Each of these company cases needs to be considered in developing, revising, or just administering compensation programs and practices. For too long, compensation systems were designed with reference to only one case, which was referred to earlier as model A and seemed to resemble the characteristics of companies like the General Electric of yesteryear. Today, there are many models; almost enough for every letter of the alphabet.

Make sure you understand the business you work for and that the work you do is appropriate for the model or models of that organization. Each case is different enough to require some special or tailored compensation programs and practices. Don't make differences for the sake of being different, but use the compensation program that is most appropriate for each case.

There are people cases as well as employer cases. In Chapter 2, the different groups of employees were identified and described. Chapter 14 through Chapter 18 dealt with compensation for different types of work performed. There are also different models of workers in the sense that they are all individuals, with widely varying personalities and personal values.

Money is important to all these people. For most people, in fact, during most of their careers, money isn't anything, but it is far more important than whatever it is that is in second place.

We don't know enough about employee cases. We also need employee cases A to Z, and they would be of practical value.

In the absence of understanding, we are well off treating all people cases the same, even though we know they aren't. In my opinion, the management of personnel in the 21st century will need to have greater understanding of employee cases. Human resources management will use that intelligence in compensation management.

Contract Workers

Reserve the letters X, Y and Z for other types of cases. Model X would be for contract workers.

What we do and what we think in compensation mostly relate to full-time, permanent employees. However, more than one-third of all workers are not full-time employees, and the word permanent hardly seems to apply anymore.

There are various types of contract status, including:

- Part time, with less than a full schedule each week
- Part time, with less than a full schedule each year
- Those hired for a specific time or for a specific assignment
- Other companies' employees who do work on your premises or in your operations
- Leased workers
- Subcontract workers

Contract workers of some type have been utilized for a long time; for example, in such jobs as security guards, cleaning contractors, and part-time workers with prescribed assignments, like public accountants or compensation consultants. In the past decade, the use of contract workers has been growing rapidly.

Contract work is a compensation matter, even when the contract workers are not your employees. If they work in your company, work with your employees, or represent an alternate form of getting work done, then their possible use involves compensation matters. You must specifically consider these people and how they are paid in fashioning your own compensation systems. There are reasons for knowing how these contract workers are paid, and you need to consider the impact of those contract workers and their compensation on your own firm's compensation systems.

Four areas of contract work are particularly important today:

1. Subcontract work
2. Leased workers
3. Voluntary part-time workers
4. Second career workers

Subcontracting is increasingly considered as a way of getting work done; an alternate to having work done by the company's regular work force. Subcontracting mostly requires having suppliers do some steps of the operations' work. The most publicized cases has been the loss of such jobs to overseas suppliers, but there has probably been as much contracting out of this sort to lower-cost suppliers in the United States—mostly to smaller companies with lower labor costs.

Contracting out work has always been a business practice. What's new is the amount of subcontract work to suppliers. Most of the loss of work has been by unionized employees in large corporations in the smoke-stack industries.

Subcontract work to households is a special form of subcontracting work. This includes the much-publicized cottage work force. This became popularized by some who noted that computer and communication technology could make work possible at home and that, therefore, this would happen. The fact is that after a number of years and much publicity, there is limited use of the cottage work force. Contracting work to the home has many problems, including legal problems. It will be a factor in the future but not the megatrend that has been predicted.

Contract leasing is a development of the past decade. The use of leased workers is now a major issue in human resources management and compensation.

The growth in contract employment leasing started in 1981. In 1990, it's estimated that there are more than one-half million employees working for contract-leasing firms. The contract-leasing companies have formed an industry association with more than 250 employer members. Conservative estimates suggest that by the early 1990s there will be more than five million contract-leased workers and that eventually at least 15 percent of all workers in this country will be employed by contract-leasing companies.

There are many reasons why contract leasing has become popular. Perhaps the most important reason is to lower the employee costs of the contracting company. Others use contract workers to get a better caliber of employees—sometimes only because of more effective recruiting and selection by the supplying company. Better benefits at a lower cost may be available to leased employees, particularly if the contracting company is small. There are no headaches from paperwork or government regulations associated with leased employees for the contracting company, and there are no severance pay costs or labor union problems for the contracting company.

In some cases, there is also greater employee stability. As contract customer A needs fewer employees because of seasonal work, perhaps contract customer B needs more. Many employees who work for a contract-leasing company are simply transferred from one job to another; in this case, from a job in contract company A to a job in contract company B.

Voluntary part-time workers are those who chose to work less than a full schedule each day or each week for your company. This category includes ''moonlighters''—those holding second jobs—and second family workers who, for any reason, only want to work part of the time. In this country today, there are more voluntary part-time workers than there are union workers. This category of work is of direct interest in compensation because these are employees. Compensation amounts and methods must be compatible with compensation systems covering those who are regular full-time employees.

Voluntary part-time employees are typically paid on an hourly basis, not as a matter of stature but because that is the only practical thing to do when these people have different work schedules. In fact, with this category of employee, work schedules may be different every week.

Usually, voluntary part-time workers are not covered by company benefit plans or retirement plans. This means they cost less than regular employees. The use of voluntary part-time workers may also cost less because there is then less overtime work by regular employees at premium rates. Part-time workers tend mostly to be employed by small or moderate-sized companies. Such firms are more willing to be flexible in their employment and work scheduling practices.

Voluntary part-time workers may be one way to deal with problems of labor scarcity. Part-time workers may also be a way to get some special knowledge or skill that would not be available or required on a full-time basis. Part-time work of this type is a way to expand or contract the work force with the flow and ebb of business volume.

A conscious and organized effort to employ second-career persons is just now starting. In this category, employment is generally an alternate to retirement.

Opportunities for second-career employment are mostly for those who are higher paid or have inherited wealth. However, there are increasing numbers of both categories in our economy today.

Some of those who seek second careers have experienced burnout, want different conditions; for example, less travel, or just want to do something different. There is usually less pay for second-career work.

The use of second-career workers usually means less payroll costs and often special knowledge and expertise that it not obtainable in any other manner by the employing company. These workers are usually salaried and may or may not be eligible for some or all benefits and extra pay plans.

There is need for more work and greater flexibility in job design in large firms to facilitate second-career workers. It seems unwise to lose highly experienced and talented people where there is needed work to be done and the persons are willing to do it, often at substantially lower compensation.

Chapter Twenty

The Management of Compensation

Compensation must be managed. Compensation is one key to a company's ability to attract, motivate, and retain the numbers and types of persons required to do the work of the company and achieve its objectives, but compensation also represents a substantial cost that must be managed. In various ways, two key elements of sound compensation have been emphasized: competitiveness and fairness. The management of compensation must also involve a third basic—the management of compensation costs. A number of important issues in the management of compensation are covered in this chapter.

Compensation Management

In my dictionary, compensation management relates to the work of compensation professionals. The management of compensation relates to compensation work done by operating managers. Compensation management must be managed well.

Compensation management involves a lot of activities. Much of what is done is administrative or supportive in nature. The list of things that might be done is very long and doesn't have to be reported. The point that does have to be made is that compensation professionals do far more than "staff" work in the traditional sense of that word.

For instance, compensation professionals make technical decisions;

for example, what survey to use, how to proceed in the solution of compensation problems, what knowledge might be needed by the company, and the best way to collect that knowledge. How compensation professionals do these things has a profound effect on the ultimate result. The compensation professional must be directly accountable for the methods used.

The compensation staff answers questions, and specific answers to questions about compensation programs add substance and meaning to a program and very much determine what those programs are. There are many of these questions and, in combination, over time, the answers have a strong influence on competitiveness, fairness, and cost.

Compensation specialists answer specific questions from employees or supervisors. The answers given by the compensation professional have an impact on decisions to a point that they are frequently themselves decisions; expert opinion becomes fact. Compensation professionals also give advice and information, and this often amounts to "effectively recommending" actions. Because they are the specialists, the recommendations of compensation professionals should carry considerable weight.

In many instances, the compensation professional is directly accountable for the design or development of new plans. The plan developed is subject to review and approval, but such reviews are concerned only with the proposals that are submitted, not with the many alternatives the professional weighed in developing the project but did not submit for consideration.

The compensation professional also exercises important elements of control. Any compensation program necessarily involves some elements of audit and control to make sure that decisions throughout the organization are reasonably consistent and equitable. It is generally the responsibility of the compensation professional to administer such monitoring systems.

Compensation professionals are involved in planning. They contribute inputs and outputs to both the general business plan and to the plan of the overall human resources management function. There also needs to be compensation planning. This should involve plans to improve existing compensation programs. In this work, there is also an element of accountability.

Perhaps most importantly, compensation is a knowledge area of business, and those who do this work have accountability for having knowledge of their field. Never be wrong on technical matters. Have data, information, or the precedents of experience to support your opinions on compensation issues.

In all these ways, compensation professionals have direct accountability for enterprise success. This is worth emphasizing, not to puff up egos or paychecks but because these are ways in which compensation work is compensation *management,* and the excellence of that work affects very much the management of compensation.

Capability of the Compensation Professional

Over the years, many different programs, practices, and techniques have evolved in all areas of compensation administration. It is crucial for compensation people to know what these alternative programs, practices, and techniques are. Having determined the needs and objectives of the company, it is basically the task of compensation experts to select from among all alternatives those that are most appropriate for the needs and objectives of the company.

To carry out this responsibility, compensation professionals must first know what alternatives exist, the details of each, and how each works in different situations. Compensation professionals must have a deep knowledge about the circumstances under which one technique tends to work better than others and the reasons for such differences. Just keeping abreast of new techniques and programs is difficult.

Compensation knowledge requirements involve more than knowledge of alternate compensation programs and practices. Compensation work also requires a lay knowledge of a number of business and academic disciplines. These knowledge areas include mathematics and a command of the use of computer sciences. There must also be a lay knowledge in certain areas of law, psychology, sociology, and economics. Increasingly, there must also be knowledge of government regulations and interpretations of these regulations.

Compensation experts today must also have knowledge about how to get knowledge. They must know how to access information that would not reasonably be possessed by any one of them or even by the entire personnel and compensation staff within the company.

One way they can do this is by networking others in the field. One of the assets of compensation professionals, besides factual knowledge, should be a range of professional contacts. Access to experts in associations, research firms, and consulting companies is part of the knowledge base of the compensation professional.

The professional must also have knowledge as to how to proceed: the steps to be taken to get a job done effectively in the most cost-effective manner. As much as anything, the compensation professional must also know how to administer and manage the knowledge at hand with great skill in execution.

Given a choice between excellence of programs and excellence of execution, the latter would always be preferable. Even a moderately appropriate practice excellently administered would be superior to the best program poorly administered.

To meet the needs, objectives, and goals described, compensation professionals must, of course, strive for excellence in both technique and execution. In this respect, they will never achieve perfection, but management's expectations of the personnel function, including compensation, certainly require continuous efforts to produce the best results possible.

There is a lot of talk these days about quality management. Those in personnel are doing a lot of the preaching. Practice quality work in compensation management by improving the quality of your knowledge. In professional work, the quality of knowledge is the essence of quality work.

Evaluating the Effectiveness of the Compensation Professional

At one of my conferences a number of years ago, the group evolved criteria by which the work of compensation professionals should be evaluated. These criteria have been used many times since and have been found to be very helpful. The items identified were as follows:

1. When management comes to the compensation department with a question, compensation professionals should usually have anticipated the question and at least have developed a sketch of an answer or recommendation.

2. When compensation professionals take a problem to management, they should also take suggestions for solving that problem.

3. Everything compensation professionals do should reflect, or be an extension of, management policy and geared to the needs of the business.

4. Some of what the compensation professional does should visibly contribute to the achievement of the strategic goals of the business.

5. Some of what the compensation professional does should help to satisfy the reasonable aspirations of employees and contribute to their job satisfaction.

6. Occasionally, compensation professionals' decisions should be to do nothing or to do something different from industry practice.

7. Compensation people should have cases where they have discontinued a practice that was no longer required or simplified some program or practice because the simpler version now accomplishes the purpose.

8. The compensation professional's work must be a part of an integrated personnel function, which, in turn, is a subsystem of management. Compensation people must demonstrate an awareness that what they do and how they do it affects every other facet of personnel, and that their work is a part of the general effort of the company to manage well the human assets of the business.

9. Compensation people should work as though they have final authority in every part of their functional area, to the limits of prudence.

10. A compensation professional should never favor a program or practice because he knows it or can administer it effectively or because it might receive high marks from his professional peers.

11. Compensation people should be business managers and personnel professionals, not just technical specialists.

12. The thinking and the work of the compensation professional must be directed to the long-term as well as to the day-to-day problems of the company.

How do compensation professionals rate in your company? Rate their work on a one-to-five scale for each criterion. Sixty is a perfect score. I think that forty is passing and any score below fifty should be cause for concern.

The Management of Compensation Work

Management must manage compensation, and in a delegative style that actually happens at every level of the organization. Executive management, supported by compensation experts, does few things: sets a salary structure, determines market-priced jobs, monitors decisions, and, most of all, sets policy. The operating managers throughout the firm make decisions, with or without counsel of compensation persons. There can't be talk now about the managers' role in compensation as there was in former years, and in earlier editions of this book. Managers decide, and the only issue now is the role of compensation professionals.

By definition, every manager should make pay decisions, but for management to do this personnel job requires experience. Supervisors must have time to do the job, and they must have sufficient authority. In most companies, probably half the supervisors do not have the background, the experience, the time, or the authority to do these personnel tasks. It is not realistic, therefore, to expect them to do the things that are expected of them. It is a basic problem of the management of people.

This is essentially an organizational problem, which illustrates again how one area of personnel impacts others. It is not an easy problem, but if there is to be effective management of people, including effective compensation administration, then it must be dealt with.

To be knowledgeable and skilled in the management of personnel clearly requires the acquisition and maintenance of a great deal of knowledge and experience. To justify the time cost involved in gaining and sustaining the required knowledge and skill requires management of a significant number of persons: from ten to thirty, depending on the level of the job managed, the diversity of work, and the technological job content of the persons managed. Compare this manager ratio with your actual company experience. In business generally, for example, in salaried positions the ratio of employees to managers is about three to one.

To increase the ratio substantially, it is necessary to flatten the organizational structure. Nine of ten large companies have eight to ten organizational levels, and at least one and as many as three organizational levels would have to be eliminated in order to achieve the required span of management. Of course, such reorganization would not only improve the management of people (and the management of compensation) but would reduce the cost of management, improve communications, and increase decision-making efficiency.

In the absence of organizational restructuring, some system of designated human resources managers must be maintained. Tight review processes for one or two levels of the management organization are the traditional method of simulating delegation in the management of compensation, when an incumbent supervisor is not able to do so for any reason. My first choice is always to deal with the issue of span of management by organizational restructuring. My second choice is the system of designated human resources managers because they then have accountability for all areas of personnel, not just compensation. Human resources unit managers and direct-work supervisors then, over time, work out systems for sharing responsibility.

However you do it, managers make the decisions in compensation and necessarily so in most work areas today. There aren't any compensation programs or any compensation staff actions that can substitute for effective management of personnel, including effective management of compensation by every manager at every level of the organization.

The Management of Compensation Costs

It is possible to pay jobs at the market average, to pay individuals better than average by pay for performance plans, and to have payroll costs distinctly lower than competitors. That might seem like a miracle, but it's very doable. The few companies that have succeeded in doing it have built for themselves a substantial competitive edge. Fair pay at a lower cost is excellence in the management of people; it reflects the highest skill in managing compensation.

The key to success in managing payroll costs is in two areas. First, the more a company is successful in identifying performance and in rewarding performance, then the more that company is likely to manage its payroll costs effectively. Second, there must be some direct cost control measures.

Pay for performance is the best method of lowering payroll costs because everyone gains. There are a number of ways to reward for performance, and these have been described in earlier chapters. Pay for performance takes management effort, the correct human resources management practices, and management skill, but it is worth doing. So lower payroll costs by paying more for performance.

The interesting thing about direct payroll cost containment methods is that many of the effective management techniques do not involve compensation practices. For example, vertical recruiting is an extremely important payroll cost containment practice. Manpower management, or compliment controls, represent another example of the critical noncompensation elements of payroll cost containment.

Specifically, there are a number of compensation practices that should be considered in managing compensation costs.

- Extend the salary review period from twelve months to a longer interval. Do this overall or for selected job categories or locations.
- If salaries are above midpoint, then establish tighter controls to retard progress in the salary range.
- Establish a quota for percentage increases of various amounts. Establish expected distribution in some form.
- Vary merit guidelines by divisions and by units.
- Pay lump-sum dollars in some instances.
- Institute pay for performance programs that are more effective in rewarding higher productivity and effectiveness of work.
- Be sure that regional differences in wages are reflected in regional pay levels.
- Include benefit cost containment efforts.

There are also human resources management activities other than compensation that can improve the effectiveness of the management of compensation costs. These often have a greater impact on compensation than compensation actions.

- Redesign the product or service to be less people-intensive.
- Utilize vertical recruiting.
- Use downsizing and other manpower management activities to make certain that compliment levels are appropriate.
- Redesign jobs to control costs or retard an increase in costs.
- Consider organizational restructuring to streamline the organization and reduce the head count.

If your company finds itself with salaries that are higher than comparable to the market, then a two-tier pay system should be considered. Start hiring now based upon a competitive pay structure. Administer salaries of new employees based upon the competitive structure. Scale back (however slightly) or stretch out (however little) current employees' pay increases so they gradually move to competitive levels.

In nonunion operations, a two-tier pay system can be used without disruption or conflict. Be certain, however, that you do not retard the pay progress of high performers whose pay is justified by the level of their performance. Look hard for promotional opportunities or redesign jobs for your highest performers whose pay may be higher than justified, based upon competitive market pay comparisons. Never penalize the high performer.

In all work on the management of compensation, remember the obvious: The goal is not the lowest compensation levels but optimum compensation levels. More specifically, what a company wants is the optimum spread between payroll generated by human effort and the payroll costs of those persons. If you can pay more but get proportionately greater output, then there is a gain. That happens whenever performance improvement is greater than a performance pay increase.

In managing payroll costs, the goal is *margin management*. The goal is to increase the spread between sales and payroll costs by any combination of increases in sales or output and decreases in payroll costs.

Human Resources Information Management

Compensation can be narrowly defined as salary administration or broadly defined in terms of the total areas of work done by many with compensation titles. The broader definition seems logical, because so many compensation professionals do work in a broad sense and are involved in all facets of remuneration, including benefits, retirement plans, and nonfinancial elements of pay. In addition, related areas of work are performed by many compensation professionals. Most particularly, work in human resources information systems that is done in personnel departments is usually assigned to the compensation department.

Human resources information systems in many companies are assigned to the compensation department, even though less than half of all personnel data is compensation data. The work must be assigned somewhere, and it does involve numbers. Compensation data also represents the single largest amount of data among all the functional areas of human resources management.

In most companies today, computerized human resources management is largely a matter of automated clerical work and the use of data. Most companies do some personnel record keeping and administrative work on computers; although most still have a long way to go. Only a minority of companies use computers for data analysis. For 99 percent of the firms in this country today, the state of the art of information management in human resources management work is far behind the use of computers in all areas of the business.

There are a number of specific objectives of personnel data management. Each of the following uses of data is now pursued by at least some companies, and all are of high value in the management of personnel.

- Computer handling of data; a far more cost-efficient manner of doing required personnel record keeping.
- Efficient maintenance of keeping records required for various reasons of compliance; for example, qualification of 401(k) plans.
- Information can be diagnostic and identify changes or trends in a firm that could cause problems. Computerized data makes possible an early-warning system.
- Personnel data can provide another set of business performance measures, such as productivity measures, manpower ratios, and benefit cost measures.
- Similarly, measures of employee satisfaction and conditions that directly or indirectly measure satisfaction can be tracked.
- Data can be a method of diagnosing and solving problems.
- Models may be built that may contribute to better work systems; and in some cases, new company products and services.

Personnel data management is a bottom-up process. Data are collected and reported at the lowest level of the organization where records are kept. Then it may be combined at each subsequent organizational level upward until there is a composite corporate information reporting. To do this, however, a uniform chart of accounts is critical.

Information technology makes it practical to enter data electronically in a uniform personnel accounting manner at all company locations. The input of required personnel data into the electronic system is no additional work.

There are required standard personnel practices that are essential to an effective human resources information system. Two examples should illustrate this point. A company must have a single salary structure throughout the organization for information purposes; it must have the same number of grades and the same between-grade progression. Similarly, all performance ratings throughout the firm should be done by the same basic system so that ratings are also a uniform accounting system.

If electronic human resources management information is to be used for management purposes, there must be a general personnel data base. Software may be purchased or programming done on a custom basis at a modest cost. The data do not have to be on mainframe computers; PCs will do very well, even in large companies.

How human resources data are used is critical. Absolute numbers usually lack significance, but trends are always relevant. For example, if a personnel ratio is now 1.0 and was 0.8 not many years ago, the change may be more relevant than either number. Such comparisons often require analysis. For example, to use personnel ratio trends, there is a need for determining whether the personnel department is required to do more work today. Also, you must judge whether the personnel department was effective when its ratio was only 0.8.

Trends may indicate not only prior experience but future likelihood. For example, the corporate office's payroll as a percentage of total payroll may have been trending up constantly for a number of years. This suggests the possibility that the corporate staff is becoming bloated. Such trends must also be analyzed. The larger corporate staff may, for example, reflect increased governmental requirements.

Personnel data may also be valuable in comparing information in one unit with other units. Personnel results achieved by some units may reflect what can be achieved by others. Here, comparability of the operating units is critical. An ideal case would be a motel chain with many units that are all the same. Significant variations in personnel data for some units can have relevance and be the clue for personnel actions to improve business results in many units. Even in this case, however, further analysis is necessary. While all motels may be the same in terms of size, structure, and operation, their circumstances may still vary. They operate in different geographic regions and are influenced by different economic conditions.

In some cases, it may be necessary to use more than one comparison method to achieve an objective. For example, combination data can be extremely useful. Combination data utilizes two data inputs in your analysis; for example, quits among high-performance people.

Clearly, there are opportunities to make intercompany comparisons. At this time, there is only one operating general personnel data exchange, but now that the technical computer capability exists, there should be many more in the future.

Intercompany personnel data comparison work has a double value. First, many companies are in multiple business areas. They can make such comparisons within their own businesses. They will also want to make such comparisons for each business unit within their company with comparable businesses in other companies with respect to some personnel data items.

Such data work adds a whole new dimension to the human resources input to the management of personnel. Now companies will be able to make judgments based not only upon how they are doing compared to how they did, but they will also be able to make judgments based upon how they are doing compared to other companies.

A personnel data exchange can collect, analyze, and report intercompany data comparisons in a number of areas, including:

- Productivity data
- The cost of management
- Number of supervisory layers
- Turnover rates
- Hiring experience
- Salary increase distribution
- Salary level distribution
- Unfilled job index
- Employment mix
- Discrimination/complaint experience
- Personnel ratios

Not all data, of course, can be compared between different businesses. One of the things that has been learned in general human resources data comparisons is the variables that must be considered in making comparisons of different personnel data items. Size of operations and the state of the economy affect some personnel data items. The type of business is important for some data items in interbusiness personnel comparisons; and it was necessary to develop a new business classification system to deal with this issue.

Developing, implementing, and improving the type of human resources management information described is an urgent job because of the need to manage personnel more effectively with a lower cost in human resources management professional work. Such human resources management information, including some form of personnel data exchange and analysis, is quality management in human resources management.

That is only the first giant step in human resources management and is of critical importance. Human resources management experts who are also expert in computer and communication technology may disagree on some specifics, but all seem to identify the following as essentials for the critically needed future development of human resources information management in personnel work.

- Expert systems in personnel must be used. There is now only a practical capability for rather simple expert systems; and in areas of personnel activities where many persons of lesser professional experience make frequent decisions of substantial importance to the company. A few expert systems in employment are used, but I know of none in compensation.

• There is a need for uniform generalized methods for dealing with human resources management issues before the use of computers in personnel will start to approach the use of computers in research (CAD) or manufacturing (CAM). But those who are responsible for human resources information management must be taking the first steps toward computer-aided personnel (CAP).

• There must also be some research and development in the handling of information in human resources management. Ours is a soft science that requires deep knowledge, and we will have fewer facts and repeatable truths than is the case in scientific fields. But we do have data, and we have the precedents of experience. These must be built on before the full capability of computer and communication technology is usable in our field. Research and development have been badly neglected in personnel; and largely relegated to academia. That must change, and true, practical human resources management experts must do some of the human resources management research and development.

• We are overwhelmed by material in human resources management. But some of what gets into print is common sense and most of it is garbage. There is a need for information handling and electronic library systems. But the first need is to screen the material for relevance. Also needed is an index or cataloging system for inputs so the material can be retrieved.

• Obsolescence of knowledge is a problem. There are no scientific laws or ageless truths in human resources management. There are no base plans that are usable forever in our field. The obsolescence rate of knowledge, programs, and practices in our field is becoming greater and greater. Therefore, there is need for information updating, and this too must be done by true experts.

• There is a compelling need in our field to focus on the needs of the users rather than on the capacity of the providers. We have had enough ''gee whiz'' magic shows and canned software. Start with user needs and user questions. That seems obvious, but when said in human resources management group meetings, the participants think they are the users. It is the managers of personnel who are the users.

The Use of Consultants

Part of management is using consultants. That includes determining work that should be done by consultants, selecting consultants to do the work, and effectively managing consultants who are doing the work.

Thirty years ago, few companies used consultants for personnel work of any kind, including compensation. Much of what might have been regarded as compensation consulting was confined to management pay. Back then, companies tended to use their law firms or their public accountants more than personnel specialists for compensation consulting work. Companies did not have their own qualified compensation people.

Today, much of the consulting work is done internally by qualified compensation professionals. When there is a need for project development work, it is becoming more appropriate to use the company's own staff to the fullest extent possible rather than consultants.

Still, even today, almost all companies use outside consultants, but they use them in new ways. The consulting field in personnel, including compensation, has polarized during the past fifteen or twenty years. There is still a need for high-value advice, problem solving, and information. However, this must be provided by highly-qualified, mature, and experienced people of great integrity, and there is a limited supply of consultants in human resources management with these qualifications. At the other extreme, there is a great demand for outside compensation specialists who can provide information or, in effect, who can function as part-time contract workers. Most of those who do compensation consulting work actually do part-time contract work.

With the widespread use of outsiders to provide data services and part-time contract work, many people have entered this field. Naturally, companies have had mixed experience with those who provide such services. Therefore, selecting the right supplier of consulting services, whatever they may be, is critical.

A company that buys compensation services should never assume that the work of all members of the consulting firm is the same caliber as that of the firm's founder or a senior member of the firm, or that the firm is as good in one type of assignment as it is in another. The selection process, therefore, must be related to the specific work to be done and to the individuals who are going to do the work.

Any consulting firm that has grown beyond a half-dozen or so consultants (plus support staff) has a quality control problem. Where analytic, problem-solving, and advisory work are involved, it becomes difficult to maintain a high quality of problem-solving consulting work in all instances.

Some companies also use consultants as third parties, on the theory that they are objective. This is only partly true. Of course, outsiders are not employees, but they are suppliers. They want to please their customers.

Particularly in management compensation, it is difficult for an outside person to recommend against something that is desired by a customer. It is difficult, for example, to suggest that the managers who are approving the bills are paid too much. It is particularly difficult if the consultant does a lot of business other than compensation for the same company. To do objective and independent compensation consulting work requires maturity and a willingness to express opinions and make recommendations regardless of the consequences.

Top Management and the Management of Compensation

Top management ultimately is accountable for the effectiveness of the compensation program. In the last analysis, top management is accountable for everything that happens in the company. This does not mean that top management needs to do everything or even many things. If anything, high-level managers have typically been too involved in the field of compensation. They have spent too much of their time doing compensation work that others could have done.

Perhaps the time top managers spend on compensation work accounts for better results. But, if nothing else, time spent unnecessarily on compensation detracts from the time available for top managers to do things that only top management can do. Furthermore, while top managers may be more competent in management areas, in many cases they know less about compensation specifics and the people affected than others do. And in some areas, such as cost control and their own compensation, it is very difficult for top management to be even-handed and objective.

There is a great need to delegate more responsibility for the technical matters of compensation to personnel people throughout the organization. It is equally important to delegate to operating managers the same degree of authority in compensation matters that is found in manufacturing, marketing, engineering, and finance.

Top management must obviously set policy, and top management must approve items having a major impact on the business in the area of compensation as well as in other areas. It must approve compensation items that involve major costs. That approval requirement has been a major problem for many companies. Too often it has meant that top management became deeply involved in the developmental work and operational decisions.

There is a way to get top-management input without getting top management too involved in doing things that others in the organization can do. Those responsible for compensation start with a number of inputs that reflect top management's thinking; policies with respect to compensation, the management style of the company, and former decisions by top management. These, in combination, are important inputs to the development of any program. The proper inputting of such matters builds in an element of approval from top management at the inception of work on a project and saves a lot of top management's time.

Another technique for building in management approval at the inception of the program involves discussions with management on any matter of substance or major cost before the project work is initiated. These discussions cannot be open-ended or philosophical but must be related to specific question areas. It is usually helpful to send key questions in writing to top managers before the discussions so they have an opportunity to think about them beforehand.

If these discussion sessions are structured properly, there are usually only about a half-dozen question areas that have to be covered, even in major compensation projects. No more than one hour needs to be spent with each executive. The key, of course, is to know the questions. It is also obviously necessary that the questioner be qualified to evaluate the answers in terms of how the answers should shape the program under consideration.

With these inputs from top management, the identified needs of the business and resulting identification of objectives, and the existing company programs and practices, there is sufficient information to develop a program that is likely to be approved by top management. Much of the approval has, in fact, been inputted at the inception of the program.

Top management can, and frequently will, do more than either approve or disapprove. Top management may have areas of concern and request more exploration of some specific aspect of the compensation recommendation, or there may be areas of doubt, in which case it may require more data or more testing. There may be a need to have the principal alternatives identified. These likely reactions of top management should be anticipated and built into the process of developing compensation programs or practices that require the approval of top management.

Top management must also review and approve some basic aspects of the ongoing compensation program. For instance, top management must approve annual salary increase budgets. Top management may also want to review and approve each year's salary increase guidelines. Such items tend to be repetitive by their nature. Therefore, with each year's experience, the compensation staff should be better able to anticipate the questions or issues in the minds of top management. The process itself should be streamlined in anticipation of top management's reaction. When this is done, then each year there is a higher probability of approval and an increased effectiveness in the approval process.

Top management must also make compensation decisions about the pay of some subordinates. Any specific decisions more than two level removed are unlikely to improve the quality of decisions—in fact, they will probably detract from the effectiveness of compensation programs—and they certainly would be using top management's time, which could be used better on other matters.

When top management becomes involved, there is a basic weakness or defect in the approval system. An effort should be made to develop compensation systems that give top management confidence in reviews by management down through the organization. Then top management can focus on specific decisions for individuals no more than two levels down in the organization.

Finally, top management must be kept informed. This must be a highly selective process. Top management certainly needs to be informed on matters that may be questioned by members of the board of directors. Similarly, division presidents must be kept advised of issues that are likely to be explored by corporate management. High-level managers must also receive briefings on important trends and developments in the field of compensation and in other basic areas of personnel as well. General managers need to be well informed about all important aspects of management, including the management of people.

Boards of Directors

During the past few years, many companies have rethought the role of directors in the area of personnel, particularly with respect to management compensation. The role of the board of directors in management compensation has been written about frequently in major journals, and some of these articles have been highly critical. The subject has also been much discussed by both top management and members of the boards of directors in many companies.

Obviously, the board of directors in every company has a legal and fiduciary responsibility. Exactly what that means with respect to compensation is a very important question today because of the possibility of stockholder questions, actions, and legal suits. Only legal counsel can advise the board as to what their legal and fiduciary responsibilities are with respect to compensation, and a company is well advised to get such legal opinion from time to time as cases are tried and new interpretations are forthcoming.

Increasingly, however, boards of directors, and particularly compensation committee members, feel they have the responsibility to look beyond those specific items of legal and fiduciary responsibility. They want to fulfill their role as *directors*. As a result, boards today are reviewing management compensation more thoroughly and more broadly.

Board members generally believe that they should get whatever information they want in the area of compensation, and particularly they expect complete information on management compensation. They recognize that their information requests must be reasonable. But they want the information they feel is necessary to carry out their role, and they want to have it in an understandable form. Boards also have a right to expect information they must review in sufficient time to digest it before they are called upon to make decisions.

Boards want to be able to use outside consultants or have access to the company's outside consultants, particularly when reviewing management compensation questions. Increasingly, directors need their own consultants, not to do projects but for information, advice, and briefings.

Some companies have concluded that it is desirable to have at least one member of the board of directors who has special personnel knowledge, training, and background. This idea is not new, but until recently few companies have given it serious consideration. Only about a dozen *Fortune*-listed companies can be identified as having such a person on their boards.

Every member of the board should, first and foremost, be fully qualified to fulfill the legal and fiduciary responsibilities of the board, and each director must contribute to the general duties and activities of the board. Only from generally qualified persons should those with special experience, knowledge, and skills be sought. This rule applies to the director with special personnel qualifications too.

Beyond considering the broad qualifications of a director, each company may seek different qualities in their directors. Companies must look for well-qualified people who bring some special knowledge that is helpful to the board in carrying out its responsibilities. They may also look for special knowledge that would be useful to the top management of the company. For most companies, one of these areas in which special knowledge and experience may be helpful, both in carrying out the responsibilities of the board and in supporting top management, is personnel.

The director with special personnel qualifications should *not* be an advocate. His role is not to "defend" employees or to be their representative. This is the job of management and the full board. Some companies have found to their regret just how serious an error it is to appoint directors who represent some special group or some special point of view. It is the responsibility of every member of the board to represent not only the stockholders but employees, customers, suppliers, and the general public.

A personnel expert who is available to the board or who is a member of the board can bring special knowledge and experience of great value to the board, just as directors with special marketing knowledge may. High-technology companies usually have one or more outstanding scientists on their boards for the same reason. Capital-intensive companies will sometimes have financial experts on their boards. Every company faces critical employee relations questions, and the director with special personnel experience would play a helpful role in answering such questions.

Boards cannot claim to be well-informed and independent in matters of executive compensation unless they have access to information and advice other than from the paid employees and paid consultants hired by executives. Never permit a situation to develop where there is confrontation and competition between management's advisors and the board's advisors. But make sure the board has independent and qualified advisors. This shouldn't require a lot of time or high fees. In fact, the fees of the board's advisors shouldn't be higher than fees paid to members of the board.

Chapter Twenty-One

Other Compensation Issues

There are always contemporary issues that are important to effective personnel management, including the management of compensation. While some of these issues may affect some companies more than others and will probably concern different businesses in different ways, some are generally applicable to all enterprises, not only at the present time but for some time in the future. These are generally the issues that are related to broad economic and political factors. Some of these that have not been dealt with so far, or where there is need for more commentary, they will be covered in this chapter. These include some human resources management issues with important compensation implications, considerations of a future career in compensation, and a look at the future.

Human Resources Management Issues of Importance to Compensation Management

Many important issues have been identified and dealt with in some way in preceding pages. In fact, the emphasis on organizing material in this book has been around issues—and answers. Increasingly, we need to deal with issues and work to determine specific action steps that can be implemented. The disciplines of human resources management have gone through the start-up and growing-up phases. There is now a broad variety of practices and experiences in areas like compensation. Increasingly, deal with the real issues with practical answers.

Here are what I consider to be the nine most important human resources management issues of the next decade that have not been covered
in previous chapters. Each has important compensation implications. In
each case, the issue is presented and there are suggestions for how the
matter should be answered.

1. Strategic management
2. Human resources management planning
3. Information technology impact on employee relations
4. Entrepreneurial pay programs
5. Educational deficiency
6. Polarization of pay
7. Communication about pay
8. Equal treatment
9. Fairness

Strategic Management

In business, the concept of strategic management means something
very special, and the business meaning is quite different from my dictionary's definition. Strategic management in business means affirmative plans
and actions that fundamentally improve the operations, resulting in a higher
level of enterprise success. In another sense, strategic management relates
to plans and actions that establish a more effective manner of dealing with
an entire class of problems, as contrasted to dealing with each case, one
at a time, as it arises.

In business, there is concern that management must focus more on
business-building activities and strategic answers to basic issues. Business
must do better at long-term investments in basic improvement and making
fundamental changes for the better rather than getting the best results this
year only—each year—and dealing with issues on an ad hoc basis when
compelled to do so. This thinking relates to every phase of the business,
including compensation.

Using the strategic human resources management view suggests some
opportunities for the enhancement of strategic management in compensation programs and practices. Here are a few examples:

• Long-term income plans for management should be based on the
improvement of the business; and for executive managers, this would mean
vesting of at least three years, with full vesting not likely until after five
years. For executive management, reward measurements would be the appreciation of stock price and improvement in stock dividends.

• There should be stock ownership by all employees.

- Place heavy emphasis on pay for performance, and do this with excellence.

- Compensation increase systems should reinforce career pathing.

- Job pricing should be market-sensitive, with particular emphasis on recruiting pay and reallocation of talent consistent with strategic business improvement objectives.

- Quick-response compensation information services (computer-aided) must exist, with access to experts outside the firm when needed.

Human Resources Management Planning

Clearly, there cannot be effective strategic management without effective planning. Similarly, there cannot be effective strategic management of human resources management unless there is effective human resources management planning. Because there is so much interrelationship of activities in the various functional areas of personnel, it is not practical to do compensation planning alone: it must be done as part of overall personnel planning.

Human resources management planning is more important today than even a few years ago, and it will become increasingly important in the predictable future. For example, in an increasingly technological world of work, the knowledge and talent of employees are becoming more important. And in an era of an increasingly rapid rate of change, the correct identification of trends is becoming more critical if firms are to deal with major issues in a timely manner. In fact, I think it is correct to say that accurate, reliable, and comprehensive information about current trends and developments in the field of human resources management is an imperative. Yet few companies of any size have comprehensive and reliable information in this area.

We know how to do human resources management planning. Human resources management planning work isn't perfect, but it can be done about as well as planning in any other facet of the business—and for the business overall. The skills and know-how used in personnel planning work are good enough, and companies that do this work will tend to do it better each year.

Companies have been hurt by not having effective human resources management planning because important changes affecting the business were not identified and addressed promptly. Many senior executives feel strongly that they should never again be surprised by such things as ERISA or EEO, both of which the author predicted in a personnel planning document published in 1966.

Human resources management planning has many distinct business values, but the primary advantages are:

• Human resources management planning is essential in order to inform management. Management wants (and needs) to be informed.

• Inputs from human resources management planning are very often inputs to business plans.

• There are occasions when human resources management planning information can provide an input toward identifying a business opportunity for the company.

• Human resources management planning information can be building blocks for action. We don't always take action in one great leap. Very often, something is identified that should be accomplished over a period of time. Then, with the awareness of that goal and that need, a whole series of actions or decisions geared to immediate problems will direct the company to the desired goal, step by step.

• Human resources management information helps companies avoid mistakes.

• Information developed in human resources management planning work contributes to the development of those who work in human resources management.

Companies must identify current human resources management trends and issues. There must be an awareness of the important current trends and issues that are actually impacting many companies and that will likely have some important impact on every organization. How could anyone do work in human resources management without knowing such information?

In 1989, there were four dozen significant trends and issues in the area of human resources management that were current in nature. Human resources management professionals in one hundred selected firms could identify only half of them. This lack of knowledge about current trends and issues in the field of human resources management and a fully reliable method of getting such information are serious problems in many firms.

For strategic management, there is only one correct process to use as a base for developing human resources management information about the future. This starts with an identification of observable and provable *current* trends. Current trends are then analyzed and logically extrapolated into future predictions.

In strategic human resources management planning, predictions of the future must be constantly monitored. If the current trend (upon which strategic predictions are based) changes, then the logical and reasonable extrapolation will likely change also. Thus strategic human resources management planning is a dynamic process.

The view of the future becomes more precise as we move into the future; until our view of a planning item is 99.9 percent certain, and what was once a strategic planning issue becomes a current trend item.

Effective strategic management requires great intelligence, the ability to conceptualize, skills in forming correct visions, and the ability to translate visions into plans and strategies to improve each business. To be effective, that process must begin with sound strategic information, including strategic information about human resources management issues. But strategic human resources management information must, in turn, be based on current human resources management trends and issues. A company must have absolutely reliable methods of obtaining continuous inputs about current trends in human resources management.

The answer to the clear need for human resources management planning (which, of course, covers compensation matters) is that every company must do it. You can buy a human resources management planning information service for less than $10,000 a year or you can organize your staff to do it. But every company must do at least human resources management current planning. Companies simply cannot have avoidable and costly surprises. You cannot take actions that seem logical only because you lack near-term current planning information and then learn very shortly that these have been costly mistakes.

Don't think you can avoid the problem or get lucky. With about fifty human resources management planning items at any one time, the odds are against you. You must do human resources management current planning.

Information Technology

Technology is increasing at such a rate that it is difficult to predict what might happen in even a few years; much less in the long term. Regardless of the specifics of technology, the single most important strategic issue for human resources management professionals involves the impact of technology on employee-employer relationships.

We know technology will be massively greater and this will create somewhat predictable changes in employee-employer relationships. Here are some illustrations of the impact of technology on human resources management:

- Most employees will be able to communicate with each other as they wish, in spite of company information systems or the company organization.
- Increasing numbers of employees will identify themselves with their technology or field of work more than with their company.
- Increasing numbers of employees will identify with smaller work groups. There will be *structurally* "higher touch" in work because of technology, regardless of what management does.

- Techno-ethics will partially replace ancient philosophies in college work and will represent new issues in employee relations.
- Communications and flat organizations will necessarily bring high-level management and low-level workers closer together.
- There will be "knowledge issues." The first is already happening—the matter of pay for knowledge. Later we may see a new version of the "right to work," which will mean that employees will have the right to use what they know.
- Working people will increasingly live and work in a world they don't understand. For many, there will be a lack of understanding about the technology of their jobs; for example, few console operators will know how computers work. This will be a factor in productivity management.

A great deal of work needs to be done in human resources management to understand the impact of technology on work effectiveness and the work experience. This work will be complete within a decade, and it will be done mostly by consultants. The action recommended here is to get at it.

Entrepreneurial Pay Programs

In business today, there is considerable interest in entrepreneurial pay. However, there are few entrepreneurial pay plans in effect, in the sense that a substantial portion of pay is geared to the strategic or long-term results of an enterprise.

The compensation of owner-managers is entrepreneurial by definition. Top people in most leveraged buyouts who purchased large blocks of stock in connection with the buyout also inherently have entrepreneurial pay. If corporate executives are to have entrepreneurial pay programs, then it is essential that the long-term income plan be based upon stock appreciation, and that the result of the plan is ownership of stock, not just more income.

Logically, to have an entrepreneurial pay program, two conditions must exist. First, the participants must have some of their money invested in the enterprise, or at least clearly have capital at risk. Second, there must be an entrepreneurial business environment. This, in turn, means that those covered by the entrepreneurial pay plan should have substantial latitude of action; equivalent to executive management of an independent company.

If these conditions exist, here are some guidelines for developing or reviewing an entrepreneurial pay program:

- Those people who are made eligible for special-purpose entrepreneurial pay programs should not be participants in other bonus or incentive compensation programs (including sales incentive compensation plans).

- There must be a clear and describable reason why any group or groups should be covered by an entrepreneurial pay program and others should not.
- Goals for payments under entrepreneurial pay programs must be beyond expected results—they should be for extraordinary achievement.
- Only when the accomplishments of a group make a substantial, visible, and measurable difference to the company or to a business area of the company should entrepreneurial pay programs be applied.
- When there is extraordinary achievement, rewards from entrepreneurial pay programs should be great—they should simulate the income from owner-managed firms. These awards should not be capped.
- The rewards should only be paid after the period necessary to accomplish the special objectives.
- Because these are special-purpose entrepreneurial pay programs, they essentially are one-time pay programs—they are not ongoing.

The fact is that few businesses have conditions required for entrepreneurial pay, except perhaps at the corporate and independent division or sector levels. Yet sometimes companies want to encourage some of the qualities and characteristics of entrepreneurship. To coin a word, they want to create intrapreneurship.

There are two variations of intrapreneurship in compensation that are far enough advanced in development and application to justify a brief reporting. One view considers persons or units as a business and compensates them for their value as a business. The closest examples would be commission pay plans, the pay of media personalities, and compensation for authors. The other form of intrapreneurial compensation links a unit and prices services to prices of outside suppliers. Then those in the unit "draw" compensation after their expenses are covered, such as any owner-manager. They also keep some of the residual profits.

Educational Deficiency

No doubt, the number one near-term and long-term issue for business in the area of human resources management is educational deficiency. Educational deficiency is such a critical problem that it should probably get a page in every book written for anyone in business, regardless of the subject. Educational deficiency is a major threat to every enterprise and to the economy.

There are no compensation systems I know of that focus meaningfully on the most important of all business problems.* Yet we have developed compensation systems that are specifically designed to deal with many disparate special issues far less important than educational deficiency is today.

For example, there are entrepreneurial pay programs, which have just been covered, designed to simulate entrepreneurial pay and create a strong financial motivation in special situations. There are thrift plans to help people save. There are day-care centers to help working mothers. There are golden parachute contracts to help executives who might experience a change in control. There are many other special-purpose plans to deal with special human resources management issues.

There has never been a special human resources management issue that is more important than educational deficiency. Isn't it time some compensation persons developed special pay plans to help deal with educational deficiency? The problems of educational deficiency will not be resolved by pay alone, but the issue is so important that everything that helps in any significant way is worthwhile.

No one has paid me to do such work, and that means that I haven't really spent time developing a special compensation program to deal with educational deficiency. Even so, in my personal study periods, I have been able to sketch some pay plans that deal in some way with the issue of educational deficiency and at the same time deal with some other clear and present human resources management problems.

One method would be a college-tuition program. My plan replaces college donation matching plans, which serve little business purpose. My college tuition plan simply provides that the company will pay tuition costs for any four-year college for children of employees and perhaps tuition costs for grandchildren of employees. The cost of the program is determinable.

The college-tuition plan has values that I think provably offset costs. It will help significantly in recruiting, has retention values, represents a unique benefit, at least for some, and will create good will.

If your company is going to provide some support toward the education of unskilled persons who are functionally illiterate, and if this costs significant amounts of money, also consider funds in individual accounts paid to success cases who come to work for your company. This plan involves lump-sum payments to functionally illiterate persons who, on their own and utilizing existing community facilities, become literate and productive workers in your company.

There are two pay plans, both of which deal meaningfully with educational deficiency, that you get for just the cost of this book. If someone

---

*There are tuition-refund programs and college-matching grants, but these do not deal meaningfully with the issue of educational deficiency.

wants to pay for developmental work, it would likely be possible to develop two more plans to support education. We need desperately to take actions to improve education.

Polarization of Pay

Even taking out the extremes of high pay and low pay, there is a great spread in pay, and it is increasing. In many firms, high-paid persons get four hundred times as much pretax as low-paid persons. Aftertax, high-paid persons earn three hundred times as much as low-paid persons.

The distribution of the working population by income has not changed that much. If anything, there are more middle-income workers. It is the spread from low to high that keeps increasing. This happens mostly because there are more very high-paid persons.

That spread from low pay to high pay has increased by 50 percent pretax and has more than doubled aftertax in only twenty years. The trend toward greater polarization of pay continues.

According to government statistics, one-fourth of all persons who work full time earn an amount annually that is such that a family of four dependent on that income alone would live in poverty. At the same time, there are ten thousand corporate executives who earn $1 million or more a year, and there are more than a million millionaires.

For lower-paid workers, these comparisons seem unfair. But the working poor have other comparisons that can also be disturbing. After taxes and after the cost of working, those earning up to two times the minimum wage have little more income than those on welfare. The spread of aftertax and aftercost income of the skilled operations worker is little if any higher than the nonskilled worker. In Miami, Florida, for example, skilled electricians earn less than airline baggage handlers.

I don't think that these are compensation issues, although some disagree. To me, they are all important issues, but the primary solutions to the problems lie elsewhere.

The problem of the high-paid executive is not just a compensation issue. The compensation committee of the board of directors must deal directly with matters of executive pay. In the last analysis, however, control of high-paid persons in all fields, including sports and entertainment, can also be controlled by taxation.

For the lowest paid, there are compensation issues that are important and which have been covered in previous chapters. I think the primary problem, however, is upward mobility, which is increasingly dependent upon such fundamental issues as educational opportunities, family values, drugs, and lawlessness.

Communication About Pay

I still get calls about effective communications as much as on any other subject. Very often the specific issue involves questions about the communication of employee pay.

It is surprising that we struggle so much to tell people what they already know.

Every employee knows how much he is paid. You don't have to communicate that anymore. In fact, you can communicate it too much.

Employees are far less interested in your pay practices and compensation technology than many human resources management people seem to think. Communication about the company's pay practices frequently sounds like a magic show to employees.

Avoid being negative about pay issues. For example, you can say that pay increases are frozen, or you can say that current pay levels will be maintained. Both statements reflect the same facts. Be positive.

At the other extreme, don't tell employees the unbelievable. Don't ask people to think they are keeping up with inflation if they don't get an increase.

Don't give employees information that isn't relevant. I'm not interested in maternity benefits, and a recent high school graduate has about the same level of interest in retirement income.

When communicating with employees about pay (or anything else), do it in the English language. Attorneys, accountants, and actuaries definitely do not speak the same English language used by most of the rest of us. Don't try to impress employees with big words. Long sentences and endless paragraphs are worse. Never use the special vocabulary of compensation; my dictionary doesn't even list many of those words.

If you feel the need for advice on how to communicate to employees in writing, hire a local 11th grade English teacher.

Communicate verbally as much as possible. Verbal communication is usually more effective than written communication.

A company communicates best when it is essentially in the mode of a transponder, and that is particularly true in communicating sensitive issues—like pay. When an employee asks a relevant question on a subject he has a right to know about, be sure the question is answered quickly, completely, and truthfully.

Equal Treatment

In my personnel planning work, equal treatment is in the top ten human resources management issues. It is a high-priority issue now; and a strategic human resources management issue of substantial consequence.

Equal treatment embodies a number of ideas and causes. Some have been around for a long time.

Equal treatment means, for example, equal pay for equal work. It means equal job pay and due recognition of performance—and nothing else. The contemporary view of equal pay means equivalency of pay for work performed, regardless of age, sex, race, or organizational affiliation.

Equal pay is against favored treatment of union members, even if they have economic power and political friends.

Equal pay under equal treatment means no preferential treatment because of race, creed, or color. Equal treatment opposes preferential treatment in pay rates for any reason, including correcting the past sins of others or someone's vision of the future world. Equal pay under equal treatment relates to fairness; black and white, by way of contrast, are colors.

Of course, equal treatment goes well beyond pay. Special benefits or better conditions for any reason other than the need for effective work are unacceptable under the concepts of equal treatment.

Furthermore, there can be no preferential hiring or promotion to gain any social goal. Employment and promotions go to the best qualified by using genuine and unbiased standards. Nothing else is acceptable under equal treatment.

Affirmative action is out when equal treatment is in. The tools of equal treatment are enlightened self-interest, absolute compliance with laws and regulations, free choice, and employer accountability.

You may not agree with some of these views about equal treatment or you may not agree with equal treatment. But if you have any responsibility for compensation, you must pay heed and, assuming I'm correct in saying that equal treatment as defined is a major trend, factor these ideas into your company's compensation programs.

Fairness

Fairness is another issue of our times. Religious leaders and politicians have been raising the fairness issue for a number of years. That makes it an issue at work also. It can be argued that there should be fairness at work because it is right. Fairness at work may be important because without it those who work in the firm will turn to unions or to the government. Perhaps most importantly, fairness at work may be essential today in order to gain employee commitment to work excellence.

Not everyone agrees that worker commitment is essential to high levels of productivity. There are also differences in view about how great the employee commitment must be to gain high levels of productivity. In fact, there is no clear relationship between the company's commitment to employees and employee work excellence. You're entitled to your opinion about the relationship between fairness at work and employee productivity. Here are some things that suggest that fairness in the work place is essential to productive work, but the most convincing should be freedom in the market.

One of the strengths of our economic system is the free choice of both employers and employees. Employers have latitude in setting working conditions, and many different working environments exist in any labor market. Some working conditions reflect fairness more than others. Employees have a free choice about where they work and, others things being equal, prefer an employer who is perceived to be fair. The result is that there is a natural labor market selection of employers by employees, and part of the employees' basis of selection is fairness. Work choices are not unlimited, and employer fairness is only one condition that employment candidates consider. However, in millions of cases over a period of time, qualified workers prefer employers known for fairness.

Workers' views of fairness are more relative than absolute. Some absolutes are expected; for example, that the company obeys the law and provides safe working conditions. What employees expect in terms of fairness is very much affected by what they (and others close to them) have experienced elsewhere. Thus in the practical sense of creating an environment for a more effective work force, fairness means being fair enough and more fair than others.

A company that has a reputation of fairness should improve. It's not that the company is going for a Nobel prize. Rather the image of fairness is a valuable asset that is translatable into higher productivity and greater income. It's important to make sure that the company keeps that asset. The most reliable way to do that is to become fairer.

Employees' perceptions of fairness are almost always intelligent and insightful. Those at work aren't easily deceived. They believe what they see and experience far more than what they are told. Deception or pretentiousness with respect to fairness can cause the condition of fairness to go from favorable to poor very quickly.

Fairness is not the same as niceness. It's nice to be fair, but employers should be cautious about niceness unrelated to fairness. A few years ago, for example, companies were being urged to be nice and to "enhance the quality of life" for those who work in the company. Such programs didn't work in any case I know of and were often costly errors.

Fairness does not create productivity; it creates the environment where those who work may be productive or improve their effectiveness. You still need management. Fairness and ineffective management mean low productivity; just like unfairness and ineffective management or unfairness and effective management mean low productivity.

Clearly, employee perceptions of the fairness of the employer are based in large part on pay policies, programs, and practices. Pay is the most visible and most frequent demonstration of fairness. Fair pay doesn't always mean fairness at work, but it is not likely that an employer will be perceived as being fair if pay is thought to be unfair.

A Career in Compensation

A very special issue of compensation for those who work in this field involves questions of a career in compensation. Many who work in the field think about a career in this field. There are some positive elements about a career in the field and some questions.

The number of people who are working in compensation today is unclear. There have been various estimates: the lowest was fifty thousand and the highest was close to two hundred thousand persons who spend all or most of their time doing compensation work. There are probably ten times that number who spend some significant part of their time in compensation work.

The compensation of those who work in the field is often high. There are probably two hundred persons working in compensation who have a salary of over $100,000 a year and probably three thousand with a salary of over $50,000 a year.

Clearly, compensation is important; important to those who are paid because it represents income and important to employers because compensation is a major cost. Compensation is important to the economy, because pay allocates scarce resources. The role that compensation people play contributes importantly to how well these important matters are handled.

Few have spent their entire careers in compensation work. That's true today because the field is still relatively new. There will likely be many more who spend all or most of their careers in compensation work in future years.

My own advice to young people would be to start their working careers in operations, then work as a personnel generalist. Only after they have had at least five years of operations work and five years of personnel generalist work should they specialize as a compensation professional. That might be for the rest of their lives or they might move on to a fourth phase in their careers (and with the career background I outlined, they would be able to do that).

Many top-level personnel people and almost all line executives share the view that human resources management professional specialists of all types should have been personnel generalists prior to their specialist experience. The knowledge of all facets of human resources management is critical to effective professional specialist work in compensation.

A career path that includes personnel generalist work contributes to effective compensation work. In addition, compensation specialist spots are increasingly being filled with personnel generalists. Opinions will vary on the need for operations experience prior to personnel generalist experience.

As you think about a career in compensation work, recognize that the job will change greatly in the future. Much of the work done by compensation persons in the future will be done by expert systems. Also recognize that the era of program development in compensation work is now mostly over. The emphasis in the future will be more on the use of technology and success in dealing with compensation issues.

Compensation in the Year 2020

In preparing this fifth edition of *Compensation,* I have had reason to look back thirty years to 1960, when the first edition was published. It is an experience to look back. A lot has changed; we have learned a lot.

No doubt, there is still a lot to be learned, and it is natural to look ahead. Many who read this book will still be working in the year 2020. It is natural, therefore, and perhaps of value to look ahead thirty years to compensation in the year 2020.

No one can predict the future with certainty. In strategic human resources management planning, it is important to identify current observable trends and extrapolate them reasonably into the future. Extrapolating observable trends must, of course, be monitored, and forecasts change as conditions change.

I have done this in my own human resources management planning work for sponsor companies, and some of my visions of the future that relate to compensation will hopefully be of value—and perhaps this is a logical way to end this edition of *Compensation.*

The income of American families, on average, will increase by one full income class by the year 2020, provided business does a reasonably good job of managing productivity improvement potential and the government doesn't mess it up. That will impact basic issues such as the mix of pay and will very likely highlight extra pay success-sharing plans.

There will be more work produced in factories by robots than by unskilled workers. Model A companies will then be the standard for compensation work about as much as we use the car with the same letter.

For the median-paid worker, salary will be about one-half of compensation. Health-care costs will be about one-half of the rest—and will have stabilized as a percentage of total compensation.

Working persons will become major stockholders in American corporations, and there will be widespread use of some type of employee-class stock. This employee-class stock will not be tax-preferred like an employee stock option plan (ESOP), but it will have legislative sanctions, like stock options. It will be common for employees to have, in combination, a block of stock that represents control, and frequently employee-class stock will amount to more than half of a company's equity.

Enterprises without publicly-traded stock won't have employee-class stock for compensation purposes. There will likely be hard work to find some equivalent mechanism, and if there is enough research and development, it will likely be successful in developing employee-class bonds.

Partly because of employee-stock ownership, American business will have its own version of glasnost. That will affect issues like communication about pay and executive compensation disclosure.

Employees at every level, not just executive employees, will have much more to say about policy issues, including compensation policies. This will be in the form of electronic town meetings and focus surveys that are done quickly and on a broad range of issues.

What are now gee-whiz magic shows with computers and communication equipment will be routine by 2020—and who knows what the emerging technologies will be then. In compensation (and in all other areas of work), one person will have at his disposal vast amounts of knowledge, almost instantaneously and easily accessed. This will include data and information about pay in the company (currently and for prior years); data and information from other companies; knowledge and experiences of experts on all aspects of compensation; and specific tools like expert systems. Many of those expert systems will be accessible to operating managers and individual employees, who will then bypass the compensation professional in their company.

Compensation experts will have many working models to deal with issues and for developing programs. Modeling will be widely practiced in compensation. People will still build the models and input information, but the models will answer many compensation questions, solve many compensation problems, and even develop compensation practices in 2020.

The life span of one form of any compensation program will be quite short. Back in the 1960s, we designed compensation programs on the assumption that they would stay largely intact forever. By the middle of the 1970s, it was recognized that the "shelf life" of a compensation program (with some exceptions) was up to ten years; and smart companies put maximum sunset dates on all human resources management programs. By 2020, programs in compensation will be in the four- to six-year range in 80 percent of the cases; and smart companies will routinely put four-year sunset dates on all new compensation programs.

Before many more years pass—or many more administrations in Washington—there will be real tax reform. In the year 2020, taxes will be simple enough so that educated people will be able to complete their own tax returns. There will be few deductions, and tax advantages for some to gain political favor will be considered politically unacceptable. The tax rate will be progressive, up to almost 100 percent on annual income of more than $10 million a year. This type of tax law will change compensation practices greatly.

Executive pay issues will be resolved by the turn of the century, and the problem of pay for executives in the '70s, '80s, and '90s will be history. There is no way to know whether corporations and boards of directors will exercise initiatives to answer the question of executive pay or whether it will be done by government controls, but it will happen.

Visions of work life, such as the sample presented, must be based upon observable conditions and trends reasonably extrapolated into the future with monitoring of the trends each year. The resulting picture of the future is clear enough to influence some decision making today, even when you're looking ahead thirty years. That is one basis for leadership. Such visions may also be helpful in personal career plans.

Compensation Issues

In preparation for this book, I contacted a random sample of subscribers to *The Sibson Report*. They were asked to tell me about important compensation issues they were working on that they felt needed some support and inputs. Then I said I would help them by talking about their problem for up to an hour on the telephone.

The purpose was to get another look at the real issues in the field of compensation and more of a sense of how well such issues were being handled. In the first eight months of 1988, I received thirty-two inquiries. I would have liked twice as many, but I didn't have more time for this activity and felt that the size and nature of the samples served the purpose well enough.

Such inquiries do not lend themselves to data or statistical presentation. However, here are the question categories and the number of times each question category surfaced. Note that there are more than thirty-two, because some questions could not be easily categorized in a single subject.

Fairness (6)
Benefit cost containment (5)
Management pay (4)
Pay for performance (4)
Variable pay (3)
Retirement plans (3)

Issues that turned out not to be compensation matters (3)
Pay aspects of labor scarcity (2)
Payroll cost containment (2)
Unit bonus plans (2)
Competitive pay (2)
Entrepreneurial pay (1)
Pay for knowledge (1)
Career ladder pay (1)
Outplacement pay (1)

All the questions were genuine. I felt that I was able to help substantially in every case, but each conversation had to be limited to an hour, and usually you can't resolve matters like these in that short a time. The important thing was that I got the input I wanted for the book, and all the firms thought they were helped a great deal.

My first impression from these conversations was that this type of networking is very much needed. I've thought of making such work part of my practice. Such networking is not available today to people in human resources management. There should be central switching systems and high-level persons available to do this work. Then people can either network that person directly or be referred to others with appropriate know-how and experience. Network information must be accessed quickly, and it should be provided in an hour to a day and not involve major project time or cost.

Another strong impression was that work in the compensation field is now often best described by the words "helter skelter." More than anything else, if you heard the telephone conversations, you had to get the impression that people were overwhelmed by what they had to do and the little time they had to do it. Most of all, I felt that the networking we had in this one case provided its greatest value by giving guidance in how to proceed as well as giving some order and direction. For the people I talked to, this seemed to be as valuable as were specific information, ideas, and recommendations.

With few exceptions, the people I contacted felt swept along without direction and without hope of ever catching up. They seemed to suggest that their work days were just one endless series of fire drills, with never an opportunity to feel good about results or get organized to do the things that should be done in a reasonable and orderly manner.

Some business novelists urge chaos in business, and it seems that perhaps they are really reporting what they see. Chaos and helter skelter aren't good, but they seem to be more prevalent than I would have guessed.

The people I talked to often felt overwhelmed by the massive amounts of knowledge needed to do the compensation job today. Most of these people were very experienced, but it may just be that today no one can have enough knowledge to stand alone, even in relatively narrow specialties.

While the thirty-two companies posed issues in fifteen categories, no two questions were even remotely alike. This also says something about the work in compensation today.

The information and the input were of value to me. Most importantly, perhaps, it got me to organize and present material in a more issue-oriented way.

Another survey for this book involved reviewing agendas and notes from conferences I have held since the last edition. There were twenty-two of these conferences in the seven-year period. All of these conferences were for small groups; the total number of participants was 285, but many persons attended a conference each year, so there were sixty-two different persons from forty-nine different companies. Attendance at these conferences is by invitation only, assuring high-level participants. The agenda in each conference is based upon the expressed interests of the participants, so the conferences are essentially issue- and question-oriented. The issues discussed in these conferences were very helpful in identifying and organizing material for this book.

In addition, I scanned my client work over the past eight years. This was also helpful, mostly as a source of material.

Finally, I sent the following questionnaire to about nine hundred compensation persons who were selected at random. More than two hundred of these were returned.

A full reporting of this questionnaire was sent to those who participated in the survey. The results were most helpful in preparing this book. The top fifteen issues determined by the questionnaire follow.

COMPENSATION ISSUES

Spring 1989

There are only 75 times listed in this questionnaire. We would appreciate it if you would indicate the importance of each to your firm.

Please check off your first impressions. If your reaction is uncertain or if the question is unclear, leave it blank.

Your cooperation will be greatly appreciated. We are asking for about 15 minutes of your time. In return you will receive a tabulation of the results and a brief report written by Robert E. Sibson outlining some of his thoughts and recommendations.

Subject	Level of Interest			
	High	Some	Little	None
1. Enterpreneurial pay plans	——	——	——	——
2. Sufficient pay for high performers	——	——	——	——
3. Management bonus plans	——	——	——	——
4. Middle-level management pay	——	——	——	——
5. Estate building plans	——	——	——	——
6. Employee stock ownership	——	——	——	——
7. Success sharing plans	——	——	——	——
8. Long term income plans for managers	——	——	——	——
9. Mix of management pay—salary, bonus, long-term income	——	——	——	——
10. Pay for superstars	——	——	——	——
11. Non-financial elements of pay	——	——	——	——
12. The Board's role in compensation	——	——	——	——
13. Non-qualified benefits for executives	——	——	——	——
14. Job pricing by use of employment experience	——	——	——	——
15. Insured benefit cost containment	——	——	——	——
16. Increasing the effectiveness of compensation work	——	——	——	——

	Level of Interest			
Subject	High	Some	Little	None
17. More useful groupings of employees	——	——	——	——
18. Better job descriptions	——	——	——	——
19. New job titles and titling system	——	——	——	——
20. Salary structure issues	——	——	——	——
21. Survey systems and methods	——	——	——	——
22. Recruiting pay	——	——	——	——
23. Vertical recruiting	——	——	——	——
24. Pay in career paths—career curves	——	——	——	——
25. Use of general salary increases	——	——	——	——
26. Better benefits	——	——	——	——
27. Individualized benefits	——	——	——	——
28. Contingent pay plans	——	——	——	——
29. Golden handcuffs	——	——	——	——
30. Golden parachute contracts	——	——	——	——
31. Special benefits for executives	——	——	——	——
32. Perquisites	——	——	——	——
33. Use of expert systems in compensation work	——	——	——	——
34. Compensation in multiple business corporations	——	——	——	——
35. Delegative management in compensation work	——	——	——	——
36. Training and development of compensation professionals	——	——	——	——
37. Total pay management	——	——	——	——
38. Pay for contract workers	——	——	——	——
39. Evaluating the performance of compensation people	——	——	——	——
40. Determining the elements of compensation	——	——	——	——

	Level of Interest			
Subject	High	Some	Little	None
41. Determining relevant labor markets	——	——	——	——
42. Career pathing for compensation professionals	——	——	——	——
43. Setting salary increase budgets	——	——	——	——
44. Use of cost of living in compensation	——	——	——	——
45. Adjusting the salary structure	——	——	——	——
46. Compa-ratio and band position controls	——	——	——	——
47. Pay increase planning systems	——	——	——	——
48. Salary levels and classes as well as grades	——	——	——	——
49. Job evaluation systems	——	——	——	——
50. Effective communication of pay matters	——	——	——	——
51. Pay of those in compensation work	——	——	——	——
52. Pay policies and practices regarding promotion	——	——	——	——
53. Technical issues of job evaluation: factors weightings, etc.	——	——	——	——
54. Performance appraisal use in compensation	——	——	——	——
55. Handling pay above or below the salary grade	——	——	——	——
56. Single rates	——	——	——	——
57. Pay increase review and approval system	——	——	——	——
58. Reevaluation and inequity pay adjustments	——	——	——	——
59. Pay for knowledge compensation system	——	——	——	——
60. Special issues of compensation for professionals	——	——	——	——

	Level of Interest			
Subject	High	Some	Little	None
61. Pay for the working poor	——	——	——	——
62. Premium payments	——	——	——	——
63. Guaranteed wage issue	——	——	——	——
64. Use of job evaluation	——	——	——	——
65. Lump sum increase payments	——	——	——	——
66. Automatic time pay increases	——	——	——	——
67. Sales compensation	——	——	——	——
68. Pay compression	——	——	——	——
69. Tenure as compensation	——	——	——	——
70. Pay of technical positions	——	——	——	——
71. Minimum wage issue	——	——	——	——
72. Outplacement pay practices	——	——	——	——
73. Pay for time not worked	——	——	——	——
74. Payroll cost containment	——	——	——	——
75. Use of consultants	——	——	——	——

Please list other items of importance in compensation that are not included in the 75 items listed above.

_____

_____

In your opinion, what is the most important single issue in compensation today?

_____

_____

What is the compensation subject of highest priority in your firm today?

_____

We will sent a tabulation of results to those who complete the questionnaire. For that reason only, please fill in the following information:

Name _____ Title _____

Company _____

Address _____

City _____ State _____ Zip _____

All responses are confidential, and will be destroyed after tabulation.

RESULTS OF QUESTIONNAIRE ON COMPENSATION ISSUES
THE TOP 15 HIGH-PRIORITY ISSUES

(Ranked from most important to least important)

1. Question 2: Sufficient pay for high performers
2. Question 3: Management bonus plans
3. Question 10: Pay for superstars
4. Question 50: Effective communication of pay matters
5. Question 54: Performance appraisal use in compensation
6. Question 16: Increasing the effectiveness of compensation work
7. Question 43: Setting salary increase budgets
8. Question 9: Mix of management pay—salary, bonus, long-term income
9. Question 4: Middle-level management pay
10. Question 20: Salary structure issues
11. Question 15: Insured benefit cost containment
12. Question 47: Pay increase planning systems
13. Question 45: Adjusting the salary structure
14. Question 49: Job evaluation systems
15. Question 52: Pay policies and practices regarding promotion

Index

(Italic page numbers refer to figures.)